Fritz Kunkel:
Selected Writings

edited, with an Introduction and Commentary, by

John A. Sanford

PAULIST PRESS
New York ◆ Ramsey

Acknowledgments

Special thanks to **Mrs. Beatrice Burch** of La Jolla, a close friend of Fritz Kunkel, who assisted me in many places in the preparation of this manuscript. **John Kunkel** also gave me frequent assistance and encouragement, and he and his brother, **Peter**, prepared the biographical sketch. **Helen Macey** of San Diego rendered her usual invaluable help with the preparation of the manuscript.

Unless otherwise indicated, biblical quotations in the sections of the book by John A. Sanford are from the *Jerusalem Bible* © 1966, 1967 and 1968 by Darton, Longman & Todd Ltd. and Doubleday & Company, Inc. Biblical quotations in the material by Fritz Kunkel are from the Moffatt Bible.

Library of Congress
Catalog Card Number: 83-62466

ISBN: 0-8091-2558-7

Published by Paulist Press
545 Island Road, Ramsey, N.J. 07446

Printed and bound in the
United States of America

Contents

IV: *Kunkel's Work and Contemporary Issues in Psychology and Religion*
John A. Sanford

Dedication

This book is dedicated to those persons to whom Dr. Kunkel dedicated his two books:

How Character Develops

To all those—young or old—who seek to understand themselves better for the sake of finding a way out of their limitations into more satisfying and useful living.

In Search of Maturity

To Elizabeth Kunkel

Books written by Fritz Kunkel

*(In the case of books originally written in German, an English translation
follows the title)*

1927   Die Grundbegriffe der Individualpsychologie (with Ruth
       Kunkel) (Basic Concepts of Individual Psychology)

1928   Einführung in die Characterkunde (Introduction to the Study
       of Personality, published as Let's Be Normal)

1928   Die Arbeit am Character (Improving One's Personality)

1929   Das Dumme Kind (The Problem Child)

1929   Vitale Dialektik (Living Dialectics)

1930   Jugendcharakterkunde (The Study of Young People's Charac-
       ter) (published in English as What It Means To Grow Up)

1931   Grundzüge der Politischen Charakterkunde (Foundations for
       the Study of Personality and Politics)

1931   Eine Angstneurose und Ihre Behandlung (A Neurosis and Its
       Treatment)

1931   Charakter, Wachstum und Erziehung (Character, Growth, and
       Education, published in English under that title)

1932   Krisenbriefe (Letters about Crises in Daily Life)

1932   Charakter, Liebe und Ehe (Personality, Love, and Marriage)

1933   Charakter, Einzelmensch und Gruppe (Personality, the Indi-
       vidual, and the Group)

1934   Charakter, Leiden und Heilung (Personality, Suffering, and
       Healing)

1935   Charakter, Krisis und Weltanschauung (Personality, Crises,
       and Views of the World)

1935   Grundzüge der Praktischen Seelenheilkunde (Foundations for
       the Practical Treatment of Personality Problems, published in
       English under the title Conquer Yourself)

1936   Die Erziehung Deiner Kinder (with Elizabeth Kunkel) (Rais-
       ing Your Children)

1939   Das Wir (The We)

1940   How Character Develops (with Roy Dickerson)

1943   In Search of Maturity

1946   What Do You Advise? (with Ruth Gardner)

1947   Creation Continues (revised edition, 1973)

1947   My Dear Ego

The Life of Fritz Kunkel

Fritz Kunkel was born on September 6, 1889 on a large estate near Stolzenberg in Brandenburg (now in Poland). His parents were wealthy land owners who led an active social life; cavalry officers and other visitors, servants and farm workers were part of his life from the very beginning. But while he was the seventh of eight children, his early years were quite lonely. The much older siblings attended distant boarding schools, and he had no companions until 1896, when a younger brother was born (who became a well-known philosopher and novelist). The two boys spent much of their time in the forests and meadows of the estate, enacting the historical dramas and social comedies that Fritz composed in the evenings. The experiences of those early years—self-reliance and imagination, closeness to nature and to books, and distance from the social whirl of the upper class—set a tone that would persist to the end of his life.

A succession of private tutors was followed by high school in the town of Landsberg. Fritz was an average student who spent much of his time pursuing his own interests in literature and history. In 1907 he went to the University of Munich to study medicine, but he continued his involvement with drama, poetry, and the arts. As a student he enjoyed an active social life and even joined a fraternity. With his friends he frequented cafes where he would compose humorous poems for payments of beer, and in general led a carefree and none-too-studious existence.

A few days after the beginning of the First World War he received his medical degree and soon thereafter became a battalion surgeon on the western front. At the Battle of Verdun, while treating wounded in the forward trenches, he was hit by shrapnel.

Eventually his left arm had to be amputated (his beloved younger brother lost the right arm).

The battle, his wound, the suffering all around him, and the months of slow recovery were profound experiences that changed his life and, more importantly, his self-image and world view. The happy-go-lucky youth without a care in the world was transformed into a serious adult who cared much for those who were troubled. From then on, position, money, and politics lost most of their meaning, and Fritz began to be concerned with the psychological and spiritual welfare of individuals. When the hyperinflation of 1922 wiped out his inheritance, he no longer cared, for he was following a new path. He turned his back on the life style of his parents and their friends and dreamed of other places. Indeed, in 1921 he wrote a poem celebrating the life of cowboys in Arizona!

By 1919 Fritz had recovered enough to try practicing medicine, but after a few weeks it was clear that a one-armed physician would never be effective. He therefore decided to study psychotherapy and journeyed to Vienna to consult the leading figures of the new movement. His appointment with Freud was canceled because Freud had a cold that day (in later years, Fritz would say that a benevolent spirit had intervened). But Fritz was deeply impressed by the man Alfred Adler and his ideas, and soon became a student and follower. Within two years, however, Fritz realized that his own ideas, which included the spiritual and religious aspects of life, were important enough to warrant expression. After some months of practical experience as a doctor in a mental institution he decided to enter private practice as a psychotherapist.

In 1924 Fritz moved to Berlin and began his work. Initially he was part of the Adlerian group, but he soon moved away from Adler's theory and began to employ his own methods and views. The parting with Adler was amiable, and the two men retained their liking and respect for each other.

The 1920's were momentous years: marriage to Ruth Löwengard, three children, a busy practice, and the growth of his own ideas. By 1928 he had developed his thoughts well enough to describe them in his first book—*Introduction to the Study of the Human Character.* During the next decade Fritz wrote twelve more books that outlined his psychology and described various practical applications in daily life. All of his books were written for the general reader and not for the professional, and while psychologists would be interested in his work, the focus was always on the intelligent normal adult who wanted to improve himself. Several of these early books were translated into English, French, Italian, and Spanish, and he soon was invited to lecture in Holland and Sweden as well as throughout Germany. Many of these books are still in print fifty years after they were written.

The 1930's were even busier. After the death of his first wife, Fritz married Elizabeth Jensen, and two more children were born. In addition to his extensive practice and frequent books, there were many students and followers, public lectures and scientific congresses. He founded his own school of "We-Psychology" in Berlin and was active in national psychotherapeutic organizations.

Like many others, he became increasingly disturbed by the restrictions being placed on psychotherapy and its practitioners in Germany. He continued to advocate the free exchange of ideas and fought for the right of psychological schools to develop their theories and train therapists. When he realized that individuals and thoughts were being repressed and that there was no hope for change, he began to look for opportunities in other countries. By 1936 he had enough confidence in his English that he accepted an invitation to give lectures at Pendle Hill (the Quaker center in Pennsylvania) and throughout the United States. Several of his books had appeared there, and his ideas enjoyed wide appeal.

Fritz Kunkel retained many of Adler's views, especially regarding the importance of the individual as a whole. But he was also fascinated by Carl Jung's emphasis on the creative aspects of the unconscious and the significance of religion. Fritz incorporated many of these ideas into his own psychology, which emphasized the development of "we-feelings" in contrast to the egoistic "I." While he never worked with Jung, the two men corresponded and had long discussions during the several psychological congresses they attended over the years.

Fritz had the rare capacity to develop his own ideas while he recognized the quality and usefulness of other people's work. He did not denigrate the theories of others because he believed that psychology was too young, and human nature too complex, for anyone to make final judgments or reach definitive conclusions. He was broadminded in his view of psychology, eclectic in his approach to human suffering, and yet certain that his own ideas were significant. In his practice he used a variety of methods, depending on what he thought was needed in a particular instance.

Fritz was intensely concerned for the healing of his clients and respected them as individuals. When his friends suggested that he should use more case material from his practice in his books, he declined because he thought that such descriptions would amount to betrayals of confidence. A master of several languages, he kept all his notes on his clients in ancient Greek in order to ensure privacy.

In the summer of 1939 Fritz accepted another invitation to the United States, to spend a year at the Pacific School of Religion and lecture throughout the country. When World War II began he decided to remain in America. He was captivated by the deserts of southern California which somehow reminded him of a familiar ancestral home. It was not until 1947, when he became a citizen, that the family was once more united, now in Los Angeles.

During the 1940's he wrote several books in English, outlining the further development of his ideas. By now he was interested not only in the role of religion in the individual's life but also in the psychological aspects of religion. Both concerns guided his work to the end of his days. They were natural steps in his spiritual development and not reflections of the California syndrome. Indeed, he often related a warning Jung had given him in the early 1930's: "Kunkel, you are too religious." But nothing would deter him from the logical conclusions of his inquiry into the human soul.

The measure of a man is found not only in his public work— in this case books, lectures, and clients—but also in his private life. Fritz had an open, friendly disposition and a great sense of humor, but he did not like parties, and had problems with small talk. He was always ready to help those who sought his assistance, but he always retained a certain shyness. He was careful not to burden his family with his projects and worries, yet he took an interest in the lives of every member. In spite of nineteen books written in the span of as many years, a large number of clients and students, and dozens of conferences, seminars, and public lectures in several countries, he retained an easy-going and relaxed manner. All of his children have been successful: the eldest, Peter, is a cardiologist in the San Francisco area; Wulf is professor of physics at the University of California (Berkeley); Ruth Maria Lipski is a psychologist in the Ocean View School District in Huntington Beach (California); John is professor of sociology at the University of Western Ontario (Canada); and the youngest, William, is an astronomer who has worked at observatories in Chile, Brazil and Spain.

During the 1950's Fritz maintained a busy schedule of therapeutic work and psychological seminars in his home in Los Angeles. There were also the usual public lectures in churches and colleges in cities across the country. He organized a short-lived Institute of Religious Psychology, but he was more interested in intellectual discoveries and adventures of the spirit than in proselytizing. In 1952 he began to write what he considered his magnum opus, a psychological interpretation of Saint Paul's life and work. Unfortunately, high blood pressure and fatigue gradually reduced his ability for such strenuous work, and the manuscript was never finished.

Yet in spite of these disappointments he retained his optimism and sense of humor. To the very end of his life he was open to new ideas and ready to try out new methods. The day before he died, he wrote his son John an enthusiastic—and characteristically humorous—letter about a new book that he thought would present novel paths to the understanding of human beings. He wrote that he was eager to follow those new paths.

On Easter Sunday, 1956, Fritz Kunkel died of a ruptured aorta.

General Introduction
Part One:
How This Book Was Born

I first met Fritz Kunkel in September 1953. At that time I was a twenty-four-year-old theological student looking desperately for someone who could help me. In the year preceding my meeting with Kunkel, the second year of my theological training in an Episcopal seminary on the east coast, I had developed such an anxiety state that I was barely able to finish the spring semester. During that traumatic year I tried to find help from a number of doctors, psychiatrists, and clergymen, but although many of them were sincere people, and no doubt helped others, none could help me. I knew I could not go through another year of school in such a state of mind, so I took a leave of absence and went to California to work as a surveyor (an old trade of mine), to try to get my feet on the ground and understand what was happening to me. This brought me to Los Angeles, and because of the healthy work things were better for me, but my acute anxiety continued and I still was not able to find help. Finally Bert Hause, an Episcopal priest, chaplain at a hospital, and a faithful friend, suggested that I see Fritz Kunkel.

I had not realized that Kunkel lived in Los Angeles, but I had read some of his books that were available in the seminary library. When his name was mentioned something clicked inside me. Before I even met the man I knew that this was the person I was to see. Dr. Kunkel accepted me as his client and we began our psychological work that month. The ensuing year became the most exciting, healing, and important year of my adult life.

7

My first contact with Dr. Kunkel was by letter. I was out of town on a survey, so I wrote to him, introduced myself, and asked if I could see him when my survey was over and I returned to the city. I can still remember his reply. In addition to saying that he would see me he suggested that I begin reading three books: C. G. Jung's *Modern Man in Search of a Soul,* Frances Wickes' *The Inner World of Man,* and his own *In Search of Maturity.* He also suggested that I begin recording my dreams. In this way I was introduced simultaneously to the psychology of C. G. Jung, to my dreams, and to Kunkel's own ideas.

That was in 1953 and I am writing this in 1982, almost thirty years later. In this interim, Kunkel's books have been out of print in the United States most of the time. Why such a long delay in the republication of his writing?

My analysis with Kunkel ended abruptly with his sudden death on Easter Sunday, 1956. Losing him as a friend and guide was a profound shock for me. Fortunately I was able to continue my psychological work and progress with the help of able Jungian analysts in Los Angeles. I had also married, been ordained an Episcopal minister, become a father, and acquired a position as assistant priest in a church, so I had been plunged into a busy and involved life. I certainly didn't forget Fritz Kunkel, but as the years went by the importance of his life and work receded from my awareness.

However, in 1980 I had a series of dreams that brought my attention back to Kunkel in a powerful way. The details of the dreams varied, but the central theme was always the same: I saw Dr. Kunkel alive and actively teaching a small group of people. It is impossible for me to communicate what a strong impression these dreams made upon me. It was as though Dr. Kunkel *really was* alive. They were so vivid that when I awoke I had to remind myself that Kunkel had actually died in 1956, his presence in the dreams seemed so real.

Of course, just as my dreams said, Kunkel *was* alive. He no longer lived in his physical body, and he no longer saw people in his study in the house on Gramercy Place in Los Angeles, but in what Jung calls the collective unconscious he still lived.

For those unfamiliar with the idea of the collective uncon- scious a brief word of explanation may be helpful. The unconscious in general refers to all the psychic life that impinges on us of which we are unaware. The personal unconscious realm includes our particular forgotten or repressed experiences, memories, and emotions. It was Freud's genius to see the reality of the personal unconscious and devise a method for bringing its contents into consciousness. However, Jung went a step further. He saw that in addition to a personal unconscious there was a vast realm of psychic life that was common to all human beings, and he called this the collective unconscious.

An illustration may help. Suppose you look out over the Arctic Ocean and see a number of icebergs. You know that only about one-tenth of each iceberg is above the water and the remainder is beneath the surface. This is roughly the way it is with consciousness and the personal unconscious. Just as only a fraction of the iceberg is above the water, so only a small part of our personality is included in the conscious mind, and the greater part of us, like the greater mass of the iceberg, is beneath the surface of consciousness. But if the top of the iceberg is analogous to consciousness, and the part of the iceberg under the sea is analogous to the personal unconscious, the ocean itself is analogous to the collective unconscious. The collective unconscious is thus a vast psychic life that affects us all, in which we all participate, and which serves to unite us all in a common humanity.

As Jung once put it, it is like an atmosphere in which we live, the unknown quantity in the world.* It was here in this mysterious but real realm of the psyche that Kunkel was alive, and here that he was still teaching, which is to say that his ideas had an autonomous and vital existence.

I knew from these dreams that the collective unconscious valued Kunkel's ideas because they had not been allowed to perish, and I also knew that it must be important that I understand their value or else the dreams would not have come to me. When the third dream of this sort came I began to realize that the dreams had a meaning that transcended my individual personality. That is, they were meant for many people, not just for me. It was then that I began to suspect that it was of great importance that Kunkel's writings come before the public eye once more.

---

*C. G. Jung, *Letters 1.* Princeton, N.J.: Princeton University Press, 1973, p. 433.

With this in mind I began rereading Kunkel's books, especially his two most important books, *How Character Develops* and *In Search of Maturity.* It was as though I had never read them before. This was the measure of how much I had grown since those days long ago when, as a frightened and immature young man, I had first seen him. I was deeply impressed with the originality and importance of his insights, and saw at once that here were important ideas that were not to be found anywhere else.

I then began to lecture on Kunkel's thoughts, and entitled my talks "Toward a Religious Psychology." Partly to deepen my understanding of Kunkel, and partly to test the power of Kunkel's ideas to affect people, I gave lectures and workshops on his material throughout the country for about two years. Wherever I went I found that people drank in Kunkel's insights the way that thirsty people drink water on a desert. The way my talks were received corroborated my perception that the dreams had come to me because it was important to get Kunkel's work into the stream of public consciousness once again.

I also found that part of my dreams could be taken literally. In my dreams, Kunkel was teaching a small group of people; this was the typical dream scenario. Now wherever I went, there were some people who told me they had known Kunkel, or had read his books, and that they still lived by his insights. Many of these people encouraged me to do what I could to have Kunkel's works republished, and I owe them a debt of gratitude for their counsel and encouragement.

So I knew what the task was, but the question was where to begin. Kunkel wrote twenty books that had been, in part, translated into seven languages. But only five of these books had been written in English, and of these five only one, *Creation Continues,* a psychological commentary on the Gospel of St. Matthew, had been republished—by Word Books of Waco, Texas. *Creation Continues* I knew to be a unique and important book, but the two most important books, *How Character Develops* and *In Search of Maturity,* had been out of print for many years.

I decided to concentrate on finding a publisher who would republish these two books. If this could be done, I would be satisfied, since the ideas in Kunkel's earlier books had matured and found their way into these two books, which were the crowning fruit of his efforts.

It was not easy to find a publisher. In Germany, where Kunkel's name is still known, I understand that many of his books have remained in print, but in this country, with a few exceptions, Kunkel was unknown. A company that republished Kunkel's books could lose a lot of money. Finally, however, Paulist Press courageously agreed to accept the risk and undertake the task. The Kunkel family was contacted and gave Paulist Press their consent and encouragement. And so the present volume was conceived.

But the matter was not as simple as simply republishing Kunkel's two books in their original form. For one thing, some situations Kunkel wrote about were no longer relevant today. For instance, he begins *In Search of Maturity* with a long section on the historical situation as it pertains to the relationship of psychology and religion. Since this was written forty years ago much of it is passé today, and some of the things for which he argued, such as the inclusion of more psychology in the pastoral work of the Church, have been resolved to a certain extent. As mentioned, this section came at the very beginning of his book. It was likely that a modern reader who picked up *In Search of Maturity* would become discouraged by this introductory material and not go on to the other chapters.

It seemed clear that Kunkel's two books should be conflated into one single volume that would contain the heart of Kunkel's psychology. This meant that we would be taking part of *In Search of Maturity* and part of *How Character Develops* and building a new book from them. But if you take parts of this and parts of that and put them together you need a cement to unite them. The introductions I have written before the different parts of Kunkel's works are intended to be this cement, and will enable the reader to read his writings as a whole. They are intended to give a flow from one section to the other.

There were other problems. Kunkel lived and wrote a good many decades ago. As a result, some of his illustrative material would appear dated to the modern reader. It was decided that here and there Kunkel's writing needed some careful editing, and this sensitive work was undertaken by the editors of the Paulist Press.

Not all difficulties can be resolved by editing, however, and in places the reader may have to forgive Kunkel for the fact that he was a man who grew up in another era than our own and so was imbued with different social views. For instance, Kunkel consistently used illustrations in which women functioned as wives and mothers. He seldom used illustrations in which women functioned in a professional role outside of the family. For this reason he appears to be unaware of the fact that women can be many things in this world and have many different capacities. This was not his personal view. His own wife was a psychologist and a professional person, and he encouraged a woman's individual development wherever it might take her, but if the reader had only his books to read, this might not appear to be the case. I can only suggest that the reader forgive Kunkel for what appears to be his dated social views and go on to the main substance of his ideas.

A happier note concerns Kunkel's use of imaginative language for complicated psychological processes. For instance, Kunkel used the term "egocentricity" to denote the tendency of people to be interested mainly in the protection and advancement of their Egos. Kunkel saw that only the idea of egocentricity could explain the Ego's insatiable hunger for security, superiority, prestige and power. In modern psychiatric parlance we might use the term "narcissism" instead. The latter term might sound more learned, but Kunkel's term is more descriptive. Also, egocentricity refers to everyone, while only specially designated "cases" are referred to as narcissistic in psychiatric parlance.

The contrast is even more marked when it comes to the terms Kunkel devised for the different egocentric types: Clinging Vine, Star, Turtle, and Nero. These imaginative names are helpful because they evoke in us immediate and vivid images of what these types of people are like. The professional psychologist today, however, might use more elaborate terms, such as "narcissistic character disorder." I suppose such a term sounds very learned, but there is much to be said for Kunkel's less pretentious and livelier language, a language that everyone can understand.

Kunkel's language also comes from his humor. Dr. Kunkel

had a sly, roguish sense of humor, and it comes into his writings in the way he expresses himself. For instance, he speaks of "Black Giants" and "White Giants" to refer to those people whom we have made into threatening or protective parent-types, and instead of speaking of a "depressive neurosis" he refers to "the doghouse" and to "minus 100." Kunkel doesn't mean to make light of the suffering of the Ego or minimize the gravity of the situation, but his humorous language helps us not to regard our plight as hopeless. There is always something ridiculous, as well as tragic, about the human situation. As is well known, when you can laugh or smile at yourself you are a free person. Kunkel knew this and preferred his ordinary, sometimes whimsical language to the burdensome language of psychiatry, which crushes a person with the feeling that he is, after all, simply a meaningless psychiatric case.

Finally there is the relaxed and unselfconscious way in which Kunkel spoke of God; for him it was natural to speak of God, and he doesn't hesitate to do so in his writings. He saw God's influence at work in human life, and perceived God's power working in his patients, himself, and the world situation. The result is that though Kunkel was a scientifically trained person and a careful clinician, he does not hesitate to speak of God in his books.

On the other hand, Kunkel did not speak of God in his psychotherapy unless his client brought God up. God was always a reality for Kunkel when he worked with his people, but he felt that to use the word would infringe upon the freedom of his clients. He did not need to use God's name to feel that his presence was there in his consulting room, and he never confused the work of the healer with that of the theologian or evangelist.

Kunkel believed that the Christian story with its emphasis on death and resurrection best represented the psychological and spiritual process through which the soul must pass on its way to fulfillment, and that Christ pointed the way personally to all those who must undergo such an experience of transformation. He also believed that beyond the suffering and tragedy of this life was a transcendental background of love best represented in the resurrection. But he could not concern himself with denominations, creeds, and churches, because his concern was with the human soul and its immediate relationship with God. Religion for him

involved constant, creative change, leading into a future development, while institutionalized expressions of religion tend to become rigid, and intent on preserving the past. His religious
convictions were rooted in his own experiences, and in his belief
as a psychotherapist that in the last analysis only creative change
heals a person. My friend Bea Burch has summarized Kunkel the
religious man very nicely in an article she wrote for the magazine
Inward Light. She also tells us of one of the powerful inner
experiences which led Kunkel to his religious point of view.

Though he investigated the past, where he felt that patterns
had been formed, he believed that the future was the important force. As the oak tree is in some unknown fashion contained in the acorn, so, to him, all future human evolution is
contained in each human individual. As the growth of the
acorn is determined by the thing-which-is-to-be, that oak tree
of the future, so, in Dr. Kunkel's view, is each human creature
pulled by his own still invisible future form, which molds his
psychological development as surely, perhaps more surely,
than past experience has conditioned it.

He had little love for the merely conventionally acceptable
action, the stereotyped, the safe, the palatable. He was too
familiar with the powerful, elemental and primitive qualities
in man—knew their capacities for both destruction and construction, and, like Walt Whitman, he celebrated them. Reckless honesty was to be preferred to cautious conformity;
daring courage was vastly better than timorous security. . . .

His spirituality lay in the vitality and immediacy of his response to all life, his openness to experience, his depth of
awareness of the relatedness of all mankind, and in his un-
shakeable conviction of the ultimate goodness and beauty of
creation, no matter how tragic or terrifying its immediate
aspect.

He told me once of his own experience of this ultimate
goodness. It was when, in the First World War, he was
seriously wounded, his left arm blown to shreds. As he lay on
the ground, waiting for the rescue team to arrive, he found
the world transformed. Suddenly he became aware, in the

tumult and terrors about him, in the battlefield with its dead and dying, of an overwhelming beauty, significance, meaning. It was, for all its ghastly horrors, part of a beauty and "love" in which he knew himself and all things to share. The immediate, transforming vision faded. But the inner certainty which it created was to last a lifetime.*

When a child is born into the world you can be hopeful, but you can't be sure what the child's fate in this world will be. Similarly, no one can be sure what effect this republication of Kunkel's work will have in our time. But for reasons I hope to make clear, I believe his ideas are more relevant today than ever before, and am confident that this book will be enthusiastically received by many people.

The Relevance of Kunkel's Thought for Today

As mentioned earlier, Kunkel was well known in Germany, and when he moved to the United States he soon became well known here during the seventeen years in which he practiced, wrote, and lectured in this country. After Kunkel died, however, it seemed as though he was forgotten, although this was not entirely true since, as I have mentioned, there were many individuals throughout the nation who recalled the man and his work with affection and gratitude. But compared to other depth psychologists of his era he is not well known, and while our present decade is full of all kinds of psychological mentors and self-proclaimed gurus, Kunkel's name is not one of them. Yet, as my dreams showed me, his work was important to the unconscious. We are confronted therefore with the question of why his work seems to have disappeared from the mainstream of conscious life.

Perhaps the foremost reason is because his was a religious psychology, which was bound to be unpopular with many people because it would challenge cherished beliefs. His psychology was religious because he believed that the meaning of a human life

---

*Beatrice D. Burch, "Dr. Kunkel and the Long Distance Analysis." *Inward Light*, Vol. XXV, No. 63, pp. 14–15.

could only be revealed when it was seen in religious terms. If his psychology was religious, it was because the psyche is religious. If as a psychologist he spoke of God, it was because he believed that the process of human development was profoundly influenced by the call to a future development that can only be aptly expressed in religious terms. Such an approach, however, was certain to meet with rejection. At the time Kunkel lived and wrote, most depth psychology disparaged religion. This was the heyday of Freud, and for Freud religion was an illusion, and a life-crippling one at that, while God was a purely human construct whose function was to support a neurosis-producing Super-Ego; not only was there no God in reality, but the very idea of God was a childish illusion perpetuated by mankind for neurotic reasons. In Freud's psychoanalysis one matured to the point where he could do without the notion of God, and stand on his own two feet in a world that had no ultimate spiritual purpose.

Of course, not all psychology was modeled after Freud. Academic psychology, for instance, repudiated Freud's depth psychology as vague and unscientific, full of ideas, such as that of the unconscious, which were unverifiable and did not fit into the materialistic philosophic approach that academic psychology assumed was the only possible scientific attitude. This branch of psychology tried to put itself on the same scientific footing as other sciences. The only hypotheses about human behavior that could be accepted were those that could be verified in the laboratory, even though the workings of the psyche can hardly ever be studied by such limited methods. Perhaps because the academic psychologists felt inferior to their brethren in other sciences they felt a need to overcompensate by attempting to be more rational and narrowly scientific than anyone else. The consequence was a rejection of depth psychology with its notion of the unconscious, and an emphasis instead on learning theory, experimental psychology, and behaviorism. Their work has produced a number of important insights and discoveries, but the human soul got lost in the process. Naturally, starting from such a rationalistic and materialistic premise, any talk of God was absurd, for the idea of God was a mystical notion, totally unverifiable, suitable perhaps for theologians to discuss, but of no importance or relevance for psychology. Therefore if a psychologist like Kunkel tried to discuss God in relationship to psychology it was best to ignore him.

One might have supposed that members of organized religions would have welcomed Kunkel, accepting the outcast from the psychological world into their midst as a friend and ally who could help them understand the way God works with people. Some of them did, but for the most part organized religion ignored Kunkel as much as organized psychology ignored him. If Kunkel was right, many traditional religious ideas were going to have to change. It was easier to brush aside the troublesome thoughts Kunkel brought up.

However, the religious world of Kunkel's day could not entirely ignore psychology, for depth psychology had mushroomed into a worldwide movement of considerable importance and was influencing our whole culture and outlook. It was apparent to many pastors and theologians that modern psychology could not be completely disregarded. Furthermore, some of the clergy became interested in the possibilities that psychology offered for pastoral care and counseling. Strangely enough, however, the psychologist who was turned to most within the Church was not the theistic Kunkel, nor even the religiously minded Jung, but the atheistic Freud. Probably the reason for this seemingly strange phenomenon is that Freud was "safer" than Jung or Kunkel precisely because his ideas about religion could be disregarded. Take Freud's psychology, eliminate what he said about God and religion, and you can use the rest without fear that it will disturb your theology. At least, not very much, and what disturbance it does bring can be brushed aside. That's not so with Jung or Kunkel; you can't eliminate the religious point of view from them because it is integral to their entire psychology. With them, psychology and religion simply can't be separated, any more than you can cut the heart out of a person and expect him to live.

So far we have considered reasons why people with a vested interest in their own psychological or religious ideas might have rejected Kunkel, but there is another reason that applies to us all: his thesis that the basic obstacle that stands between us and our personal growth is our own egocentricity. We shall soon discover what Kunkel means by this. For now it is enough to say that, all our protests to the contrary, it is our own ego-centered position that puts us in opposition to creative change and is the cause for the perpetuation of our difficulties. People don't like to hear this. We prefer to believe that we are innocent victims of circumstances beyond our control, objects deserving of sympathy and compassion, who should be cured in some painless manner.

To be sure, there is Kunkel's good news that there is also a genuine Self in us full of creative power, but he makes it clear that first we must submit to the bad news before we can realize the good news. The crucifixion comes before the resurrection, but who wants the crucifixion if it can be avoided? It is Kunkel's point that for many of us it can't be avoided, that some people can only get to heaven by going through hell. If anyone can offer people a psychology that purports to give us the benefits of the whole life without requiring that we undergo the difficulties of overcoming our egocentricity it is bound to be popular. Kunkel didn't do that.

So it was that Kunkel's ideas were for the most part like seeds that fell upon hard and stony ground. While he was alive and the direct influence of his personality was there to reinforce his teachings he commanded a following, but when he died the seeds of his ideas continued to live only here and there in a few people, and, as we have seen, in the collective unconscious where his work was not allowed to die.

Though the world was not ready to receive Kunkel in 1956, it may be ready to receive him now, for today the state of mind is different, and the times have a different feeling to them. I think there is a reason why the dreams that came to me in 1980 and 1981 did not come earlier; the time was not ripe earlier for the reintroduction of Kunkel's thought. Now the mental and spiritual climate may be more receptive.

Since Kunkel died, interest in psychology has gradually increased, and in recent years it has grown significantly. In Kunkel's day, Freudian psychoanalysis dominated the stage, but today Freudian psychology has passed its zenith and many people are looking for other psychological perspectives. Of course a great number of people still look for a convenient psychological "package" that will solve all their problems while at the same time requiring the least effort and change from them, and plenty of prophets are willing to step forth to offer these people what they want. But there also seems to be a growing number of people with more mature psychological goals. For whatever reason, there are now people who seem to have both the need and the sincerity of purpose to embrace a psychology that points the finger at their own egocentricty, provided that psychology is meaningful.

There also seems to be an increased willingness on the part of many religious people to entertain a new idea about how God works among people. While the walls that protect cherished theological ideas are certainly still there, there also seem to be many people who are willing to stand outside those walls, but are unwilling to give up the idea that there is an intelligent direction to life as a whole. These people are open to a religious psychology in a way that was impossible some decades ago.

Finally, help has come from another direction: the psychology of C. G. Jung has begun to influence us. When Fritz Kunkel was living and working in Germany, so was Carl Jung in Switzerland. During the 1930's and 1940's Jung had more of a worldwide reputation than Kunkel, but compared to Freud, Jung was a dark horse, a psychologist whose work was either unknown or only dimly understood. There was, to be sure, a devoted group of people who were enormously attracted to Jung, and many of these people were themselves creative and capable individuals, but they existed only as individuals or in small groups. While psychoanalysis, for instance, had become a worldwide movement, highly organized, with training centers and a system for accrediting psychoanalysts, Jungian psychology had none of this. Slowly Jung's personal reputation grew, and gradually his books were published and read by the daring and venturesome, but there was nothing like the movement engendered by Freudian psychology. And while Freudian psychoanalysis made heavy inroads into psychiatry, and, as we have seen, even into pastoral counseling, Jungian psychology was either unknown or overtly rejected by both collective medicine and collective religion.

Partly this was the way Jung himself wanted it. He distrusted organization. He did not want the collectivization of his ideas. He feared that acceptance of his thought by the power structures of his day would threaten his psychology with erosion and corruption. Only late in his life, when the fact of his death seemed imminent, and under pressure from his colleagues and friends, did Jung finally assent to the organization of a school for the promulgation of Jungian psychology and the training of analysts: the C. G. Jung Institute of Zurich.

Nevertheless, Jungian psychology was growing. Like all important scientific ideas it could not be permanently denied, and the seeds of Jung's thought, scattered here and there by his books and by personal contact, began to take root in the minds of more and more people.

Jungian psychology grew like a bulb grows under the ground. The bulb lies invisible, hidden in the earth, but gradually grows and expands until at the proper time it pushes its way through the earth's crust and sends forth its stalk and flower. So today Jungian psychology has emerged into public view. Jung's name is now well known, his books are widely read, and his thoughts have influenced an increasing number of psychologists, theologians, and lay people.

The emergence of Jungian psychology will be a great aid to the acceptance of Kunkel's psychology, for Kunkel's psychology can be understood much more readily in the light of what Jung had to say. In many respects, Kunkel's ideas rest on Jung's ideas. Certainly Jung's ideas make a good background against which Kunkel's contributions to psychology can be seen.

As has been noted, Kunkel studied Freudian psychology, worked personally with Adler, and knew Jung. The influence of all three of the originators of depth psychology can be seen in Kunkel's psychology. Kunkel shares with Freud an emphasis on the importance of early childhood experiences in determining the course of adult psychological development. He shares with Adler an appreciation of the importance of the Ego, with its striving and ambitions. But it was Jung's idea of individuation, the lifelong process that impels a person to develop into a whole person, that most nourished Kunkel's idea of the creative Self that lies at the center of a person's psyche. Kunkel frequently acknowledged his debt to Jung, and saw where his ideas and Jung's overlap, though there were places where he sharply disagreed with the master psychologist from Zurich, so much so that he himself never became a Jungian.

One of the refreshing things about Kunkel is that he never claimed to have invented a complete psychological system, to the exclusion of other psychological points of view. He perceived that without the work of Freud, Adler, and Jung his own psychology would have been incomplete, and therefore managed to avoid the messianic pretensions and inflations that befall many psychologists who take their particular, limited bit of truth and make a monolithic psychological world view out of it. Kunkel made his attitude toward his contribution toward psychology clear in the introduction to *How Character Develops:*

> The relationship between the We-Psychology and other systems of psychology is not one of competition but of completion. . . . The We-Psychology is not an attempt to supersede other psychological systems. . . . It does not pretend to be more right or nearer the truth than such systems. In fact, it tries not to be a complete unit at all. It simply calls attention to certain things in our psychic life which have been too much neglected heretofore.*

It should bring a sense of relief to the reader of this book to know that he is not going to encounter a new self-proclaimed messiah. For someone who comes from a Jungian point of view it should be possible to integrate Kunkel's perspective into Jungian psychology in such a way that something is added but nothing is lost. For the religious person, it should be possible to read Kunkel and accept his ideas, free from the fear that he will have to replace his faith in God with an allegiance to a self-styled new prophet.

Now for a word on the organization of this book. For obvious reasons, the book begins with the biographical sketch by John Kunkel, followed by this introduction. The next section is a concise résumé of Jung's most important psychological ideas. The reason for this should now be clear: since Jungian thought provides a foundation for a proper understanding of Kunkel, it is good to begin with a description of Jung's psychology. Those readers who are already familiar with it may wish to pass over this part of the book, although I think if they read it they will be glad since it is part of a proper introduction to what follows.

The next part is the heart of the book: the reprinting of the

---

*Fritz Kunkel, *How Character Develops*. New York: Charles Scribner's and Sons, 1946, p. xi.

major portions of Kunkel's two most important books, *How Character Develops* and *In Search of Maturity.* Three hundred and eighty-three of an original five hundred and fifty-eight pages have been reprinted, and these three hundred and eighty-three pages include, I believe, all the most important elements of Kunkel's thought.

As I have already mentioned, I have written introductions to each of the major sections of Kunkel's books that are reprinted here, for the purpose of preserving continuity and to lead the reader from one section to another in an organized way. In addition, I have some ideas of my own that have emerged from my study of Kunkel and comparison of Kunkel with Jung and with Christian thought. These ideas are found in the final part of the book, a series of short articles in which I comment on the relevance of Kunkel's ideas for biblical study, Jungian concepts, dream analysis, and many other points of interest. In this final section, the first articles are of primary interest to the Christian world, and the last to the Jungian world.

I regard the last part of the book as a little like dessert after a good meal. If you like dessert you eat it, but if you don't like dessert you're happy anyway because you've just finished a good meal. If you only go through Kunkel's own material you will have gained most of what is to be gained from reading this book, but if you are interested in the way Kunkel's thought impinges on Christianity and Jungian psychology, you may wish to read the final section as well.

General Introduction
Part Two:
The Psychology of C. G. Jung
in Relationship
to Fritz Kunkel

In Galatians 2:20 St. Paul says: "I live now not with my own life but with the life of Christ who lives in me." In this statement, Paul tells us that his personality has been reorganized in such a way that it no longer revolves around his Ego, but around a larger center within himself that he calls the Christ within. This is the essential thought of a religious psychology, namely, that in the course of our lifetime our personalities are to be transformed and reorganized in such a way that the Ego, with its ambitions and goals, is no longer the main reference point. Instead, the guiding element in our personality is to be the will of God, which in psychological language we call the Self or Center.

Such a psychology is religious because it involves the recognition of a higher power than the Ego, a power that the Ego must recognize and serve, but it is also psychology because it is possible to describe empirically, and study scientifically, this process of personality transformation, and to find evidence for the reality of both Ego and Self.

The Swiss psychiatrist C.G. Jung observed such a process of transformation taking place in himself and in his patients and gave it a name: *individuation.* Individuation is the lifelong process that goes on within a person and seeks to bring into being a whole,

23

completed, and unique personality. Jung says that he used the term individuation to denote a person who has become a psychologically undivided and therefore whole person, that is, a person in whom the conscious and unconscious dimensions of personality are in harmony. Individuation means individuality, an embracing of our own innermost and incomparable uniqueness, and thus implies becoming truly oneself. If we expressed the meaning of individuation in religious language we would say that it means becoming what God intended us to become, and that it necessitates following God's will rather than our own will.

It should be emphasized that individuation is not a process we consciously decide upon, but is thrust upon us by our deepest instinct: the urge from within to become whole. Individuation does not start with the Ego, but from a source within us we know little about. Therefore we say that the source of individuation is the unconscious.

Jung was aware of the religious nature of this process. This is why, in an oft-quoted passage, Jung once said that he never saw a problem in a person over thirty-five years of age that was not in the final analysis a religious problem. In one of his letters he wrote: "Individuation is ultimately a religious process which requires a corresponding religious attitude—the ego-will submits to God's will.*

The religions of the world have represented the individuation process in theological or metaphysical language. Jung, however, was a scientist. He did not come up with the idea of individuation because he felt that it had been revealed in somebody's sacred scripture, but because he observed it taking place in his clinical experience and in his own inner development. He also believed that he saw it represented symbolically in spontaneous products of the unconscious such as dreams, myths, fairy tales, and alchemy. Since he was a scientist he came up with a scientific language to describe what he saw taking place as people became whole. We will now look at some of the more important scientific terms that Jung devised for his purposes.

We have already used the term *Ego*. The Ego is the "I" part of us. In fact, in both Latin and Greek the word Ego occurs with

---

*C.G. Jung, *Letters* 2. Princeton, N.J.: Princeton University Press, 1975, p. 265.

this meaning. The Ego is that part of us with which we are consciously identified. When we think of ourselves we think for the most part of our Ego. It has been called the "executive of the conscious personality." The Ego is that part of us therefore that does the willing, choosing, and suffering in life, and that has a certain continuity of memory.

While this part of us that gives rise to our self-consciousness can be said to be the Ego, we must not make the mistake of assuming that we are aware of the way our Ego functions. To the contrary, as Kunkel will make clear, many of the processes of the Ego are unconscious to us. Nevertheless, as an approximate rule of thumb, it is safe to say that there is a close affinity between Ego and consciousness, so that the Ego may be regarded as the center of the conscious mind.

We have already used the term *Self.* In common parlance we speak of "myself" or "yourself" in a loosely defined manner as though it is almost a synonym for the Ego. But in Jung's psychology the Self is used with a special meaning to denote the whole personality (while the Ego, in contrast, is only a portion of the personality). In Jung's psychology human personality is partly conscious and partly unconscious. The Ego, as we have seen, refers to consciousness, but the Self refers to the totality of the personality that includes all that belongs to us, both consciousness and the unconscious.

The Self can be thought of as the center of the personality, its midpoint or inner unity. In fact, we sometimes will use the word "Center" as a synonym for the Self (Kunkel often uses it). Roughly defined, then, this Self is our Center, our wholeness, our totality, and our uniqueness, but we must also think of the Self as the circumference of our personality, that which bounds everything and contains everything within it. This shows that the Self is a psychological hypothesis or construct that must be evoked in order to explain a great many psychological facts, but is concerned with a reality so paradoxical that it escapes our rational comprehension. When we see later on how the Self is not only the center of *our* personality, but exists between us and others, its paradoxical quality will become even more apparent.

We are speaking of the Self as something already existing, but we also must think of the Self as a potentiality striving to become realized in us. The Self gains expression only through a life that someone actually lives. While the Self is always there, it becomes operative only in the life of the individual.

It should be clear that the Self is much greater in scope and more difficult to comprehend than the Ego. In fact, no one can say that he understands the Self, for no one has succeeded in becoming completely whole or making conscious all of his personality.

It should also be clear from these definitions that there is a special relationship between the Self and individuation. Individuation is the process in which the Self seeks and achieves realization, but this means that there must be a special relationship between the Ego and the Self, and that the realization of the Self can only take place in and through the Ego. The Ego must therefore lead the correct kind of life, and achieve a certain consciousness, if individuation is to occur.

Thus Ego and Self need each other. The Ego needs the Self because the Self is the support, foundation, and source of life for the Ego. On the other hand, the Self needs the Ego because the Ego is the proper representative of the Self in life. Without the Self, the Ego is powerless and ineffective; without the Ego the Self is unexpressed. This unique relationship between the two can be represented in the following diagram:

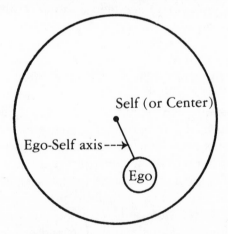

In this diagram, the Self is represented by the larger circle and the Ego by the smaller circle. The Self is also represented by the center of the the large circle. This shows its paradoxical nature as both circumference and midpoint. Clearly, the Self is larger than the Ego, and the Ego is contained within the Self. This is true even when the Ego is unaware of the Self. The optimum relationship that can exist between Ego and Self is represented by the line connecting the small circle with the center of the large circle. This line is called by Jungian analyst Edward Edinger the "Ego-Self axis." When this connection exists between Ego and Self, the Ego is positively connected to the Self and experiences it as a creative will other than its own. Many methods are used in both religious disciplines and in psychology to create this Ego-Self axis. Some of the more common ones are prayer, meditation, and the analysis of dreams.

However, the relationship between Ego and Self may not be correct; then the Ego-Self axis will not be functioning. This state of affairs is represented in the following diagram:

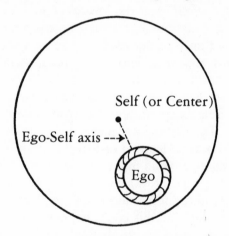

In this diagram, the inadequate connection between Ego and Self is represented by the broken line. The extra thick line around the circle that represents the Ego symbolizes the egocentric Ego, which is isolated behind its defenses that are like thick walls around it. The Ego inside of these thick, rigid walls is unaware of the existence of the larger reality of the Self even though it is contained within it.

Another term we need to introduce is the *Shadow.* The Shadow consists of all those psychic qualities within us which, because of their incompatibility with conscious goals and attitudes, have been denied access to consciousness, and therefore denied expression in life. These qualities could have become part of our conscious Ego structure, but because we fear or distrust them they have been banished from consciousness into the unconscious. They do not, however, cease to exist. Instead they form a secondary personality within us, an alter-Ego, an autonomous "splinter personality" that carries on a life of its own even though we may know nothing about it. The Shadow is thus "that part of our personality which has been repressed for the sake of the Ego ideal."*

The Shadow is the object of our fear, hatred, loathing and dislike, but also is the object of our secret longing and desire, for the urges that the Shadow represents have a certain fascination. It is the Mr. Hyde to our Dr. Jekyll, the dark and dreadful inner man or woman whom we nevertheless long for in a secret way.

Because the qualities of the Shadow could have been incorporated into our conscious Ego structure, the Shadow appears in our dreams as a figure of our own sex. So in a woman's dreams, the Shadow will appear as another woman, usually disliked or feared, and similarly with a man.

The Shadow has a special relationship to the individuation process. Without a recognition of the Shadow, individuation cannot take place. The reason for this will become more apparent when we consider what Kunkel had to say on the subject.

Jung's psychology is, in many respects, an optimistic one, for the individuation process brings with it an experience of meaningfulness. To experience individuation taking place in us, or even to intuit that something like this could happen, is to acquire a sense of purpose and meaning to life that can give a person hope and courage. This is true even if things are going badly. Individuation is an encouraging idea because it implies that life has a meaning, and that there is an intelligence to life, beyond that of the Ego, that can guide us through life's difficulties.

However, in practice, individuation is far from simple. For one thing, individuation is not a process we can ever say we have completed. We never become whole; we can only perhaps ap-

---

*Edward C. Whitmont, *The Symbolic Quest.* Princeton, N.J., Princeton University Press, 1978 paperback edition, p. 160.

proximate wholeness. Moreover, for reasons that will become clearer later on, we can function in a whole way one day and the next day lose our contact with the Center and once again be woefully incomplete.

The path of individuation is like a path through a dense forest that we can easily lose; then we wind up wandering and lost instead of finding our way. It is a tortuous path, full of unexpected twists and turns. It goes like a serpent crawling on the ground, not like a bird that flies in a straight line through the air. It takes us now here and now there, and sometimes we discover that just when we thought we were on the path, we have lost it. As my friend and colleague Robert Johnson once said, "I climb up two steps and fall back three but I get there anyway because I was going the wrong way in the first place."

Why a process that is apparently so desirable should be so difficult is partly due to the hardship of finding our way through the twists and turns of a life that is constantly changing and demanding new attitudes and potentialities from us. But when we look more closely into our difficulties we will see that the Ego itself is a large part of the problem.

We have already seen that if the Self is to be realized it must be expressed through the Ego. We may compare the Ego to the neck of a bottle of wine, and the Self to the contents of the bottle. Clearly the wine is the important thing, and the neck of the bottle is only important as a means of getting the wine out. As long as the neck of the bottle is clear, all goes well, but if for some reason the neck should be obstructed the wine can't flow. The Ego is like this. It is either like the neck of the bottle through which the wine of the Self flows, or it becomes an obstruction to the process, in which case we might speak of its being a "bottleneck," an impediment.

It was not lost on Jung that the Ego was necessary if individuation was to occur, but that there were bottlenecks. His method of analysis was intended to clear away these bottlenecks and help the individuation process take place by enabling the Ego to become conscious. As long as a person is unconscious, he is blocked as far as individuation is concerned, for an unaware person can't help but be a bottleneck to individuation.

To become conscious means many different things; in fact,

the process of becoming conscious is basically indescribable though we can say certain things about it. It involves becoming aware of one's own psychological nature, including both our potentialities for development and also our dark side, like the Shadow. Everything about ourselves of which we become aware adds to our range of consciousness. It also means becoming aware of other people and who they are and what they are like and of the nature of our relationship with them. It means the expansion of our thoughts, feelings, and emotions, and becoming involved in the issues of living. It can be seen that life itself is a sort of arena in which we can become conscious, and that becoming conscious is a main function of the Ego.

The function of the psychotherapist, Jung felt, was to help his client become conscious. In the analytical process, interactions with others are examined for their meaning, and so are manifestations of unconscious psychic life such as slips of the tongue, dreams, and emotional outbursts engendered by our inner complexes. The psychology of our childhood is explored to help us understand ourselves better, and we look for indications of unrecognized and undeveloped creative abilities. Jung felt that psychological analysis was so important that one might get the idea that without analysis a person can't individuate, but life itself is the great teacher, and anyone who lives life completely, experiences bravely its sufferings and joys, and learns its lessons becomes a more whole person.

In stressing the importance of becoming conscious, Jung stands firmly in the tradition of all depth psychologists from the time of Freud. It was Freud who discovered that certain types of psychologically induced problems could be cured when underlying but unconscious psychological processes were uncovered and brought into awareness. From experiences like these came the confidence of depth psychology that if only a person becomes more conscious, the negative and life-defeating symptoms will vanish and a cure will result.

In Christian theology we speak of "soteriology," which means "salvation theory." Soteriology is that branch of theology that discusses why people need to be saved, and what it is that saves them. As far as depth psychology is concerned, what we need to be saved from is ignorance, especially of ourselves, and what saves us is becoming conscious. In early Christianity, the importance of *knowing* in relationship to salvation was stressed by the Gnostics, a group of people who believed that only if you were "in the know" could you be saved. The very word "Gnostic" comes from a Greek word "gnosis" that means "knowledge." There were Gnostics in the early Christian era who had nothing to do with Christianity and were part of a movement known as Gnosticism, but there were also Christian Gnostics, such as Clement of Alexandria and Origen, who were part of the life of the Church. These people were "Christians-in-the-know" and emphasized the importance for the Christian life of achieving knowledge of oneself and one's proper place in the cosmic scheme of things.

At first in Christianity, the Gnostic Christians and the other Christians who emphasized faith to the exclusion of gnosis existed side by side, but later in Christian history the Gnostic element in the Church was rejected. It is an interesting thought to speculate that the rejected Gnostic element in Christianity has reappeared in the guise of depth psychology. For this is certainly the mainspring of analysis: to know is to be saved, or, at the very least, makes it possible.

However, even with an expanding psychological awareness the process of individuation often seems to be thwarted. The truth is that the Ego actually seems to resist the process of becoming whole, and this resistance can't be explained on the basis of ignorance alone. Even persons with a great deal of psychological knowledge and acumen can resist becoming whole in devilishly subtle ways. In the same way, seemingly sincere Christians, possessed with all the credentials that should produce a state of salvation, can fail to be whole. Something seems to be wrong with the Ego; for some reason it seems to keep getting in the way.

The truth is that the Ego is a great cheat, and is so clever at it that it can cheat at anything. The Ego can use the best of religion—be it Judaism, Christianity or some religion from the East—and in spite of becoming an expert about it, it can still cheat. It can use psychology, even Jung's psychology, and still cheat at the process of individuation. People can acquire a great deal of religious understanding or psychological insight, and master all kinds of philosophical or psychological concepts, can even become learned gurus or successful psychotherapists, and still be cheating.

Something strange is going on!

This is where the importance of Fritz Kunkel and his work enters the scene, for Kunkel was the one who saw most clearly that the Ego was cheating and why. It all has to do, he said, with egocentricity. Early in life, Kunkel argued, we are forced into an egocentric pattern, and it is the perseverance of this egocentric pattern that defeats the process of individuation. The more ignorant we are of ourselves and our egocentricity the more complete the defeat of life's process will be, but even if we see some of our egocentricity we may continue to remain stuck in it. Since the reality of the Self can't be expressed through an egocentric Ego, the matter is of great importance. In religious language, an egocentric person can't do God's will but can only try to fulfill his own will.

Kunkel's life work studied egocentricity: how it starts, how it functions, what forms it takes, and, most important of all, how we can be cured of it. Kunkel also had a gift for describing vividly the contrast between the rich and creative life that comes from the Self with the cramped life that comes from egocentricity. It's time now to introduce the first portion of Kunkel's own writing, and let him tell us in his own words what he saw to be the problem, and the solution.

Section One

THE EGOCENTRIC LIFE
AND THE
LIFE OF THE REAL SELF

Introduction

How Character Develops was written before *In Search of Maturity,* but we begin with two chapters from *In Search of Maturity* because these chapters present us with Kunkel's main thesis: that we live either a creative life from the Self, or a constricted life from the egocentric Ego.

Kunkel presents his thesis scientifically, but also uses imaginative and colorful language. He is trying to help us grasp the difference between the creative and the uncreative life not only intellectually, but also with our imagination and emotions. Only if we are affected on a deeper level than our intellects will we find the energy and faith that will enable us to break free of defeating egocentric patterns that have become entrenched through years of false living.

Most of us are so habituated to our narrow and defensive egocentric lives that we mistake this for the norm. After all, we have been living this way since we were children, so we are not aware that this egocentric life is not the real life.

Imagine that you have lived all your life behind huge walls that are so high and thick you don't know there is anything on the other side of them. In fact, it never even occurs to you that these are walls; you mistake them for the limits of reality. For this reason you don't try to get through them to the other side, but live all your life within their confines because this is all you know.

Now imagine that someone comes along who can help you understand that you are living a confined life behind walls, and that on the other side of them is a vast and beautiful country. If this person is sufficiently skillful and knowledgeable he might inspire you to make an effort to get through. Or, at the least, he

35

might create in your mind the new thought that the life you are leading isn't the only life possible for you. Most of us are like people living behind such walls, and Kunkel is a man who can help us see our plight, and help us understand that there is a much more vital life possible for us. That is what Kunkel sets out to do in the two chapters that follow.

Creative Power

Human life needs help; otherwise it may destroy itself. The more resourceful we become and the more we develop the technical means of making life beautiful and happy, the more destructive and bloody grow our moral catastrophes, our crimes, revolutions, and wars. We know more or less how to raise and handle cattle, but we do not know how to deal with ourselves and our fellowmen.

Immense hidden powers seem to lurk in the unconscious depths of even the most common man—indeed, of all people without exception. It is these powers, when put under pressure, that are responsible for all great creative efforts, whether in the form of a new technical invention or a work of art. Some of the most important books in the world's literature have been written in prison. The same forces—in people who are driven to despair—turn men into criminals, are responsible for addictions and obsessions, all kinds of madness, and suicide. Where large groups of people have to face this pressure—as is the case during economic depressions, religious persecutions, class struggles and national wars—there arise, on the one hand, heroes who perform the highest deeds of courage and loyalty, while on the other hand thousands or millions of lives are wantonly destroyed. Such is the origin of powerful empires and worldwide religious movements.

What is the relation between the destructive and the creative power? And what are the conditions which make people either creative or destructive? If we want to help ourselves, our friends, and our governments, we should know more about those hidden powers.

We understand, or think we understand, a large number of human reactions. We usually interpret them as the expressions of hunger or love, self-preservation or race-preservation. The exact meaning of these words may be questionable but we comprehend their implications because we have similar experiences in our own lives. That an individual is afraid of losing money or falling sick, that he enjoys being popular or being successful, is taken for granted. In the last analysis, however, it remains difficult to explain what kind of motive or cause may prompt our reactions, attitudes, and developments. And especially in the case of conflict between self- and race-preservation, we do not understand what makes one of the antagonistic motives or forces prevail.

In our discussion, the blind forces of nature not related to any living form shall be called energies (such as electricity and gravitation). They can be understood and used in terms of cause and effect; no moral values or goals, as far as we can see, are involved. And the "life forces," whether they are motives, instincts, or drives, shall be called "powers," and shall be considered in connection with biological or sociological forms. We have to describe them in terms of means and goals, though their highest ends may remain incomprehensible to the human mind.

As soon as we understand the word "preservation" as related to the present form of life, we have to admit that self- and race-preservation can explain only a certain part of human activities. There are evidently other tendencies, desires, or powers, which force us to create and to believe in new ideas and forms. Almost every century produces new visions of individual life and of society, and every time this happens thousands of people are ready to die for these new values. These creative powers are again related to forms, future forms—and the groups motivated by them are inclined to sacrifice the existence of the individual and even of large parts of the race for the sake of a future society of the Golden Jerusalem beyond space and time.

We see then that, besides the power of self-preservation and race-preservation, we have to acknowledge a strange and daring power of self-development and race-development which may one day compel us to become martyrs for values which we do not yet know.

Moreover, we find frequently in young people, and especially primitive "red-blooded" people who are still living close to nature, a peculiar longing for danger, adventure, and if necessary for sacrifice of health and life. It sometimes expresses itself as an exuberant desire to meet with the danger of death. The mountaineer realizes a sharpening of all his senses, and a deeper awareness of his being alive when he embarks on a climb which may prove fatal. The good hunter prefers to hunt lions rather than rabbits. The healthy boy likes to swim across the roughest waters or to drive a hundred miles an hour. And the healthy girl throws herself, even against her own better judgment, into an impossible love affair.

To most of our psychologists this tendency seems to be so strange and inexplicable that they simply explain it away as deviation, neurosis or criminality. They believe that the striving for security is the basic human instinct. And they cannot see that here, where nature still is "red in tooth and claw," bloodshed and sacrifice are the half-conscious, misunderstood, but all-powerful expressions of a central and creative impulse.

Most of us are Hamlets nowadays:

Thus conscience does make cowards of us all;
And thus the native hue of resolution
Is sicklied o'er with the pale cast of thought,
And enterprises of great pith and moment
With this regard their currents turn awry,
And lose the name of action.

We are afraid of this natural urge for danger and adventure, but we may sometimes, as Hamlet did, enjoy its queer excitement and almost prehistoric atmosphere. It tells us that life is useless, that money, reputation, family are worthless, unless we take our life in our hands at least once and throw it deliberately and consciously at the feet of the gods or the demons, regardless of whether they may bless us or destroy us. It is primitive religion, an unconscious groping of blind people attracted by the light.

England has always had the opportunity of sending her young

daredevils all over the seven seas. From the other European countries the young and the stout of heart used to come to America where they became pioneers, golddiggers, or gangsters. All of them threw themselves at the feet of the demons, and many of them found God beyond the demons. They probably would not have found him if they had stayed at home.

This crude longing for deeper experiences is the best part of primitive life; it is the compass pointing to danger and adventure as the shortest way to spend the primitive forces and to reach the higher level of culture. What will happen, however, to this longing, how will this power express itself if improving civilization does not allow conquistadores, pirates, gangsters, and pioneers? How will the untamed nature of red-blooded people behave in a "pale-blooded," so-called Christian society? It will start one revolution after the other, unless we find a better way which leads from nature "red in tooth and claw" through the encounter with sacrifice and danger to inner maturity and real religion.

Our inner, unknown power has to face an adequate outer situation in order to be lived out, experienced, and consciously developed until it reaches a more creative level. The potential hero is looking for the possibility of becoming his best self, and, if his environment prevents him from so developing, his true life is not lived and his hidden talents turn into the negative, driving him around like a madman. Unconsciously he tries to find or to create the fire which can purge him; he forces people to fight him, because nothing else can teach him the truth. The more he has gone astray, the more dangerous and painful must be the outer situation for the fulfillment of his inner life—until finally his "power of darkness" will change into the "power of light."

But what about us—the more pale-blooded people, the good citizens with good consciences and good reputations? We do not know much about those demoniac powers. Are we actually less powerful? Has life withdrawn from us? Are there no demons to lure us into danger and crisis and through suffering into fuller life?

Yes, we harbor the same powers in a more subtle form, but not less dangerous and not less helpful. Only it takes more psychology, indeed depth-psychology in the true sense of the word, to explore the unconscious capacities, to unmask them, to

lead them and to change them into creativeness. We are more at
the mercy of the dark powers than we know. Everyone, even the
coolest and calmest moralist, is their slave. And to master consciously our unconscious forces is the only way which can help us
to replace our bloody so-called civilization by real culture.

There are many signs indicating to each of us that our
unconscious power is waiting for release. Even trivial incidents
betray its pressure. A person is in a hurry to get to a movie;
impatiently he buttons his coat and one of the buttons flies off.
His reaction is anger. With a furious kick he sends the rebellious
button under the couch and then spends ten minutes trying to get
it back. The more he hurries, the more excited he gets, and the
more he delays his departure by giving vent to his excitement.
This reaction may be comprehensible to most of us. We would
feel a similar impulse, but at the same time we deem it ridiculous,
uncontrolled, and inadequate. A mature person does not behave
in this way. But the willful and impatient impulse scoffs at our
maturity.

Words like "primitive," "childish" and "immature" shed
some light on the pattern of such a reaction. But they give no
explanation of the source and nature of the explosive power
which is involved. We may only guess that its destructive form is
not the genuine one. Originally, haste may have been the proper
reaction to pressure of time; here, however, it leads to blunders
(tearing off the button), creates delay and greater hurry and
further blunders. The power which produces the "haste" seems
to have a history and a development which branches toward either
the good or the bad. Yet we are unaware of it; it remains
unconscious, until its results confront us with disaster.

Imagine that someone tells a story at your expense. You may
laugh and simply consider it out of place. At another time you
may resent it, but answer it with a better and more ingenious
joke, thus defeating the aggressor. In a third case, you may feel
deeply hurt and be unable to control yourself. Sometimes such a
joke may work like a spark which is dropped into a barrel of
gunpowder. A terrific explosion may be released by a small
stimulus. This power is evidently stored in our unconscious mind.
Its release can be postponed and led into different channels. The

good answer, the creative joke, or a destructive fight may be the result. By whom, how, and with the help of what other force can this power be controlled?

Nobody likes rats, mice or bugs. Some people resent them so much that they find their presence literally unbearable. One day, so the story goes, a large meeting of belligerent suffragettes in London could not be controlled by the authorities. The policemen were scared to death by the shouting and gesticulating ladies. One of them, however, was a wise man. He released a mouse in the midst of the women and three minutes later the meeting place was empty. Who can explain the power of the mouse? Who knows its origin? It seems a demoniac power.

Sigmund Freud has pointed out that some of our blunders, such as slips of the tongue, and at least part of our forgetfulness are due to unconscious tendencies which conflict with our conscious intentions. For example, a woman who is very anxious to have children always reads the word "stock" as "stork." That happens against her conscious will, and is caused by the deeper instinct which controls her reactions more than she knows. Innumerable examples of this kind have been analyzed during the last fifty years.

Then there are the strong tendencies which support our so-called bad habits. If a person unconsciously toys with a spoon when he sits at the table or "doodles" when listening to a lecture, he may try very hard to overcome this habit. He probably will not be able to do so. Careful analysis usually shows that these are not casual happenings. Bad habits frequently express unconscious tendencies which cannot be mastered or suppressed. They have to be accepted, assimilated, and developed into something better. Otherwise they will continue to disturb the individual.

Similar to the bad habits are the cravings and addictions like alcoholism and gambling. They often turn out to be substitutes for improperly used or unused possibilities of life. The born artist, if he does not know that he is an artist or does not allow himself to be creative, may become a drunkard or a gambler. And the same is true with regard to sexual passions and perversions. They also represent the "unlived life." The unknown power is led into the wrong channels. It becomes destructive and finally may result in neurotic diseases or crimes. Life, as it were, has entrusted us with great capacities. If we misuse them they turn against us and destroy us and themselves.

Here we are confronted with an important theoretical problem. It is indeed the problem on the solution of which depends our practical mastery of unconscious power, and therefore the failure or success of human development. It is the question: What is the relationship between ourselves and our "power"? What do we mean when we say, for example, "I do not want to smoke, but my urge or craving or vice is stronger than I am, and so I smoke against my will"? Who is "I," and what is "it" which is stronger than I? Am "I" part of "it" or is "it" part of myself? Or are both "it" and "I" separate "entities" of equal standing?

The popular answer to this decisive question is usually given in terms of Freudian psychoanalysis: "I" is my conscious personality; "it" is the unconscious energy (libido) which is cut off (repressed) from consciousness. For a beginning this crude application of Freudianism may be sufficient. It gives us a vague idea that there is a conflict within our psychic life and that unification or integration would be the way out. Yet a more careful investigation reveals very soon that we need a better description. What we call "it"—the powers, instincts, tendencies we have to deal with— is not completely unknown and in most cases certainly not unconscious during the time that "it" controls us. The smoker who does not want to smoke is aware of his vice. He may even understand its meaning, origin, and final goal. And still it is stronger than what he calls "I."

On the other hand, this "I" is not entirely conscious. It is known only to a certain extent, and its "shadow-side," the less agreeable qualities (for example, greediness, envy, irritability) may be excluded from consciousness, like the "unlived life" which expresses itself in the addiction to the cigarette. The demarcation line between the unconscious and the conscious does not coincide with the border between our "I" and the powers which we want to explore. Further investigation is needed.

A taxi-driver had a quarrel with his colleague. Later when he was asked by the judge why he had hurt his friend, he said, "He accused me wrongly, and then my Irish got me—one of my grandparents was Irish—and so I just let him have it with my fists." The taxi-driver's explanation in terms of inheritance may be completely wrong, but it indicates that he is aware of his temperamental pattern. Sometimes he may try to master it, but sometimes he allows it to run away with him. Then he is identified with "it." He is then, as it were, completely Irish, and he may say, "I am like my grandfather—I will kill you!" In this moment the word "I" denotes his fury, and his other qualities and attitudes which prevail at other times now are superseded. They are overruled like the minority in Congress and have to wait until the party in power collapses—the relationship between "I" and "it" is unstable.

The next step in our investigation seems to add a new difficulty. Both the "I" and the "it" can be found as expressions of group life as well as of individual life. "I" then is replaced by "We," yet the instinctive power remains the same, its nature becoming more evident. Finally this new aspect of the problem will lead us to decisive discoveries.

A teacher arouses the patriotism of her class. The waves of enthusiasm are running high, and she is proud of her achievement. "Everyone must be ready to die for his country!" The boys are excited: "To hell with the cowards!—Let's kill the enemy!" They yell and scream. "Hurrah!—There he is!—Get him!" The teacher becomes afraid. She shouts, "Order! Quiet! You cannot serve your country without discipline!" But hell is loose already and her angry voice stirs the fire like a pair of bellows. The boys jump on the desks and an inkpot flies against the wall. "Hurrah!"

The cry for discipline, the anger of offended authority on the part of the teacher, and the patriotic courage turning into riot on the side of the students—both are different channels for the same power. The waters of a river are divided by an island. Behind the land they meet again now coming from opposite directions, and they clash like inimical forces. The striving for discipline and the striving for unbounded expression of energy are in the last analysis the same river which contradicts itself.

Both the teacher and the students identify themselves with their respective emotional attitudes. The teacher says: "My anger is justified. I *must* be angry. If only I could express my feelings more adequately the boys would understand and obey." And the students say: "It is fun to feel as excited as this; and even if we were to try to stop ourselves, we couldn't do it." Here we find some kind of collective personality. The students would not say, "I am excited" but "We are excited." The collective power has submerged, at least for the time being, their different individualities.

This phenomenon leads us into the problems of group-psychology and mass-psychology. And we have to solve these problems if we want to understand history; and we have to master these collective powers if we want to control the development of the future. The next step, however, on the way to this almost superhuman goal has to be a simple investigation of facts. We have to explore the points which the psychology of primitive tribes and the psychology of our own unconscious have in common. This will shed new light on the intricate problems of the collective power.

A primitive tribe can be excited to collective emotions such as fear or hatred or joy. The cause may be an outer reality like thunderstorms, eclipses, wild beasts, enemies, or visitors. Or it may be the inner readiness and expectation of the community aroused by religious ceremonies or magic achievements. The reaction is the emotional discharge of a super-individual power. The individual cannot refrain from participating in this experience. And the proper description is not that the individual has or realizes the excitement, but rather that the emotional excitement seizes and obsesses the individual.

Later the same people may find themselves in quite a different mood. They may have gone through utmost fear and despair yesterday. And today after a magic performance of their medicine-men they may be filled with courage and confidence. Looking back and trying in their own mind to understand the change, they may ascribe the fear and the courage to the presence of super-individual entities. Demons, spirits, gods can animate and support the tribe or forsake it, blind it, and lead it into annihilation.

The medicine-man who propitiates the spirit of war and exorcises the demon of fear or—even better—sends the demon of fear into the enemy's camp, can master the fate of the tribe almost as an artist masters his clay. And there is not much difference between the medicine-man of ten thousand years ago and the political propagandizer of our time. We call the demons and gods by other names, confusing them with other facts, speaking of patriotism or duty or war-hysteria or mass-phobia. The instinctive power is still the same. And even the mysterious test of its presence, well known to modern psychology, does not change. Three men spellbound by a super-individual spirit can achieve much more than these same men could do under separate impulse with their strength simply added together. The group is more than the sum-total of its members. Where does this additional power come from? The demons are still alive, and they are nearer to us than we usually admit.

The most important of all of them is the great and bloody god, Mars. He was in disfavor for a long time. The poets ridiculed him and the scientists explained him away. The causes of war were supposed to be economic interests, the need of markets, or of raw materials, or the class struggle, or the ambition of the generals. But then the god shook his head, the nations clashed, and the scientists admitted that all the explanations they could think of did not fully account for the slaughter. It seemed evident that nobody wanted the war but that it had happened nevertheless. Our fear, it is said, creates what we want to avoid. This is the pattern of our neuroses. But if wars are neuroses of mankind, we have to investigate the power that prompts them all the more. And this power, until we find a better name for it, may be called Mars.

The name does not matter. Instead of Mars we could say just as well Ares, Thor, Vishnu, or even Lord Sabaoth, the Lord of Hosts. But looking at this row of gods or demons of war, we discover another fact, namely the indistinctness, cloudiness, and plasticity of the collective powers. The biological basis is always the same. The readiness to fight seems to be a general human quality, though different races share it in different part. The outer forms, however, differ according to technical means and moral standards. The bushman with his club, the medieval knight with his splendid armor, the modern parachutist with his elaborate equipment—all of them are inspired by the same collective power, or they will fail. All of them are courageous but the style of their courage and the goal of their exploits differ. They may be more bloodthirsty or more magnanimous, more daring or more cautious, more ingenious or more stubborn. In spite of all these differences they are psychologically—at least in the moment of combat—in a similar situation. Their "I" is more or less replaced by "We," and this "We" is identified with the power which we call Mars.

Here we have to deal with collective powers which master the style of life in groups, movements, social classes, and nations. They are like enormous billows coming up from the depth of the ocean. Our private instincts, convictions, ideals, and fears then represent small waves and shallow cross-currents which may influence the surface of the water only for a short time. The "man in the street" who constitutes "the mass" has little or no "private waves." He is controlled by the huge billows of the herd instinct. The individualist consciously holds private opinions and inclinations which may contradict the herd instinct, although unconsciously he may still be moved by the collective powers. The so-called great men and the leaders of mankind are those whose individual wave is in accordance with the rising tide. They do consciously what the mass, because of their lack of consciousness, can never achieve. They solve the problems of their century and their success changes our civilization. Such were St. Francis and Luther, Washington and Lincoln, Shakespeare and Goethe.

The greatest historical events, however, have always appeared as startling cases of insanity or crime to most of the reasonable onlookers, the rising tide of the ocean being then in discord with the individual waves as well as the big billows. Alexander the Great was a powerful criminal, an aggressor, and conqueror without legal rights; but he plucked a fruit which was ripened by history. And all his predecessors and successors, all the Nebuchadnezzars and Caesars, did the same. Jesus of Nazareth, on the other hand, was deemed to be an obsessed fool, and even nowadays some people think of him as a paranoiac. And it was the same with Buddha and Lao-tse before him. But Jesus was the turning point of the tide. The flood now rises in spite of all the waves and billows. There was no room for a second one like him. The Caesars condemned him but he did not condemn them. He is still waiting for them.

The terrific red-blooded power that inspired Alexander's legions to sacrifice their lives on the battlefield, and the other power, the shining love which filled the Christian martyrs with joy when they were torn by beasts in the Roman arena, these two powers shake and illuminate our own world even now. And they seem to be as young and dynamic as they have ever been. We must study them, understand them, deal with them; indeed we must choose between them or we shall be lost in the chaos.

Ego

Our problem is rather involved. We have mentioned the fact that the psychic power is always related to form. Development, change, destruction or preservation of special living forms is always intended. A second observation, previously mentioned, must be recalled here—namely, that this power cannot be understood in terms of cause and effect. Causality can explain only an unspecific kind of destruction—a falling stone may cause the death of a person. But growth and development imply more. The Tea Party in Boston, in addition to many other "causes," prompted the War of the Revolution. But this result was not the unavoidable effect in the sense of a natural law or mathematical necessity. It was a creative reaction of individuals and groups who were inspired by a growing vision of a growing future. Human life has to be understood in terms of means and goals.

But the highest goal remains unknown; it is an infinite value. We think of the goals not in the sense of rigid, mechanical forces determining the means (this again would exclude freedom, responsibility, and creativeness). We think of the goals of life as values which may or may not be reached, which can be interchanged or replaced, and which build an infinite pyramid pointing to the unknown highest value which is the purpose of creation and the will of God.

Here many questions arise which cannot be discussed in this book. Only some of them may be mentioned. What is the relation between the powers we are talking about and those infinite values? Are they identical or opposite? Are they dependent on or independent of each other? Are all the destructive powers derived from constructive ones as it has been suggested with regard to obsessions and addictions? How many powers are there? Are they creating or created (*natura, naturans,* or *natura naturata*)? And

last but not least, is there one Creator, God, to be assumed behind
all this mysterious life? Is it unavoidable to assume his existence?
And if so what do we know about him? What is his will with
regard to us? And how can we do his will if we are controlled by
those super-individual powers which we do not know?

The last question is the basis of the present book. How can
we do or even find the will of God if we are largely controlled by
unknown unconscious powers which may cause us to do what we
do not want to do? But before we can try to answer this question
we have still to ask another question. Who is "we"? What about
our consciousness? Are we, the conscious individuals who ask and
answer, identical with the psychic powers we try to explore? Or
are we identical with the values and goals of development? Or are
we something different? Who are we?—Or, using the formula of
the foregoing chapter: what does the individual mean when he
says "I"?

The problem of the human "I" cannot be separated from the
problem of consciousness, though, as we have said, consciousness
and "I" are not identical. You cannot say "I" without being
conscious, but you can be conscious without being completely
yourself. You can honestly say, "I am not I in this moment." An
artist in the depressed state of mind which often occurs in the
interval between two creative achievements may be clearly conscious of his momentary impotence and shallowness. He suffers
because he is conscious of his not being himself, that is, of not
being creative. What he calls his real Self is, as it were, not awake;
it exists, but temporarily it does not work.—Our consciousness is
changing every hour. It can be clear or dim, rich or poor, dynamic
or static. What we call our Self, however, seems to be there as
long as we live. It does not cease even when we sleep. Sometimes
it is creative and sometimes it hides itself. We do not feel it then,
but it is there.

What we mean by the word "I" in a given moment may be
very different—and has to be distinguished psychologically—
from what we mean in the next moment when we say "I myself as
I really am." The temporary "I" looks at the deeper and more
essential "I myself" much as "I" looks at the emotional power
which it remembers from yesterday. Or with regard to consciousness someone may say: "I am conscious of the fact that I am dull

and sleepy today, but I know that I could be wide awake, courageous, and creative. If my real Self would awake to consciousness
I would be different from what I am now."

The human mind is accustomed to seeing—and indeed wants
to see—definite forms. Therefore it remembers the collective
powers in the form of images and very soon ascribes to them the
dignity of independent entities. The images become "objects"
and are believed to move around in space and time. In this sense
the patriotic enthusiasm of the home-front or the super-individual
fury of the battlefield is seen as a collective spirit which seizes the
individual minds; and soon it is symbolized as a super-human
figure, and, by a primitive mind, idolized as a god or a demon. In
a similar way our own remembrances and ideas about our own
"real Self" are seen as an image. And very soon this image
becomes an "objective reality." What we think of ourselves becomes more important than what we really are (because we know
the images of ourselves, but we do not know what our "Selves"
really are).

Thus we may say: "I cannot concentrate on a book when
there is noise. I need perfect calm. This is one of my innate
peculiarities. It is a quality of my real Self." How can we know
whether this is a quality of our deepest "Self" or of our temporary
"I"? For thousands of years men have taken it for granted that we
have to hate our enemies. This seemed to be the most natural
reaction of every human Self. Then the man from Nazareth
taught us that it is possible to love our enemies. And now more
and more people are discovering that the closer they come to
their real Selves the more it is impossible for them to hate their
enemies. They change when the Self emerges; they look at the
world with different eyes; they act differently; and the world
reacts differently too. Reality changes.*

---

*The same person, having gone through the amazing experience which changed his
hatred into love, may find himself furiously fighting again. Now he fights his former
enemies, knowing that he loves them and that he has to change them in order to help
them. Thus Jesus fought the Pharisees and the Sadducees, relentlessly and undauntedly.
The creative fury of such a fight is the exact opposite of hatred. A fighter who hates is a
poor marksman; his emotion blinds him. The sacred fury of creative men is the same in the
artist's study, on the speaker's platform, and on the battlefield. This fury, originating from
the very center of mankind, provides unlimited resourcefulness, endurance, creativity and
often clairvoyance.

The real Self, now, seems to be a goal of development rather than an immediate experience. It may be the channel through which the infinite highest value draws us toward the top of the pyramid of means and goals. But then it is infinite itself, and cannot be pictured as a definite image. It is not possible to have an adequate image of our real Self—just as it is impossible to have such an image of God. We are infinite like him, and increasingly so the more we are aware of our real Selves.

Our ideas, therefore, concerning the inherent qualities and conditions of the human Self are necessarily incomplete. And we have to discriminate between the image of the Self and the real Self. We call the former the Ego, and describe it as the sum total of what we know or what we think we know about ourselves. The Ego is a system of statements concerning our goals and means, gifts, capacities and limitations—statements such as: "I would be a good musician if my parents had given me the proper education." "I will become famous, rich, or morally good if only I can get rid of my present handicap." "I am a loyal friend, but when my friends laugh at me I feel like hitting them."

The Ego-image is the part or aspect of our real Self which has become conscious in earlier years. It may have been partly forgotten again; it has usually been misunderstood; and worst of all it is considered to be a stable object which can be described like a house or a tree—while actually the Self is indescribable, impenetrable and inaccessible to our research.

In the vague manner of popular philosophy we may call this Self the source of our most creative and most vital actions, the core of human personality, or, following the unanimous tradition of the mystics: the inner light, the soul's deepest ground, the empty center of the inner universe—but we only realize the more vividly that we do not know its true nature.

The psychological statements which we can make so far about the real Self are not so much the result of scientific observation as the result of philosophical thought and religious experience. They are more negative, stating what the Self is not, than positive, defining what it is. It is important, however, for our later discussions, to explain carefully what we think about this mysterious center of the human personality.

The Self (in the sense in which we use the word here) seems

to be essential to human life. In animal life its presence is questionable. We don't know whether a dog has a Self. But we are enticed to ascribe a certain kind of Selfhood to a *community* of ants or bees rather than to the individual insect. And the same is true with regard to primitive men and little children. They seem to have merely a "tribal consciousness," and their Self, the source of their strength, and the center of their impetus, belongs to the group and not to the individual.

The Self is invisible, just as consciousness and life itself are invisible. We know them only from our own *inner* experience. Or we infer them from outer results. The Self can never be made an object. If we try to explore it, it escapes. If we handle it, as we handle dead things, it eludes us. If we formulate its qualities, and the laws of its reactions, it suddenly shows different attitudes and behaves in a way which could by no means have been predicted. It is incalculable and free because of its creativeness. Here the "nomic method" is the only adequate approach.

The Self exists and works in time but it cannot be located in space. It certainly is connected with the body as long as the body is alive. But it has no special organ as its residence. Its efficacy depends on the inner glands as much as on the central nervous system, and on blood and blood circulation as much as on the solar plexus. Yet in spite of all this it acts independently, using the body and its glands and nerves creatively, as a strategist uses his army. Like him it is limited by the deficiencies of the instrument; but like him it can achieve the most astonishing results with weakened forces in a stroke of unexpected ingenuity.

What we know about this enigmatical Self we owe to the fact that it frequently contradicts the instinctive powers which constitute our unconscious life. In every man's life, as we have pointed out, there is a time when he may say, "If I am myself, I want to do this; but sometimes my emotions get the better of me and then I find myself doing just the opposite." This conflict therefore will be the starting point for our further investigations.

Our religious ideas about the human Self have a better basis in real experience than the philosophical statements. Religiously we may say we can realize that our true Self is more than our conscious personality. The more a person finds himself, the more he discovers that his personal interest is replaced by his responsibility for the whole. He is really himself only as far as he is a member of his group; and his group is alive only as far as it is related to mankind. The real Self therefore is not "I"; it is "We."

Moreover, the human Self is not only human love and brotherhood; it is at the same time the creativity of the Creator, working through human individuals. He who really finds himself finds God. And he may say, as St. Paul did, "It is no longer I who live; Christ lives in me."—In this sense our true Self is the final goal of our religious development. At first it is "I"; then it becomes "We"; and at last it will be "He."

However carefully we may look at ourselves, we can never discover what we really are. We may discover some of our present qualities, and putting them together with remembrances of earlier experiences we may achieve a self-portrait which bears some similarity to our real Self. Our desires and fears, however, will distort the picture, in addition to the fact that always the larger part of our life remains unconscious. This inadequate self-portrait, this image or symbol of our real Self, is what we call our Ego.

There would be no need to take this Ego-image seriously and to give it a special name if it remained just an image, an idea, developing when we develop, and changing when its model, the real Self, changes. But the Ego tends to lead a life of its own. It remains, as we have said, an independent, rigid "object," while the Self changes or, more exactly speaking, displays new qualities and growing maturity. In many cases the Self and the Ego develop in opposite directions.

A person may have quite an optimistic Ego. "With me everything is all right—nothing bad can happen to me." Yet his real Self may grow more and more desperate. He does not really believe in the egocentric mask that he wears, but he is able for a long time to deceive himself and his friends. Here the conscious personality is centered around the optimistic Ego-image; the truth, the desperation of the Self, remains unconscious until the mask breaks down and the truth comes to light.

Even this self-deception would not be too serious a mistake and would not last long if our actions and decisions were controlled by the original center and source of our life: the real Self. Yet, as soon as our consciousness is dominated by the Ego-image, our behavior-pattern and our new decisions become "egocentric." They serve the Ego instead of the Self. They apparently originate in the Ego, and are shaped by the Ego's vision of life (for example, the crude optimism mentioned above). This is what we call egocentricity. The opposite attitude is characterized by the fact that actions and reactions flow from the real center and are shaped by the creative instincts and intuitions which surround the real Self and serve as its genuine channels of expression. We describe this attitude as creativity, and we assume that egocentricity, in spite of a certain resourcefulness, will always remain barren and uncreative.

Suppose you want to write an important letter to the board of directors of a large organization. Your Ego demands that you make a good impression, not hurting the feelings of Mr. A, nor contradicting the convictions of Mrs. B. And here you sit writing out six different drafts and rejecting them all. Your ambitious egocentric goals are not yet satisfied, nor your subtle egocentric fears appeased. You try again; but now you are tense, you get excited, and you fail even more than before. The Self would write the letter easily, honestly, courageously and successfully. But the Ego does not allow this. As long as the Ego-pattern is the basis of our activity we are bound to fail, sooner or later. The Ego is helpless, rigid and shallow as compared with the inexhaustible creativity of the Self.

The collective powers are to be found on the side of the Self, while the strength which is available to the Ego is limited to shrewd cunning and sentimental excitement, cleverly used, but not at all creative. Where an egocentric person explodes in fury and rage he already comes close to the collapse of the Ego. The power of his outburst is already due to collective powers which may get the better of him very soon. He still uses his fury for the sake of his Ego, but already he feels insecure in his own house, and the more insecure he feels the more furious he becomes.

Our Ego, therefore, has to defend itself not only against outer enemies, competitors and exploiters, but also against inner dangers such as emotions, desires and thoughts which would destroy the Ego-pattern from within. Where the Ego-pattern says, "I am a good boy, I stay at home," there the desire to explore the world, to have all sorts of adventure, and to face all kinds of danger—a healthy boy's desire for self-development—has to be discounted, fought off, and finally repressed into the unconscious. On the other hand, if the Ego-pattern prescribes being a bad boy, breaking windowpanes, doing mischief and never telling the truth, then all inclinations toward honesty, loyalty and kindness have to be repressed.

Thus a large part of our functioning and of our inherited collective powers remains unconscious, under-developed and primitive, because those activities would conflict with our egocentric pattern of life. The Ego is not only the insincere mask which overlays the real Self, it is also the censor and appraiser who casts aside into the unconscious or admits into consciousness our inner impulses, creative thoughts, and emotional reactions.

The Ego is the factor which determines our outer fate and our inner development more decisively than any other factor in life. And its influence as we shall see is always unfavorable. The study of the Ego is therefore as important as the study of the collective powers. In fact we cannot understand one without understanding the other. The Ego keeps the powers unconscious, and the powers, threatening to destroy the Ego, force it to defend itself with all its shrewdness and cunning. The solution of this inner conflict would free the imprisoned powers, lead them from negative to positive expression, and replace the Ego by the real Self—the goal of our religious endeavor for centuries.

The investigation of egocentricity has been one of the main objectives of depth-psychology for as long as this psychology has existed. We know how egocentricity begins in the life of the individual. We do not know, however, how it began in the life of mankind. We have sufficient evidence for the statement that the newborn child is not egocentric. The baby is as trustful and as responsive as the members of primitive tribes—though the individualistic psychologists of the last generation cannot believe it. Egocentricity is not innate nor inherent in human nature, but it can easily be induced by outer influences.

Egocentricity begins in early childhood as a natural adjustment to the child's egocentric environment. It is a normal reaction to an abnormal situation—the abnormal situation being the average situation. The abnormality of the child's environment may be described generally as the absence of the right kind of love. This abnormality carries over from one generation to the next.

We certainly love our children. Our love, however, is egocentric and therefore incomplete. It either lacks wisdom—we pamper our children; or it lacks warmth—we are too strict and too demanding. And where exceptional parents happen to be more or less mature and able to avoid those two mistakes, other educators come in and teach the children the erroneous lesson of our civilization, that only egocentricity enables them to live.

Many parents are convinced that the child compelled to live in an egocentric world must first of all learn to defend himself. And this self-defense they can only imagine as an egocentric attitude. They teach their children egocentricity on purpose. "You must beat your competitors! Be smart! Be at the top of the class! Excel in popularity!" These are the semi-Christians who think that the Sermon on the Mount holds good only on Sunday, but that during the week we must kill or be killed.

Every generation, not so much by words as by actions, forces the next generation to become even more egocentric. This unintentional teaching is a fiendish process. It affects the very center of children's lives. And it is much more successful than any other educational endeavor. We more or less destroy the creativity and happiness of those whom we love most; yet we have a good conscience because "we do our best," and we simply cannot believe that we participate in the common human fate of transmitting our own deficiencies and weaknesses to the next generation. We may admit that our parents did this to us, but we cannot think that we do it to our children.

We talk rather glibly about the deviation and the guilt of humanity. But here where a large part of our own guilt may become visible we prefer to say that all children are born as egocentric individualists and that we try to soften their "hard-boiled egos." The truth is the opposite: they are born soft and responsive, and we change them into hard-boiled egos by our own egocentricity. Yet guilty in this case is not just one father or one mother or some teachers; guilty is our whole generation, and the former generation also. Our private guilt is part of our collective guilt, and we have to pay the penalties as collective debtors.

Our children appear on this earth, as far as we can see, in a state of actual innocence, neither good nor bad themselves, and equally ready to develop good and bad qualities, according to circumstances. During the first period of their lives they are so completely a part of the higher unit, the group, that they express like mirrors the emotional situation of their environment. In a nursery, if one baby cries, all cry; if one laughs, all do the same. If the mother worries, the child is depressed; and where the parents fight with each other (even without betraying consciously any sign of their conflict) the children are inwardly disturbed and insecure.

This important fact, which adds so greatly to our parental responsibility, was first discovered among primitive tribes. If one of his fellow tribesmen is hurt or offended, a bushman will feel it. Whatever happens, happens to the tribe and not to the individual. All experiences and reactions seem to be more or less collective. The individual has not yet emerged out of the tribe. Consciousness is still a tribal and not yet an individual quality. The group feels, thinks, and wills; the individual, as separated from the others, is dull and callous. "We" has not yet become differentiated into "I" and "You."

The French ethnographer, Lucien Lévy-Bruhl, has carefully investigated these facts, terming them "participation mystique." We find the same attitude in all our babies, and we cannot see any mystery in it. They behave like little savages, it is true; they are organs of a higher organism, the family, like tribesmen; they are loyal, and at the same time unreliable, wise and stupid, creative and narrowly limited—and therefore bound to go astray, unless they are led by better leaders than we are.

We call their inner attitude the "original We-feeling," and we assume that it arises from their real creative Self which still coincides with the real Self of the group. The small child is not yet conscious of his center; but he is closer to the real Self and therefore to real love and creativity than any other member of the group. The adults are conscious of their centers—but they have exchanged the group center (the Self) for the individual center (the Ego). Therefore they have to become like children again, discovering anew that their real center is the group and behind the group the whole, and finally God. And they should go this way, back into childhood, without forgetting their adult consciousness and their individual responsibility. Then, out of the child's "original We-feeling" and the adult's "individual consciousness" will arise the "creative We-experience" of the mature and fully responsible personality.

The We-feeling of the newborn baby is potentially complete, but it is plastic and weak. It immediately mirrors, as we have said, the warmth or the lack of warmth and the wisdom or the lack of wisdom of its environment. The child lives out of the real center, yet in a very primitive way. It needs help, it needs the real We-group; yet the family is a sham We-group, a group perhaps with forty percent genuine We-feeling and sixty percent egocentricity. In the family the real Self has been replaced by an association of Egos with limited liabilities. And the newest member of this association has to accept the conditions of membership. The child therefore either has to give up its spontaneity, its original Self, and a large part of its collective power, or it has to give up its membership in the group. Anticipating later results we may say that the child has to choose unconsciously between God and the family, since the family is alienated from God. And the child always chooses the family, and that means egocentricity. The reason for this empirical fact is very simple.

The child cannot yet distinguish between the parents and God. To him the parents are God. The love for man and the love for God are identical. Subjectively the child does not realize that there is a choice. He accepts his parents as they are and applies what he learns from them to life and mankind and God. They are his encyclopedic knowledge of religion.

Here is the point where religious education begins. If we destroy the early We-feeling of our children, we destroy the basis of their religious faith. If we are bad parents, the child learns that God is bad.

Many psychologists tell us that monotheistic religion is "nothing but" the projection of the father-image into the universe. This is true in many cases but only as far as the poor pedagogy of egocentric parents distorts the children's imagery, represses the collective powers, and replaces their creative Self by fearful and powerless Egos. The parents exchange within the children "the glory of the immortal God for the semblance of the likeness of mortal man" (Romans 1:23). Later we shall see how God and his creative powers destroy the wrong religious ideas and finally replace them by truth.

Here are two drastic examples showing how egocentricity is transferred from one generation to the other and how the wrong conception of God is an integral part of the wrong vision of life.

In the first example the father, a successful businessman, pretends to be a very good Christian. This, however, does not prevent him from unscrupulous competition in business and reckless tyranny in his home. His wife and his three sons tremble at his rage. Nobody dares to oppose his wishes and whims. The family goes to church twice every Sunday. The two older boys very soon learn to say "yes" and to do "no." They read funny stories during the sermon and the second boy develops an admirable talent as a cartoonist, drawing caricatures of all the pious people in the church. These two sons were alienated from Christianity for almost a lifetime. They assume that a cause supported by this kind of a paternal tyrant cannot be a good cause.

The mother and the youngest son are of a softer constitution. They take religion seriously; they are startled when the father shouts that according to Scripture disobedient children will burn in everlasting fire. They try to be obedient but it is impossible. The father tells them to wear new clothes, but to spend no money. They have to cheat him, and that means to cheat God.

For them the image of God is characterized by the same features as the father. He is a furious and revengeful God, jealous of his rights, and inexorable in his judgment. When they read the Bible, which they do constantly, they always find this picture of the thundering Jehovah. They are not able to see any kindness in his character. The word "forgiveness" is empty and meaningless and the expression "our Father in heaven" means simply "our terrible judge who knows our guilt."

The youngest son had to go through a painful religious crisis of several years before he—at least partly—overcame his wrong ideas about God. Whether his brothers and his mother have ever found the way out is not known.

In the second case, both parents were lenient, weak and mild. They brought up their two children, a boy and a girl, without any harshness, discipline, or constraint. This was their interpretation of love. They believed that it was not necessary to struggle and to toil since God gives to his children what they need. Their understanding of non-resistance to evil was: if the boy at the age of five climbed on his father's desk and stepped on the letters and the books, and spilled the ink, the father had to take it as sent from the Lord. He should try to rejoice in it and he certainly must not punish the child.

Other people, however, had different ideas about education. In kindergarten and Sunday school the children behaved as they did at home, but they met with disaster, and the catastrophe was the more terrible because it was entirely unexpected. The only explanation was: "These are bad people; we and our parents are good. We serve God; the others outside our family serve the devil." Their God became a tribal God, a family protector, as in the most primitive religion.

The parents allowed them everything and gave them all they wanted. And the parents received everything from the family God. This God seemed to be a kind of department store where the good family had infinite credit—until one day the father lost his job and a few weeks later the mother fell ill. Not being accustomed to any disappointment they found the darkness so black that it was incompatible with the existence of any God. The family God had failed. It was a crisis of utmost severity. Finally they decided that there was no God at all, and the government with its WPA had to take care of them.

In both cases, the original "We" had been destroyed very early. In the first case, the children learned that there was a group of good people represented and headed by the infallible father but that they themselves, being bad, did not belong to this group. Therefore they developed a strong feeling of inferiority and guilt. In the second case, the children learned that they were good people themselves and that the world was bad. Therefore they developed a feeling of moral superiority. Later, however, they discovered that the good group grew smaller and weaker; and finally God himself proved to be on the side of the bad people—if he existed at all. The children felt forsaken and utterly helpless. In spite of all their righteous pretensions, their moral superiority was no defense against the feeling of utmost insecurity.

In both cases, the "good group" exists only subjectively in the children's imagination. Objectively, it is a "sham-We group," an egocentric group with a moral façade. In the first case, this group is destroyed from inside by the tyranny of the father. In the second case, it breaks down under pressure from outside. The group of righteous children of God cannot protect its members and God himself evidently does not desire that they be protected.

The result is the same in all cases. The child is finally left without the support of any group. Loneliness, the necessity of self-defense, the unending fight against deceitful enemies, and the distrust of unreliable friends are the outstanding features in all the different forms of egocentricity. And worst of all, the child has already sacrificed a large part of his capacities, and in most cases has renounced the very source of his creativity, his real Self, before the struggle began. So, he has to defend himself without adequate preparation.

He has lived for some time in a "sham-We group," namely in his family, against his original nature. He was not allowed to develop his collective powers. His creativity was not wanted. In our first case, the father did not tolerate the children's creative ideas. In the second case, all sound development would have had to surmount the narrow limits of the family, but the outer world was too dangerous; safety was preferable to creativity.

More generally we may say that in both these cases the hard task of the growing human mind, the journey from original We-experience, through loneliness and individuation to the mature wisdom of a conscious We-group, was imposed on the children too early and too suddenly because of the deficiencies of their parents. Thus, the parental egocentricity is handed down to the next generation. Its outer form may vary; sometimes in the succeeding generation it assumes an opposite shape (the son of a miser becomes a spendthrift, and vice versa). Yet the degree of deviation remains the same, or is increased: God "avenges the sins of fathers on their children and their children's children, down to the third and fourth generation" (Exodus 34:7, Moffat).

Moreover, the very essence of "sin" becomes evident. It is the substitution of a sham center, the Ego, for our real center, the Self. And that means three things:

1. Our genuine membership in the group—or the sense of love and brotherhood—is replaced by loneliness, callousness and distrust, the Self being the identical gravitation point of both the group and the individual.

2. Our positive relation to God is replaced by the self-sufficiency of our Ego. We do not know him anymore, and where we still acknowledge his existence intellectually we try to exploit him in the service of our Ego (for example, by egocentric prayers).

3. The subjective experience which results from this double deviation is anxiety. We find anxiety—conscious or unconscious—at the bottom of all egocentricty. Anxiety results from the fact that we are cut off from our creative center, the Self, and thereby cut off from God as well as from our fellow men. This center still exists; it still supports our lives; but we do not know it. We have repressed it; it has become unconscious; and—though objectively speaking it remains positive and creative—from the viewpoint of our Ego it appears as negative, destructive, threatening the Ego. Together with the repressed collective powers it seems to constitute a fiendish group of evil spirits, endangering the Ego with passions and addictions, errors and blunders, too much or too little emotion, and, worst of all, with a rising flood of half-conscious anxiety.

Anxiety may be defined as the opposite of creativity. It is the power of creation flowing in the opposite direction: creation being a centrifugal force; anxiety, centripetal. In the state of anxiety the intensity of life increases but its scope decreases. Consciousness becomes keener but its contents disappear. Anxiety is the opposite of life in the normal sense of the word; and, at the same time, it is the opposite of death, if death means quietude due to complete absence of consciousness.

Our creative center, the Self, is our positive relationship to God. Our Selfhood is the experience of our dependence on and our support by the Creator whom we know only partially. We realize creative power if we live from our real center. Then we are channels of creation. If we lose our Selfhood and our positive relation to the Creator, we are cut off from any new influx of power. And the power which is left, as it were, flows back into eternity. This ebb of creative power is what we feel as anxiety.

THE ORIGIN AND NATURE OF EGOCENTRICITY

Introduction

At the conclusion of the last section we were introduced to Kunkel's idea of egocentricty. Now as we go on to read the major portion of his book *How Character Develops* we will learn much more about the origin and nature of egocentricity.

Kunkel believed the egocentric patterns that would shape our later life began in childhood. In his emphasis on the importance of childhood, Kunkel is more like Freud than Jung. Jung devoted little attention to childhood (although some of his followers did), but Kunkel felt that the influence of childhood on us was definitive. Kunkel saw the child, however, quite differently than Freud. Freud saw children as perverse creatures who had to be shaped by education and social pressure into some semblance of agreeable human beings. Kunkel saw the child as naturally tender and trusting—until betrayed by egocentric adults into his or her own egocentric patterns.

In this section we also learn that the Self is not bounded by the individual, but includes two or more individuals in a single unit. That is, to be "our Self" is not to be isolated, but necessarily means that we will be bonded and connected to others. Consequently the subject changes from "I" to "We." This is why Kunkel called his psychology the "We-Psychology."

As far as I know, Kunkel's thoughts about the *We* are original. They cannot be found in Freud since, for Freud, there was no Self in which others could be included. The thought is implicit in Jung, but Jung seldom speaks of the importance of others in the emergence of the Self except when he refers to the need we have for other people in our lives in order to see and understand ourselves. But Kunkel goes beyond this notion. Other people are necessary in our lives because the emergence of the Self necessarily includes them as it brings about a vital change in our frame of reference from egocentricty—which is always concerned with "I"—to the creative life—which always embraces others in a creative "We."

After Kunkel has discussed the importance of childhood and the nature of the "We-Psychology" he goes on to describe the four basic egocentric patterns: Clinging Vine, Star, Nero, and Turtle. Here we find Kunkel's use of imaginative language at its best as Kunkel helps us grasp with imagination as well as intellect what it means to be egocentric.

—————————————————
—————————————————

The "We-Experience"

Let us imagine a huge football stadium where the teams of two great colleges are matched for a championship and in the stands seventy-five thousand spectators are massed. Every movement of the ball, every skillful play creates a wave of excitement which surges across the crowd and, almost like a visible force, thrills the fans of one team or the other. Sometimes the feeling runs so high it engulfs even those who are not ardent fans, and those little interested in football. They, too, find themselves tingling with excitement, keenly responsive with the other spectators to the movements of the players. For the time being they are enthusiastic rooters.

Ordinarily, the spectators fall into two groups, supporters of one team or the other. But there may be a time when these two, despite sharp differences in loyalties, become more or less unified. Let some player give a display of fine sportsmanship or carry the ball eighty yards for a touchdown. The spectators join in an ovation for that player. Rivalries are forgotten for the moment and there is little or no division in the crowd. It is unified by a common admiration, a sense of oneness in paying tribute to achievements which reflect credit on humanity. Even those whose partisan loyalties may keep them from openly showing their admiration are inwardly stirred by the feeling which the group displays. When the game is ended thousands of spectators feel as if they had won a victory or had been defeated. The truth is, of course, that only the teams have been victorious or beaten. But even after all have gone to their homes, many of the more ardent fans will say with glee, "*We* won," or with equal regret, "*We* lost."

As is well known, these reactions have been described in terms of a so-called crowd or mass psychology. Psychologists explain them by saying that the crowd shows less reason and is more easily swayed by emotion than the individuals who make it up. Mass psychology is right so far as we deal with an accidental or casual gathering of persons moved by a momentary interest, such as curiosity, anger, hunger or joy, but it fails to explain this football game.

These thousands of spectators not only share in this feeling of victory or defeat, they are self-disciplined in that they accept the rules of the game and observe seating and other regulations imposed upon them in the stadium. They may be said to be capable of sacrifice. In paying admission, they have given up something in order to be a part of the group witnessing the game. They may have sacrificed their comfort by sitting where cold winds blow or waiting in line to get a seat. They are capable of responding to the needs of their fellows, even at the cost of some discomfort to themselves. Let a woman in the crowd become sick or a spectator faint, and willing hands will serve their needs even in the excitement of the game.

Now, a mere crowd is never able to observe rules, to restrict itself, to renounce something. It cannot forego its own wishes or satisfactions but is bound to its urges like an animal. The reaction of the spectators to the superb play or a grossly unsportsmanlike act in this football game is better understood by thinking of it in terms of what we call a "We-experience." It consists in a mutuality of participation—a sharing, at a given point, of the total experience. In this case, it includes sharing on the unpleasant side of defeat as well as on the pleasant side of victory.

The reaction in a We-experience has something in common with the feeling involved in a sense of honor. Broadly speaking, it is not only the honor of the team but also that of the school, the country, and all amateur athletics which is at stake, and so the spectators may react as a unit on levels above the mere interests of a team or a school, reflecting their feeling of united concern for the good name of their city or country, or the good reputation of all amateur sports. Suppose that there is a suspicion that the game has been "fixed," or let one player be caught consistently fouling his opponents. Notice the widespread resentment among the spectators regardless of their loyalty to one team or the other. Here is something greater than either team—a common sense of values. And thousands respond to it in a We-experience uniting otherwise partisan opponents. Here is a situation which merely sheds some light on our subject. The concept of honor is not sufficient to explain this inner unity which we describe as the We-experience. So we must go on to further investigations.

In so doing we note that these reactions are more or less fully conscious. The spectators sense that they are united; they dimly or clearly recognize an inter-relationship in which they have common interests, purposes, ends and values. We call this consciousness of the We-experience "We-feeling." It is an important part of a We-experience and may sometimes be one and the same thing, though it is not indispensable.

Very often the We-experience includes actions and reactions which remain unconscious for a certain time or even forever. Suppose you try to comfort a person who has lost his father by death. You will be aware of your compassion in general. You will be touched or even deeply moved, and all your words and gestures will be, as it were, imbided by your We-feeling. You will be conscious of the fact that you are motivated not by private emotion, but by a common reaction to a common loss. Yet the We-experience may reach much deeper. You may not until much later understand that the person you comforted has become your brother, and that you are connected with him to a new unit, since you have looked together into the depths of human life. That is We-experience.

In athletic contests the We-feeling of the spectators usually is restricted to passing or superficial events, but the team itself may be profoundly affected for many years by their We-experience. Its members may be bound in a firm, lifelong comradeship. In such cases, the individuals are so changed by their We-experience that afterward they cannot react as mere individuals. Each man has come to feel as a part of a unit, an organ in an organism, and his feelings and decisions are not to be explained by his purely private interests. They point to something else which we call the "We-experience." The person acts as if a larger entity, greater than his private personality, has come to life within him, and this is what we call "We."

Now the fact is that, by virtue of his birth, every man is a part of a We—the great human family, so whether he realizes it or not he is linked with the lives of others of the race. There is no entirely satisfactory or accurate way of describing this relationship, yet it is self-evident that nobody can live without the help of his fellow men. That is true not only because of the necessary division of labor, but also because of our longing for mental communication. Robinson Crusoe in reality would become crazy. Solitary confinement is the most cruel torture, and ultimately mankind could not survive without the desire of man and woman to meet each other. Even from the viewpoint of zoology, man is not a solitary animal.

As to the inner side of this fact, the average human being realizes that he sympathizes with other people more vividly as he becomes nearer to the person who undergoes suffering or joy. If he sees his brother or his best friend in difficulty, he feels as if he were himself in his place, but if the relationship is merely that of an acquaintance, the other's suffering must be more severe in order to have so great an effect. The fact that foreign people suffer does not bother us too much—usually—because we do not know them and, what is decisive, we do not see them.

Suppose you have an enemy—one, let us say, who is bringing a series of lawsuits against you. Imagine now that you see him die in agony in an automobile accident. Would you feel pleased? You would be gripped by quite different feelings. You never could forget his blood running in the street; you would hear his last cry in your dreams again and again. Why? Not because he is your enemy or your friend or an unknown person, but solely because he is a human being as you are. It is mankind, it is our common blood which reacts. You are a part of this great human We, and it does not matter whether you know it or not, or whether you like it or not. Your blood, your soul, your unpremeditated reaction will prove it. There is in you that which compels you to share, at least inwardly, in the life of others.

The consciousness of this relationship comes first in the family, and even there it may be very dimly and imperfectly sensed. Frequently it does not seem to extend much, if any, beyond the family. But other individuals are recognized to have been strongly conscious of their being a part of the whole We.

The deepest We-experiences are found in great political and religious movements where it is clear that one may be a part of a larger unit—a We—which strongly influences what one does long before one becomes aware of it. We may describe the process by which this relationship is realized—the process of one's becoming aware of the We—in two ways. It may be said that when the individual realizes his membership in the larger unit—the We—it seems somewhat as if he had walked out of a small room into a larger one. He leaves the former narrow and individualistic attitude and feels himself to be an integral part of the greater whole with responsibility for its highest interests. We could say just as well that the We manifests itself in his inner life, causing him to realize that he is a part of a greater unit, and this realization works a change in his feeling and thinking, his aims and valuations. The resultant We-feeling pervades and fills his being as the light, diffused through the air, fills a room. The former Ego-centered personality now becomes more and more We-centered. The We is alive within the individual, and the individual within the We.

This is not an expression of some foreign idea coming from outside the individual. (When that is the case, the group may very soon be broken up again.) On the contrary, it is an actual, inner psychological reality displaying itself. We become conscious of something which always existed in the deeper layers of our being, and which only seemed to have been asleep. The individual becomes aware of his own nature and discovers what he really is. To find oneself means at the same time finding the We—and to find the We is to find oneself.

This awakening of the We often occurs at a time of major crisis in the life of the individual—a time in which the foundation of one's being seems more or less shaken. The political and religious forms of this awakening, and also the "great" love, the intense, overpowering We-experience of lovers, means the breakdown of former ideas, feelings, aims and valuations. The finding of the We also means change, renewal, a growing and ripening personality. Therefore, the way to the We very often has to pass through inner and outer difficulty, even catastrophe. It often takes a serious crisis to make us feel the need of a change in our thinking and living. Otherwise we do not seek and are not receptive to the new ideas, feelings and valuations involved in that deeper insight into one's nature afforded by the awakening of the We.

In order to understand the We-experience psychologically, it is useful to observe some simple situations in everyday life. For our investigations these have real advantages. Everyone has observed them and to some extent understands them, perhaps because of his own experiences. Even the most egocentric man may have a certain understanding of them. If only by envy of, or longing for, them, he has to deal with the idea of these natural We-experiences.

Let us consider a typical illustration. A mother is bathing her baby. Even though she herself is not in the water, she says to the baby, "*We* are taking a bath." Then she feeds the child, saying, "Now *We* are eating," although she does not take anything herself. At last she puts the baby into its cradle, saying: "Now *We* go to sleep nicely." But she remains awake. She has a direct feeling of being in a We; it is as if she and the child were different parts of a higher entity. She senses, assuming that she herself has not been spoiled or distorted, what the child needs. She knows when the baby should be in bed, when he ought to get up, and when he should be taken outside.

We see here the same kind of sharing as in our former illustration, the football game, but here the We-feeling seems to be more highly developed and displaying more subtle ramifications. The child, for example, is disturbed and weakened if the mother undergoes serious difficulties; and the mother feels uneasy, to say the least, when the child is endangered by sickness. They react almost as if they were one being.

Here, too, we find sacrifice and sharing. That the mother has to bear suffering and pain for the child is self-evident, but the child, assuming that he still reacts naturally, also puts himself at stake courageously. The two-year-old boy attacks anyone who threatens his mother, not reckoning whether the enemy may be larger or stronger than himself.

Science speaks in such cases of "instincts," but we maintain that instincts may develop into good or bad behavior. There are mothers who abuse a child by using him as they would a piece of jewelry or a plaything. Of course they say that they love the child tenderly, but they do not do what the child needs, or, better, what would serve the common welfare of mother and child. Instead they do that which serves their own Egos without regard to the welfare of the child, even when that might injure him. They dress him as nicely as possible, but not hygienically, and take him into crowds to show him off to other people, instead of going into the woods where less admiration but more health may be found. The child pays his mother in the same coin. The three-year-old already abuses mother love in order to obtain by artifice chocolate or toys, flattering or presuming upon the mother in order to have his own way. In this case the love of the mother and the tactics of the child may be called egocentric. Their natural instincts are misdirected into Ego-serving channels.

Consider another illustration. The mating instinct can lead to an inexpressibly fine We-experience, but it does not necessarily do so. A husband and wife may find that together they are vastly more than either one could be alone. Marriage may seem to be not merely an addition but a multiplication of their resources. In sharing their lives in this basic We-experience, new energies are released, new ideas are produced, new courage is developed—in short, both lives become much more creative and productive. Both may be so keenly conscious of the enrichment of life in this We-experience that they marvel at the change which has come over them.

On the other hand, the mating urge may be utilized in the most egocentric ways. A man may gratify his desire to dominate another, subjecting his wife and children to the rule of a domestic Nero. A woman may use her sex as a means to find some man to whom she may cling, like a vine, for the rest of her days, helplessly depending upon him to think for her and make her decisions, as well as to provide food and shelter. The mating instinct can be put in the service of the Ego to elevate, satisfy or preserve its unsound demands.

The We-experience, therefore, is not identical with any natural instinct. It is one of the possible directions in which the instinct may be directed.

We-feeling is actually closely connected with (or close to) real love, but it is more than love. It forms the foundation of all mutuality—of all community—in the sphere of common honor as well as in the sphere of affection. It is a specific psychic reality of which love gives proof—a peculiar experience, difficult to describe and yet very powerful. And, fortunately, it is also very widespread.

Let us make this preliminary statement for the time being: The We is the psychic reality which constitutes the basic unity of a group whether its members are conscious of it or not.

The Original-We

Let us proceed to investigate the qualities and laws of this We-experience, since almost no one would doubt its reality or importance.

In the first place, we must consider the nature of the We-relationship in which every individual has his first We-experience. It is the one which exists between mother and child, and we call it the "Original-We."

As soon as a child is born, the biological unity of the mother and child is demonstrated by the fact that the one organism produces exactly what is necessary for the other one, namely, milk, and even later on we may observe a kind of mutuality which gives the impression that there is no psychic dividing line between mother and child. Sometimes, for instance, we see a child about a year and a half old taking food out of his own mouth and putting it into his mother's. If the mother is mature enough, she does not feel disgust; on the contrary, she may have a thrilling sense of unity.

As has been said before, we call this a We-experience and say that it and similar ones are expressions of the "Original-We." The Original-We does not acknowledge any barriers between its members, and that is the reason why there is no disgust. The deepest unison—not only harmony but full consonance—is the essence of the Original-We.

However, this deep unity may be disturbed. Suppose the baby cries because its mother has not had enough milk for him. The mother, understanding that she is the cause of his distress, will be unhappy, but the more upset she becomes the more her milk will fail, and the greater her failure the more the distress of the child. In this way each increases the other's unhappiness. This breaks in upon the complete unison of the mother and child. It is a disharmony—a "Breach-of-the-We"—which we will discuss later. For the present, we simply say that not only consonance but also fragility is a characteristic of the Original-We.

Any disturbances of the Original-We arise from within. Attempts to disturb it which come from outside are successfully warded off. Suppose mother and child are disturbed by a noise when singing, or their walk is spoiled by rain, or their toy is broken. They will laugh together or lament together, yet their harmony will not be endangered. They react conjointly against the disturbance; they do not react impatiently against one another. Against the outer world the Original-We shows a great resisting power. Its capacity to endure common hardship and suffering is almost infinite, and its best quality displays itself, even in the moment of outer danger, in its creative power and its capacity for development.

Between mother and child creativeness often shows itself in play, in telling fairy tales, in painting pictures and in inventing playthings. In serious situations, as when the child becomes sick, this creative source proves itself to be really inexhaustible—always presuming that the mother and child actually are still bound together in the Original-We and remain so. If a little child must have an operation, one can observe that he not only withstands the shock, but even takes a step forward in his development provided that the mother remains courageous, that she does not weep, tremble, or faint. But if she fails, or if a physician with little understanding sends her away, then the We is broken and the egocentric part of the child's development is fostered. The child begins to develop in ways which are very difficult to change, much as they will need correction.

Thus loyalty, as well as courage, creativeness and endurance, is one of the essential characteristics of the Original-We, and, as we have already noticed, so are fragility and the condition of being easily upset.

We find the Original-We first in primitive life. For example, in certain Negro tribes in Africa we find that if a member breaks, say, his right leg, all members of the tribe wear a bandage on their right legs. This apparently senseless custom becomes quite understandable when one considers that even the adults in such tribes are yet in an Original-We relationship. The tribe is a psychical unit—a Primitive-We.

This relationship in this Primitive-We is shown in the old ideas of blood vengeance. Suppose a member of one group killed a member of another. The death might be avenged by killing any member of his group. Obviously, we have here again the Original-We unity persisting, as it did in primitive society, into adult life. The individual has not yet emerged out of the community of the group; therefore the group is responsible. The injury was one to the tribal We group and was avenged by any similar injury to the other tribal We.

In the Old Testament we find still another illustration (Dt 25:5–10). A brother was expected to marry his sister-in-law after her husband's death if there were no children. The brothers were viewed not as individuals but as parts of a whole whose best interests were served by the production of children. The living brother represented not himself but the Primitive-We of which both he and the deceased were members.

Many vestiges of the Primitive-We relationship have been described by Tacitus in the clans of the old Germans. Nearer to us such vestiges are found in some Indian tribes of our day. Consider, for example, certain communal customs under which the owner of the soil is not the individual but the tribe. The tribe decides how the fields are to be cultivated, where the hunters shall go, and how the game is to be distributed. The group is responsible for the welfare of its members, and if a person offends the gods, not just one sinner is guilty but the whole tribe, and the tribe has to make the necessary atonement.

There is another person-to-person attitude in which the Original-We may be observed and studied, even though it does not last long. It may be found in the behavior of the couple in love. The so-called "first" love and still more the "great" love show in their very beginning a disregard for many so-called "sensible" and "grown-up" rules of conduct. These two people may really behave like children. Rather often they speak a kind of "baby-talk," calling one another "Tootsie" and "Wootsie," or some other endearing baby name which fond parents apply to mere infants.

The lost paradise of the old childish Original-We seems to be regained. The deep harmony and easy productiveness mentioned before give them the wings of a new life. The capacity for common suffering and loyalty and the courage to fight against outer difficulties are plainly recognizable. So, too, are the dangers of being disturbed by inner discords and even the fragility of the We-relationship itself.

Turning back to the Original-We is like discovering the fountain of youth. It not only renews psychic productivity so that new ideas and often new talents suddenly awaken, but it also makes the lovers "younger" physically, so to speak. On the one hand there is often a greatly increased capacity for expression in words; good poetry or lyric prose may be written almost for the first time; ideas flow more freely and are of a loftier order and more beautifully expressed. Love often seems to release the inarticulate one from his lack of words. On the other hand old bodily disorders which have lasted for years sometimes suddenly disappear because the whole organism apparently acquires new energy through a happy love experience.

Even the laws of hygiene sometimes seem to be set aside for a while by the We-experience. In the early spring or in the late fall sweethearts may sit late on a cold night upon some park bench or on a porch without catching a cold. Their parents and doctors (if they knew) would be convinced that these tender young things who are always in need of so much consideration will get pneumonia, or at least catch a bad cold. This fact involves important consequences in the sociological field. Perhaps one thinks of parades and ceremonies in the open air for which thousands of people often stand in the rain many long hours. The more these people are enthused and united by Original We-feeling, the less will they fall sick. If colds and numerous infections arise, there was not much We-feeling in the gathering.

Fighting troops in World War I often stood days and nights in water to the knees, but sickness, at least in the beginning of the war, was ten times less than it would be if one would repeat such an experiment today for the sake of gathering statistics. The egocentric hypochondriac who goes through the rainstorm wrapped up in his overcoat and taking cold tablets has already granted home rule to all the bacilli that enter his body.

The Maturing-We

Turning for a time from the Original-We, let us consider later developments, using again the mother and child for our illustration.

The mother teases her child, disappearing behind her apron and reappearing again. The child now looks anxious and then joyful, but he is slowly realizing that the sudden absence of the mother does not mean much. It is like a shadow passing over the bright picture of play. In this way the child learns what is, perhaps, the most important thing that can be learned in our world, namely, that the darkest clouds are passing and that the sky is still blue and bright behind them. Sorrows and disappointments are only shadows on the foreground, while the background of our life remains serene and dependable. Loyalty reaches further than danger.

If, on the other hand, this teasing by the adult is exaggerated or is done too roughly or for too long a time, the child has the opposite reaction. Life seems full of uncertain dangers and darkness. All bright lights, all joys pass over the foreground like a deceitful will-o'-the-wisp while the background remains dark. The Original-We is destroyed and the tragedy of life begins.

It is part of the natural attitude of the child that he tries to conquer the world. He observes, fingers, studies everything. As soon as he can walk nothing is secure. The books in his father's bookcase, the dishes in his mother's cupboard, the toys of his older brothers and sisters are all discovered and conquered with the same will to power and joy with which the adult discovers and masters strange continents, primeval forests, deserts and mountain summits. Even before the child walks, when he can only sit on his mother's lap, he likes to touch and to hold everything that he can reach. He puts his hand into the applesauce and turns over the dish of soup with shouts of glee. The child is right in doing so, because he is really only doing what his growing life directs, obeying his very nature. There is—the first time at least—no bad will, no challenge to the adults, no feeling guilty for his behavior.

On the other hand, the mother is right, too, when she curbs the child. She defends the mode of life of the adults somewhat as a policeman protects the property and life of his fellow citizens. Moreover, she says to herself that the child must learn, as soon as possible, the limits of his rights and powers and how to respect the rights of others, too.

But how can we preserve the loyalty, the confidence and the creative power of the Original-We if the mother must, in almost every moment, curb the enthusiasms of the little conqueror? The way of the child and the way of the adult are in conflict—an unavoidable conflict. The broadening and ripening of the Original-We relationship which had its imperceptible beginning in the teasing play between mother and child seem to be endangered in this new phase of development.

In spite of this necessary and inevitable conflict, it is possible for a productive (We-feeling) parent to find the way out. In fact, it is in just such a situation which has the appearance of being an "unsolvable lesson" that the creative power of the We proves itself most distinctly. Let us take a simple case. Suppose a child pulls down some books which his father wishes to keep in a certain order on his shelves. What shall be done? It would be easy for the father to become irritated, even angry, and clearly show it to the child. Such a reaction pits father and child against each other. They are not a We-unit—the We is broken. But it is possible to find a better—a creative—way which maintains the

We-feeling between the parent and child and still leads to teaching adult orderliness to the child.

In dealing thus creatively with the child, the father might, first of all, say to the child: "Now *We* (not you) have done something which is not good. We have spoiled the nice arrangement of the books." Thus, the father may be a bit sad (not irritated) about the disorder and draw the child into sharing (in the We) that feeling. Thus, the child feels childishly sad. But he still remains within the father–child We instead of outside it, as would be the case if the father became angry and said, "See what a bad thing you have done," or otherwise created a breach between the two of them.

The father might join with the child in putting the books back on the shelf, acting together in such a way that the child feels that he is freely using his own energy. Perhaps, when the books are replaced, they can be arranged according to color, or in some other simple order more readily apparent to the child. If the father does not like this new arrangement—he may call it disorder—he must realize that it is, perhaps, an orderliness much better suited to the educational needs of the child than the original one.

The pressing problem for the father is not to teach the child immediately to place the books in adult order. It is to deal with the child in a way that maintains We-feeling and at the same time carries the child through a creative, educational process to the time when he ultimately has learned the proper order.

After working with the child in replacing the books, the father may lead the child to other tasks, asking him to handle old bottles or boxes or anything else which may be explored, conquered and put in their proper place. Now the child helps us to maintain the order, provided it is comprehensible to the child. Moreover, he becomes a firm supporter of that order. He objects, for example, to each change in setting the table; he scolds if one speaks loudly after dinner while the father takes a nap.

Gradually a new pattern of living has to be developed. It is the pattern of family life as a synthesis of the adult's style and the child's style. The conflict between the child's pattern and the adult's has to be settled by developing the right style of family life which fuses the two into a new style. This new one cannot be rigid—it has to be flexible, changing and growing every day, and the adults, as well as the children, must conform to it.

The We—the family—includes persons who are quite different: masculine and feminine, young and old, strong and weak, educated and uneducated, clever and stupid. All of them are organs of this living larger organism called the family, and by their We-feeling they have a part in the common life of the whole. They share not only in its duties, but in its joys. The boy, radiant, says that he has watered the flowers, and the adults are glad with him. The father explains that he has had to take the place of a sick associate and do twice the usual work. The others understand what that means. The oldest daughter repeats a good joke cracked in her high school and all laugh understandingly together.

By such signs, we perceive that the Original-We has changed by invisible steps into a Maturing-We. The simple and full unison between mother and child has grown into the rich harmony which unifies parents and children, and perhaps cousins and aunts, in spite of, or even because of, all their different qualities. This new unit is a living and productive one. This development rests upon a basic principle—individual differences may increase, but the community increases still more.

Quite similar tasks and solutions are to be observed wherever an Original-We develops into a Maturing-We. For instance, children of a kindergarten class may build up a real community with the help of a warm-hearted teacher who has taught them to share in joy and distress.

But how will this We retain its harmony in the face of the differences which stand out more and more in later years? The group may include children who are gifted and stupid, aggressive and retiring, interested in science and in sports, and, unfortunately, very rich and very poor. Ideally, all should remain the We-feeling members of a unit. The spirit of unity should prevail. The question is: How may differences contribute to the strength of the We in spite of endangering its unity?

The answer to this very difficult problem can be indicated by taking our kindergarten class through an imaginary situation. Suppose in the fourth year of their school life that the class undertakes to build a model of a country, or a part of it, in sand

and stone and wood. One boy, the son of rich parents, gives some money. Another boy, whose father is poor, contributes some wood. Sand, stones, plants are collected by the entire group. The young carpenters do their work; the painters paint; others make placards; those who can draw make drawings. The teacher takes care that everybody, without exception, puts his best effort into the project. When, finally, the project is finished, it is *"Our"* model and *"We"* are proud of it.

The We-group has taken advantage of all the differences in its members, and thereby it has, perhaps, built something that no member of the group could have built by himself. It certainly has achieved in the We-feeling something which no individualistic effort could bring about. This principle of cooperation is central to the notion of group process. Its true significance may be better understood when considered from the viewpoint of the We-psychology. Thus considered, efforts to apply it will be more practical and more successful.

The Breach-of-the-We

In the Original-We the child is wholly dependent, so closely linked with the mother that he at first seemingly does not realize that he is a separate being. The distinction between "I" and "You" has been made, if at all, very vaguely. Sooner or later the child must realize that he is a separate person and learn to act on his own initiative and assume responsibility himself.

From the child's viewpoint the sense of unity in the Original-We may seem so complete that there is scarcely an awareness of separate identities. Soon, however, that awareness develops, but it does not necessarily mean disunity. The two individuals, mother and child, remain entirely harmonious in a unity which fully recognizes the separate personalities, yet binds them together despite their differences. That unity is, as we have seen, the Maturing-We. It becomes a constantly more inclusive group expanding itself to include in its We-feeling all members of the family and a widening circle of friends, acquaintances and others. In this form it is a living social group—a dynamic reality.

The child can gradually pass from this original sense of unity to the larger one of the Maturing-We without any feeling of a break in the We-relationship between himself and his mother. He can become completely aware of his individual existence without feeling at odds with the You in the We. He can also develop, as a separate individual, very many differences of opinion, of goals, of skills—and more—yet be strongly bound by We-feeling to the group, the We, which he feels is more important than himself. Becoming aware of his individuality and developing his distinctive differences he does not necessarily create disharmonies which destroy the We-feeling upon which the We rests.

Such is the ideal, but in practice it is never realized. The transition from the Original-We to the Maturing-We does not come about without the child's suffering from a more or less serious injury to this sense of harmony. It is caused by what is termed, in the We-Psychology, the Breach-of-the-Original-We, or, for quick reference, the Breach-of-the-We.

It will be remembered that the Original-We is resistant against attacks from without but is endangered by conflicts arising within itself. Therefore, there is danger of the Breach-of-the-We whenever the child's style of life (in spite of his We-feeling) is contradicted by the mother because of her We-feeling. This tragic conflict is possible because the viewpoint of the Maturing-We is higher than the viewpoint of the Original-We, but it becomes dangerous only if the We-feeling of the more mature person is not strong enough to overcome the conflict by a creative synthesis.

A pediatrician, for instance, may say that the child—perhaps a three-year-old—should not drink at night. The child is thirsty, but the mother is not allowed to fulfill his wishes. How can she manage it so as not to destroy the We-relationship? There is theoretically always a possibility of solving even the most difficult problem of this kind, but the solution of every problem presupposes a degree of patience, productivity and love on the part of the mother which cannot be found on our earth. She would have to be as capable as an angel of unadulterated We-feeling, and we know that no human being is like that. Therefore, we say that, regardless of theory, in practice every child and every mother must come to the Breach-of-the-We.

The Breach-of-the-We does not arise solely in the conflicting demands made by the child and the adults upon each other. It is not, for example, simply a matter of drinking or not drinking, taking the books off the shelf or leaving them there, going for a walk or staying in the house, handling the dishes or not touching them. The We is destroyed only if the tone of the "no" or the expression of the face in saying it indicates in itself that which is the essence of the Breach-of-the-We—the betrayal of the faith of the child, the real lack of love on the part of the mother.

As long as the mother remains friendly, trustful, reliable, it is possible to deny the most important wishes of the child without destroying the We. The decisive thing is that the mother be creative, which means that she must be We-feeling enough to invent again and again new ways of soothing and compensating the child. The moment that she becomes impatient, helpless, angry, or even hopeless the We is broken, whether she wishes it to be or not, and she cannot conceal that fact.

Training the child to be clean, punctual in going to bed and getting up, and especially teaching him good manners at the table and in social intercourse involve so many conflicts that it is extremely difficult to find the creative way of the Maturing-We in every case. Moreover, there are special problems such as the sickness of the child or of the parents, the birth of another child, trips, changes in the environment, visits of grandparents or other relatives. In short, our life includes so many adjustments, and the egocentricity of ourselves and others is so great, that we may state one thing with mathematical certainty: if the Original-We has not yet been broken by the mother (or father) in the first two years of the child's life, others will break it afterward (unconsciously, of course). They will destroy this original harmony and confidence between the child and the adult sooner or later, gradually or suddenly, but in every case effectively.

With regard to the future form of the child's personality, it makes a great difference whether this Breach-of-the-We occurs early or late, quickly or slowly, cruelly or mildly. In all these cases, the child learns that he cannot rely upon adults as a whole in the way he had formerly assumed he could. The We in which he lived and believed was an illusion. It is true that adults act again and again as if the We did exist, and they also demand the We-feeling behavior from the child. Nevertheless, they betray this We and break it every day. In fact, they are much further away from it than the child is.

Consider for example three-year-old Gretel, who is sad and aloof. The mother notices it and thinks her child has lost her former frankness. She speaks in a friendly manner to the girl and says she may tell her mother everything that happens. The child again enters the We-relationship and quite freely tells her small troubles. The next morning she is playing in the living room when she overhears her mother talking to her father: "Yesterday I discovered Gretel's secrets at last. I got her to tell me her troubles. They are very childish ones, of course, but she is so very reserved already. I am afraid she may have told me only half of the whole truth."

This conference between the parents is well intentioned and reasonable, but it is done in a tone of voice which to the child completely contradicts the We. She feels betrayed once more, especially by the mother's distrust. Unconsciously she leaves the We again and builds up the walls of her aloofness higher than they were before. She and the mother had made a new treaty of loyalty and confidence, and this new We is broken again. The mother seems to be a betrayer on purpose; now it is almost impossible for the child to build up a new We once more. She becomes stubborn or whines. She cannot help it, for she feels compelled, as by a power outside herself, to defend and indemnify her little Ego against the investigation of the adults and their concern in her affairs. The child has become egocentric.

Educational science describes a so-called "age of obstinacy" which is noticeable in the third and fourth year of almost all children. Part of this may be grounded in the wholesome development of the child's personality within the We of the family. The child claims his own proper place in the circle of his brothers and sisters, and also in the ranks of grown-ups. He wishes to do what he is able or nearly able to do himself, without the help of others. He does not want to remain a baby, and that is right. There is a natural inner urge to grow up. This may be the sound kernel of the "age of obstinacy," but mostly the child's stubbornness or apparent listlessness (the other side of the same egocentricity) goes beyond the limits of sound development. The child says "no" where the We-feeling person must say "yes." Often one has the impression that he says "no" only to enjoy his own power. The power of saying "no" is the only power of one who feels weak and helpless, as the child feels in the broken We. This new negative attitude indicates that a vastly important fundamental change has taken place in the whole system of the child's thinking, feeling and acting.

The values in the child's world may remain the same. A doll is nice, an apple is sweet, shiny pennies are desirable after the Breach-of-the-We, as well as before. Formerly they were something to be enjoyed by the We; now they are for the pleasure of the individual. We say that "the enjoyer of the values" has changed.

Formerly, the child thought: "*We* would like to eat; therefore *We* need the apple. *We* wish to play with the doll. *We* will put the coin in *our* box." Now he thinks: "That is *my* doll; no other may play with it. *I* claim the apple. *My* coins belong in *my* box and not in *yours*." The difference between my things and yours has become apparent, but this discovery unfortunately is made in a way so that the child does not learn first to respect the property of the others. On the contrary, he demands that everything belong to him.

Private property in the development of the individual and of society is understood first as "my property," and the defense of one's property is the first and most important task of the new-born, egocentric policy. The property rights of another are acknowledged only if the other defends his right very vigorously. Even this respect for the rights of others is chiefly shown in the way represented by the egocentric sentence: "If you do not take my things, I will not take yours." A real, living and well-understood right in property is to be found only within a Maturing-We and in its service. Under these circumstances property is a means to We-feeling service by the proprietor, possible only when the distribution of the goods is a sound one.

The mother has fine dishes because she knows best how to handle them. The father is the owner of books because he is able to read them. An older sister, being an expert in knitting, has all the pretty yarn. The child feels that she has the little watering-pot because she is capable of watering the flowers. Each one remains responsible to the whole—the family We-group—for his own private property. In such an early education of the child within a maturing family We, social problems might find their first solution.

The Breach-of-the-We is felt by the child as a struggle with an adult. The superior power of the adult and the child's weakness and dependence upon the adult make this a grim reality and often a terrifying thing for the child. It always gives rise to the fear of the We-relationship being dissolved. The dissolution involves a sense of helplessness of the "I" and makes for enmity toward the "You."

When the breach first occurs, the child feels that the world is unfriendly and invincible and that he is helpless and abandoned to it. The expression on the face of the adult who pronounces a prohibition may be a terrible thing to the child. The expression may mean anger, hate, lack of love, enmity, or other attitudes which make the child feel that he is being attacked and must defend himself yet cannot hope to do so adequately.

The Breach-of-the-We must come. It may come slowly and by degrees, beginning with little more than a normal realization on the part of the child that he is an individual different from his mother yet harmoniously related to her. Or the breach may come suddenly, violently, dramatically, and if so it generates a terrifying feeling of fear, helplessness and estrangement. Beyond doubt this is the most terrifying experience of childhood. In psychopathological cases there are always indications that the child fears a parent or one in the position of the parent. It is not difficult to understand the dreadful nature of this fear and its far-reaching results.

The educational problem of every parent is to help the child make such a gradual transition from the Original-We to the Maturing-We relationship that he does not suffer from fear and is not endangered by any of its unfortunate results in later years. But every parent is more or less egocentric. One is therefore limited by the weaknesses of his own egocentricity and inevitably fails in some measure to solve this problem. The more rigid and unsound one's own Ego is, the greater the damage unconsciously inflicted upon the child.

Isolation

The results of the Breach-of-the-We are often scarcely notice-able. Both the child and the adult take care after each quarrel to restore the former peace—"to be as good friends again as they were before." A slight increase of stubbornness, of whining, or even of docility and tenderness may be the only sign which the adult layman can observe. In more serious cases, to be sure, the children often obviously show increasing anxiety, shyness, greedi-ness, envy, malicious joy over another's misfortune, and other symptoms of egocentricity. All these qualities can be kept in check only by will power in the service of higher egocentricity.

Greediness, for instance, may encourage a boy to want to take away the candy his sister has received for her birthday, but in order to avoid punishment he restrains himself. This outer atti-tude, perhaps, is polite or even chivalrous—as long as people see him. He restrains his egocentric greed by his will power in the service of his egocentric goal of being rewarded or praised, or at least not blamed. What we call "well-educated" very often means only having a well-working system of egocentric rules and habits in order to play the role of a "perfect gentleman or lady." It does not mean—as it should—the system of insights, skills and habits in the service of the Maturing-We.

The decisive fact is that in all cases, including apparently rough, energetic and robust people, there is a wound under the scar left by the so-called healing of the Breach-of-the-We, and this wound remains exceedingly painful and irritable. If you felt as a child that you could not trust yourself to those nearest you, you will develop an attitude which will influence all your later deci-sions and reactions. The Breach-of-the-We involves just that feel-ing. In experiencing it you have had, so to speak, an encounter with the spectre called "Isolation," and you cannot forget it even if you do not think about it every day. Feeling that you were alone and helpless, you have faced the innumerable and apparently dangerous things in the unknown world which seemed to be the terrible chaos of reality. The primeval fear of mankind has laid its hand upon you with greater power than is justified by our human situation and your tender years.

We are very small parts, it is true, in a vast world, but it is not a chaos. It is sensible and orderly, even though we do not always understand this order. Our task in life may be very difficult, yet there is a way to complete it, and that truth makes us humble and secure. In spite of this, the childish fear seems to persuade us that we are surrendered senselessly and accidentally like helpless victims to a blind chaos, or even to a cruel and omnipotent deity. Primeval fear shows us where Isolation may lead us. Reality, however, shows that Isolation itself is an error, since our later life is partly the correction of this wrong presupposition of our egocentric behavior and partly the invigoration of the opposite principle—the We. In the end, life encourages neither egocentricity nor isolation nor fear. Life supports and favors courage, community and We-feeling—even where our first impression (seen with egocentric eyes and judged by a pessimistic soul) seems to prove the opposite.

In the light of these facts, it must be apparent that the best preparation for a healthy-minded and correct understanding of the world is to postpone the Breach-of-the-We and to diminish its harshness. Here, in the experiences of early childhood, not in later instruction, is to be found the root of religious living. For in these early experiences the child may be made to feel that his world, in spite of its hardships, is supported by the love that permeates the We-feeling family. In such cases the background of his existence is bright with hope and confidence, not darkened by fear and distrust. And this makes for a deep-rooted faith in a loving God and a basic outlook of confidence and hope upon life itself.

The more a child's soul has been shaken by the Breach-of-the-We, the more he is in danger of seeing himself, his fellows and especially the relationship between him and them, in a false light. He has realized that the most important presupposition of his life—the We group—in which he feels at home is imperiled by unknown dangers. The child cannot determine what these dangers are and, therefore, he cannot avoid them. Some kinds of play which seem quite natural to the child may bring about a sudden and forcible interference by an adult. At once all joy is spoiled, and it is impossible to continue playing.

In such a case, the We is renounced by the adult whose attitude is such that the child is burdened with a disturbing experience. He cannot forget the threatening voice of the adult: "If you do that . . ." "Well," thinks the child, "what may happen if I do that? I am afraid that something unpleasant, perhaps terrible and irreparable, will happen and I cannot protect myself against it." Seen from the outside, this happening may be merely a reproachful or a severe look. The inner meaning to the child is that he has been turned out of the We. The little bird has been thrown out of the nest.

We call the role which the adult plays in this tragedy that of the Black Giant. The expression, taken from the fairy tale, indicates reasonably well the mood of the child at such a moment. The child is one half of the Original-We. The Black Giant is the other half—the person who turns out the child. The We is divided into "You" and "I." The You is a giant, and the I is a helpless dwarf. Therefore the emergence of the Black Giant is always the beginning of the so-called inferiority feeling.

The first Black Giant is usually the mother or father. Later other persons—a policeman, teacher, or others in authority, or even public opinion—may take their place. They are the persons who wound the child—tease him more than he can bear, punish him too severely, treat him unjustly—or who lay prohibitions upon the child—deny his wishes—in a way that arouses his fear. All such persons remind the child of the forbidding attitude of the Original Black Giant and the fears it aroused. The experience itself may be forgotten, or it may be ineffective for a time, but unconsciously it remains a powerful influence which makes harmlessness, gaiety, successful activity and real bravery more or less impossible. Only exaggerated audacity or concealed cowardice is "allowed."

The teacher says peevishly: "If you make this mistake once more . . ." She does not complete the phrase. But the child has heard the same tone in the teacher's voice which sounded years ago in the mother's words when she became terribly angry. Then the child's emotion completes the sentence: "If you make this mistake again, I shall punish you terribly." And a cruel witch seems to grin from the teacher's chair. Is it the witch of the dream of last night? Is it the nightmare itself? Is it a distorted picture of the mother when she becomes furious? It is all this together. It is the symbol of the Breach-of-the-We—the Black Giant! Yet the poor teacher does not guess what role she is playing, and therefore she cannot handle the excessive and "unreasonable" reaction of the child.

At the same time that this kind of reaction occurs in the inner life of the child, the opposite—and not less egocentric experience—usually takes place. The child is afraid of the anger of one adult and flees into the arms of another. There is not only the Black Giant, but also the White Giant. The child feels—in the exaggerated manner of the discouraged—that there must be a bright, friendly power which not only protects the helpless dwarf but fulfills all his wishes. Sometimes the grandmother or an uncle or an aunt can play this role. Thus certain demands, expectations, and claims, which cannot be satisfied in reality, are developed in the child's personality.

Sooner or later the White Giant must disappoint the child, failing in some way to fulfill his wishes. Perhaps even the White Giant becomes irritated, angry, domineering. Then the color is not—as might be expected—merely a little darkened or stained. No, it becomes as black as the night. The protector disappears; the We-breach is split open anew. That is why certain children weep despairingly over some small unimportant matter as if their whole life depended on it. To the child, his life does indeed depend upon the white or black color of the giant. The security, peace of mind and happiness of the child depend upon whether he remains in the We that protects him and fulfills his wishes or is cast out.

The so-called "good" relationship between the child and his White Giant, of course, has to be distinguished from the real We. It is a sham We, built up by two equally egocentric individuals, and that is why it cannot last.

In spite of this crude opposition of "black" and "white," both colors may be seen in the same person alternately. The mother can be a White Giant when she tells fairy tales, but she changes into the Black Giant if she asks who has eaten the missing apple. The child's attitude may be as tender as possible during the fairy tale. Unconsciously for the child, and perhaps even for the mother, this tenderness may conceal the fear and the danger that the mother may suddenly take up the role of the Black Giant. The tenderness in such cases is somewhat exaggerated, since it is supported by unconscious mistrust, and perhaps by a guilty conscience.

Similar childhood experiences account for the fact that some adults always feel obliged to agree with the opinion of everybody. They are unable to say no. If they have to tell their superior something disagreeable, they turn back three times before they dare to enter the Black Giant's room. The diplomacy of their lives is to save the white color—the smile—of all the different giants, and to avoid, at all costs, the change to black.*

We find the same situation in all the different fields of our biological existence—for instance, in learning to walk. We cannot remember how and where and why we fell as a child, but we involuntarily obey the rules we learned by falling down; nothing must be done to disturb our center of gravity. If you learned to ride a bicycle or to skate, you realize how difficult it is to change these rules. One cannot consciously make the mistakes or awkward movements once made in learning to keep one's balance, or do a "heel-and-toe spin." These rules are guaranteed by the main interest in self-preservation.

Imagine a boy who always does what he is expected to do. He has been trained to be a model child, and his giant is public opinion. Obeying it, he feels praised. It is white. His value seems to increase. If he acts in opposition to this public opinion, he feels blamed. The giant is black. The smallest violation of the rules of conduct laid down by public opinion is at the same time a violation of the inner egocentric law unconsciously enacted by the boy himself.

Suppose his friends go out to steal from a store. Now the boy is caught in an inner conflict. "Should I go with them? Isn't this the demand of comradeship? On the other hand, one must not

---

*The whole procedure, as we said, is usually unconscious. We do not need a long explanation of the conception of the unconscious. It means simply the store of experiences, collected in our lifetime, which helps to direct our reactions and which cannot be purposely reproduced in their entirety. If the theory of C. G. Jung is right there is, below the personal unconscious, the store of race-experience or mankind experience, the so-called collective unconscious. The We-psychology is inclined to adopt certain parts of this theory.

steal." The boy is living in two sham We-relationships at once. The one tells him to violate the laws of the other. The result is an acute anxiety, for he realizes that he is not at home in either sham We. His egocentricity makes him rigid and unproductive, and he is unable to make a decision.

Back of the rigidity of his rules is fear—and the fear here is the fear of the Black Giant originating as a consequence of his Isolation, which can be understood in turn as the consequence of a very early, or relatively early, Breach-of-the-We. He is isolated because the We was broken too suddenly, and he is unproductive because he is isolated. This is the pattern of that terrifying sense of isolation growing out of the child's feeling that a once friendly relationship has been broken. As a consequence he feels alone, helpless, and likely to suffer at any moment from the sudden and unpredictable disfavor of one he depends on.

Our attitude, therefore, is the result of remembered or forgotten experiences, forbidding us certain ways and allowing us others. We have many guideposts and warning signs in our inner life. Originally they have nothing to do with morals or conscience, though in time they come to influence the development of these systems. They originate in our childhood experiences, their chief purpose being to avoid the repetition of the Breach-of-the-We, and to escape the fear that arises when we feel we are heading for a breach. They are rules or laws which we have imposed upon ourselves without realizing it, and which we unconsciously obey in order to protect our Ego from encounters with an evil world, or, speaking in our terms, with some Black Giant. They serve our Ego.

Here is a person, for example, who has lived many years according to the rule that one should not confide in anyone. His blind confidences in childhood brought him bitterly unhappy disappointments, so now he cannot help being distrustful. Other persons cannot keep any secrets. They feel compelled to blab their affairs to everybody because they found this the way to buy the favor of their White Giants in childhood. One person cannot relax when he is alone because as a child his relatives quickly changed into Black Giants on the slightest excuse. Another does not go to sleep except in the presence of a friend because in his childhood there was always an adult—a reliable White Giant—who indulged him. Unconsciously he now relies upon his friend as a substitute White Giant. Another person works like a Trojan and cannot stop, since his former giants used to praise him for his assiduity. Still another is unable to concentrate and always feels distracted because he realized painfully years ago that all his diligence brought him no favor from his Black Giants.

It is significant that all these rules, "laws," or compulsory patterns may be stated negatively. Not even the chatterbox is a person who *must* chatter, but one who simply *cannot* keep things within himself. All these patterns are restrictions upon life, limitations upon productivity, hindrances which should be overcome. One may object that lack of rules and patterns of this kind would lead to recklessness and arbitrariness, and therefore these patterns are necessary. The decisive point, however, is not the content but the rigid form of the rules. The child should be able (and willing) to restrain himself from touching the matches, but he should not be bound to do so by compulsory inhibition. His own judgment and his free will should decide.

Not all, but very many, characteristics in personality which we usually and falsely feel unalterable are actually the result of these restraints. Such characteristics are not inborn but are created by later influences. We cannot change them simply by decision and strength of will, because behind them lies hidden the unconscious fear of the Black Giant, and that means the human primeval fear—the fear of helplessness, friendlessness, isolation and death. We unconsciously expect and dread the attack upon our Ego of some Black Giant.

All these egocentric restrictions work automatically and outside our conscious control as if they were natural laws. They are not. Fortunately, there is a possible development which may lead us through crises and pain to a new state of mind where all egocentricities are overcome and where these restrictions are removed. Of that we shall write later.

The strangest thing in this connection is that these restrictions do not fulfill their purpose. They should avoid a repetition of the Breach-of-the-We, but they cannot annul the consequences of this break, and they do not. Moreover they cannot wipe out the consequences of a breach that has already occurred, for the fear it engendered still remains. The so-called "laws" operating as restrictions or inhibitions are only a means adopted as a protection against the discomfort caused by stirring up this fear. They may conceal the breach with its terrifying feeling of isolation, but in the end the veil of deceit is torn asunder. Meantime, there is only a pretense that the We has not been broken and the relationship is a Sham-We, the egocentric mask of a real We.

The Remainders of the Original-We

Everywhere we find persons who try to disavow the Breach-of-the-We in their own lives. They pretend that former conflicts passed without serious consequences and that everything is all right now. For various reasons they are unconsciously seeking to maintain the Original-We, its substitute or its corpse, as long as possible.

Consider, for example, a mother who, having lost her husband, clings to her only son with all her affection. He has become, in a sense, a substitute for her husband and is unconsciously loved by her with greater intensity than he would be otherwise as a son and, to a certain extent, as a mate. For her the normal transition from the Original-We to the Maturing-We requires a separation and alienation which she feels she cannot bear. She is always afraid of losing her child. It is as if the normal, increasing independence and responsibility of a growing young person must end good relationships between parents and children. Though this is not true, the mother clings to her son as if it were. She would, if she could, keep him a child always, or at least in childish dependence upon her. She may go to extremes, such as taking him to school every day even when he is ten, or keeping him much too long in short trousers, and she may succeed in keeping the relationship between them—on his part as well as hers—largely as an Original-We.

Strange as it may seem, there are many cases in which the essential feeling in the Original-We of childish dependence upon the mother is prolonged far beyond the time it would normally disappear. Consider some actual cases—a daughter who at thirty will not make a date without asking her mother's permission; a son who, remaining unmarried, lived with his mother until her death and then when he was thirty-five killed himself because he "could not live without her." Consider, also, a daughter who has not married because her mother "couldn't get along without her," or the fifty-year-old woman who was not allowed to buy things herself or go walking alone.

In all such cases we call this too anxious clinging of parent and child to each other—this undue prolongation of the Original We-feeling between them—the Embalmed Original-We. In such cases, too, there is a danger actually impending of a second or third Breach-of-the-We, which will not be a half but a complete break. The mother and child are so frightened by this danger that they are ready to sacrifice everything in order to save the inner peace and harmony of their We (which is, as we know, a mere Sham-We relationship). They give up in this way, without realizing it, their own further development, but they obtain, or rather think they obtain, what they wish to have—the full harmony of the Original-We in their relationship.

They do not understand, however, the price unconsciously paid for this sham harmony in their own lack of development. They think honestly that they love one another, feeling it is self-evident, right and unquestionable that they defend their community against all intruders, new ideas and new feelings. They don't look at one another as human beings with changing age and growing experience; they behave as if they were statues or dolls doing the same old things, saying the same nice old words and having and awakening the same feelings—something like phonographs playing the same old records. This love without courage is a sham love, and the result is also a Sham-We—a We without differentiation and without real fruit.

This sham Original-We—this Embalmed-We—is defended against all outer influences. Outsiders and outer influences would disturb the peaceful paradise and therefore must be kept away like enemies. The members of this Sham-We are especially afraid that one of them will lose the other by death. This fear is, correctly understood, an egoistic one, being not fear for the one who dies, but for the survivor. As another fear, there is always the knowledge that the "child" could marry, a situation which should be prevented by all possible means, since the son-in-law or daughter-in-law would be an invader in the Sham-We.

As a rule, the fear engendered in the Breach-of-the-We is for adults the same menacing spectre which was, consciously or unconsciously, feared so greatly in their childhood. In the case of the Embalmed Original-We it is especially vivid for reasons which are easily illustrated. Suppose one of them should break out of the rosy prison in which this sham "love" holds him, or suppose that death takes one member of the inseparable unit—then the other may fall into such despair that insanity or suicide seems to be the only way out.

One who remains in the Embalmed-We is not prepared for anything approaching normal independence or responsibility for himself. The development which should have been going on for years cannot be suddenly made up in a few months after such long neglect. The degree of independence which is necessary at this particular stage can be developed, as we shall see, only through long efforts in the school of crisis and suffering. The Maturing-We has not been built up. Therefore, all persons must, at this time, be considered as enemies and malicious betrayers.

This abnormal attitude which is characteristic of the Embalmed-We carries its own future catastrophe with it.

Lesser forms of the same deviation are to be found in so-called "family pride," and "hometown pride"—both of which sometimes represent a familar psychological structure. Moreover, certain cases of exaggerated conservatism—the inclination to preserve old habits and opinions in spite of their obsolesence—may have root in a similar Sham-We.

Many people display slavish devotion to certain standards of conduct. Their attitude rests upon an extreme deference to a supposed or real public opinion. Their devotion is, however, a symptom of the same We-sickness. "One" has to wear certain clothing—be in style—or to say certain words under certain circumstances—have good manners; one must go to the country in the summertime, or have six bridesmaids. "Otherwise, what would people say about us?"

Easygoing and irresponsible submission to the opinion, real or supposed, of a group of people such as a family, a class in school, or so-called fashionable society is not We-feeling behavior. It is a lack of that genuine independence which a person in a Maturing-We would have. This submission is not disciplined self-control, but fear of disagreeable differences or quarrels, and, in the last analysis, it is a fear of being turned out, which means a fear of the Black Giant.

Such docility is basically as egocentric as its opposite, namely, boasting assertiveness in order to put oneself forward and to become popular or a celebrity. We-feeling independence, which is necessary in all the different forms and degrees of the Maturing-We, is exactly the opposite of the egocentric longing for the good old Sham-We of our early childhood.

In many cases, there is not enough courage remaining to attempt to restore the Original-We. The desire or longing for it persists, and it can be so strong that it does not leave one during one's lifetime. Such a yearning may make (out of this grown-up child) a poet, a philosopher, or a utopian politician.

The sentimental feeling which sometimes calm and poised persons experience, for instance when they see something reminding them of the Original-We (their lost paradise), is an unmistakable sign that this desire is still in their lives. Sometimes the feeling is aroused by a scene of childhood, a little song, a canary, a Christmas tree, perhaps a childish scene in a movie, and in spite of all his critical powers and self-possession the spectator begins to cry without knowing why.

Most people allude to this longing for the lost Original-We. They speak of the "good old times" which never return, or of the sound and virtuous life of our great-grandparents. The religious doctrine of the sinless and painless beginning of human development is often misused in the service of egocentric longing for the Original-We, and all the social theories which follow the "back to nature" emphasis of Rousseau have to be placed in the same class of egocentric utopias. All these are dreams of the Original-We.

The last class of these dreams—the social utopias—has one interesting and significant characteristic. As everybody knows, the realization of a dream is expected in the more or less distant future, and it is the supposed beginning of sound social development. The Original-We, as the ideal situation "where the lion and the lamb lie down together," has to be restored by social reforms or religious rebirth. Such dreams are dangerous because they ignore or avoid consideration of the real facts, and the solution is too simple, too idealistic—and too poor. These dreams prevent men from coming to grips with the problems of reality by turning them aside into some bypath of human thought.

The true course of human development does not lead us back to any kind of Original-We or substitute for it. It leads us, on the contrary, to a more complicated, better differentiated and therefore far richer form of We-relationship. Different characters, different gifts, and even different valuations will make the life in the future We, which has to be a Maturing- (but never mature enough) We, less agreeable and more productive than these utopians imagine. In this relationship, the independent and responsible personality will unfold itself and use its powers in the service of the Maturing-We for the development of that We.

There is no place in an Original We-relationship for this kind of personality, but it must be recognized as a goal of human development. Such personalities are the highest type of human beings, and only such personalities can play the part that persons must play in the development and maintenance of the highest social order.

The future We-relationship must be built up with the help of innumerable independent, responsible individuals, bearing this We-feeling within them as a characteristic of their personality. It is necessary that they feel responsible love toward one another and toward the community, love that is not the emotional attachment so often meant by the word, but rather a sincere, intelligent, courageous concern for the common welfare.

In the Original-We the individual is, so to speak, not yet born. There is little or no awareness by its members of themselves as individuals. It is not I and You, but We; therefore, there is no genuine individual responsibility. The only responsibility in the Original-We is that of the group for its members. The later form of the We, called the Maturing-We, on the contrary, is characterized by the responsibility of every member for the whole group.

The Development of the Egocentricity

The Breach-of-the-We is, as we have already said, practically unavoidable. Theoretically, however, we can imagine a way of rearing a child which leads the individual straight out of the Original-We on through a sound development to what we call the Maturing-We. The principal thing that prevents this ideal development is the egocentricity of the parents or those in a parental position who, broadly speaking, serve as the educators of the individual. The more they are impatient and domineering the earlier will be the breach. The more they are soft and indulgent the deeper it will be.

Even in the most favorable case the mother is a part of the Original-We only to the extent of being the mother of the newborn child. At the same time, she must live in many other relations, for she is her husband's wife, her older children's mother, her parents' daughter, and so on. All their relations are more in the form of the Maturing-We unless, as is usually the case, they are of the egocentric type.

The baby with his Original-We attitude has, so to speak, come into the world about thirty thousand years too late! He behaves as if he were a member in a tribe of primitive men whereas the child is living in a civilized society in which the customary ways of living for adults often alienate them from the child. Notice, for example, that the mother in primitive life is usually in constant intimate association with her baby, sometimes even carrying him strapped to her back while she works. In our civilization the mother may be forced to leave her baby in a day nursery while she goes to work. Such behavior by adults may seem to the child like a betrayal. Some mothers themselves feel this clearly when they leave their babies to go shopping or to visit a friend or to go to work. The problem of bringing up the child without any seeming treason (i.e., without a Breach-of-the-We) appears to be insoluble in our day, with our methods of education and our egocentric society.

The second reason why the Breach-of-the-We cannot be avoided is to be found in the differences in human beings. Even if parents belong to the same race, they carry in their genes so many different possibilities that sharp differences may be expected in the inheritance of their offspring. So, too, children may have quite different characteristics, even if parents are physically quite alike. Parents may bring into the world children who are greatly varied mixtures of the parental genes, and children may develop characteristics which were hidden in their parents and came to the fore only in the second generation.

Family life, therefore, means that one has to live in a Family-We with three or four persons of quite different natural endowments and varied subsequently developed personality patterns. One member of the family may be lively and unrestrained; the second, passive and dull; the third, an introverted artist; and the fourth, a practical man of affairs. The pure form of the Original-We presupposes a certain homogeneity and similarity in psychic reactions, but this homogeneity is not found in our level of culture, even in family life. Thus the concept of the Original-We serves us only as a theory which helps us to understand reality, but which is only approximately realized in everyday life.

The question now is how the members of that family may accommodate their differences and even make use of them. The more they recognize these differences, and the more they learn from each other, the richer their We-relationship becomes. However, if the active boy worries the passive girl, because her passivity "gets on his nerves," the We must decay in spite of the parents' pedagogical knowledge and endeavors.

The decisive difference in the so-called "constitution" may be described in terms of different degrees of sensitiveness or delicacy of nerves. There are people endowed with inborn robustness and others with natural tenderness, just as there are thoroughbred race horses with slender limbs and farm horses with thick, heavy-set bodies. The race horse, put to the plow, will be damaged, and the farm horse cannot be successful on the race course.

The same thing is true of children. A tender young fellow brought up in a group of rough comrades will be destroyed root and branch, and a robust youngster among tender and highly bred companions will be thoroughly spoiled. In both cases the We-relationship must be broken early and deeply. The task is always the same in any mixed group of robust and tender children. One has to secure everybody's rights or, better yet, one has to enable them to defend their own rights and respect the rights of others.

As the last of the causes of the Breach-of-the-We, consider the differences in degree of vitality. Often vitality is the more inferior as the more sensitiveness has been developed. Everyone knows delicate descendants of very old families who scarcely have enough vitality to meet the needs of everyday life, and who fail as soon as they are called upon to meet higher demands of life. On the other hand, there are coarse, thick-boned people with very little vitality, living phlegmatically and gloomily. Moreover, there are occasionally sensitive people gifted with very great vitality, who are often the stuff of which artists and scientists are made.

The degree of vitality frequently varies within the individual's life. One can increase it by sound living or decrease it by unwholesome behavior. The child of low vitality cannot hold his own against his environment, whereas the child of great vitality is able to assert himself successfully. The relative strength of the child's vitality and that of its educators (parents, etc.) is, as we shall see later, of very great importance in determining the form of Ego which the child will develop.

There are in every child's life definite zones in which the Breach-of-the-We may occur very easily. One of these is the training in toilet habits and personal cleanliness. Others are found in the problems of learning to eat properly and of forming regular habits for rest and sleep. All the tasks of developing an increasingly orderly system of living are in this general class. Very often the birth of younger brothers or sisters is another danger zone. Still another is the changes in environment due to starting in school, death of relatives, change in residence, making trips, and similar experiences. The last to be noted here is the well-known period of difficulty at puberty.

In all these zones the task of the educator is to save the child from increasing discouragement, or, what is the same, from feeling that he will be betrayed. Here we are not concerned with any question of guilt or innocence in his behavior. Even if the child has really done wrong, the grown-up should by all means try to avoid the Breach-of-the-We, remaining loyal to the child even if the child is disloyal to him. It has already been pointed out that being loyal is not the same as being indulgent and easygoing. Within the frame of the We it is possible to handle the child very firmly and even severely; but one must remain kind, serene and objective even though very firm.

This requires genuine We-feeling. Otherwise, in attempting to be just, one actually becomes the betrayer—the one who destroys the faith and confidence of the child—and, in this way, one transmits his own egocentricity to the next generation.

This short summary already proves that the causes and therefore the ways of the Breach-of-the-We may be extremely different. As a result, egocentricity displays itself in different forms, with varied symptoms and at different times. In spite of these differences, in the last analysis the same thing always occurs.

The sound development may be described as the discovery of the Self within the We, and as the deliberate assumption of personal responsibility in the service of the We. It is also the transition from being a member with no sense of one's individuality in an Original-We to being a member in a Maturing-We in which one is conscious of his own separate Selfhood and at the same time of his inter-relationship with others in the We and his responsibility for it. As has been said before, this picture of sound development represents an ideal which sad to say is almost never fully realized.

What actually happens is always a leaning toward one of two extremes in this development. Either one so clings to the Original-We that he does not discover his individuality and therefore cannot enter into the Maturing-We, or the individuality is stressed so much that it no longer remains in the service of the We and deviates—becoming rigid and autonomous in the form of the Ego. From then on, the person acts and feels and even dreams exclusively in the service of the preservation or elevation of his own Ego. The We-relationship disappears and what remains is mere egocentricity.

We have already said that the first extreme—the perpetuation of the Original-We—also leads to its decay later and then to egocentricity just as in the case of the second extreme. The reason is that there is no stopping point in human life. Clinging to the Original-We in an attempt to save its poor remainders is just as certainly an error as the later wish to save the Ego, for in both cases a basic mistake is involved. It is the assumption that the current of life can be brought to a standstill. The fact is that life constantly moves on, which means that change is continually taking place. It leads us either directly through egocentricity and its painful consequences into the Maturing-We, or it leads us by a long detour through the effort to remain in the Original-We into a similar kind of egocentricity and then, if life is long enough, also into the Maturing-We.

The differences between these two cases are to be found only in the degree and rigidity of the egocentricity and the length of the way into it. In the latter situation the individual travels a longer and more roundabout route. He moves from the Breach-of-the-Original-We back into its remainders, thence at length into egocentricity, and finally (if at all) into the Maturing-We. Observing others it is sometimes difficult to realize that in both cases the individuals are on the wrong track.

Consider some soft and tender child who shares all his sweets with his mother in contrast with the stubborn and often antagonistic egoist. It may be hard to feel that one is really as much lacking in true We-feeling as the other, yet the apparent tenderness of the child may be only an attempt to retreat into the old Original-We and preserve its remainders. The seeming We-feeling is really a means of controlling the mother. That it is not love but tyranny may be much more apparent later when the same child forces his mother by tears to remain with him.

The simplest definition of egocentricity has already been indicated. The values, themselves unchanged, are desired now in the service of the Ego only. Before the Breach-of-the-We, they were desired in the service of the We. The We as the enjoyer, so to speak, has been superseded by the Ego. It must be borne in mind that to the individual his Ego seems to be himself; therefore, we could say that the We as an enjoyer is superseded by the I. The values are sought for the advantage of the individual rather than the group.

Let it be put in other words. The active agent, the doer (the subject which, in the grammatical sense, is acting), was formerly the We. Now it is the individual, the I, a part of the We, which has asserted its independence. It acts as if it were, in itself, the entire We. It does not acknowledge that it is a part of any larger or superior unit.

This setting up of the Ego as an independent I means, so to speak, that a part has been tied off from the whole. It inevitably causes a certain limitation of interests, understanding, feeling and productivity. The I is now more or less cut off from the common source of life, somewhat as a hand, bandaged too tightly at the wrist, might be deprived of the life-giving blood supplied by the whole unit of which the hand is only a part. The individual thus cut off must be more superficial and less vital than the We from whose vitalizing energy he is separated. It is not enough, however, to speak of this situation as if it involved nothing more than a lack of nourishment for a part somewhat cut off from the whole. We must recognize that in egocentric living the real I is replaced by a Sham I—the Ego—a something that seems to be genuine but is only an illusion and a poor substitute.

Thus, one's vitality and sensitivity may be either restricted by increasing egocentricity or released in the Maturing-We. This result influences further development. The less a child is vital, the more he is discouraged by his stronger mates, and this discouragement in turn inhibits anew his vitality. One consequence of this lack of vitality is, of course, a more or less distinctly arrested development. Some aims which should be only a means to an end—the service of the We—now become ends in themselves. They are taken as absolute values and they are detached from their proper relationship to the whole of life. Thus, for example, money, power, popularity, and glory may be accepted by an egocentric person as being in themselves the highest values in his life—the most desirable achievements—the supreme goals.

The further egocentric development proceeds the more we see that the highest value of every egocentric life is, in the last analysis, a negative one. Self-preservation of the individual is the presupposition of all other values, for other values—riches or anything else—are a value for the rich man only if he is alive, and therefore his greatest concern is to preserve himself. However it must be remembered that even though the Ego is the individual's inaccurate conception of himself, it seems to him to be what he is. Upon careful analysis a student of psychology may realize the general truth that the Ego is only the Seeming-Self. Even so, it is very difficult for him to apply that truth in his own life.

It follows that all the thinking and striving of the egocentric person is basically concerned with avoiding all damage to his cherished Ego—his Seeming-Self. In whatever he does or plans, he always feels, consciously or unconsciously, the possible advantage or danger to his cherished Ego. He constantly fights against the breakdown of his Ego because its collapse seems to him to mean the destruction of his very Self, but by these defensive efforts he inevitably brings about that breakdown which he dreads most. This is the result of the so-called vicious circle which we shall consider later.

In his consciousness the egocentric person may feel that he is secure and successful, but unconsciously he feels that some critical moment for his Ego is close at hand. Being increasingly cut off by his egocentricity from the We—the source of real life—he suffers from a lack of inner psychic vitality and becomes less and less creative. This makes him insecure and anxious first in his unconscious and then more and more in his conscious mind.

Seemingly inexplicable inferiority feelings, irritability, sensitiveness and other signs of increasing "nervousness" always stand out more distinctly. The more the individual comes to feel that egocentric goals probably will not be attained, the more he seems to attach value to them, and now he strives for them more than ever. The unconscious anxiety—or, what amounts to the same thing, the unconscious feeling of guilt—whispers to him more distinctly in the form of bad dreams, melancholic or troubled moods or even physical disturbances. At last they speak out loud, and mercilessly say that in spite of all endeavor and apparent success he has really failed. Life is passing. Perhaps much has already gone, but he has not yet really lived.

But now these symptoms which seemed to be bad and inimical, namely, this anxiety or guilt, prove themselves to be helpful and friendly, for they intrude themselves in order to bring healing by awakening this living yet unalive person. They are the voice of this life which is not lived, and their force is the power of life itself. They are the messengers of the We which represents this power of life, even within the egocentric mind.

The Clinging Vine

Our purpose now is to investigate various forms of egocentricity. In doing so, we must proceed from one decisive question: How does the individual look at the remaining parts of the broken We? In other words, how does the I feel toward the You? Let us pause to recall the fact that the individual acts the role of his Ego. His Ego is the mistaken image of himself—the inaccurate conception of his value and what he can or cannot do, but he is unconsciously misled into acting as if the Ego were actually the Self.

It becomes highly important, therefore, to see the differences that arise, through the development of the Ego, in the attitude of the individual regarding his own value and that of others. At first this attitude may change rather often, depending upon the varying conditions to which the child is subjected. Gradually, however, it takes a more definite form, and at the beginning of school life, or at the latest at puberty, it is possible to distinguish four fixed and well-defined types of egocentric attitudes.

These four types are dependent in their origin upon the interaction between two basic factors. The first is environment. Whether it is soft or harsh considered from the viewpoint of the child's nature is the decisive matter, and it is also a relative one. What seems soft to one child may seem harsh to another. The second is the vitality of the child in comparison with that of the adults upon which he is dependent. The important point here is whether the child's vitality is superior or inferior to the adults', and again it must be noted that this is a relative matter. The vitality of the same child may be quite inferior to that of certain adults and superior to others.

From interaction of these two factors, we may get four different situations:

1. The child of comparatively superior vitality in a relatively soft environment;

2. The child of comparatively inferior vitality in a relatively soft environment;

3. The child of comparatively superior vitality in a relatively harsh environment;

4. The child of comparatively inferior vitality in a relatively harsh environment.

Out of these four situations we find as many different attitudes developing. They give rise to the four types of Ego patterns which we are about to discuss.

Before doing so, it should be said that one thing stands to reason: All possible mixtures and changes from one to another of these attitudes are to be found. It is also true that in childhood several types of attitude may be developed at the same time, simply because the child may be in a different position with respect to the different adults with whom he has to deal. With respect to one he may be inferior in vitality but superior to another, and so he forms simultaneously different attitudes that later may be displayed one after the other. Many so-called contradictions in human personality, many seeming "changes in character," may be explained in this way.

Suppose now a child that has been brought up in too soft an atmosphere, pampered, spoiled, protected against all the hardships of life. At the same time, let us imagine that this child is inferior in vitality to his educators—his parents. He is in a way overwhelmed by love—and almost stifled by too much care, finding no opportunity to display his own powers or to explore and conquer the world of reality on his own initiative and by his own resources. Moreover, suppose that this child has been startled several times, for instance, by being left alone, and that he has experienced fear that one day he will lose his life without being prepared for it. After the Original-We has been thus broken the child has been pampered again as he was before. (The Breach-of-the-We is the presupposition of the egocentric pattern. Without this breach the attitude could never become so rigid.)

Such a child learns that without help from others he is not equal to the tasks of life. If we consider the inner meaning of a typical experience, we can see how this is unwittingly impressed upon the child. Imagine that he is playing with blocks trying to build a tower. His hands are unsteady and his skill limited, so the stack of blocks is uneven, totters and falls. Now mother rushes to the rescue and, thinking to show the child how to place one block evenly upon the other, builds the tower for him. The lesson she teaches may not be at all what she intends, for the child may learn simply that he cannot build the tower and must rely upon others for help. He feels weak and helpless.

Again, the efforts of the parents to protect the child and the excess of their concern for his safety may teach the child that reality is to a very large degree dangerous and fearful. The well-meaning cautions of the parents, "be careful," "watch out," "you might get hurt," and like admonitions tend to create in the child a sense of distrust and fear of life. Reality seems to be more dangerous, the more the child withdraws.

Further than this, the child may learn that, because of his weakness and helplessness, he is entitled to be helped. His own weakness and helplessness become identical with the obligation of others to help him and his right to receive that assistance. The child himself may come to feel that without this help he would suffer in a way unbearable both to himself and his parents, and their overconcern for him may cause them to look upon any hardship which the child might be called upon to endure as unbearable both for him and them.

At first sight, this parental attitude looks like genuine love, and therefore We-feeling, but, looking closer, one finds in the parents an egocentric attachment which is sometimes called "apes'-love." On the child's side one finds the exact counterpart to this attitude, namely, an unconscious egocentric diplomacy. He uses his own weakness and dependence, and, if necessary, his suffering and fear, to work upon the sympathies of others to the end that he must be comforted or permitted to have his own way. Thus the child unconsciously learns to cling to others for help and to wheedle them by one means or another into doing things for him or humoring him. This type of behavior reflects, of course, the child's Ego-pattern which, because of his clinging tendencies, we call the "Clinging Vine."

A child with such a Clinging-Vine Ego coaxes his father to give him things that the latter does not like to give. If the father is strict, the child flees to the mother and by pitiful laments or weeping silently gets what he wants. If his egocentric goals cannot be easily attained, he may unconsciously resort to more drastic measures. He cries out in his sleep, he vomits after breakfast, he does not sleep well. His excitement and half-conscious fear cause many sorts of physical symptoms. His glands function poorly, and his blood circulation is out of order.

The family doctor is called. The Clinging Vine lies in bed with the expression of a suffering madonna. Without knowing what he does, he achieves his unconscious aim, remaining the pet of the whole family, the center of their attention and the object of their concern. In this case, the way to egocentric success is through suffering.

All Clinging Vines are well-trained, so to speak, in suffering. They feel pain more than other people, and at the same time they are less able to endure it. This suffering is real. It is no sham torment, and mostly not even exaggeration, but it serves their unconscious egocentric goal—and does it successfully for the most part. Later on when there is no one to pity or to comfort them, they pity and comfort themselves. A propensity for sweets, dependence upon certain comforts such as music, flowers, and fine clothing, or a compulsive desire for alcohol, morphine, or other narcotics is very often the later attitude of a Clinging Vine. The individual in a sense clings to such things for the comfort he craves.

As a rule the Clinging Vine and other egocentric attitudes demonstrate a certain increasing enhancement which can be understood as the result of a vicious circle. It is rooted in the fact that no egocentric aim can be attained again and again without considerably intensifying the means necessary to achieve it. The Clinging Vine, for instance, depends upon the tender-heartedness and compassion of his fellow men. And he must display new and always more pitiable forms of helplessness or suffering in order to appeal to these sentiments in his associates. Otherwise, they will become accustomed to the usual degree of the Clinging Vine's weakness and no longer respond to it. Soon no one will raise a hand to do anything unless he is reminded of the fact that the Clinging Vine cannot help himself, and this may be called back to mind only by new and surprising misfortunes befalling this unfortunate, helpless person.

Some increase in suffering and in complaints about his unhappy state is therefore necessary to maintain the Clinging Vine's position. Such increases are, however, as little purposely brought about as the original state of distress. It is the unavoidable result of the reaction of the Clinging Vine's associates. From time to time they become weary of helping him, and again and again he feels himself forsaken, betrayed and endangered by the indifference of "the world." The terrible danger of being left to his own resources and of being placed at the mercy of a wicked world without help throws the Clinging Vine into an extreme state of fear and apprehension. It is, therefore, no wonder that he suffers from anxious dreams, sleeplessness, lack of appetite and depressing moods.

The more the Clinging Vine depends upon the help of other people, the more he suffers from the fear that the helpers might some day stay away. The more he is filled with such fear, the less he develops his own powers, which would make it possible to live without depending upon outside assistance, and the less he is actually able to live without this help. Furthermore, the less he develops his own powers, the more he becomes dependent upon others and the greater his fear of losing his helpers. The fear is aggravated by its own consequences. Thus the ability of the Clinging Vine to live independently is decreased by his own attempt to maintain his hold upon others by increasing his helplessness, and therefore his dependence upon them. This is the vicious circle.

At last, the sense of difficulty and distress is enhanced to such a degree that life is no longer bearable. The vicious circle necessarily leads to a crisis in the affairs of the individual. The Clinging Vine becomes more helpless than ever. The helpers themselves see ever more clearly that nothing good can come out of this Clinging Vine. They understand that he is a failure—all help seems to be in vain, and they give up the hopeless case. Eventually—often with a bad conscience—they withdraw their support, whether it be moral or financial or both, preferring to use these means to help more hopeful cases. In the end the person who is almost completely the Clinging Vine may become a public charge, living miserably upon relief. Only insofar as he hungers is he alive.

The Clinging Vine needs a regular supply not only of money, but of pity, sympathy and even admiration. Others must be touched by his fate, and therefore the climax—the crisis of difficulty—comes when others withdraw their sympathy. A very well-developed Clinging Vine said one day: "Nobody's fate in the whole world has been so wretched as mine. If people realized this, they would put my picture in the newspaper."

Thus the way of the Clinging Vine is the path through egocentric satisfaction in meekness and misery to a glory of gratification, even though it is the glory of wretchedness. When this splendor can no longer be attained by the unconscious trick of enjoying one's misery, a profound change may occur. The Ego may collapse totally. The attitude which has become his second nature disappears and now his real nature may assert itself—the living, creative, We-feeling Self of mankind. The process of this change must be referred to a later chapter in which the nature of that psychological development which we call "The Crisis" is discussed.

Finally, we should remember that there are very few people who are always and completely Clinging Vines. Most of them behave in this way only to some degree, or for a time, or on certain conditions, or in relationship to certain persons. On the other hand, it is probable that nobody is entirely lacking in this form of egocentricity. Every reader, if he wishes, can discover the Clinging Vine in one corner or another of his own personality.

At this point it is well to add a note of caution regarding the use of the term Clinging Vine, or any of the other names used to described the various types of Ego. For convenience in quick reference and easy writing we have been speaking of a person as a Clinging Vine, but this is not strictly accurate. He simply has come to think of himself in that pattern. He is actually a very different being. At the heart of his personality is the Self—the essential core of every individual—the genuine I. This Self is rich in potentialities, with vast and unguessed possibilities of being creative, productive, courageous, loving and sensible.

Speaking scientifically, these are the natural endowments of every normal person. In a very real sense that is what he is. No person really is a Clinging Vine. That term and others which we shall define and use only describe a mistaken system of thinking about the Self—the reality that is actually what the person is. The danger in using these terms is that we unconsciously come to think of persons as being what these terms imply.

In these pages and in conversation one might, instead of speaking of the "Clinging Vine," always refer to "one who thinks of himself as a Clinging Vine," but the sheer clumsiness of such expressions makes facile speech impossible on any such level of accuracy. The risk must be run of confusing the Self (the real person) with the Ego (the Seeming-Self) which is only a false image of the reality. The best one can do is to point out this very important distinction in terms with the hope that it will consistently be borne in mind.

The Star

Let us imagine next a child who has been pampered and cherished much as the Clinging Vine. The Breach-of-the-We may have taken place already and the facts and circumstances of the breach may have been forgotten. In the case of the Clinging Vine, the relatively scant vitality of the child was overpowered by the greater vitality of the adults. Now we will suppose that the child's vitality prevails. He does not feel restricted and hampered by the overattention of his parents, but he considers himself well served by them. He has come to seek, in a sense, sovereignty, wanting to be acknowledged, respected, admired and obeyed by his relatives. He feels that he is a very important person who is entitled to have his needs and wishes served by others.

As a whole, the atmosphere between him and his parents is very mild. He attains his egocentric aim of dominating the family by clever and peaceful means. He is radiant, compliant, coaxing, joyous as needed to secure his ends, and not at all the whining, lamenting Clinging Vine type. He plays the part of the gracious ruler, and, without realizing it, those about him play the role of his courtiers. They are charmed if His or Her Majesty is gracious. "How delightful, how enchanting, how irresistible the Prince or

Princess is." They are always convinced that this sovereign is the most gifted, if not the most beautiful, in the world, so it is small wonder that they hasten to serve at the call of their Royal Highness.

In this atmosphere and with this treatment, the child learns that there is no need for him to make arrangements with the harsh outer world all by himself. His courtiers will do that for him and, moreover, they will consider it an honor and a privilege to be permitted to serve him—the royal child.

We call this type—this pattern of thinking about oneself—the Star Ego-pattern. In doing so, we are thinking not so much of the really great artists as of their caricatures in the comic strips (and sometimes also in reality). In behaving like the Star he mistakenly thinks he is, the child displays certain amiable and enjoyable traits, but he also shows the mean, fussy and shabby qualities which the layman expects to find in every prima donna. The Star is vainglorious, conceited and fickle. If you do not admire him, you fall into disgrace. He is touchy and peevish, upset and driven mad by the smallest trifle that is not as it should be according to his ideas. He is jealous. A second Star near him is completely unbearable, for as soon as his stardom is in the least endangered, he feels it necessary to resist the danger with the most powerful weapons at his disposal. Calmness, tolerance, objectivity are not to be found in his personality. When he is offended he scolds, threatens, rages, boasts, lies, calumniates or denounces, and if he were not frightened and cowardly, as egocentric people mostly are, he would not shrink from using poison and dagger to defend this Ego that seems to be his very Self. All means to this end seem right to him. Since he feels that he cannot live without being recognized as the foremost, most important and cleverest of men, he fights for the first place as desperately as any drowning man struggles to save his life. If his stardom is acknowledged, his behavior is quite different. Now he is a splendid companion, an amiable host and a radiant, gracious, magnanimous conqueror.

The vicious circle which determines the fate of all egocentric people is to be observed in the life of the Star even more distinctly than in other Ego-types. Let us consider an example.

Everybody knows the harmless kind of a person who must satisfy his need for recognition by telling the newest jokes, thinking that his value depends upon the fact that people laugh at his drolleries. He almost believes he would have no excuse for existence if he could not make them laugh. The newest jokes, however, are often the feeblest ones, and sometimes what he thinks are new are not so at all. His weapons are constantly in danger of failing him, for the more he exerts himself to amuse people, the more he runs the risk of annoying them. Perhaps they will laugh not at his jokes but at him. They do not think him witty, but silly and absurd. He, however, is so much interested in his egocentric success that he is ready to sacrifice himself. He plays the role of the clown, and in order to keep the attention and applause of his audience he does whatever seems to be agreeable to it. Thus the career of the Star often leads to the sorry fate of the fool.

Usually the caricature of a type is the best means of showing its weak and strong points most distinctly. Thus when he becomes a fool, the Star proves that he was really dependent upon the favor of his hearers and that his starry grandeur was absolutely dependent upon his admirers. He supposes that he dominates them and that he is able to sway them as he wishes, yet, as a matter of fact, he is obliged to avoid everything which deprives him of public admiration and to do everything that could secure it for him. The Star must rule without offending his subjects. If he becomes offensive (like a Nero) a new breach (a Breach-of-the-Seeming- or Sham-We) could occur and the Star would be deserted by his admirers. Naturally he avoids this danger. Therefore the Star, very often without knowing it, develops very good insight into human nature. He knows how to handle the public. His inner dependence, however, makes him insecure and, as it were, servile, but neither the Star himself nor his courtiers know this hidden fear. In the last analysis he does not fight so much for applause as against the diminution of his glory.

Consciously, of course, he never admits that there is any possibility of being laughed at, or even of being hissed off the stage, but, unconsciously, he is never free from the nightmare of this possibility. What he does not avow in daytime tortures him nightly in his dreams. Withered laurel leaves, bombardments with rotten eggs, a terrible running the gauntlet of the sneering looks of a crowd—these are typical of the usual materials of his dreams. They illustrate the shallowness and emptiness of the Star's superiority.

The ordinary dream of finding oneself half dressed at a ball, a parade, or a concert, may indicate the same inner fear. Everyone who has this kind of a dream should ponder whether his egocentricity has not, to a certain degree, taken the form of starhood.

The hidden danger expressed in the fear of failure speeds up the operation of the vicious circle. The more it matters in a given moment to achieve a triumph, or at least to protect one's stardom by avoiding a defeat, the more one exerts himself to play the role of the Star quite faultlessly. At the same time one is, consciously or unconsciously, more seriously alarmed by dire fears of threatening catastrophe. These fears appear again and again at the borderline of consciousness; try as one may they cannot be turned away. It is as if a trembling voice whispers continuously, "Do not fail now! The slightest mistake at this time means the collapse of all our fortune! It means execution and damnation!"

Thus one's attention tends to dwell more and more upon this fearful picture of failure. The imagination is filled with spectres of the terrible possibilities which one is trying to avoid, leaving no room for a vision of the positive goal which one might try to attain. One strives to collect his wits, but the more he strives the more he is upset by the anticipation of failure. The fear increases, the exertion increases, the limbs tremble, the heart becomes agitated, the thoughts are confused—and defeat becomes unavoidable.

In such a moment, the real basis of all stardom comes to light. It is the fear of the repetition of the Breach-of-the-We. All sovereignty, all superiority, all security, and all high hopes are broken down, and there remains only a miserable person begging for mercy. The Star has become a Clinging Vine.

The Nero

If a child lives in an overly harsh environment, the Ego develops in quite a different way. The Breach-of-the-We occurs against another background, but it cannot be said that this harshness leads to worse results than softness.

The child, in this case, learns rather early how to deal with the difficult circumstances of life and in this way often builds up attitudes that are quite suitable for what may be called "practical" success in later years. Any attitude originating in this way, however much it may contribute to this type of success, is (and must be) poisoned through the same egocentric roots that bear all the Ego forms we have been discussing. This way of life, as well as the way of the Clinging Vine and the Star, leads to the We-feeling aims of human life only through difficulty and crises.

As an illustration of this situation, let us take the son of a very ambitious but discouraged businessman. The boy has been brought up in a harsh and strict way. Now school life begins. The father thunders: "If you don't get good grades . . ." The boy, whose vitality is superior to his father's, looks for a way to avoid his father's wrath.

In spite if the harsh Breach-of-the-We he is still able to be productive, but his productivity is befouled with egocentric aims. It is placed in the service of the Ego, and the result is somewhat like the situation when a pure spring becomes choked with rubbish. The flow of the water is not altogether checked, but what does trickle through is no longer clear but murky with mud and perhaps stained with some mineral dye from the dirt dumped into the spring. So when the spring of productivity within the Self is clogged and defiled with egocentric aims its flow may well be halted, and whatever stream does escape is so soiled and stained that it is difficult to realize that it is really the clear, sparkling spring water defiled by egocentric aims. This polluted flow becomes only that resourcefulness often found in egocentric behavior. It is merely a negative productivity—a productivity misdirected in the service of the Ego to what are essentially negative ends.

If we suppose now that some of the water of this choked-up spring finds an outlet to one side of the rubbish dumped in it we have an illustration of another situation found in human personality. In this case there is some flow of unspoiled water in addition to the murky seepage. Here we have illustrated the fact that there may be some objective living—some unspoiled expression of productivity, some use of it in the service of the We—even in a strongly egocentric personality. The powers of the Self may at times work their way around the rubbish of egocentricity, finding an outlet through which they display themselves unspoiled, and this is always in the service of the We.

Returning now to the boy's situation we note that the father is the Black Giant, not too tall it is true, but as black as can be. Therefore, the boy decides—or, better, the decision turns up in his unconscious mind—to avoid at all costs the bad grade. So he makes various arrangements, among them being one with a classmate to help him do his arithmetic in return for a piece of chocolate every week. The pennies he needs for this business he steals out of his father's pocket while he sleeps after dinner.

The father is a harsh, ruthless, egocentric businessman, and the son is similar to his father. One difference is that a certain surplus of vitality increases his egocentric keenness and craftiness in a very dangerous, yet, we have to admit, rather successful way, if we consider that it serves his goals. He outwits his father, masters the situation, dominates the environment.

In younger children the same reactions can sometimes be easily observed in a simpler pattern. Imagine a situation where the child does not receive the attention he should have, his needs and wishes not being attended to as they ought to be. He is harshly dealt with by indifferent, careless or even antagonistic parents, and now the child feels that others are against him—that he can expect no help but only neglect or even hostility from them. Yet the child is not crushed, for in spite of the unfriendly appearance of the world, he seeks his own ends and discovers ways to achieve them.

No child, of course, ever analyzes his situation as we are now doing. No child would ever describe his own reactions in words, but if he could, and did so, he might be supposed to say something like this: "Others are against me, they neglect me, they do not care for my needs or pay attention to my reasonable wishes. But never mind! I'll have my own way anyhow. I'll find the means to make them serve me in one way or another. I'll dominate them in spite of themselves."

So the determined youngster discovers a way to manage his parents. He pesters his mother until she gives in to him to get rid of him. He goes into a temper tantrum—he kicks and screams and perhaps holds his breath until the harassed parent lets him have his way. He cries at his nap hour until he is picked up. He wheedles his mother with many wiles and artifices or even threatens until she bends her will to his and meets his wishes. "If you don't do what I wish," he may say, "I will throw this crystal vase on the floor." Meantime he swings it over his head until his trembling mother gives in. The willfulness of such a child is at the same time both active and rigid in the sense of being inflexible and unbending. We have to do with a young tyrant who develops arbitrary and ruthless ways of attaining his egocentric goals by violence or craft. His highest principle reads "My own will be done."

We call this pattern of Ego the Nero type in spite of the fact that the historical Nero also showed some of the traits of a Star Ego. He was not a pure example of this kind of egocentricity. The most typical characteristics of the type, however, may be indicated clearly by this name. They are the wish and the ability to dominate for mastery's sake and without regard to the welfare of those who are dominated.

All the small Neros growing up in our families and claiming the first place in their school classes and youth groups can be distinguished from their Star competitors by one fact. They go at things harshly and are not nearly so easily disappointed and discouraged (as Stars are) by opposition and defeat. Often they show a kind of seeming objectivity, and only later does it become clear that their own personal power means more to them than the well-being of their group. Sometimes it is difficult to say whether we have an egocentric Nero bearing the mask of objectivity or a really objective and We-feeling leader who honestly serves his group and who only displays some remnants of egocentricity. The truth appears when the situation calls upon the individual for sacrifice.

Consider, for example, a man like Lincoln. One of the marks of his greatness was his willingness to subordinate his own prestige and glory for the sake of achieving results which he felt were in the interests of the common good of the nation. Within his own cabinet he tolerated men who were mistrustful, jealous, detractors. They were almost open enemies who lost few opportunities to impugn his motives and belittle his fame. Their attitude and acts were not unknown to Lincoln, but he counted no personal humiliation too great a sacrifice to further the ends he sought. We-feeling and his passion for the service of the We left little place in his life for egocentric pride or love of power. Even though his own associates found it almost impossible to understand these qualities in him, they were forced to respect them, and history has recognized what we would speak of as his capacity for We-feeling as the very essence of his greatness.

In contrast with this, place the life of the egocentric man who at his death called himself F. Donald Coster.* A career of cunning manipulations mostly under his own name, Philip Musica, brought him more than a million dollars as a comparatively young man. But it involved him in convictions for bribery and grand larceny, an indictment for conniving at perjury in a murder case and a desperate but unsuccessful attempt to flee from the United States to escape charges of swindling New York and European banks of huge sums.

Afterward there were some years of mystery in which Philip Musica completely disappeared. Out of them came a suàve, astute man, still vastly cunning, who under the name of Coster rose to unquestioned control of the third largest drug corporation in the world—an $86,000,000 concern. More than a decade of amazing connivance, stranger than any fiction, brought fame, power, social position, command of great wealth, and at last the disclosure of vast frauds including, among other things, the creation of a subsidiary company with fictitious assets of $18,000,000 manipulated to his great financial advantage. Frantic, he again sought to escape only to find that the captain of his private yacht had drained its fuel oil tanks for winter storage. Then, standing in a room where he could see officers entering his palatial residence to take him into custody, he ended his life. When his kingdom was at the point of collapse, when fame was about to become infamy, when prestige was about to be replaced by disgrace and when wealth was on the point of taking wings, he chose death rather than the sacrifice of his pride and power. To his Ego the value mistakenly

---

*F. Donald Coster was a notorious impostor whose forged credentials hoodwinked bankers, business executives, even the editors of *Who's Who*. On the basis of his fabrications Coster was elected president of McKesson & Robbins, a drug firm. [Editor's Note]

placed upon money, power and fame seemed so essential to his very being that life was unbearable without them.

Psychologically the adult Nero may be described as a person who in childhood comes to feel that his fellow men do not help him, that he has to help himself and—what is most important— that he is able to do so. To him others are only his tools and, in the last analysis, his enemies. He is ruthless in using persons to secure his purpose, exploiting them without a scruple. He concedes some recognition to them only as long as they treat him as their superior, but as soon as they begin to assert themselves, as soon as he thinks he cannot trust them anymore, he rides over them ruthlessly. Friendship, gratefulness, love and loyalty are strangers to him. Indeed, he is for the most part directed by an inner law, unconsciously enacted by him, which flatly forbids him to have any such feelings at all or to make the slightest display of them to others.

There is not a complete lack of something akin to courage in his outer life. On the contrary, he knows how to face physical dangers, and sometimes he is even able to stake his life for the sake of his glory or power or popularity. The inner motivation, however, is primarily a reckless determination to dominate at all costs—quite a different urge from that genuine courage displayed by one who jeopardizes comfort and perhaps even limb and life in the service, not of an unlimited craving for mastery, but of the highest interests of the We. That is something of which the Nero knows nothing because his inner egocentric attitudes have so completely restricted or contaminated the expressions of the real courage latent in the Self which is at the heart of his individuality.

His We-feeling is almost entirely inhibited by unconsciously developed attitudes. He values nothing higher and holds nothing more sacred than his own success, and he knows as little of genuine living honor as he does of real love. So far as affection is concerned he has not learned to love simply because he does not permit himself to yield his heart to anyone in trust, affection and devoted service. Instead of these We-feeling reactions, he has developed an inordinate desire for glory—a need for recognition and acclaim which exceeds all reasonable limits.

Thus the Nero and the Star show the same excessive esteem

for themselves, the same unlimited confidence in themselves and a like pretentiousness. Both of these forms of egocentricity are active, yet their goals are diametrically opposed to each other. The soft Star wishes only that people shall speak well of him. His goal is popularity and if necessary he is ready to resort to stupid tricks or to commit a crime in order to make a name for himself. The hard Nero, however, strives for real power. If necessary, he foregoes glory for the pleasure of ruling the destiny of as many people as possible, even though he is not known or seen. The anonymous power behind the throne in high financial circles, whom no one knows, may be the best illustration of this concealed Neroism. He delights in making thousands of people happy or unhappy by one stroke of the pen or by a single act, but he does not feel accountable because nobody knows that he is the doer of these deeds.

A mixture of Star and Nero personality traits occurs rather frequently, the longing for power and for mere popularity often blending with each other. In such a case the person looks for power in order to gain popularity. He may, for instance, need power to reward those who serve him, and he needs popularity and so-called friends to obtain power. Thus a man may seek enough popularity to be elected to high political office for the sake of obtaining power to dispense the favors which help to maintain his popularity.

A temporary alternation in the roles of Nero and Clinging Vine is also often observed. Here, for example, is an egocentric Nero who rules his office like a thundering Zeus. His underlings tremble and the windowpanes rattle when he fights to defend his omnipotence. At five o'clock, however, he comes home like a broken-down person, scarcely having the strength to eat as he ought. His wife, his daughter and some aunts must wait on him with great solicitude and protestations. "Do eat a little bit! Some soup at least! You poor boy, how this terrible business has worn you out. You are the heart and brains of the whole organization. You don't get anything except ingratitude." His blood pressure mounts to 200. The physicians are alarmed. The patient enjoys wearing at the same time (without realizing it) his office crown as a Nero, and his home halo as a Clinging Vine, with people moving about him on tiptoe in his home even as they do in his office.

Throughout, the Nero faces the necessity of maintaining himself through fear. This necessity urges him on to new fearsome deeds. To remain a tyrant he needs to find new and perhaps increasingly awesome means. If he does not create new fear around him, he will be overthrown very soon. His slaves know that he is not concerned with the welfare of the We and that he will abandon them when they are no longer useful to him in pursuit of his egocentric goals. They serve him out of their own egocentric fear.

Therefore the Nero is surrounded by an atmosphere of harsh, unbending egocentricity. The better he understands the nature of this atmosphere, the more his fears increase, leading him into a short and terrifying vicious circle which he might express thus: "In order to dominate I have to find new means to make others continue to fear me as much as, if not more than, ever. The old means tend to lose their effect and to fail me more and more because of their long familiarity. I must increase the pressure I use to create the same degree of fear. All this really means that I have to keep alive and even intensify my servants' hatred against me. I have to foster their rebellion and my ruin. I cannot help doing so, even if I understand what I am doing."

When the crash comes, when the servants become enemies and the tyrant is overthrown, then we find the active form of egocentricity changing into a passive one. The mighty Nero becomes more like a small, helpless and threatened child. He who was feared as a Black Giant by so many people now becomes a dwarf who in time of need appoints one of his former slaves to be his White Giant. Now he clings to the White Giant and desperately begs him to give the former Nero all that the Nero needed yet did not know that he needed: help, love, patience and understanding. The unknown or despised We shows once again its inescapable and irresistible power. Even the Nero realizes, when his outer shell of egocentricity breaks down, that he, like other men, is a part of the We, and that he cannot live if he forgets it, but the way in which he now seeks to experience the We-relationship may be childish or inadequate because of the remnants of his egocentricity.

The Turtle

The Nero Ego evolves in a harsh environment when the child's vitality is superior to that of the adults. If, however, the child is weaker, the harshness of its educators (parents and others) leads to much worse results. The situation now is one in which the child feels, like the Nero, that others are against him, that the world is unfriendly, that his needs and wishes are neglected, but unlike the Nero the child has not discovered any means of compelling others to serve him. To him it seems that those around him are unmindful of his needs and wishes and that he can do nothing about it.

One result of this feeling is a retreat from life, so to speak. The child experiences only disappointments and frustrations. His repeated efforts to satisfy his needs and wishes are fruitless and lead only to the pangs of defeat. Quite naturally the child comes to abandon effort, to forego its wishes and even to minimize its needs. All is unprofitable and, perhaps, painful, so why exert oneself? Why even permit oneself to have desires or needs? Why not avoid all the pains of disappointment and defeat by ceasing altogether to strive? What else, indeed, is left for the helpless victim of a harsh, unfriendly world?

Thus, unconsciously, the child comes to develop a type of Ego which is almost a negation of life itself. Its capacities are undeveloped, restricted by all sorts of inhibitions. The Nero developed in unwholesome ways, but this child may be said to be undeveloped—to be little more than a mass of mere inhibitions. And it is self-evident that the few functions which do develop in spite of all these restrictions must be egocentric.

There is no entirely satisfactory English word by which to designate this type of Ego. The nearest approach seems to be the word "Turtle" with its implications of being a simpleton—a dull, slow, listless person with seemingly no mind of his own, but even here we do not catch up all the peculiarities of this type of Ego as indicated in the subsequent discussion. However, we shall use the word to designate this type of extremely rigid Ego.

The Breach-of-the-We, involved in this Ego, usually comes about in the form of a series of severe disappointments. The results of the first of these may be described in the formula, "Do not touch that. You are not permitted to do so." Later on the formula usually changes. Now it is: "Do not touch that. You are too clumsy to do so." However, nobody stops to think that the clumsiness of the child is the result of the lack of practice enforced by the injunction, "Do not touch." Now it seems to be inborn.

In the beginning, the adults were the Black Giants who forbade the child to follow his natural inclination to conquer the world by developing his own capacities. Later on the Black Giant is replaced by the mere danger of failure. It is not the Giant who says: "You cannot do that," but the child who says to himself, "I am unable, I cannot do that." The Black Giant is superseded by something more generalized which we may describe as "the black situation." Failure seems as if it were unavoidable, and all attempts to attain the goal and to evade impending misfortune seem to be useless. Thus, only one kind of tactic remains—to withdraw.

The child's retreat from life at first consists in the simple fact that he gives up striving for the fulfillment of his wishes. Very soon, however, the wishes themselves are felt to be painful since both the wish and its renunciation are experienced by the child at the same time on account of his frustration. Thus, he learns renunciation even before he becomes aware of the wish.

Imagine that the child sees his comrades at play in the garden. Formerly he would like to have played with them, but he would not have believed that he could share in their games. Indeed, the attempt to do so would have been so clumsy that defeat was certain, so, without understanding why, the child prefers the attitude of the famous fox who found the grapes too sour only because they hung too high above him. The child asserts peevishly that he does not like to play with other children because they or their games are "too silly." Or he accuses them of injustice, or finds other excuses. Neither the adults nor the child himself is aware of the fact that behind this stubborn or refractory mask an ardent and hopeless, though quite unconscious, longing for community and comradeship is concealed.

The longer this withdrawal continues, the more it becomes a complete renouncement of life. Since all normal exercise of his forces in the struggle with reality is lacking, the child's inferiority feeling—his conviction of not being equal to his tasks—must increase, and the ability to solve the problems of everyday life must decrease from year to year. Thus the vicious circle compels the child to develop more and more its Turtle strategy, and in accord with this principle a hard and passive egocentricity slowly develops into behavior which now seems quite similar to, and may be mistaken for, genuine and somatically conditioned feeble-mindedness. Yet for us it is self-evident that the Turtle is often supplied with a natural endowment of sensitiveness which makes for attainments of an unusual type. Unfortunately, the more sensitive a person's endowment—the more he is of the high-strung racehorse pattern—the more he is in danger of becoming a Turtle.

Fortunately, one hundred percent Turtles are not very numerous. As educational insight and skill increase, the egocentric commands and mechanical fault-finding are replaced by treatment growing out of We-feeling comradeship. The further this replacement is carried in the home and school the fewer Turtles we shall have.

It should also be noted that bad social conditions account for some Turtles. Sometimes when children are very young their parents die or are separated from them a long time by sickness or imprisonment, and in such cases the children may be cared for in institutions that cannot or do not nurture them sufficiently. Here we observe a natural development of the same kind of Turtle egocentricity which we find in families of the highest social level and the best education. It seems to be an important indication of the order of human life that the son of a millionaire who has too many teachers and tutors is as much endangered by being oppressed from outer life as the poor boy of the unemployed woman who must leave him alone in order to get her relief. Both of them may develop the same inactivity; both may become Turtles.

There are partial Turtles in all the different fields of human life. Imagine, for example, a child who develops on the whole as a Star, yet in one single field, let us say in mathematics or music, this successful and sunny egocentric boy suffers a defeat from the very beginning. Quickly and without a struggle he gives up further attempts to wipe away this ugly stain on the white shield of his glory as a Star. He prefers to maintain his stardom in an easier way more in accord with his discouragement. He asserts that failure in this particular field is only the "reverse of the medal," that it goes along with his genius and that the world simply must accept and admire the Star, notwithstanding this dullness which only serves to throw his brilliance into sharper contrast. This partial renunciation becomes part of his unconscious diplomacy—part of his second nature—and the longer it lasts, the more this negative attitude is necessary simply because it is increasingly difficult to make up for the lost practice.

Thus many sensitive and well-educated people display striking and sharply defined deficiencies which are often regarded as a lack of natural endowments. In reality, they are deficiencies of training. Sometimes we find the same kind of deficiencies in the personality of Neros and of Clinging Vines and in all the mixtures of these types, all of them showing partial Turtleness. In fact, one may say that there is scarcely a reader of these pages who is entirely free of Turtle inhibitions.

There are Turtles in music, in mathematics, in social arts, in athletics, in love, in religion and many other areas of life. They all affirm it to be sound and natural to have in this or that field neither understanding nor feeling. Unconsciously, however, they are envious of everybody who has developed skills in these fields, and they often take revenge for their own defeat by most energetic, willful and arbitrary criticism of all that others do along these lines. For one who is a Turtle at love, all tender and warm emotions are silly and sentimental, and the finest love song is childish babble. The Turtle in religion judges every possible experience with God as medieval superstition or hysterical deceit. The Turtle in patriotism assumes that all expressions of national feeling are mere egocentric interests or, at best, the intoxication of mass suggestion, and the Turtle in social consciousness cannot discover any social injustice in the world.

No one of them or anybody else tries—as far as he is egocentric and therefore rigid—to cure his own blind spots. On the contrary, each one tries to explain them from the egocentric viewpoint. Through such misinterpretations he prevents his own healing, and thus brings on a crisis and a more or less complete breakdown of his egocentric system.

In the Turtle we can observe better than in other types the complications which develop wherever a person feels compelled to step over his inner psychic, self-imposed limitations. Imagine a gifted man—a Star or Nero—who is a social Turtle. This inner law (his egocentricity) reads: "Accept not invitations because you certainly will make yourself ridiculous." From his egocentric viewpoint ridiculousness is worse than death; therefore, he must avoid, rudely or politely, yet very carefully, all situations in which he might be exposed to such disaster. On the other hand, as a Star or Nero he feels compelled to look for influence or attention. How can he achieve these goals if social appearances are almost, if not entirely, impossible because of his feeling of fear and insecurity? Here is a conflict of two egocentric urges. Egocentricity is endangered by egocentricity. Crisis is near.

The way out is the natural result of the dangerous situation. Each invitation may disturb this man very much. He feels his heart pounding and he cannot sleep. In his thoughts he anticipates impending defeat and feels almost crushed by this unbearable situation. He has headaches, high blood-pressure, cramps, so his doctor comfortingly says, "Stay at home." Now he has to refuse the invitation because of bad health. He or his unconscious is more resourceful than he imagines.

For a moment he has faced the deep insecurity and anxiety which everyone must encounter when his egocentric shell is shattered. They are, as we know, an offspring of the primeval human fear. We should not wonder that in all these cases nature finds a way to avoid this fear or restrict its influence as much as possible. The state of excitement caused by feelings of insecurity and anxiety is converted into symptoms of disease which seriously threaten his physical or psychic well-being. Whether his feeling was consciously anger or fear, it was unconsciously fear, as we know, and now it turns into nervousness.

In group life the partial Turtles are not conspicuous or striking as long as it happens that the group problems make no demands upon their deficiencies. However, some day the group must demand acts or functions which were in the beginning forbidden to the Turtle by his egocentric law and which are now actually impossible because of lack of training. Then comes the most severe conflict and the catastrophe occurs.

The college, for instance, may require that the land-Turtle swim. He has never tried to swim since, when he was eight years old, his older brother had almost drowned him, and now he has to face this Black Giant, the water, or even the spectre of this cruel older brother, and he feels entirely unequal to the task. Military service may compel the sleep-Turtle to sleep with thirty comrades in one room, but his inner, egocentric law tells him not to fall asleep unless he is alone and safe behind well-locked doors, because fifteen years ago his cousins startled him by barking and roaring like animals when they slept in his bedroom. In such cases, the Turtle feels strongly impelled to conquer his own limitations. However, this is only possible when under strong pressure, and a complete change in the form of his psychic life must come about. He would have to alter the patterns of his personality, and that means he would have to face the dreadful old fear we mentioned before.

A crisis, which outwardly takes the form of a nervous break-down or a series of acute neurotic symptoms, is unavoidable. Inwardly it is, so to speak, a revolution of the whole psychic system, so therefore people try to avoid it at all costs. But he who endures this crisis experiences a sort of rebirth. He makes a new start. New productivity and new courage are his, and perhaps for the first time in his life he knows what We-feeling is.

It is self-evident that a leader or a teacher is only able to complete educational tasks of this kind if he is himself "We-feeling," productive and understanding. Otherwise, he cannot recognize and evaluate the symptoms of approaching crisis, and he cannot deal with people who have to undergo this difficult yet creative development.

The Shell

Having considered carefully the various Ego patterns, it must be obvious that the individual is greatly misled by them. The difficulty is that the person actually feels these mistaken ideas about himself to be facts—that he actually is what he mistakenly supposes himself to be, according to the pattern of the particular Ego form he has developed. The Star, for example, feels that he is a very important person deserving to be praised and served by others. The Turtle, on the other hand, feels that he is a worthless and helpless person who is entitled to nothing and from whom nothing can be expected.

The meaning of this situation for character development grows out of the fact that the individual consciously and unconsciously plays the role of the person he supposes himself to be. If he thinks he is important and entitled to deference, he adopts a grand manner and shows his resentment of treatment from others which does not properly recognize his position. If he considers himself a Nero, he assumes a dominating attitude and vigorously assails those who do not submit to him. In innumerable ways, in what he does and says and even the manner of his bearing, a person reflects the conscious and, sometimes, unconscious feelings he has about his value and worth. His Ego is the mental mold into which he constantly pours his energies in the effort to be and do the things which he feels he ought to be or do, because of what seems to him to be the very nature of his being.

To the feelings of value and worth thus embodied in the Ego, the individual comes to add other feelings about his capacities—what he can or cannot do. Many illustrations of this have already been pointed out. Let us take the case of a small boy we shall call Johnny. He had an older sister well trained as a musician, and the family liked to gather Sunday evenings around an organ and sing hymns.

Johnny, however, could not sing. He could not "carry a tune in a bucket." Childlike, his voice wandered off pitch to the very great annoyance of the musically sensitive ear of his sister. "Johnny," she burst out, "you can't sing. You are a nuisance. You spoil our music for us. Go off and leave us alone." So Johnny ruefully went away—cast out of the We by his big sister—and sat disconsolate and, worse yet, defeated. He had ventured out on a little journey of exploration into this world only to meet with a painful experience and discover a limitation. Now he accepts his sister's dictum: "You can't sing," and on account of her unpleasant rebuff he is even afraid to try. Thus Johnny actually built into his Ego the idea that he could not sing. That idea became an inner law enacted, so to speak, by himself on the motion of another, which he faithfully observed, having no notion whatever that he had only been misguided into passing such a law. It was not until many years later that Johnny actually developed enough insight into the processes by which his own personality was constructed to understand his mistake. Then he repealed the law. He no longer said to himself, "I can't." He no longer inhibited the expression of the inherent capacities of the inner Self, and with some training he learned to sing well enough to join in ordinary group singing.

By such a process various other mistaken ideas regarding what one can or cannot do are likewise unconsciously enacted into self-made laws. They become inner rules of behavior to which the legislator more or less rigidly adheres. In effect they place artificial limitations upon the natural productivity of the Self—limitations which the individual accepts as valid, genuine, real. As long as he does so they have exactly the same result in his life as if they were realities instead of mere creations of the imagination.

Feelings about one's value and worth and ideas about what one can and cannot do are embodied in the Ego. So distorted and inaccurate are they that the Ego is always a false image of the Self—so false that it bears little or no resemblance to the Self, yet to the individual it seems to be what he really is, and he acts accordingly.

In seeking to understand the effect of this Seeming-Self upon the life of the individual, it is helpful to think of the Ego as something in the nature of a psychological shell encasing the Self which may be thought of as the heart at the center of personality. No figure or comparison can ever be relied upon to depict fully the reality we are discussing; in fact, the greater one's grasp upon the truths of the We-psychology, the more one realizes the futility of words and images to describe them. At the moment the figure of the shell encasing the "heart" serves us well in understanding the psychological situation.

We see that this shell, with all its mistaken feelings and inaccurate ideas, does indeed wall up the Self. The more firmly these errors are fixed—the more inflexible one's ideas and feelings—the thicker and more rigid this wall is. That means that the Ego limitations placed upon one's productivity are greater and more inflexible, and the Self is more and more restricted in its expressions. Life is less rich and meaningful and creative than it might be otherwise, yet the individual often has no idea of how great his limitations are, how much of real life he is missing, how vast are the unrealized potentialities of his being.

Considering this figurative shell further, it is obvious that every human being is unconsciously cooped up in one. Without realizing it, he is shut up within a system of mistaken ideas and feelings which thwart the fullest expression of the powers of the Self. They add to the necessary limitations of the natural laws of his being which he must take into account. His eyes, for example, are sensitive only to certain frequencies of vibrations in the so-called ether. Moreover, he cannot see distinctly at night as a cat or an owl does. His ears are attuned only to certain degrees of sound. They do not register what the robin or the hound seems to sense—and the sensitiveness of one pair of human ears, it seems, may be different from another. In many other ways the natural conditions of his body and of the universe restrict what he can do. These are real limitations which one must accept, but they do not involve the handicaps that they are often supposed to impose. Consider, for example, a deaf mute who learns to talk in spite of a natural defect that seemed insurmountable, or a surgeon who trains his fingers to a sensitiveness far beyond anything they might have been supposed to have.

The individual is also limited by the defects of the culture of his time. Its biases, prejudices, unscientific assumptions, historic errors, mistaken beliefs all bind him with fetters that seem to be unbreakable and often are never discarded. The man reared in a world that believed the earth was flat and that the sun moved around it was bound by chains of cultural errors that few even thought of trying to cast off. The woman living in the day when a black man was deemed fit only to be her slave and chattel was limited by prejudices whose reality few even questioned, much less escaped. These latter limitations may be said to be the part of the limitations of a faulty education—an education that was unwittingly begun at birth by one's parents and carried on continuously thereafter by all the forces of the family, the school, the Church and society as a whole. Such is our human fate that however good may be the intentions of our educators, in the broad sense, we suffer from the mistakes they unconsciously reflect in their dealings with us. Being human, all such persons express in their behavior the mistakes of their own Ego and unconsciously influence us accordingly.

Under that influence we accept their own errors for ourselves, or develop other mistaken ideas to counterbalance them. We enact these errors and mistakes into laws which we unconsciously accept and submit to as the natural laws of our being. Thus we come back to the basic psychological truth that the Ego is a shell limiting more or less severely the expression of the capacities of the Self. We are vastly more than we realize. There are potentialities in us beyond all our surmises. The creative, productive capacities of the Self far transcend the Ego-centered limitations we unwittingly set up for ourselves.

Now it follows from all this thinking that one basic task of a person is the removal of this shell. As long as any traces of it remain in any individual's life he has found, to some degree, less freedom and been less creative and productive than he might be. One lifelong problem of humanity is the discovery of the errors built into the Ego, for only by discovering them does one come to crack his shell and remove its limitations even piecemeal. This discovery grows only out of the realization that one's system of living does not work. At some point the individual comes to see that something is not, to some extent, as it should be. The fact may dawn upon him rather quietly as some sun of truth rises in his mind and the errors before hidden in the dark of ignorance stand out clearly revealed. In such a case, the man may feel that the sunrise has been gloriously beautiful indeed.

The quiet insight into human nature gained from reading and observation may be the source of this sunrise. It is possible for one to learn his mistaken ways from the reasonably calm contemplation of his life in the light of kindly observations by a friend or helpful suggestions in a book. One can discover the limitations of the shell by methods involving no discomfort, no distress, no suffering, but something much more may be necessary. We must distinguish between an intellectual insight into some error or the broad fact that the Ego is only our second, not our real, nature and the actual breakdown of the shell. Even the discovery of this difference between the Ego and the Self presupposes, in almost every case, a certain though rather small degree of suffering, and in only a very few instances is insight alone sufficient to remove the shell. Most of us must suffer rather seriously in order to feel what we understand very well so far as our thinking goes.

Frequently it takes an encounter with difficulty, hardship, frustration, bitter discontent, and even anguish to crack the shell at any point. One strives for some goal only to find that, when it is reached, there is no lasting satisfaction in attaining it. The fruits of victory turn to ashes in one's mouth. Life sours. One is lifted up by some much-sought conquest to heights of elation only to be dashed down into envy, regret, disappointment, unhappiness. Things go wrong. One suffers.

As long as things go well, there may be little inclination to change one's ways. Why trouble even to look for mistakes? Why make the effort to correct them? What difference could it make anyhow? Is not life flowing along smoothly and pleasantly? But when life brings pressure to bear, things are different. When we are distressed, when we suffer perhaps acutely, we are more likely to look for the error in our ways and seek relief from it. It may be said that then the shell is cracked and it becomes possible to remove some part of it. Moreover, then we may be eager to do so.

In the end, however, it seems that nothing short of the severest kind of pressure is enough to shatter the shell completely. Something more than minor distress is necessary to bring about a realization of the full extent of our errors. The Ego embodies a great collection of mistaken ideas on which one builds a complete system of living. Life's attack must be along a wide front and with tragic fury to demolish the entire system—to shatter the entire shell—to make the unsoundness of all one's mistakes apparent at one time. Here is something which may seem to be so tragic in its far-flung destruction of all that one has built his life upon that it seems to be like death itself. The destruction of the Ego—the Seeming-Self—does indeed seem to be the end of one's being.

This drastic experience we call a major crisis, and its nature and course shall be considered fully in the next section. Meantime, it is enough to say that all egocentricity leads toward it. Moreover, it should be welcomed if the shell has not otherwise been broken down, for through its suffering, as will be seen, we may move into that joy and peace which comes from releasing the

Self within from the limitations of its shell into the creative, productive, courageous, loving expressions of which it is capable. That is indeed the abundant life.

If we change the figure, we may find another helpful comparison. Considering the human personality, we see the individual living on two different planes. He engages in two basically different kinds of behavior. One includes the things he does in playing the role of his Ego—in acting out the part of the person he supposes himself to be. The things he does in doing so we speak of as being "egocentric." They are centered in his Ego. He is acting upon—and because of—the various feelings and ideas gathered up in his Ego. Since the Ego is his Seeming-Self, he believes he is acting as he ought to act.

It must be obvious, however, that he is being misled. He is pursuing false goals, cherishing false values, clinging to false ideas. Consider how this works out in the life of the Nero, for example. In playing his role, he is unconsciously acting on the idea that all others are against him, that the only value in life is dominance over others, that the proper and chief goal of his existence is the exercise of masterful power. To these he may add equally erroneous notions about his own super-ability in business, industry, or some other area of life.

Any man who acts on such mistaken ideas and feelings must be seriously misled. He is following a will-o'-the-wisp which can and does lead him into the swamps of disappointment, frustration, defeat, bitterness, envy and other negative attitudes and, maybe, the quicksand of despair, for in the nature of things there is and can be no permanent, lasting satisfaction in living guided by false goals, false values, false ideas. At the same time he may become the victim of a curious form of self-deception. His Nero attitudes and acts tend to and may actually forfeit his wife's affection, estrange his children, and cause his friends to renounce their friendship. Such is the normal outcome of a domineering attitude toward others. When they appear the Nero has created just the reactions he expected in others. They are indeed against him, and thus in spite of all the errors in his thinking it seems to be sound. Being wrong he seems to be right!

The second kind of behavior is on quite a different plane.

Here he is expressing now and then something of the true nature of the Self—the heart within the shell. Figuratively speaking we may say that somehow, here and there, the Self finds a crack in the walls of the shell which leaves it free to move out in some direction, or maybe it breaks through some thin spot, and so he acts kindly, courageously, wisely, lovingly. He is genuinely creative and productive, perhaps only for a brief act or quick remark. In some quick surge of kindliness, even the ninety-nine percent Nero may show mercy to his victim, say the generous thing, do the submissive deed. Almost as quickly he may lapse into his old behavior, wonder how it was possible for him ever to have done anything which seems so foreign to what he feels to be his nature, and hasten to repair the break in his shell.

Such behavior—the Self finding outlets from its shell—we speak of as "objective." It expresses the Self; it issues from the heart within the shell and is characterized by genuine We-feeling. It is always in some degree behavior in the service of the We, and in it are always found genuine love, courage, wisdom. Viewed in the light of this comparison, we say that the psychological goal of humanity, the lifelong task one faces, is to become less and less egocentric and more and more objective in living.

Behavior on these two planes is associated with and motivated by quite different emotional reactions. It is helpful to think of them as a horizontal plane with a perpendicular plane intersecting it midway at right angles. The horizontal plane is objective behavior—the kind that springs from the Self, the "heart" of personality. The perpendicular plane is Ego-centered behavior, the kind that is rooted or centered in the mistaken ideas of the Ego. On the basis of this symbol we may construct an imaginary thermometer for the measurement of egocentric feelings. For this we shall use the perpendicular plane and scale it in units, say of five degrees, from zero at the point of intersection with the horizontal plane up to +100 (plus 100) degrees at the top and a −100 (minus 100) at the bottom.

As an illustration of the use of this thermometer, let us take a situation found in the egocentric living of a Nero. Perhaps he is some Napoleon of finance ruthlessly fighting his way through to his goal of financial mastery. Now the members of some group marshal their forces to block his progress and do so for a while. Being thwarted, he feels injured, discredited, dejected and otherwise "low." To him defeat is an unbearable situation. He is emotionally, say, -100. In an outburst of furious effort, enraged beyond words, he forces his opponents to capitulate, and now he is $+100$, feeling his triumph, proud, elated, haughty, vainglorious.

The -100 and $+100$ of a Clinging Vine involve quite different reactions. Suppose we considered one who is called on to do the work of an office mate absent on a vacation, work involving some degree of initiative, independent action and decision. To a Clinging Vine this is far from a welcome obligation. The Star would relish it, but the Clinging Vine shrinks from self-reliant efforts. He has unhappily learned to feel that he is relatively helpless, that he cannot rely upon himself, that he must count upon someone else to do for him what others do for themselves.

So now, facing responsibility, he feels -100. He is fearful, dismayed, discouraged, despondent, even becoming resentful and rebellious toward his employer or his associate. Why should his boss expect him to do "double work"? Why didn't his fellow worker take care of this problem before he left? What right has the boss or an associate to impose upon him in this way? By such devious reasoning he may become very sorry for himself or vindictive toward his co-worker. In any event, he is overwhelmed with negative feelings. At length the vacation is ended, and the hated new responsibilities are no longer his. Instead of having them, he even manages to get his office mate to do some things for him. He complains about the hardships of the vacation work and contrives to make the vacationist feel under such an obligation that he does something for the hard-working stay-at-home. Perhaps the office mate expresses admiration, offers sympathy or helps Clinging Vine do his work. Now Clinging Vine is emotionally $+100$, feeling secure, properly deferred to, and perhaps even a bit proud of the attention shown him by his secretly unwilling Tree.

These illustrations are sufficient to emphasize a few important matters in this connection. First is the fact that for every person there is some situation in which he feels -100. There are many variations in these situations, although in the main they are dependent upon the Ego-pattern and the past of the individual.

Since there are many possible combinations of the various types and many different degrees of any one type, and innumerable unhappy, distressing experiences in early childhood, the -100 situations are numerous beyond description. But for every person there is at least one kind of an experience that makes him feel -100.

In the second place, we note that this -100 feeling seems to be unbearable. The individual looks upon the situation as something of a yawning abyss into which he has fallen, a terrifying place in which his very existence seems threatened. It may even seem worse than death, for death would be preferable to life in it. When he is out of it, the fear of falling into it is appalling, and the very thought of doing so impels him to seek by every means, fair or foul, to avoid that disaster.

The reason for this fear is to be found in the supposed effect of the situation upon the Ego. Since the Ego seems to be the Self, a threat to the Ego apparently imperils the Self and is feared and resisted as a matter of Self-defense. The fear is without real foundation, arising because one attaches unnecessary value to some ideas built into his Ego. The Star's conception of his great importance is, for example, one reason for his -100 reactions. To him censure, criticism and even indifference are an abysmal affair, but they are so solely because of the mistaken ideas of importance incorporated in his Ego. Correct them and the abyss closes. The -100 no longer exists. What is true of this particular Star situation holds good for all other sources of -100 reactions, which are always related to some misconception in the Ego.

A third point is the fact that egocentric behavior involves one in a constant recurring cycle of emotional ups and downs. One is continually oscillating between $+100$ and -100. Perhaps one day the emtional temperature is -20, the second day $+50$, and the third -75. It may descend in some crisis to -200, which indicates grave danger of suicide, and it may rise to $+300$ with perhaps a delusion of grandeur. One feels he is, for at least the moment, Napoleon or even Jehovah.

Fourth, the individual frequently seeks to become $+100$ at the expense of making someone else -100. The Nero exalts his own Ego at the expense of others. He gains his $+100$ through triumph over another by exploitation, by crushing him, by forcing him into some subordinate and, perhaps, humiliating position in which he must approach − 100 or even sink lower.

There is no element of concern for the well-being, comfort or happiness of any other in Ego-centered living. The sole test of all egocentric behavior is the exaltation of the Ego. Regardless of what happens in the lives of friends or foes, the supreme concern is the protection of one's own Ego. Here we have a source of great difficulty in human relations. Men and women are so much preoccupied in the service of their own Ego—with defending and exalting it at all costs—that they are in constant conflict with each other. Stars are pitted against Stars, Neros against Neros. Clinging Vines compete with each other for the same Tree. Turtles withdraw from any trustful, warmhearted relations with others. All are so much concerned with egocentric goals that they usually find cooperation, mutual good will, and comradeship largely crowded out of their lives and always difficult to maintain even in the family where manifestations of We-feeling ought to be most in evidence.

From this consideration of the egocentric plane, we turn to the objective plane, the level on which one is freed from the feelings of +100 and − 100. One's reactions are not based upon the mistakes in the Ego nor are they primarily concerned with it. Instead of some egocentric emotion, such as exultation, pride, rage, envy, fear, inferiority feelings, and the like, one experiences quite different emotions.

What they are is readily understandable when we consider that on the objective level behavior is an expression of the powers of the Self. The dominant note is We-feeling. Objective behavior is always in the service of the We, not the Ego. It is characterized by a genuine concern for the well-being of the We, and the individual recognizes that the highest interests of the Self are identical with the highest interests of the We of which it is a part.

Out of such We-feeling behavior grow the deepest and most lasting satisfactions in life. Associated with it are the noblest emotions in human experience. As the Self finds outlets through the shell—as, figuratively speaking, cracks or gaps are found or formed in these restraining walls—life moves out into ever fuller and richer self-realization. The individual experiences more and more satisfactions of courage, love, kindness, patience, peace, poise. Life is creative, productive, richly satisfying, positive, never negative.

The objective person knows the sadness of failure to attain some We-goal, but he never despairs, never loses hope, and never lacks courage or fails to find some new and hopeful approach to his problem.

Fortunate, indeed, is the fact that life tends to release the individual from his shell. Sometimes one quite spontaneously acts objectively. Something takes place that we can think of as the "heart" bursting through the shell at some point by virtue of its own powers pressing outward from within its mistaken limitations. In such cases there are two important factors. There is, so to speak, the pressure of the Self from within. On the outside there is a strong appeal to the Self as a part of the old, forgotten We. Consider, for example, murderers who kill several persons—let us say a farmer, his wife and two servants—and then spare the life of a six-year-old boy because they are touched by his pleading. They may do so understanding that this outburst of We-feeling may enable the police to apprehend them. Outside of their shell was the appeal to the Self made by the boy who may remind them of their own childhood and perhaps some few minutes of We-feeling love during an old Christmas season. From inside comes the response of We-feeling they are longing for without knowing it.

No shell seems to be thick and rigid enough to prevent this. In the life of even the person most ruthlessly seeking Neroistic goals, there are moments of We-feeling in some degree. Life simply will not be altogether denied an opportunity to find outlets for the capacities embodied in the Self. Good will, kindliness, sympathy, cooperativeness, and other expressions of We-feeling display themselves unexpectedly and sometimes seemingly against the will of the individual. Often their appearance proves to be such a surprising and keen source of satisfaction that the person is prompted to do again the things that caused so such enjoyment. Thus one may learn, by experience, to be more and more objective in living just because of this tendency of the Self to burst through the shell now and then.

Life also tends to release the individual from his shell by bringing pressure to bear upon it. In one way or another the tasks of everyday living force one to face mistakes. The walls of the shell are attacked by truth. The pressure of reality may cause its collapse at points or as a whole.

Fortunate indeed is the fact that there are cracks or crevices in the shell. At some point one's concept of himself must be reasonably accurate. The Ego considered as a whole is a mistaken image of the Self, but in some respects there is sound thinking which may be represented in our figure of speech as cracks in what would be otherwise a solid wall of error. Through these breaks in the shell, the Self finds outlets in the objective behavior which affords the deepest satisfactions in human life.

The Crisis

Egocentricity in any form—Star, Clinging Vine, Nero, Turtle, or any mixture of these patterns—always leads to difficult experiences which we call the crisis. These experiences may be extremely tragic—so much so that they are nothing short of a temporary catastrophe to the individual—while, on the other hand, they may be mere minor disappointments, frustrations and vexations which have nothing in them of the serious meaning commonly implied by the word crisis.

In any form the crisis simply leads to the realization growing out of uncomfortable experiences that there is need for a readjustment of one's thinking and behavior. The individual comes to feel that he must do something different. Old ways of behaving are no longer satisfactory, so new ones must be adopted. A turning point has been reached. There may be a total collapse of the whole Ego-pattern or merely a minor modification of some one of its elements. In the former case, the crisis is catastrophic indeed. In the latter, it is really a matter of little concern to the individual. It is a turning point, but the need for a change in direction may be small as compared with the complete turnabout involved in more serious readjustments.

These minor crises need no particular discussion here. They are a part of the common experience of everyone, resulting in the correction of some error in the Ego, or perhaps the substitution of another error. In the latter case we have simply a change at the periphery of one's life and not the center. It is the evasive way of improving one's habits without actually correcting the mistake in the Ego. After some painful experiences in telling lies one may renounce that form of deceit and resort simply to saying nothing. But the egocentricity is the same as before. Whatever the result of these minor crises they are at least an opportunity for a change from egocentric to objective behavior, but they involve no complete breakdown of the Ego.

No one ever becomes entirely objective. It is theoretically conceivable that one may grow bit by bit into relatively complete objectivity without experiencing more than the minor crises of everyday life. In practice, however, the higher degrees of objective living usually evolve, if at all, only out of a collapse of the Ego forced by the experiences of the major crisis to which we now turn.

There are many differences in the timing of the crisis and in its inner form. Sometimes it begins rather early, let us say about puberty, and lasts for ten or twenty years, rising and falling in intensity like waves. In other cases, it is delayed until old age appears. Then often fear of death or fear of senility causes a climax. In a few instances it seems to be avoided even until the moment of death. Whether the experiences in dying replace the major crisis or are the major crisis itself is a question we cannot decide from an empirical viewpoint. We only know that people die easier, assuming that they are conscious at or shortly before death, if they are less egocentric.

To the completely Ego-centered person death is identical with the total loss of his Ego, which seems to him to be what he really is. His egocentricity, therefore, increases his fear of death and his struggle against it until it may be an utterly terrifying prospect to be endured only in agony of soul, if not of body. Here we can clearly see that the Ego, as distinguished from the Self, is indeed only a conception—a creation of the mind without ultimate reality—a mistaken system of ideas regarding the Self. The more the Self is freed from the limitations of these Ego ideas, the

more one becomes conscious of it, the more it finds expression in
one's life, the more one is prepared to undergo the crucial
experience of dying.

The differences in the course of the crisis and its severity
depend more upon the degree of rigidity of the Ego than on the
nature of the four types described above. We can only say, in
general, that the active Ego forms, Star and Nero, are usually first
changed through a lesser crisis into the passive Ego forms, Clinging Vine and Turtle. Then these passive forms are changed
through further crucial developments until the complete passivity
of the major crisis is reached. The inner course of all these
changes is, however, always the same from the viewpoint of the
We-Psychology. The Ego is shaken like the throne of a monarch
in a revolution. In a minor crisis, his power is restrained, checked
by new privileges granted the parliament. In a major one, the
crown is replaced by other authority.

However, before the very essence of the crisis is described,
we should consider the conflict between different types of egocentricity, since this conflict is one of the most important reasons
why the crisis occurs. Since there are four Ego forms, there may
be six combinations of them involving the conflicts we have in
mind. We must restrict ourselves to an analysis of only one of
these, leaving it to the reader's observation and imagination to
depict for himself the other combinations. The conflict between a
couple, one of which has the Star Ego pattern and the other, the
Clinging Vine, will serve admirably.

Two Stars cannot live together. That is self-evident. Marriage, for instance, cannot last between them. They must separate
soon unless one of them changes into a Clinging Vine. The
alliance between Star and Clinging Vine usually has a very good
start. The Star finds in his Clinging-Vine mate just what he craves,
namely, unqualified admiration. On the other hand, Clinging
Vine finds (but only for a time) what she, too, wants—a protector
who defends the helpless creature with shield and sword against
the harsh and dangerous outer world. In this situation, it does not
really matter whether the husband or the wife is the Star or the
Clinging Vine.

As long as things go well with the Star, as long as he feels
content, the Clinging Vine has a part in his glory and feels secure

against all harm. As soon as the Star begins to fight for his stardom, he becomes ready to sacrifice even the most loyal Clinging Vine if he could thereby obtain any advantage for himself. Sometimes we see a man making fun of his wife, or a wife of her husband, in the presence of others in order to win new laurels or to freshen those that are withering.

The Clinging Vine, of course, must feel betrayed by the Star's attitude. A new and unexpected breach of what was felt to be a We-relationship once more shakes the foundations of her life. No wonder that an outburst of pain, despair and fear is the result of this disappointment. Whether it comes to open reproaches by the Clinging Vine or it brings about acute disorders such as headaches, sleeplessness, and fits of anguish, the situation remains the same. The Star understands very well that his mate considers him a traitor. Her judgment does not fit at all into his role as a generous and radiant protector and therefore he becomes irritated and indignant. For him the sudden suffering of his former admirer is only a loss of his indispensable admiration and applause. Such a loss for him is a Breach-of-the-We relationship which he, too, felt to exist between them, but which is only a Sham-We built up by an artificial equilibrium and substituted for the Original-We destroyed many years ago. Nevertheless, the Star also feels betrayed and as injured as the Clinging Vine.

Now two wounded persons look grievously and painfully at each other. Both of them feel offended anew by the other's complaints, and both are vastly irritated by the other's irritation. Altogether there are three vicious circles in this situation. One turns within the Star, who is losing his stardom by fighting for it. The second turns in the Clinging Vine who destroys her protection by seeking it. The third one involves the couple as a unit. The Sham-We destroys itself by its attempts to save its remnants, and thus egocentricity conflicts with egocentricity and produces a crisis. Life sees to it that two or more egocentric persons become involved in a conflict which leads to crisis and the possible breakdown of the Ego. As Luther said, "God punishes one rascal by another one."

In order to indicate the great wealth of egocentric forms which are everywhere observed in life, we may mention here a rarer kind of threefold vicious circle. There are Stars who find their glory in helping other people, yet in doing so they want spectators. If their deeds are not noticed by many, at least the receiver of their benefits must be endlessly thankful—far beyond any normal gratitude. We speak of them as the Benefactor Stars, the Charity Stars, or the Nursing Excellencies.

Sometimes the friendship or marriage between the Star and the Clinging Vine lasts only as long as the latter is sick or weak or needy for other reasons. Now suppose that the Clinging Vine, in spite of his being a Clinging Vine, would be audacious enough to become sound and healthy as the result, say, of the Star's excellent nursing. Then the Star would feel uneasy or even injured, and unconsciously he would wound and torture the victim of his charity by reproaches and complaints until the Clinging Vine fulfills once more the task incumbent upon him, namely, accepting benefits and overflowing with praise and admiration. Thus this Star unconsciously destroys what he consciously built up.

There are other cases in which a husband plays the role of the Clinging Vine in his office, but at home he is as pretentious a Star as possible. His wife, as his counterpart, is the Clinging Vine at home, admiring her Star-husband and in turn winning admiration and laurels for herself outside of her home as the Star in charity organizations or in her job. Indeed there are a few cases in which the husband and his wife alternate with each other in the role of Star and Clinging Vine.

At length, however, all these couples are led into their crisis. The artificial equilibrium in the Sham-We destroys itself as we have noted before. If the vicious circles do not work out swiftly enough within, life brings its daily tasks and demands from without, and neither the Star nor the Clinging Vine is able to meet them, to safeguard themselves against the impositions consciously or unconsciously practiced upon them. One who needs money asks the Star for a loan of a large sum of money, saying many pleasant things about him and his magnanimous nature. The Star finds it difficult, if not impossible, to deny the request simply because he cannot withstand the flatterer. So, too, the Clinging Vine cannot withstand the Nero. He cannot say "no" because he cannot bear the bad mood of the other. Thus both the Star and Clinging Vine fall easy victims to the demands of others. They lose money, are cheated and otherwise taken advantage of in

numerous ways. In short they are forced to bear the bitter consequences of their own egocentricity. They may cunningly delay the
crisis but they cannot entirely escape it. Life is stronger than their
egocentric evasions.

The more egocentricity develops the nearer it leads to a
major crisis, but egocentric people try by all means to avoid this
crisis. They do not know that this painful way may take them to
the end of the former mistakes and the beginning of new productivity.

The means by which the crisis is resisted may be described as
evasion. Consider, for example, the person who roams about the
world looking for adventure. We often observe that he is not a
We-feeling and courageous individual but is really egocentric and
evasive. He evades staying long in one place because he is consciously or unconsciously afraid that others will at length come to
understand him, to see through him and to offer criticism. His
apparent longing for new experiences proves to be, in the last
analysis, something quite negative—the fear of being seen for
what he is. That which seemed to be the outward sign of courage
turns out to be the product of fear.

In order to distinguish whether we are dealing with a courageous and enterprising person or with an egocentric vagabond,
we would put him to the test of staying a long time on the same
job without changing his residence. The objective, We-feeling
person is able to do this even if he would prefer something else,
but the egocentric one is absolutely unable to do so. The We-
feeling person is able to do one as well as the other. The reason is
that objectivity and We-feeling are identical since the We is the
real frame of our life. Therefore the We-feeling person is able to
adapt himself even if the outer circumstances of his life are
unsatisfactory and to find satisfaction both in improving them and
changing his own ways. The egocentric person, however, is rigid.
If the needed adjustment touches his Ego he is unable to change
himself or improve his circumstances. He shrinks from profound
inner changes and even those less drastic, and he avoids the outer
changes which he might otherwise enjoy because he fears they
may bring about an inner transformation.

In the later years the extreme fear of the possible maturing involved in such changes always expresses itself in terms of longing for rest and peace. This is a fear of change in which uncertainty of the future plays a large part. We cling to our outer situation and even more to our inner situation. This is the rigidity previously mentioned. "Leave me at rest" is the typical motto of these older egocentrics. They are not less egocentric when the "rest" means a pleasant family life or an admirable comradeship. They say: "With the old everything should remain stable. We cannot adjust ourselves to new circumstances. We are too old." This wish is another expression of the old egocentric device, "My will be done." They demand that the goal of any higher unit—of mankind, or even of God—should be worked out only insofar as it conforms to the egocentric goal of the individual.

Since they demand an unchangeable so-called peace, we know that they are egocentric, living only in a Sham-We relationship, whatever it may be. The real, living We seeks development, transformation, differentiation, and expresses itself in the life of an individual in a desire for that which is just the opposite of this "peace." What egocentric people mean by peace is the satisfaction of their own egoistic wishes and goals—the undisturbed gratification of their Ego-centered desires.

Life, however, changes all these attempts to preserve the Ego into the very opposite. The desire for rest increases in proportion as one becomes more fearful, and the more it becomes difficult to defend the Ego, the more somatic symptoms of fear and restlessness develop.

At last there is only one way of avoiding the crisis. One has to cling to the given situation even if it is very disagreeable. One has to avoid any change—to cling to the present situation and never leave it. Thus develops the "sticking attitude" which every person has learned to know from his own experiences. For example, one may stick to the book he is reading even though he is so tired and sleepy that he does not grasp the meaning of the words he reads. To change the situation, to approach a different object (the bed), to do something different, requires a higher degree of productivity, so to speak. It is easier to stick to the old situation and the old object, the book.

Many people know very well that they should change their whole life. They long for a person who would come to rescue them from entanglements in the difficulties of their egocentricity, even though they do not understand the reason for their troubled state. Perhaps they dream of wars or earthquakes in order to escape their psychic fetters. They might even have a dim idea that a major crisis is indispensable, yet they do not do anything to bring about a change. On the contrary, they stick to the old situation like flies on flypaper. Rumors about impending economic or military disasters sometimes originate, in part, in these negative attitudes. There are people who assert, maybe every three months or so, that a world catastrophe is now to be expected "by objective necessity." There are quarterly pessimists just as there are quarterly drinkers because of their own peculiar egocentric development. The vicious circle drives them into despair and desperation now and then.

This sticking, or clinging, to a situation is a tragic, crucial affair because the human being seeks thereby to maintain his Seeming-Self—his Ego. The tragedy is that he seeks to preserve a false conception of himself which should really be destroyed, but his belief that it is the Self always makes it painful even to contemplate surrender. Thus as the crisis becomes more acute there is a certain vacillation which we call "fluttering." The individual is driven again and again to the verge of abandoning his Ego. He feels that all is lost. Then, terrified by that feeling and the uncertainty of the future, he turns back before the final renunciation to his Ego—he clings anew to its mistaken system.

Thus the individual does not find any rest and may move through increasing degrees of agitation. He gives up every interest. He has no hold of anything. He cannot settle down to reading or writing. Desultorily, without any purpose, he bustles about, driven partly by physical restlessness, partly by the primeval fear we have described. He cannot be alone, yet he cannot bear the presence of others. He seeks quiet, yet finds it unbearable. He weeps without knowing why. He anxiously clings to some agreeable person, but does not know what he expects of him. He may give the impression of being almost insane, confusedly laughing, crying, chattering, scolding, and he may even fall into a state of semi-consciousness.

In all the varied manifestations described thus far, we see the outer side of the crisis as it occurs, not only in neurotic cases, but also in the life of normal, average individuals. We observe similar events in the great catastrophes of mankind—in earthquakes, battles, plagues, and also in financial panics or stock-market collapses. On such a black day many "normal" people undergo such a crisis and show many of these symptoms. The thinker may ask himself whether the task and burdens of life are not more than human beings should be expected to bear.

Our answer is clearly, no. The more we are egocentric and therefore rigid the less we are able to bear life's burdens. This is as it should be, since the breakdown of the Ego—the collapse of the system of mistaken ideas which like a shell encase the Self and limit the expression of its powers—is one basic aim of human destiny. Thus even the suffering of the rigidly egocentric person under life's seemingly impossible burdens is as it should be, for it brings him to the crisis, and the crisis is the door of opportunity. It is the point at which he may turn about in his life, lay aside his former limitations in part at least, and become more productive and courageous than ever. The human path to new We-feeling, courage and daring productivity is through egocentric difficulty and, perhaps, well-nigh hopeless fright.

This is the crucial matter in the development of individuals, nations, cultures, religions. Each of them must sooner or later deal with it. Many of them fail and perish because they do not dare to expose themselves to the pains of suffering, crisis and rebirth. Only those who go through the crisis, only those who endure the "perils of the soul" and dare to brave the unknown dangers of the future find the way to new, mature and productive life. They attain the experience of the Maturing-We and they help this We even if they sacrifice their lives in joining it. They find themselves and they find the We—the We being their Self. Even if they lose their lives, they will find them.

In spite of all outer differences in the forms and in the course of their development, the crises of egocentricity show so many and important similarities that we are able to describe their common nature. This, however, does not mean that we can explain them as a natural science does.

In these crises, as in all living reactions, there remains a certain unexplainable, irreducible reality. The only thing we can do is to point it out, to describe it as best we can and say, "So it is." No definition or explanation can comprehend it and analyze it thoroughly. We have to admit that we stand here before the same ultimate riddle that we find in all living processes. The major crisis of egocentricty shows this "miracle of life"—and especially the miracle of human life—more clearly and more in detail than do any phenomena in the entire range of biology and history.

Let us try now to get at the very essence of this major crisis of egocentricity. The first point may be stated thus. The egocentric form of psychic life breaks down because it proves to be erroneous in its content and too rigid in its form. The attempts of the individual to save his Ego only lead him nearer to the crisis. This clinging to it is a form of rigidity—an inflexibility of thinking, an unwillingness to change an idea or accept a new one—which is the greatest danger to the Ego. In other words, an essential quality of the Ego becomes the cause of its breakdown. One might say that in the service of egocentricity it would be useful to be less egocentric! Increasing egocentricity destroys itself! He who tries to save his life kills himself!

That this breakdown is or can be connected with a new start is self-evident to anyone who knows something about biology. Everywhere in life springtime comes after the fall. This is true in general in human life, and yet it must not be true in every case. We admit that the new start seems to be impossible from the old viewpoint of physics or chemistry. It is, however, natural from the viewpoint of biology, human history and religion. Moreover the new viewpoint of physics and chemistry seems to be quite different in this respect from the old. While the observer may with all hopefulness look for the rebirth—the new start—the person who undergoes this crisis feels no hope. It seems to him to be a real death, for the Ego disappears forever. For him it seems to be the Self, the only form of life that he knows, and therefore he believes its collapse is death. Thus he believes he faces the end of his life.

There is no help for him in the fact that the We transcends any individual, because, to the egocentric person who approaches his crisis, the We does not exist at the moment of which we speak. Objectively it is a reality, but unrevealed, unknown, like a hidden treasure; therefore, he does not feel himself a part of it. At the most, it is mere theory for him, and therefore the We cannot help him. He knows himself only as the Ego. The values, insights and experiences which make up the whole system of this Ego are the only ones that seem to be real. It is exactly these egocentric values and experiences which lose their validity. They are no longer useful. They yield no satisfactions. They break down, and their collapse is the breakdown of the Ego. The Ego has to abdicate like a despot who has ruined his country, leaving a chaos out of which it seems that nothing new and sound ever could arise.

Thus we understand why the major crisis of the Ego very often involves thoughts and sometimes threats of suicide. However, it rather seldom occurs in these cases because as egocentric values fade there remain only indifference and desperate dullness. At that depth such a person has lost not only all feelings of desire and aversion, but of need and the sense of privation. In complete indifference he lets all things go. Out of this state no impulse leads to any deed. Suicide demands a much higher degree of activity. As long as he complains and rages or threatens to destroy himself or others, the crisis has not reached its climax—the deepest point of its despair.

Let us try to imagine one who has come to this state where all his former values seem to be worthless and where he is completely indifferent and without aims of any kind. Perhaps one can recall such a state in his own life, if he ever passed through it. In this state suppose he sees written on a paper the equation $3-3 = 7$, or imagine that he sees a rank weed grown high in a flower garden. Without being any the less indifferent, he could not help judging that the equation is wrong or that the weed does not belong in the garden. So, too, the sight of a beggar, a sick person, an unemployed person or another unfortunate human being would not stir his compassion, since feeling is impossible in this situation. Yet he is aware that something is not as it should be. This insight, the statement of a truth, is still possible even if all feeling and striving has disappeared, but it includes a new understanding of human nature and of this person's situation in the world. A few days or even hours before he would have felt malicious joy or he would have drawn far-reaching and wrong conclusions such as "Since this is possible, there is no God" or

"Evil prevails in the world." He would have found new food to feed his pessimism. Now he simply notes: "This is wrong."

It is necessary to distinguish two paths through the crisis to a new start. We call the first one the human or earthly path. It ends in a certain sense of fellowship in a We that consists of humans—an earthly or human We. The second one may be characterized as the religious path. Its outlet is—at least in our time—Christianity with its sense of the manifestation of God in the We.

In the first case, the person has renounced all the former aims and values of his Ego. In anticipation this process seemed to be death itself, yet now, having passed through it, he realizes that he is alive in spite of the terrible breakdown. Now he sees that the world is quite different from what he formerly believed it to be. He seems to look upon life with new eyes, seeing connections, facts, values, goals, ways, possibilities he never saw before. A serious offense which yesterday seemed unbearable is now a mere trifle. Like old clothes, worn out and worthless, his egocentric prejudices, notions, and ideas have been discarded for something better. Formerly it was supposed that without these egocentric values life would be empty, meaningless, nothing at all—that when these old egocentric ideas had been dropped nothing would be left, that the rest of life would be emptiness. But now the person discovers how mistaken he was. For a new world opens up before him with a whole new life, richer and more colorful and more differentiated than anything he knew before.

This appearance in his life of the new values, new feelings and new aims, which completes the new insight into the actual realities of life, is the very essence of the crisis, and perhaps the essence of human life itself. It is inexplicable, and we must limit ourselves to describing it as carefully as possible. In the case of the human or earthly path through crisis, we come to feel that this "miracle of rebirth" seems to be a natural element in human life. In the case of the religious path, we feel behind the sunrise of the new life a higher living power who brings it about.

As an illustration of this human path we may imagine a desperate person weary of life who has gone through the loss of his egocentric interests, feelings, values and goals. Fear and depression have gone, too. In complete indifference he looks around, awaiting his death. Then, by chance he sees two boys quarreling about a ball they lost. Each thinks that the other one lost it. The desperate man, not being diverted by egoistic interests, knows that the quarrel is useless and that the only problem is to find the ball and not to argue about who was guilty of losing it. Quite mechanically, without being interested, without any feeling at all, he looks around to see where the ball may be, and without realizing what he is doing, he says: "Maybe we can find the ball in these weeds." Perhaps we should not say that he speaks but that the We speaks through his mouth, since we know already that it is the We which expresses itself through him. Now he makes the first step toward the weeds without any conscious interest, and likewise a second step. In a sense the We, of which he is not aware, moves on his legs. The boys seek; the man seeks. The quarrel is over. "*We* are looking for this damned ball." At once a joyful voice shouts, "Here it is." The boy throws it to his mate. They rejoice. "Come play with us," they say to the man and suddenly throw him the ball. Before he has time to say "yes" or "no," he catches the ball and throws it back. Then half angry, half astonished, he plays ball with two children instead of waiting indifferently to die.

A new awakening takes place. The We revived within leads him to understand that he must find many lost balls and reconcile many fighting boys and people before it is time to think of death or suicide.

In this imaginary case we have illustrated an indispensable step on either path through the crisis. It is the discovery of some human need to which one may minister. Better said, it is finding one's place in the service of the We. Life now takes on a richer meaning because one realizes that he is a part of the We. We-feeling quickens within, and because of it one's outlook is now out toward human need, toward working relationships with others for the highest ends of the We. No longer is he preoccupied with the false demands of his Ego. No longer does he suffer the frustrations and disappointments involved in the pursuit of the false goals imposed upon him by mistaken Ego-centered values. The satisfactions of genuine We-feeling experiences begin to be his.

Thus he comes to realize the deeper meaning of the great

paradox, "He that would save his life must lose it." It is true, indeed, that one must lose that which seems to be his life—the system of mistaken ideas and values which are embodied in his Ego—in order really to live, to release into life the creative, enriching, productive powers of that portion of the We which we call the Self.

In one way or another, the individual who finds his way out of the crisis must make this discovery. Somehow he must come to find himself in We-feeling relations to others—in genuine service of the We. The validity of this fact is amply attested by the actual experiences of human beings. How frequently we see the men or women whose whole life seems to have collapsed about them forgetting their woes in the radiant happiness of finding themselves anew in some We-service.

Perhaps it is the Star dashed from her pedestal of admiration by some crushing fate who finds a new and unsuspected richness of life in a quiet, inconspicuous routine as a teacher. Maybe it is some Clinging Vine deprived by a tragic death of the husband to whom she clung for years, and now, to the surprise of all, she becomes a creative, productive, independent person in rearing her family. Perhaps it is some Nero whose kingdom of wealth and prestige has been taken away from him by the onslaughts of a depression. Yet one discovers him later, not miserably suffering but delighting in the We-feeling satisfactions found in striving to make himself not dominant over, but quietly useful to, his fellow men. Finally it may be some Turtle timidly retreating from the world, dreading its terrifying demands, who is suddenly forced by some adversity to make his own way in it. He now becomes increasingly courageous, productive and happy in some humble role as a helper and friend of the helpless and friendless. Always, in any event, there is a loss of all old egocentric values and a rebirth into living anew in the We.

The earthly path through the crisis of egocentricity seems to be the way most frequently taken, but it does not lead to the highest state of human maturity. This is reached only through the religious way. Here, as far as we see, the individual senses the presence of the living reality, God, who works behind the We, and who through it shows at least a fraction of his power without disguise. To the student of the We-Psychology this reality seems to display himself in all crises and to serve as a guide on all the paths out, but in traveling what we have described as the human path the individual does not recognize his presence or sense his power.

The first steps on the religious path are the same as in the other case. The emptiness and indifference resulting from the collapse of the Ego and the complete loss of egocentricity enable the individual to discover the very foundations of his life and of human life in general. He sees that man is powerless and important at the same time, that he is part of a larger unit and responsible for it. Furthermore, he realizes—and this is the decisive insight—that he himself as well as the larger unit, the We, is created, sent, supported, endowed and used by a higher reality who rules the world and in whom he and others live and move and have their being. Thus he feels himself gripped, influenced by God and charged with a concrete task. He feels like a tool seized by a strong hand, or like a knight commissioned by his king with a definite commission. His reaction at first seems to be a mixture of fright and joy, or of grief over the past and confidence for the future. Later come new strength, new insights, new goals, new productivity and, above all, new love, and with it comes obedience to what is felt to be the "divine commission."*

There are three elements in this new inner life which in the last analysis prove to be only one. They are: the Self whose powers lay latent within the shell of the Ego, the We which is the very essence of the Self, and this mysterious power which theologians and religious people will think of as the light, or the voice, or the grace of God. Those who are mere scientists engaged in pure psychological research may feel that they cannot philosophize regarding the ultimate nature of this reality. Nevertheless, they have to respect it as an unknown, irreducible, inexplainable, incalculable, but overwhelming and creative power.

---

*Here we have as a classic illustration the life of Paul with his strong sense of commission (after the experiences of his crisis on the road to Damascus), and yet with the varied feelings of fright, joy, grief and confidence which he so clearly displayed.

Section Three

THE WAY THROUGH THE CRISIS

Introduction

In the last section we ended with Kunkel's description of the crisis that occurs when our egocentric life patterns no longer work for us. What Kunkel had to say about the crisis, and how we can go through it successfully, is probably his most important contribution to religious psychology. However, there is no single place in any of his books where we can find everything that Kunkel had to say on the subject. Consequently, this part of Kunkel's works includes five different sections composed of passages from both *How Character Develops* and *In Search of Maturity.*

Each of these five parts concerns a different aspect of how we can find our way creatively through the crisis. The first concerns "The Shadow and Negative Life."

The reason we begin this part of the way through the crisis with a discussion of the Shadow is that we *must* come to terms with the Shadow if we are to find our way through. Although Kunkel did not write very much about the Shadow, what he did say was of great interest and importance. In this part we have included most of the relevant passages in which the Shadow is discussed. Here we find that the discovery of our Shadow helps us find the way through the crisis first because it erases our false egocentric image of ourselves, and second because the energy of the Shadow can revitalize us because it is closer to the Self than the egocentric Ego. The whole topic is of such importance that one of the commentary chapters which make up Section Four of this book discusses the subject of the Shadow at some length, and its relationship to Jungian psychology and Christianity.

The second part of this section concerns methods of self-education in order to help us through the crisis. The fact that

Kunkel emphasized self-education so much is important, for it reminds us that in the final analysis we are our own doctors. Of course there is a great deal that medical doctors, psychotherapists, and spiritual directors can do for us, but ultimately we must take responsibility for the health of our own bodies, minds, and souls. Furthermore, though experts may guide us from time to time, the true healer lies within us. Kunkel knew this, and this is why he stressed the importance of finding ways of helping and educating ourselves.

In this respect, Kunkel is more like Jung than like Freud. Classical Freudian analysis called for the patient to see the doctor three or four times a week; in this process the patient was relatively passive. Jungian therapists, however, often see their clients only once a week, perhaps less, and in between visits to the therapist the client is encouraged to keep a journal, record dreams, reflect and meditate upon them, and engage in forms of meditation, active imagination, drawing, sculpting, and other means of self-education and therapy.

In Kunkel's discussion of self-education the Jungian oriented person may miss Jung's emphasis on dream interpretation. Kunkel relied heavily on dreams, but didn't shed new light on the subject in his books. Neither did Kunkel discuss Jung's technique of self-therapy called "active imagination," but he did make valuable contributions in other ways to the subject of self-education, and quite correctly stressed its importance. For Kunkel knew that the health of the soul, like that of the body, depends on lifelong habits of learning to live creatively with oneself.

In the third part we discuss "Idolatry and the Attempt To Escape from the Crisis." Here we learn of the importance of Kunkel's ideas about the Shadow for social science as well as for individual psychology, for Kunkel tells us that if we turn someone into an Idol for us then we can (seemingly) cast aside the burden of having to face and deal with our own Shadows.

Perhaps nowhere is Kunkel more timely than in his analysis of groups and particularly of the group that centers around the Idol. Our century has seen many disastrous examples of groups centered around an Idol, ranging from Hitler's Germany to Jonestown. In Kunkel's ruthless exposure of egocentric groups for what they are he does all of us a great service. His analysis of the

Idol, and the false group life that is a distortion of a genuine We group, is original with him. We include it in this part of the book because flight to such a group represents a false attempt to find a way out of the Crisis.

Kunkel has shown us how the Crisis develops, has pointed out that we can take positive steps to help ourselves, and has warned us that we must not take a false way out of our dilemma. In the fourth part, "The Creative Way Through the Crisis," he tells us how the Crisis can become a positive experience.

We begin with a chapter from *In Search of Maturity* that seems deceptively simple. From time to time we may even get impatient and feel as though we are reading things we have read before. We may wonder if this is all there is to be said about the way through the desperate situation our egocentricity has created. Then it comes! In the last part of the chapter that Kunkel has entitled "The New Life" we read what I regard as the most important seven pages in all of Kunkel's writing. It is so deceptively simple we wonder why we had not thought of it ourselves. The way through the Crisis, Kunkel tells us, is to go *through* it rather than try to avoid it.

Face the darkness, go through it, Kunkel urges us, if we wish to overcome our egocentricity. It may sound simple, but it is also painful. It is the last thing our egocentric nature wants to hear. We had hoped, perhaps, for something more complicated. Surely an interesting case like ours is deserving of a more interesting solution than this! The very simplicity of Kunkel's prescription for psychological and spiritual health is an affront to our egocentric image of ourselves.

We are like Naaman the Syrian, whose story we find in the fifth chapter of the Second Book of Kings. Naaman was a Syrian general afflicted with leprosy, who went to the prophet Elisha to be cured. When Elisha told him to bathe seven times in the Jordan River he was disdainful. Why should he bathe in the muddy old Jewish River Jordan when the waters of his own country were so much purer? Just the same he did it and was cured.

So it is with us. There must be some more glorious way of curing ourselves than bathing in our own muddy waters! But it seems that this is the only way to be cleansed of the leprosy of our egocentricity.

At this point Kunkel and Jung are in agreement. The way of Analytical Psychology, Jung's method, is the way *through the darkness*. The way to heaven, Jung once said, is to go through hell. So Jung, as well as Kunkel, encouraged people to meet the darkness, to face their dark dreams and nightmares, and learn the bad news about themselves. It looks like the last thing we would want to do, but when we *do* go through the darkness we discover a great thing: our inner enemies are now willing to become our allies, and the dreams that used to be so disturbing now become supportive. In short, what we thought was the devil turns out to be God, and what we thought was God is, in fact, the devil.

This bring us to the fifth and last part, "Practical Aids on the Way Through." We have already seen that Kunkel stresses the importance of psychological self-education. In this part Kunkel gives us some practical suggestions. It is characteristic of Kunkel that he not only takes us up into the heights from where we can get a grand overview of our spiritual plight, but he also leads us back to solid ground, and gives us concrete suggestions that we can use in working out our problems.

It is also in this part that Kunkel discusses the importance of faith. Faith, so often disparaged in what purports to be scientific psychology, and even sometimes denigrated in Jungian thought, is pointed out by Kunkel to be essential in the healing process. It is an important point that we will have occasion to return to in one of the chapters in the commentary part of the book.

Part I:
The Shadow and Negative Life
The Ego and Its Shadow

We have described the original We-group which is usually, though not always, identical with the family. And we have mentioned the early "breach of the We," the destruction of the child's

We-experience, when the egocentric adults betray the We-feeling child. This catastrophe, we said, causes the child to replace his real Self by an Ego-image. From this point on his life pivots more or less around Ego-preservation and Ego-enhancement.

Thus, every We-group dissolves sooner or later and more or less thoroughly into egocentric individuals, and afterward is maintained only as long as the egocentric interests of the members are better served by staying together than by scattering. There is no inner power, no living loyalty which could protect such a "sham We-group" against eventual decay. And it is important to realize that in this connection morality is powerless. The group is recognized only as long as the Egos can profit from it. To the degree that its members are egocentric no sacrifice for the sake of the group can be expected. On occasion, outwardly good behavior can be enforced by sanctions which would endanger the Ego's own interest—hence the system of reward and punishment in all egocentric societies.

We have said that the members of the We-group—before the breach of the We—are represented by inner images within the conscious or unconscious mind of each member. The "inner We," the set of images within the individual, corresponds to the "outer We," the group of individuals. It is for this reason that the center of the individual, his highest value—or better, his source of values—coincides with the real center, the highest value and source of values, of the group. The inner images within the individual are balanced around the same hub as are the actual individuals in the outer world. This hub is the real Self, although the members of the group may call it variously "our cause," "our mission," "our way of life," and sometimes even "our God." It is the source of power and creativity which enables both the individuals and the group not only to meet all outer challenges but also to solve creatively all conflicts between the inner images and their contradictory interests. The mother may be torn between the baby that needs its diapers changed and the husband who needs lunch. Only her creative center, observing and combining the two inner images, husband and child, can solve this problem and turn impending irritability into laughter and creative comedy.

Now, the question arises as to what happens to the inner imagery of an individual when the outer We-group breaks down.

His real center is replaced by an Ego-image. The gravitation point is shifted, the hub is superseded by an eccentric and artificial "highest value," namely Ego-preservation. The real Self—which is not an image and can never be seen or influenced as if it were an image—seems to disappear or to be entirely blacked out. The images, however, cannot vanish. They will remain, if not in the conscious mind then in the unconscious.

We have already seen that images can be repressed, that they can deteriorate, lose their power, or turn into the negative. But we do not yet see what this fact means with regard to the relation between the individual who harbors the decaying imagery, and his fellow men in the outer world. In order to answer this question we have to begin, of course, with the special image which becomes the new—and wrong—center of the egocentric individual, the so-called Ego-image.

The Ego-images are rather simple, at first, expressing immediately the Ego's pretended superiority or its fear of being inferior. "I am the good son of good parents"—the Ego-image of feudal or moralistic aristocrats—simply means "I am better than others, and this is (or should be) proved by my blameless behavior." "I will reform the bad world, including my bad parents" means: "I am better than everybody; not the superiority of my tradition but the new self-evident value of my own personality is the basis of all my claims." Feudalism has been replaced by rugged individualism.

Before the breach of the We, the child does not know the difference between good and bad. He only knows that he is "the little boy," an essential part of the group and in harmony with all its members. Then the requirements for membership in the group are raised, and raised again. He is supposed to eat spinach; not to eat the applesauce first, though it was on the table all the time; to clear away the toys; not to wet the bed—and all this seems to be the arbitrary command of a dictatorial adult rather than a genuine need of the We-group. At the very beginning, in the cradle, it was quite different; the paradise is lost.—Shouldn't he rebel? Why comply with the whimsical adults? To hell with the group if the group means losing the paradise!

The innocent "little boy" image has split, has differentiated, into two little boys of opposite value. One is the "good boy," siding with the adults, in harmony with the group as it is or ought to be now, and ready to sacrifice, forget or repress everything which interferes with the inner peace of the group. The other is the "bad boy," a rebel, a daredevil, and if necessary a criminal. To him life is worthwhile only if it is lived recklessly and dangerously, defying the adults, scoffing at their dreary morality, acknowledging no standards, no authority, enjoying all kinds of mischief and sabotage, laughing even at pain and death—the negative hero, loyal only to his Ego-pride and, to some extent, to his fellow-gangsters.

The moral differentiation of the original images is as old as mankind. The motif of the two fighting brothers, one good and one bad, is to be found in primitive religions, myths, and fairytales all over the earth. In the Old Testament it recurs almost like a musical "theme with variations." There are Cain and Abel, Abraham and Lot, Jacob and Esau, Joseph and his brothers; and on the feminine side, though less elaborate, Eve and Lilith, Sarah and Hagar. In depth-psychology we call this motif the problem of our negative (inner) twin or the Ego's shadow. And we assume that since everyone has an Ego-image everyone probably will have its counterpart, the negative Ego-twin-brother or Ego-twin-sister, too.

In a few cases the twin images remain equally conscious and available. Some children are extremely good when at home and extremely bad when with their playmates, or vice versa. They live as it were in two different worlds alternately. But usually one of the images is consciously and officially accepted while the opposite is rejected, condemned, and repressed into the unconscious.

The good boy develops all the qualities which seem to be desirable for harmony with the adults; he is as they want him to be—or rather, as he thinks they want him to be. This attitude becomes his second nature. But the other half, the bad half, of his first nature still exists. There is a slight possibility that he may "forget himself," that is, forget the ideal image of the good boy, and have a tantrum, or steal some chocolate, or take the radio apart, or put a frog in grandma's bed. The bad twin, the Shadow, turns up like a ghost, haunting the good child and asserting that—fortunately—the other half of reality is not entirely lost.

From the viewpoint of the Ego the resurrection of the bad

twin means utmost defeat. The whole Ego-pattern would explode if we would acknowledge that this bad behavior is as natural to us as the ideal Ego itself. Therefore, to preserve the Ego, we call it "not I," my weakness, my vice, or the devil. The proper psychological name is the Ego's Shadow.*

The Shadow is a possibility of behavior and experience which completely contradicts or excludes the consciously acknowledged Ego pattern. If your Ego ideal is to excel in smartness, fine clothing and brilliant conversation, then your Shadow may be illustrated by the following scene: You come to join a party on a rainy day. Your car has to stop three feet from the curbstone. You try to jump, elegantly, in front of seven well-dressed ladies who look at you in admiration. You jump, you slip, and there you lie in the mud in your new evening clothes. For the one who wants to be rich the Shadow is his extravagance which makes him poor; for the ambitious one it may be ridicule; for the spoiled child it is exposure. It is the "doghouse," the situation which makes us wish to be swallowed up in the earth; and usually it is the unavoidable result of our egocentricity.

From the viewpoint of depth-psychology, as we shall see, the acceptance of the Shadow means honesty and confession, and leads to the experience of forgiveness, which is the only way out. But under the tyranny of the Ego there is neither honesty nor confession nor forgiveness. There is only condemnation and fear. For the reconciliation of the twins would transform both of them, and the reign of the Ego would come to an end.

The Ego-image seems to represent all the desirable values of life—honor, righteousness, power, reputation, or security, wealth, and indulgence in all the good things. The Shadow, on the other hand, appears as a symbol of all that is repulsive,

---

*The term "Shadow" is taken from the Jungian Psychology. (Cf. Frances Wickes, *The Inner World of Man.*) We use the word in a more specialized sense than the Jungians. To us it means the crystallization point of all the powers which are repressed into the unconscious. The term "Ego" is used by Jung in approximately the same sense as we use it. The only difference is that we ascribe to the Ego certain unconscious functions which serve its purposes while Jung uses it exclusively with reference to consciousness. The "Self" for us is a metaphysical reality which exists not only all through the individual life but also beyond space and time. Jung thinks of the Self as an entity which comes into existence only through the process of integration. We would say it awakes, or should awake; he would say it should be brought into existence through our personal development.

detestable, and unbearable. In both cases the image symbolizes our own attitude as well as the outer situation. If the "doghouse" is represented by disgrace, it does not matter whether the individual is disgraced through some fault of his own or through outer circumstances; but it would not be felt as disgrace, it would not be "Shadowy," if the Ego-image were not endangered by it.

On the thermometer of our egocentric values, the ideal Ego-image marks the point $+100$; the negative twin, the Shadow, corresponds to the point -100. If we know one of these two points we can determine the other one with almost mathematical exactitude.

In this way our egocentric striving for $+100$ (superiority or security) and fear of -100 (inferiority and insecurity) are related to our inner images. And since even distorted and deviated images are still channels of power we may understand that our egocentricity, together with its Shadow, is strong enough to wreck not only individuals but groups.

Negative Life

The most destructive feature of egocentricity is its rebellion against time. Complying with time means growing older and more mature, slowly and patiently. It requires creativeness, or at least flexibility. The egocentric patterns, however, are rigid and defend with fearful stubbornness the momentary Ego-image without admitting any possible change. Sometimes the Ego-image is related to the future, but it is not therefore less rigid. "I will have this kind of family, this much money, this much influence." What the future has to be is decreed arbitrarily from the viewpoint of a timeless but egocentric valuation. The Ego, as we said, tries to be God; God is beyond time; therefore the Ego does not submit to time. To wait, to fail, to grow old, to die, is unbearable for the Ego. And the worst of all words for it is "too late."

Suppose the Ego-image in a certain case is "good little girl." By the time the child is four or five, this limited and one-sided image constitutes already a grave error. It would be better for her if, in addition to being the sweet and admired little pet, she would act occasionally as a nasty little mischief-maker. Ten years later she is still the nice little girl; her Ego-image, being rigid, has not changed; she speaks and feels and acts like a precocious child of about five. Older people think she is "cute," and the aunts praise her for being virtuous; but the boys don't like her. Again ten years later, her Ego-image is still five years old. She cannot grow up. She is good and kind and meek, but she cannot stand any difficulty, nor can she take responsibility on her own. And thirty years later she is a completely ridiculous creature, a white-haired baby, trying desperately to be cheerful and "cute." Her Ego-image is entirely out of tune with reality.

Cases like this are rare, fortunately; but they occur. However, in a more diluted form, we find this sort of "arrested development" in every egocentric personality, which means practically everywhere. The Ego-image is located in a position in the inner We-group where it does not belong. The mother may have the Ego-image of a little girl. The father may behave like a youngster. And, looking more closely, we find that more intricate Ego-patterns outnumber the simple ones. A mother, for instance, may live emotionally on the level of a child; mentally she may be mature but completely masculine; while physically she is a healthy woman of her real age.

The opposite sin against time is possible too. A small boy may anticipate the dignity of fatherhood (especially if his father lives the life of an egocentric child). The boy then does not learn that he is the "little one." On the contrary, he finds out, by practical experiment, that he can have his way, if only he screams and yells loudly enough. The child, of course, does not know what happens; the psychologist, however, may see unmistakable signs of the "choice of the wrong Ego-image." There is a look in the boy's eyes and a tone in his voice which at the age of two already herald the future boss or dictator. His whole attitude says, "You do what I want you to do, or I smash you!" His father, the sissie, admires the aggressive boy. His unlived life, his repressed desire for power, his inner twin brother, seems to become reality—in so mild a form, and without any danger to the father's effeminate Ego. So the father lets him have his way.

Later the father understands that his boy will do in earnest what he, the father, never could do because his egocentric pattern did not allow it. The daredevil, the egocentric conqueror, develops with amazing rapidity. Now the father is afraid, he despises the boy's behavior. He terms it bad taste, or even immorality. But preaching does not help; and punishment increases the evil. The boy is and remains the bully. He takes the place in which the father should have stood. He is the shadow of his father's Ego, materialized in the outer world.

Psychologically speaking, if in the outer We-group the place of the father is empty, then the father-image in the child's imagery is, as it were, "unemployed"; it does not find a lodging place in outer reality; so it becomes easy for the boy to identify himself with the vacant father-image, and to transfer the image of the sissie boy to his father. Thus he anticipates the advantages of adulthood without paying the price, that is, without accepting the disadvantages such as responsibility, hard work and sacrifice. The egocentric pattern, then, shows a second mistake in addition to eccentricity and rigidity, namely the wrong location of the Ego-image.

Unfortunately this mistake of anticipating the future cannot be corrected by time. Thirty years later the boy will be just as immature a bully as he used to be at the beginning of his egocentric career. The father-image which he assumed as the "ideal" of his Ego was not that of a grown-up father. It was an egocentric father caricature. It was distorted from the very beginning; and it will be more distorted thirty years later. He may have children, then, but he will bully them and exploit them, and force them into another kind of egocentricity.

Yet the choice of the Ego-image can be even worse: it can confuse the masculine and feminine side of the family group. The girl may feel that it would be much better to be a boy. As a boy she would be allowed to climb trees and to go with her brother's gang to steal apples. If she is very discouraged she decides that she is and has to be a girl, which means that she feels inferior, insecure, resentful and bitter. (All girls are "bad," then, in the sense of inferior, underprivileged.) But if she still retains some courage she decides: "I will be a boy. Believe it or not: I *am* a boy!"

She identifies herself with the image of boyhood as she finds it within her imagination. She talks her brother's slang, walks like a trooper, throws things around as her father sometimes does, and refuses flatly to knit or to play with dolls. Of course, this masculine Ego-image may be remote from real boyhood. The negative features, such as roughness, swearing, and even cruelty, are exaggerated, and the positive ones, chivalry, helpfulness, endurance and fortitude, are missing. The image, however, is usually strong enough to change the girl into a complete tomboy. And even the inner glands are sometimes influenced to a certain extent so as to retard puberty or to decrease the development of breasts and hips.

In the opposite case the boy would understand that life is too dangerous for him, and that girls are less exposed to this danger. So he prefers—especially if the place of the "big boy" is taken already by an older brother—the Ego-image of the girl. He becomes a sissie, and, in the extreme case, a homosexual. He avoids fighting and calls his cowardice a Christian virtue. He cannot stand disharmony, and terms this weakness a love for peace. He develops good taste, a definite sense of beauty, but no patience and no efficiency. Physically, of course, he remains a man, but his potency is usually underdeveloped, though he may consider himself as highly sexed.

In some cases the picture is more complicated. The Ego-image is then masculine in one layer and feminine in another. The boy may be a sissie physically and emotionally, but a bully or even a tyrant mentally; or vice versa. And the girl may be very masculine in her mind as well as in her physique, while emotionally she may be over-feminine (the type of certain hysterias); or vice versa. The respective Ego-images may be the oversensitive scholar, the prizefighter, the emotional suffragette, and the sentimental mother. The right image has to be discovered in every case individually. All generalizations are wrong.

There is no limit to the choice and the combination of our Ego-images. Every place in the family scheme of father, mother, son and daughter can be usurped by every member of the family. But life becomes the more miserable for ourselves and for our fellow men the further our Ego-image is removed from our natural position in our group. Moreover, the strangest mixtures of images occur, real monsters with the sweet intentions of an angel and the cruel appetites of a devil; and, as we said before, different images can be used at different times.

We can easily imagine, now, the extreme case of a completely reversed family. This caricature may never occur in reality; but again we have to say that less severe cases of this kind, with more diluted egocentric intoxication, are not so rare. The father plays the role of a helpless little girl; he is oversensitive and needs a guardian to fight off the hardships of reality which he simply cannot stand. So he has married a tomboy whose Ego-image happens to be a tramp. He mistook her carefree behavior for strength, and her big words for reliability. Later she turned out to be totally unreliable, which made him feel even more insecure and therefore inclined to lean on his eldest boy. This boy learned very early that he could not trust his parents. They could not help him. Therefore he does not trust anybody but himself. At the age of five he is already a tyrant; at ten he assumes the leadership in his family and at fifteen he is the undisputed and completely egocentric boss. His younger brother, being excluded from government and power, excels in stunts and jokes. He amuses the whole family and makes them laugh when the inner conflict becomes critical. Like a mother he preserves peace, but he does it on a merely egocentric basis. Because everybody likes him or even needs him, he is allowed to do as he pleases. He takes the best sweetmeats, gets the finest clothes, and is as touchy as the prima donna in an old Italian opera.

The four members of the family are equally egocentric. And the Ego-image of each is in an opposite place from its rightful one. The father is an egocentric girl. The mother is an egocentric boy. One son is the egocentric father, and the other is the egocentric mother. They will torture each other until all their egocentricity breaks down.

When people complain about their inner difficulties such as nervousness and irritability, or inhibitions and fears, they frequently use the word "tension," or similar expressions derived from the same root. They say, "I am tense, I cannot relax, my nerves are highly strung." And their outer appearance reveals that they are right. They frown, they clench their fists, their movements are abrupt, and they easily develop intestinal cramps. Even where physical symptoms are missing the intensity of their speech and the defensiveness of their reactions seem to indicate some kind of mental or emotional tenseness as the underlying evil of all these more or less "nervous" attitudes. Here "tension" is evidently something bad, something to be avoided.

In other cases the same words are used with an opposite meaning: people complain of not having enough intensity. They are slack, listless, indifferent; and they wish to be more interested, more intensive, more tense. Or they say that the intensity of modern life wears out their nerves. They cannot bear so much tension, they are not strong enough. And if the stress and strain persist, a nervous breakdown may be the result. Or a married couple confess that they do not feel any sexual tension, and that this lack of tension is lack of love, or at least lack of happiness. Here "tension" means something good.

All these expressions are borrowed from the "tension" of the strings of musical instruments. If the strings are too tense or too slack the instrument is out of tune. Our nerves have evidently been misunderstood as resembling musical chords. But with reference to the more complicated picture of the human mind which we have developed in the foregoing chapters we need a more careful terminology. Therefore we will use the word *tension* with regard to the Ego and all its manifestations. (For example, the ambitious student is tense and his tension endangers his success; he should learn how to relax.) And *intensity* will be used in relation to the real Self and the inner images as far as they are still (or again) in genuine relation to the center. (A man and woman who are intensely in love with each other feel not only the growing intensity of their own relationship, but of all their functions and reactions in life.)

The complaint that modern life is too intense for our nervous constitution has now to be formulated in a rather disconcerting way: Life is intense; it demands the creative reactions that issue from our real Self. If an egocentric person tries to meet this demand he may succeed for a certain time with the help of reckless cunning and tricky devices, but sooner or later he will fail; his Ego will be endangered; he will feel tense, irritable, nervous, and finally he will break down. The less he is egocentric or the more he overcomes his Ego and brings to light his real Self, the more he will be creative, intense and equal to the task. His presence of mind will increase the intensity of life—and make it less comfortable for his egocentric fellow men.

All egocentric tension can easily be traced to our striving for superiority and fear of inferiority. We survey a task, and the more we are afraid of failure, the more we overestimate the energy which is needed. Here is a piece of black wood, weighing one pound; you mistake it for iron, expecting it to weigh some ten pounds. In lifting it you not only spend unnecessary energy jerking it up too fast and too high; but you also waste energy re-establishing an artificial equilibrium between the upward movement and the downward pull. In our example you would have to add a downward pull equal to nine pounds by straining your own antagonistic muscles; otherwise the movement would be uncoordinated and probably a failure.

Imagine a person walking easily and carelessly along a mountain path. Suddenly he sees a sign saying that there is danger of a landslide. He discovers the cracks and crevices across his trail; he begins to move with utmost care, slowly and cautiously. He spends ten times as much energy for each movement as is necessary; therefore his muscles are tense, his breathing is irregular, and where he should walk fast and lightly as a dancer would do, almost without touching the ground, there he is going step by step resting his whole weight on the unreliable soil. And worst of all, the more he is aware of his mistake the less he is able to do better. He is caught in the vicious circle of egocentric fear, and only a miracle can save him.

Most people are psychologically in exactly the same situation when they try to pass an examination with outstanding grades, or to apply for a job which they desire very much. If they were less anxious they would meet with more success. And many people—not only neurotics but normal average people—live on a general level of egocentric tension high above their natural intensity. To them every new task and every normal day mean an additional strain. A vacation means only relief from this *additional* tension, not the disappearance of their habitual amount of tension. They always behave as if they had to carry a load of fifty pounds on their shoulders. The normal work of everyday life to them means ten more pounds; they carry them faithfully, and after having done the job they are glad to be freed from the additional ten pounds. But the invisible fifty pounds remain; they try to rest, but no genuine enjoyment, no thorough relaxation is possible; and finally they are glad when the vacation is over and they can shoulder the additional ten pounds again.

What are the mysterious fifty pounds of habitual tension? They represent our egocentric fears, based on our unconscious central anxiety. Since our creative center, our real Self, is out of commission we have good reason to feel insecure and inferior. Every moment life may ask us: Be creative! Answer this question! Invent something new! Solve an unheard-of problem! And we would be completely unequal to the task, not because human nature is not creative enough and the task is superhuman and therefore unreasonable, but because of our own egocentricity.

Here is the point where our feeling of inferiority coincides with a vague but very deep and genuine feeling of guilt. We are not "legally" responsible for our egocentricity. Yet we have to bear its consequences. Life confronts us with the checks which our ancestors have signed and we have to pay. "Be creative; overcome thy Ego and theirs; or perish!" We may consider this unjust, unfair, impossible; we may rebel with all the little strength which our Ego still possesses. Rebellion only creates new tension and therefore makes things worse. If we could recognize the higher (namely, collective) responsibility and the super-individual justice which controls human history, we could easily cooperate with the creative powers of life and our sickening egocentric tension would be superseded by living intensity.

Theoretically it would be possible to annihilate the Ego and dissipate its whole system of defense mechanisms within one minute of horrible crisis. It would be a sort of spiritual death, the breakdown of the whole past, all valuations, fears, and hopes, and the immediate birth of a new life. We do not know whether this has ever happened. The classic example which is usually quoted in this connection, St. Paul's conversion at Damascus, seems to prove the opposite theory. His egocentric pseudo-religion certainly was critically challenged by the death of Stephen; and his "breathing out threatenings and slaughter against the disciples" is a significant symptom that his innner crisis had already started. He "made havoc of the Church" because the Church was making havoc of his Ego. That is the pattern the Ego usually follows.

The long period of incubation preceding the crisis is due to the fact that our Ego develops in the course of time the elaborate system of defenses which we have already mentioned. The citadel of the Ego is surrounded by strongly fortified barricades and pillboxes, just as the real Self is surrounded by powerful images which may be understood as secondary power-stations. The difference, however, is evident: the egocentric fortifications serve a merely negative purpose, the defense of the Ego. The original images, on the other hand, are the positive expression of creativity. We cannot even say they serve the Self; because the Self, if it is real, serves the group and through the group, God.

The creative power of the real center, as far as it expresses itself through the channels of our undistorted imagery, is realized subjectively as the intensity of life. Its significant qualities are colorfulness and aliveness; and even if things are going wrong there is a sense of the presence of immediate value. The same power is subjectively felt as tension if it is misused in the service of the Ego. It may help to postpone the fate of the Ego, and may therefore evoke the sensation of triumph or pride; but it always destroys life and therefore carries a vague feeling of bad conscience. Tension is always concomitant with uneasiness and imminent danger.

The outer line of egocentric fortifications consists of rigid rules and regulations which can easily be understood as parts or functions of the Ego-image. We usually call them *inhibitions.* The good boy, for instance, learns: "I must not fail; I have to avoid all disapproval of adults; I must win the highest praise, outwit my rivals and secure the first place in every contest." These laws unfold new implications almost every day. *Differentiation* is working as fast on the negative side as it does on the positive.

The boy learns that he cannot take any risk unless he has the complete guarantee of success. And if certain situations prove to be treacherous with regard to this guarantee they are simply written on the blacklist of things that must not be faced. To recite a poem, for instance, may be dangerous in spite of the most careful preparation. Some criticism might still occur. Then the Ego had better decide not to talk anymore before any audience. The decree is issued, the machinery of Ego defense is geared accordingly, and—the result is a speech-inhibition which prevents this dangerous situation with the precision and thoroughness of a perfect automaton.

In a similar way the same person may be prevented from saying "no." To reject an invitation, for instance, would mean to provoke disapproval. This has to be avoided at any cost. So the invitation is accepted, though it may include the necessity of speaking to an audience. The Ego, now, can neither refuse, nor do what it is asked to do; it is caught in the intricacies of its own legislation, thus proving that further development on the negative side only leads deeper into the tragedy of Ego-destruction.

The original positive imagery is consistent. Wherever its development leads into apparently insoluble problems, a new and creative idea may turn up and provide an unexpected and astonishing solution. One of the best examples is Jesus' answer to the Sadducees' question concerning immortality (Mt 22:23–33). But the Ego-image is not creative. Its development is artificial and shallow. It is as if a small amount of color were spread out too thin. The color loses its tone, becomes weak and insignificant, and finally disappears completely.

The same is true with regard to all the other inhibitions. Some people cannot make decisions, some cannot show their feelings, and some cannot feel at all. Others cannot think clearly and others cannot stop thinking. Practically any function of body and mind can be at least partially inhibited.

Sometimes the inhibition hits a function which is constitutionally weak, and sometimes one which is exceptionally strong. A person, for instance, with a definite inhibition in the field of mathematics may have a mathematical endowment far above average, or far below. No test can prove which is the case; but careful analysis of the unconscious structure may reveal some vestiges of our "hidden talents." And only the collapse of our Ego, the central crisis, can bring them to life again.

Wherever two tendencies of the human mind contradict each

other we find the danger of blunders and bad habits. Suppose a girl has a boyfriend who usually sees her home when she leaves her office. She decides to give him up, and with much effort writes him a letter that he should not come anymore. Her decision is reasonable, but her feeling runs counter to it. However, when she seals the letter she feels relieved; she has done the right thing. Next day the boy is there, waiting for her as usual. He has not received the letter. She is furious. Finally she finds it in her handbag. And immediately she knows: "I forgot to mail it because I wanted to see you again! I hated to write it. Thank God I made this mistake!"

Here is a man going downtown. His wife asks him on his way back to stop at the grocery and to bring two pounds of carrots. His first reaction is, "Am I a messenger boy? Why doesn't she go herself?" Then he understands that she is busy with the children, and tired—of course he will be glad to help her. But he forgets the carrots, remembers them when unlocking the door, hurries back to buy them, and brings them triumphantly to his wife. She looks, and is offended: "I see I cannot expect the smallest help from you. Oh, of course you do what you can for me; you bring the carrots—but you don't help me at all! They are half rotten!" And she cries bitterly. She has understood his unconscious resistance, and all his reasonable excuses do not comfort her.

Examples like these can be found everywhere in ordinary life. There are no bad imps or benign spirits involved, stealing things from our pocket or our memory and restoring them when we deserve it. There is no need even to resort to divine guidance to explain these happenings. Psychologically they are not amazing at all. They are simple expressions of the fact that our unconscious is a little more alert, more courageous, and has better memory, insight, and foresight than our conscious mind.

The situation, however, is not so simple that we could say: heed all your hunches, obey every inkling of your unconscious, and you will be guided perfectly. Neither is the unconscious entirely wise and good while the consciousness is egocentric and bad, nor vice versa. The former is the wrong assumption of those who ascribe to the Holy Spirit all the thoughts which turn up during a period of prayer or meditation. They are just as wrong as the others who ascribe all interfering ideas to the Ego or some evil spirit. The problem has to be investigated more carefully; it is exactly as intricate as the structure of the human mind itself.*

First of all, we have to say that not all blunders are significant. Many of them are valuable symptoms, it is true. They can and should be understood as tokens of our deeper desires (the case of the unmailed letter) or expressions of our discouragement (the case of the rotten carrots). In these cases the blunders indicate a tendency which at the time is unknown or unacceptable to the individual. But we have to admit that in innumerable cases the mistake may be merely casual, that is, caused by irrelevant circumstances such as fatigue, ill-health, or interference of other occupations.

If you forget to mail a letter, the reason may be an unconscious or half-conscious desire not to mail it, or incipient influenza, or the sight of a beautiful woman who catches all your attention just as you pass by the mailbox. Thus you can choose your alibi; you will always find at least half a dozen different explanations which are equally acceptable. But if you are hunting for the truth rather than for excuses you had better assume that an unconscious tendency was involved. And if you cannot discover it this time wait until the next blunder occurs.

The decisive insight which we may attain from the proper analysis of our blunders is due to their connection with the different strata of our mind. In the case of the unmailed letter, the girl's mother would say: "Your conscious resolve to send the letter was good, objective and moral; the opposite tendency, to forget it, was egoistic and bad. Under the disguise of forgetfulness your egoism got the better of you." Her lover, however, would say: "Your egoism told you to obey your family, to be the good girl, faint-hearted though apparently unselfish. But your unconscious instinct, your love, your daring heart got the better of you, and so you didn't mail this cowardly document."

The girl herself could probably find an even more bewildering inner situation. She might discover some egocentricity and some objectivity in both tendencies, to mail the letter and not to

---

*It is the merit of Sigmund Freud to have discovered the deeper meaning of blunders. His interpretation, quite un-Freudian (that is, not yet related to sexual drives), is excellent, though not deep enough. (Freud: *Psychopathology of Everyday Life.*)

mail it. Her Ego wants some sexual satisfaction in kissing the boy in addition to a virtuous crown bestowed by her mother and aunts for giving up the sinful love affair. And on the other hand she sees objectively and honestly that there is real value in avoiding sensuous stimulation as well as in the further development of her sincere relationship with the boy.

The way out is difficult to see as long as we talk about tendencies, drives and needs. It becomes quite obvious, however, as soon as we relate the tendencies, drives and needs to their underlying imagery. The Ego-image of the spoiled girl is very apparent. She wants everything, satisfaction of the senses and of her religious ambition, the heavenly crown for her head and the thrill for her inner glands: the Ego-image is undoubtedly the spoiled child, the pet, "Her Majesty, the baby." And here again we see that the Ego-image produces contradictory claims and is not creative enough to reconcile them. Therefore it resorts to a special form of negative life, the blunder—a poor and sterile attempt to satisfy the two contradictory tendencies at once: to write the letter without doing so, to serve both masters, to be the sweetheart and the nun. And all this in complete innocence, without any consciousness of the Ego's refined diplomacy!

As far as the Ego is concerned it has caught itself in the meshes of its own net. There is no way out. But, as soon as we look for the objective and creative images which may be found in the deeper layers behind the Ego-image, the whole picture changes immediately. We call this process searching for the virtue behind the vice. We try to unearth the creative power-image behind the sterile Ego-image. And if we succeed it may help us to discover even the real center, the Self, behind the Ego, and thus to reverse the whole development of egocentricity.

The latter result, however, can be expected only if the blunders (or whatever the negative results of the negative life may be) originate so much suffering that a real crisis, the breakdown of the Ego and the beginning of a new life, becomes unavoidable. The blunder in such a case would lead to catastrophe, and what at first sight seemed to be a superficial mistake would turn out to be the fatal action which changes the whole life.

Suppose, for instance, that the girl in our example were to argue with her friend about the unmailed letter, and in trying to get rid of him, in a moment of utmost despair, she were to hurry across the street just when the lights change and a car knocks her down. Psychological half-suicides like this are not rare. They always show the exact structure of the blunder as we have described it.

During the crisis that follows, the Ego-image would lose its rigidity. The girl would "turn and become like a child," the real, creative, undaunted child rather than the spoiled pet. And the image of the growing, loving, conscious and conscientious girl would emerge and lead her to the simple yet creative discovery: "I love the boy, and therefore I want to see him. But we should not satisfy our mutual and egocentric desire for sexual enjoyment. If we cannot find a way of being together without going too far and too fast in our caresses—then we'd better quit until we grow more mature."

All his egocentric objections she would sweep away smilingly: "I hate the selfish little boy you are! Because I love the mature man you will be. Don't come to see me before you are a grown-up man!"

If you object that this creative and courageous attitude could not be expected from a young girl, you may be right. But this only means that usually a young girl in such a situation does not really face her crisis. She does not suffer honestly and does not know her own "heart's sincere desire." Neither her mother nor her lover can help her, both being equally lost in their own egocentric mazes. And life, being patient and kind, does not yet put her to the crucial test of being run over by an automobile. Therefore the girl probably will blunder along, serving two masters, writing letters and not mailing them—until her negative life in the course of the years heaps so many failures and disappointments on her shoulders that finally her Ego breaks down and she stops blaming others and begins to discover her own responsibility.

The Ego, as we have seen, is in a desperate position. Like a bad government it braces itself against outer troubles, but it chooses the wrong way, runs into inner troubles, and therefore collapses when the outer troubles grow serious enough. The inner difficulties which we have described as "negative life" are the result of our inner conflicts between the Ego and the repressed images. They provoke outer difficulties—and often just the kind of difficulties that they are supposed to prevent.

Our distrust induces people to leave us alone; then we feel betrayed, and think that our distrust was justified. Or we attract people by our excessive friendliness, then our repressed vanity explodes in an outburst of anger, or, even worse, hurts them secretly by half-conscious calumnies and unjust criticism. Thus, we unconsciously destroy what we consciously build; the weapons of our Ego-defense become the means which finally annihilate the Ego.*

The most dangerous of these weapons is the transference of our earlier experiences to similar current situations in the form of rigid expectations, fears or claims. Generalized prejudices must lead to disappointment, quarrels, offenses and anger. If you believe that all teachers are hypocrites because your first teacher really was one, or if you expect all doctors to treat you gratis because your family doctor did so when you were a child, you will certainly run into trouble. Yet, less obvious and more subtle transferences may have an even more disastrous effect. If you pursue the unconscious policy of hiding your intimate feelings, because your elder brother used to ridicule them, this inhibition will poison all your friendships and stifle your marriage.

Life asks us new questions every day. Our former answers have to be revised time and again. We must be creative, discovering new aspects of the truth, and developing new forms of life— or we will perish. A reaction which is right at the age of twenty may be wrong at forty; and a principle of business or politics which was successful in 1925 may be disastrous in 1980. Time, the changing outer circumstances, is against rigidity; egocentricity, the artificial inner equilibrium, is rigid, because rigidity seems

---

*The so-called "suicide of the Ego" can be understood in many cases as the result of the Ego's one-sidedness and rigidity without resort to unconscious influences. In some cases, however, the interference of the Shadow is so evident that its contribution to the final development of the whole personality cannot be overlooked. The reason a drunkard drinks, for example, is only in its outer appearance egocentric: his Ego rebels against restraint. The real power of his vice belongs to the Shadow. Therefore he cannot be helped unless or until his Shadow is integrated.

to be its only means of survival; therefore time will destroy the Ego, the changing outer circumstances will abolish the rigid patterns of our inner life.

The citadel of egocentricty is attacked from outside and inside at the same time. The new outer situation which requires a new adjustment, and the old inner conflict which makes the new adjustment difficult, seem to cooperate purposefully to defeat the Ego. Then the Ego musters its last reserves for a last-ditch stand, and again the result is a betrayal: the last reserves turn out to be enemies. The student who has put off writing his paper until the last day is caught in a vicious circle. The more afraid he is of failure, the more tense he grows; his tension prevents creative work; he worries; time elapses, unused; his fear increases; and the final mobilization of all his will power creates only anger against himself, new tension, new excitement—and no work at all.

Many psychologists have observed the "law of reversed effort." It is usually described as the fact that an unusual conscious effort brings about an opposite result. The bicyclist who strives to avoid the stone will hit it. If this were the whole truth the law of reversed effort would mean the definite collapse of all ethics, moral education and even civil legislation. The law tells you that you should not steal; you try to obey, and the very attempt to avoid theft causes you to steal. This fortunately is not true, in spite of St. Paul's experience: "The command gave an impulse to sin, and sin resulted for me in all manner of covetous desire" (Rom 7:8).

The "law of reversed effort" should be replaced by the "law of materialized fear." The bicyclist hits the stone not because of his desire to avoid it, but because of his fear that he may be unable to avoid it. His Ego-image tells him to avoid the stone; the Shadow whispers: You certainly will break your neck. If the Shadow prevails, the latter will happen. The fear of failure on the part of the Ego means distrust in its own strength and the growing conviction that its inner enemy, the Shadow, will one day win the upper hand. The Ego's fear increases the strength of the Shadow.

Here we are confronted with the central question as to where the power of the Ego and the Shadow originate, and which agency or rule is responsible for the distribution of power and therefore for the final victory or defeat. There is no doubt that the original source of power here again is the real center, the Self. The Ego, the Shadow, and all the other images, repressed or not, deviated or not, are mere channels of power. The more they preserve their original connection with the Self the stronger is their activity, whether conscious or unconscious. The more completely they are cut off from the Self the more they wither and finally become atrophic like the muscles in a paralyzed arm. The Ego-image is usually separated from the Self by rigid walls, and the conscious life of the egocentric individual therefore gradually loses its zest and creativity until finally he himself admits that he does not really live. His life, as far as it is conscious and egocentric, becomes shallow, unreal and meaningless. The real center and the real value remain inaccessible to the Ego, behind the walls in the depth of the unconscious.

The Shadow is separated from the Ego by the same walls, which means it is repressed into the unconscious together with the real center. But the connection between the center and the Shadow is not seriously damaged. Therefore the Shadow does not wither. Its repression turns its power into the negative direction. It becomes destructive, as we have said, but it remains young, primitive and vigorous, like the oppressed peasantry in a feudalistic country.

At the beginning of the egocentric development, the different channels convey an equal amount of power. Ego and Shadow are balanced. Later the Ego declines in vigor because of its separation from the center, and the Shadow becomes comparatively stronger because, as we may now say, the center supports it, in spite of its negativity, while the Ego is gradually forsaken. This is why the egocentric person appears to be satisfied, successful and even happy during the first half of his life. Later, however, his rigidity increases, and his whole occupation becomes Ego-defense. The inner enemy, the Shadow, seems to grow, and the fact that it remains unknown (that is, unconscious) increases the danger. Then all kinds of doubt, skepticism, distrust, fear, hypochondria and anxiety foreshadow the impending breakdown.

The startling fact is that the real Self favors the Shadow in opposition to the Ego, in spite of the Shadow's destructiveness. Consider the drunkard. He may be a pious hypocrite as long as he is sober. Then he drinks. His Shadow usurps the throne for a short time, yet long enough to destroy thoroughly the sham-values of his egocentric life: his reputation, his career, his family life, his friendships break down. He cannot resist the temptation; in spite of all this disaster, he drinks again. His destructive Shadow is stronger than all his egocentric "good will"—because, and as long as, his "good will" is nothing but an egocentric device. He will lose the battle time and again; the powers of evil, his addiction, will be stronger than his best purposes and his most holy promises—because, and as long as, his egocentricity, hypocrisy, and self-deception are the more dangerous evil.

The strategy of the power of life is far from being one of acquiescence and appeasement. Life has to be lived, and destructive life, bad as it is, is still preferable to seeming death. Destruction arouses overwhelming forces on the positive side, anxiety can be turned into creativity, and hatred can be redeemed by love. But unlived life is worse. To bury the talent is a greater sin than to misuse it. Average egocentric people, "whitewashed tombs, looking comely on the outside," are in their unconscious filled with buried talents, repressed possibilities, which have turned into the negative and now are "dead men's bones and all manner of impurity." If we do not find an antiseptic way, a religious way, to cleanse our tombs, the impurity will come out into the open. That will be bad, but better than the whitewashed lie.

Every egocentric person denies these statements, calling them ridiculous superstition or unscientific speculation—unless he is sophisticated enough to accept them theoretically and to all practical purposes shelve them, together with other "interesting psychological remarks," by writing a book about them. If the statements are right, however, neither sophistication nor ridicule can invalidate them. Tension and sleeplessness, inhibition and irritability, will do their work. The hounds of heaven, by the Ego called the hounds of hell, will corner us. The crisis, the breakdown of the Ego, will begin.

Then all the disasters of human life seem to clamp down on us in the same moment. Our friends fail us; our health fades away; the doctor shrugs his shoulders, and his silence seems to say "cancer." Our opponents' lawyer starts a new lawsuit; our work lags and the boss is impatient. Well, we may know that most of this is our own apprehension, but the insight does not help us. We feel like a swimmer tossed about by the dark waves of the ocean, exhausted, hopeless, and about to sink.

In such a situation we are ready to pay any price. The slightest relief would be accepted gladly even if the whole Ego had to be sacrificed. Survival in any form, under any condition, even death itself, would be welcome, if only this nightmare, which has now become reality, would disappear—or if reality, now a nightmare, would only change.

And then, there are voices offering help. There are always several voices. And we choose one of them. It is no conscious and deliberate choice; we are worn out, tormented, and grasp the hand which seems to offer the quickest relief. And in almost every case the choice is wrong. We make a new blunder. We choose the tempters, the pseudo-saviors, the "false Christs, and false prophets" who "bring forward great signs and wonders" (Mt 24:24). The crisis stops short of the utmost catastrophe, our anguish is relieved, our old individualistic Ego is replaced by a new ready-made group-Ego, and the second half of the crisis is postponed for a long time to come.

Part II:
Self-Education
The Principles of Self-Education

One conclusion drawn from our investigations thus far is that in the course of the development of human character one ordinarily moves from the state of the Original-We over more or less lengthy detours which we describe as egocentricity to a new and higher kind of We-relationship—a We-centricity called the Maturing-We.

If we accept this conclusion, we must face some important questions. Is it possible in everyday life to avoid the detours or to shorten them or to accelerate the passage over them toward the

Maturing-We? If so, to what extent may this be done and by what means? And what about escaping the crisis altogether? We have already described the complete breakdown of the egocentric shell—the Ego—as the major crisis, and we have added that this catastrophe may be replaced by several minor, or even by minimal, crises. The question then arises: By what means could we replace the greater crisis within our own lives by smaller ones or even avoid them entirely without losing their effect?

Many useful consequences can be drawn from the application of the theories of the We-Psychology to education, mental hygiene, and psychotherapy. We shall, however, restrict ourselves here to the most difficult and perhaps the most important side of the problem, namely self-education. By this we mean the process by which a human being may deliberately and purposefully deal with his own deeply rooted egocentricities so that character develops or matures.

It must be obvious that improvement in our behavior is often possible with little effort. Almost as soon as our attention is called to some shortcoming, we are able to correct it. This common experience seems to be due to the fact that the mistake we undertake to correct is not felt to be a vital part of our lives. It is not directly or indirectly related to the Ego, and there is, therefore, little or no resistance either to the criticism which points out the error or to giving it up for a sounder viewpoint. This type of minor improvement often comes about through a person's own efforts to understand himself and is in one sense a form of self-education, but it is not that self-education with which we are concerned here. We are dealing with genuine egocentric reactions which are much more difficult to understand and to modify or replace.

In We-Psychology self-education is more meaningful than elsewhere. For us, the individual Self is part of a higher unit which consists of many and different Selves. We call this unit the We and we think of it as a growing or, better, an increasingly dynamic entity. Thus, the way to participation in the Maturing-We is through the increasing realization of the potentialities of the Self. The rigidity of social and moral forms—that one has to dress or to behave in a certain way or paint or write in a certain style—is or should be replaced by comradeship, social conscience, solidarity, love, inventiveness, and other attitudes and behavior resulting from We-feeling. Since the development in the Maturing-We eventually includes all these, the education of the Self, as we use the phrase, means something like the next practical steps in the direction of religious and social progress. These now become a matter of normal growth rather than something superimposed upon an inherently weak and defective Self.

We need to find out these steps not only because we should be better prepared to help suffering mankind, but because we must either take them or suffer ourselves. However the wish to be better prepared to help mankind has often proved itself in the course of human history useless as a motive in spite of its ethical soundness. The efficiency of moral principles as motivation presupposes: We-feeling persons. The appeal to these principles presupposes what they create. One, for example, who has not already developed a sensitivity to human need does not readily respond, if at all, to an appeal in its name.

The point at which the egocentric person is most readily touched is his egocentric welfare; therefore, the original impulse toward self-education often must be formulated as an appeal to our egocentricity, wherein a strange paradox becomes apparent. As a matter of fact, we must face the alternative either of suffering the consequences of our egocentricity even to the extent of experiencing a major crisis or of taking this next step in the direction of religious and social progress. The paradox is that even from the egocentric viewpoint it seems advisable to decrease our egocentricity for the sake of decreasing the suffering from it. Whoever realizes that this is true has already begun to "educate himself," and the egocentric era in his life comes nearer to its end.

This paradox is the very kernel of our theory of the crisis. Even egoism itself recommends that we become less egoistic. Here we meet the first principle in the art of self-education as the We-Psychology is to display it. Its name is "pressure."

The task of character development is the destruction of our own egocentric shell in order to set free and develop the We-feeling productivity which was shut up within the shell. That would be a nearly impossible task without the help of some power coming from without. At first the shell is realized in the form of the Ego. When I say I, I usually mean my Ego. The imprisoned Self is felt—if at all—as an It, a kind of unknown, almost foreign force that one ordinarily fears. Thus the task is that I, saying I, should not identify myself—as formerly—with the Ego, but now with the Self. My viewpoint should shift from the Ego-center, the Seeming-Self, to the true center, the real Self.*

If this were possible by mere will-power the shell and the egocentricity would not be what they are—the old fortifications against anguish and fear. They seem to us to be the walls behind which we suppose the tigers and lions wait ready to seize us if they could get out. Suppose I have learned that I have to be the "good," the obedient, child. In playing my egocentric role I am impelled to look for approval and to avoid everything which may displease my friends, but when I lay it aside I display the courage and We-feeling qualities of my Self by opposing injustice and objecting to my friends when they are wrong.

Insofar as I act my egocentric role, I feel afraid that my reactions might be inspired by We-feeling and courage. I fear such reactions because they seem to be dangerous to what seems to be my best interests seen from the viewpoint of the Ego or the Seeming-Self, and I hate these possibilities of being We-feeling and courageous as if they were wild beasts waiting to attack me. The greedy Star fears his kindly impulses because they tend to separate him from his money, which seems so essential to his stardom, and the Nero fears his We-feeling impulses because they represent weakness which would make others less fearful of him and therefore less submissive. We unconsciously oppose the destruction of these walls—these egocentric fortifications—even though we are consciously trying to demolish them and to laugh at them as being obsolete, useless, and childish.

We cannot pull ourselves out of the swamp by our own hair as the famous knight in the fairy tale did. We cannot succeed unless an outer force—the pressure—comes to our assistance. Mere idealism, or moral endeavor, or, in most cases, even insight would not be sufficient.

---

*In the later stages of development, when "I" has grown to mean the Self, the Ego is—not always but sometimes—realized as the It, i.e., the bad old habit, the moral weakness we repudiate, or even something like a temptation.

Imagine that you have recognized for a long time your bad habit of putting off disagreeable things and especially answering letters. You have decided many times to replace this procrastination with a better habit, but even though you know what it means—that it is a symptom of egocentricity and that you should correct the mistakes of your Ego—all your good purposes and decisions have failed. Let us imagine also that you discover, in your business or professional work, that the consequences of this carelessness have become dangerous to you, and that you are now able to find the way out and to "educate yourself." The motive for your change was not strong enough as long as it was a mere "moral" one. Now it becomes real, powerful and evokes egocentric fear as well as objective suffering. Life itself helps self-education by punishing mistakes and rewarding progress. This punishment—this corrective influence—inflicted by life is what we call "pressure." It represents life exacting the penalty for the violation of its laws.

The individual becomes aware of pressure—feels it—as a disturbing situation which he more or less correctly understands. Considered from the viewpoint of the individual's reaction to pressure, we may describe it formally as a disturbing situation which is immediately and exactly realized. It is necessary to say "immediately and exactly realized" because there are many dangerous situations not realized at all. Medieval painters sometimes represented a person unwittingly dancing with Death just as today some cartoonist pictures a speeding driver with Death at his side. The situation is very dangerous even if it is not understood by the dancer or driver.

Our problem sometimes is the same, perhaps less urgent or more so. There are people who think themselves well situated—healthy, successfully married and widely respected. They do not suspect that their comrades laugh at them, that their mates betray them, their children hate them and that they are neurotics or worse. On the other hand, there are people who feel an immense pressure from life itself. They lack money, an advantageous job, friends, health. Or they are just afraid without knowing what they fear.

From the psychological viewpoint their situation is better than that of the dancer with Death. They are aware (as the dancer was not) of something foreboding—the pressure. But the trouble is that they do not recognize *exactly,* that is correctly, the source of the pressure and what it means. They accuse the outer world, their bad luck, their family, their friend, and their spouses. They do not understand that they cause the major part of all their difficulties by their own egocentric behavior. Sometimes they pretend to be the worst kind of personalities, lost souls, hopeless failures—excusing by these exaggerations their complete lack of self-education.

To discover the real source of most of their difficulties in all these cases is to discover, besides certain outer circumstances which may present serious problems, the egocentric shell as the decisive inner condition. A person's own wrong attitudes are the very essence of most of his suffering. At the moment this discovery is made the pressure is realized and becomes efficient. It becomes the motor of further research, the increasing stimulus for attempts to get rid of the wrong attitude. Up until this moment one remains blind to the real causes of his difficulties.

The pressure must be felt immediately. The schoolboy who prefers to play instead of doing his schoolwork may feel the impending pressure of tomorrow, yet the sparrow in his hand seems more valuable than the pigeon on the roof. He does not care about tomorrow, for his reality is the present moment. The next morning he will feel the pressure as present, but almost without connection with the sunshine and the forgotten schoolwork of yesterday. In such a case self-education is not yet possible, because the boy cannot yet *feel* (though he may understand intellectually) that the distress of tomorrow may outweigh the pleasure of today. This is a problem of maturity. The mature person anticipates the consequences in the right way. The neurotic is very often inhibited by too much anticipation, an exaggerated fear of what *could* come.

Pressure should be felt as present, or an earnestly foreseen or anticipated future difficulty. To be rightly dealt with it must be correctly seen in its relationship to one's own inner problem—to egocentricity and self-development. Many things may supply the original impulse to self-education. There may be the bad results of inclinations to gamble or drink or the unfortunate consequences of an aversion to certain persons or to an occupation.

There may be the bad results of an egocentric defense of the Seeming-Self or of efforts to enhance its prestige. There may be blunders and failures which arise from the inner conflict between different egocentric tendencies. The discomfort or suffering resulting from these bad results gives the original impulse to correct the faults as soon as it is realized that these faults are the real cause of the discomfort or suffering.

The original impulse leads to reflection, observation, and better purposes, but new frustrations are often encountered. They prove that the correction of the fault is more difficult than it seemed to be in the first moment of realization. One has to examine his own life more carefully, has to collect new experiences and, first of all, to find out the source of the pressure. Otherwise, it will increase and someday bring about a minor or even a major crisis.

Pressure is inevitable. Egocentric living involves acting on mistaken ideas, pursuing false goals, being swayed by unsound emotions, and all this leads to difficulty and distress. Life cannot be lived on untrue premises or filled with deluded behavior without creating pressure sooner or later even though it be felt only in the haunting fears or vicious nightmares of one's dreams. Life is so organized that unsound living cannot lead in the long run to that poise, calm, courage, and peace which is the opposite of pressure. One cannot act on mistakes and pursue false goals without violating basic self-executing laws of life, and these violations always result in some form of difficulty and distress which is characteristic of pressure.

It follows, then, that one ought not to rebel against pressure. Like bodily pain, this psychic discomfort is unpleasant and should be relieved as soon as possible by dealing wisely with its cause. But like pain, it is a beneficent thing, because it warns of danger. It points out an unwholesome condition which might otherwise go unnoticed far longer than it should. The distress of pressure calls attention to unwholesome conditions, thereby making it possible to correct them. One of the first lessons in self-education is that one should welcome the discomfort of pressure because of the opportunities for growth which it is capable of revealing. A person ought not to be sorry for himself but rather glad that some source of difficulty in one's life may be disclosed by the pressure.

In discussing pressure we see that it is difficult to know when real pressure, as opposed to mere imaginative suffering, is at work and to what sources it can be traced. It is hard to distinguish between the two in order to know when we have to deal with nothing more than neurotic, imaginative suffering. The sham-pain of a Clinging Vine, for instance, sometimes leads to attempts at self-education. However they must fail since the Clinging Vine seeks suffering as a means of moving others to pity or serve him. Therefore it is difficult to foresee which suffering is genuine, and what attempts to change one's inner structure may be useful and not a neurotic bluff.

A certain amount of objective research is a necessary part of the self-education that develops character. Unconscious connections must be discovered and cleared up; faults, weak spots, fears, or aims of which we were not hitherto aware must be explored. We must look at them with the curiosity of the scientist, not with shame or moral devaluation or even horror.

If we are not scientifically impersonal and dispassionate in searching out our faults, we shall never be able to dig up out of the deeper and unknown layers of our inner life the very thing that must be changed. When we look at our lives from the viewpoint of the Ego, we strive for superiority as the person we seem to be, or at least for security. Now if some unrealized attitude of forgotten experience in my life would, at the moment of its appearance in the light of consciousness, be condemned as "bad," I would not, because of my egoistic thinking, acknowledge it as mine, in order to avoid an increasing inferiority feeling.

Therefore, a moralistic standpoint strengthens the egocentric resistance against self-knowledge; we never see what our mistakes are if we wish to be "stainless." The most serious errors in the Ego will not be realized as such because they are an essential part of this Seeming-Self. The only way to escape self-deception and to unmask ourselves successfully is to suspend all moral and ethical judgment until the investigation has been ended. Thus, the second principle in self-education is in accord with the saying in the Sermon on the Mount: "Do not judge." However we must add at once a psychological observation very important in our days. Many persons have what we call "reversed valuation." The mistakes of their Ego are such that they would not have inferiority feelings even if recklessness or sensuality or wantonness were discovered in the depth of their unconscious life. On the contrary, they would be pleased. In these cases the egocentric goal (+100) is something such as being the Don Juan who conquers the greatest number of girls or the "good fellow" who drinks the most wine or the shrewd trader who "gets ahead of" every person he deals with. Those who pursue such goals would feel devalued if this research would prove them more "moral" than they want to be. They disown their virtuous inclinations, which they deem ridiculous, just as the moralizer disowns his "lower impulses." Consequently, they pretend not to be afraid of the "immoral specters" which are to be found in their inner life, but they are, nevertheless, afraid of what may turn up out of their unconscious, since it would be something "moral."

From the viewpoint of their Ego, they cannot value loyalty, kindness, righteousness, love, and religion. For them, all the We-feeling qualities seem related to inferiority. They are "forbidden" and repressed or suppressed and seem intolerable when viewed from the viewpoint of the Seeming-Self. To recognize and value these We-feeling tendencies would threaten the breakdown of the Ego. Therefore, even in these cases it is necessary, if a person would discover his mistakes, for him to suspend all valuation of a situation as moral or immoral.

On the other hand, this unconscious defense of our Ego—the Seeming-Self—against everything that, by reason of criticism, seems to be an attack upon us may be very helpful in our efforts to investigate our own lives. It may supply us with an important clue as to our own weaknesses. The more we feel offended by what we interpret as a reproach, the more it is probable that the criticism hits the nail on the head, even if we do not at the time find anything in our conscious life to support the reproach. We are resentful or angry because we see ourselves as the most objective Self in the world or at least one who is very little misled.

Strong negative emotions like anger, irritation, and indignation usually but not always indicate that our weak spot has been touched consciously or unconsciously. The more we protest the more likely it is because the Seeming-Self appears to be endangered, and the nearer we are, if we are discerning, to our goal—the destruction of the Ego and the consequent release of the Self.

In order to discover our true inner situation, it is necessary to overcome our own egocentric inner resistance in the form of some negative mood. We should, therefore, learn to understand and handle them. To that task we shall turn in the next chapter.

It is not only interesting but important to know as much as we can about our own personality, yet it would be far too optimistic to believe that, by self-knowledge and nothing else, we could improve the attitudes and overcome the faults of our Ego. We cannot achieve that result even though we use the best Freudian methods to bring the unconscious contents of the mind to consciousness. Some slight symptoms may disappear simply by becoming aware. But more serious faults—the bad inclination, passions, and inhibitions—the average troubles of average people—cannot be overcome unless the indispensable self-knowledge leads to real changes in reactions, behavior decisions, in short to new and sound experiences.

However we cannot study We-Psychology without asking ourselves what type of egocentricity may be ours.* We should not be satisfied with our own or our friend's first reactions, for very often more reflection and further research reveal quite a different type from the one we first take for granted. Moreover, we must remember that no human being is ever one hundred percent true to any one pattern. The Ego of any one of us is a mixture of two or more of the various types. In some situations and at some times one might well discover in himself behavior that fits more than one Ego pattern.

Yet, in the main, the Ego conforms more or less to one single pattern, and it is ordinarily possible for a person through self-observation to recognize which role he is acting, even though it is true that appearances are deceptive. It seems almost as if the Ego were a living being seeking to deceive us by wearing a mask so lifelike that it is almost impossible to distinguish it from the reality it covers.

The best way to conduct this Ego investigation is to ask ourselves what goal we would like to attain, if we could choose. It

---

*Sometimes it is useful to try to recall one's earliest recollections in order to find out what kind of fear or wish may have been developed. Our experience has shown that the choice of our early recollections is influenced by our Ego and therefore our idea about our earliest recollections may reflect our egocentricity and help us discover our type.

is important to make this choice alone or together with some very good and completely understanding comrade, but not in the presence of moralizing friends or relatives who expect us to be heroes and very virtuous. What we are trying to do is to understand our egocentric reactions, uninfluenced by what we feel we ought to choose or what would be expected of us by those who set ideal attainments for us. We must be prepared to recognize a choice which may seem embarrassing to us, which we should not care to disclose even to a good friend simply because it would not be approved of and might even be condemned. Frankly, perhaps even jokingly, we should imagine ourselves in the situation in which we should really like to be, laying aside all idealism. Otherwise, our moral or philosophical or religious convictions would likely keep us from being honest.

If we understand what is involved in such a choice it will be vastly easier for us to face frankly and honestly the things we may find in exploring our thinking and feeling in this connection. This choice is bound to reflect the mistakes in our Ego; in fact, the very reason we try to make such a choice is because it will help us understand our own Ego pattern. We seek that understanding because we are misled and deceived by these mistakes. In playing the role of the person we mistakenly picture ourselves to be in the Ego we are bound to be betrayed into some unsound decisions and to seek some unwholesome goals.

Here we must have something akin to Paul's reaction (Rom 7:15–17). We feel like saying, "It is I and yet not I. This choice seems to represent what I am, yet it is not. If I were freed from the influence of my egoistic thinking, I would choose differently. I would be no longer egocentric but objective. I would see clearly. My Self would be free from its shell, and my choices would be sound and wholesome. Until that freedom comes, I, like all others, am the victim of the human process by which the Ego is developed, and I am misled as they are." That is the fate of every human being. All others have had the same experience. If we could really know their egocentricity, we should discern mistakes and errors on the same level as any of ours even though of quite a different type. There is no necessity of judging ourselves harshly if we find that we are seeking that which should not be sought. Our responsibility in character development is to study our situation honestly, to face what we find unflinchingly and when we have become aware of mistakes to correct them as soon as we can.

This is the purpose of our attempt to understand our Ego pattern. To understand it is simply to become aware of what some of our mistaken ideas may be. The implied goal of our inquiry is the escape from the limitations of those mistakes—from the handicaps and discomforts of egocentric behavior—into the full and satisfying living of which the Self, freed from these deceptions, is capable.

Suppose now that, pursuing your inquiry in this spirit, you discover you feel you want to be secure, peaceful, unpretentious, left alone in calmness with sufficient supply of food. Are you acting objectively as a follower of Rousseau and a priest of pure nature? Or would it be more honest to admit that you are thinking of yourself in a rather well-formed Turtle Ego pattern?

If your goal, your highest value, is security with indulgence and the protection of a good, reliable, strong person, if you are looking all the time to see whether this godlike person—a priest or employer or husband or wife—may find you (without thinking too much of trying to find him or her yourself), are you then a loyal and modest servant of the good? Perhaps you are reacting according to the passive and dependent Clinging-Vine pattern.

If you dream of laurels, fame, glory, and riches in order to be admired, or of splendid achievements in arts or sciences, probably you are playing the role of an egocentric Star. You may object that good achievements are objectively necessary for cultural progress and that you wish to serve the whole race and not just your Ego. Well, that may be. If so, you would not be offended if you invent something greatly beneficial to mankind and another person becomes famous because of it. Suppose you create a beautiful role on the stage and some director is credited with giving you the idea and by his direction inspiring your work. Could you imagine this without rebellion? And if you could, you must somewhat distrust your reaction and be ready to recognize some egocentric remnants in your We-feeling attitude. Even the martyr to injustice may be acting a Star role.

Finally, if power is what you want and you think you want it for the service of humanity, don't trust your thinking too much. It is better to test it carefully. Imagine, for example, that you do everything necessary to form and build up a new and needed organization, but someone else, who has done nothing, is made president and exercises many privileges, great authority, and extensive influence. Would you be satisfied? St. Francis built a monastery and then lived in it as a simple monk, one of the others being the abbot. He seems clearly not to have had a Nero type Ego. And you? The more you really want the power for power's sake only—and that means for your own sake—the less you would feel you could tolerate such injustice! And the more you are playing the part of a Nero.

The next step in verifying or correcting our idea about what type or mixture of type we are is to consider the matter which we call the question of the abyss. For all of us there is something that seems to be an abyss into which we must not fall, an experience or situation so dreadful that we can scarcely bear to imagine it for ourselves. It is too terrible, too frightening, too unbearable. This abyss is always closely connected with our Ego. It is the depth of life which is the very extreme opposite of the heights of experience which our Ego leads us to seek. Therefore, to know one's abyss is to know much about one's Ego type.

Some questions are very helpful at this point. What would be the most unbearable, most horrible situation in which you could imagine yourself? What seems worse than death? Is it more the loss of esteem and recognition (the preacher who is laughed at), the loss of power (the officers whose commands are not obeyed), the loss of security and protection (the spoiled rich woman who loses all her money), or the loss of seclusion and privacy (the official who retired early but who is called back to service again)?

We should work out this part of our investigation as carefully as possible, preferring always to think of the concrete situation— the scene, the immediate experience—and not of the abstract term or name for our reactions and apparent qualities. Only at last, having collected many memories and made many "experiments by imagination," can we come to see what intermixture of types are involved in our Ego.

As an outer aid to this inner process, and as such only, we give a rough outline of the highest values and the abysses of the four Ego types as they appear to the self-investigator. Again it must be said that in real life one finds a thousand different kinds

and shades of egocentric attitudes. However, this elementary
outline may be useful to the new student of We-Psychology in
classifying his memories and the products of his imagination.

	THE GOAL	THE EGO TYPE AND ITS "THEME"	THE ABYSS
PASSIVE	Absolute security granted and guaranteed by a reliable and mighty protector.	Clinging Vine. Strives for security and protection, a hothouse plant seeking warmth.	Loss of protection. Being forced to depend on one's own resources.
	Absolute privacy and calmness; to be undisturbable.	Turtle. Wants to be left alone.	To be disturbed; to be touched, stirred up to emotional reactions.
ACTIVE	Greatest popularity, recognition, and applause.	The Star. Wants to be admired.	To be laughed at, despised, ridiculed. Loss of dignity and esteem.
	Absolute power, blind obedience by and devotion from followers.	The Nero. Wants power for power's sake.	Loss of influence; not to be obeyed, or even to have to obey.

To the various means of self-education mentioned here we
must add another which is a special form of what may be called
meditation. Since it is much better to describe the process than to
define it, let us suppose that I am facing some Black Giant and
trying to discover its origin. At length I understand that my first
Black Giant was my father. Now I strive to remember everything
about him, and especially my negative reactions to him, and as I
do so I find that other impressions come in, or had already come
in during my childhood. They are impressions out of fairy tales or
old bad dreams or myths or superstitious gossip. My emotion was
not only conditioned by my father's real attitude, but at the same
time by certain images, imaginations, and vague apprehensions
which had been evoked out of my inner life by other experiences.

On the other hand there was a quite definite wish—almost a

demand—that the father should display certain qualities which would meet my needs. This longing for the "good father" increased, became exaggerated and created at last an ideal of fatherhood which apparently was superhuman. Yet, in spite of this enhancement, my "image of fatherhood" became an avenue for understanding the essence and the different attitudes of paternity. Meditating this way, behind my own ideal of fatherhood, I gradually discover the objective idea and the emotional and mental reactions which are or should be connected with this experience. At length I may for the first time, even if I have been a father for several years, come to know something like a human father who represents all human fathers, and I understand better now the full range of a father's reactions. His joys, frustrations, responsibilities, influence, and limitations are seen from the inside as they appear to human fathers collectively.

Age and sex and social situation present no serious obstacles to this kind of meditation. We can find the way to "see from inside" the opposite sex, old age, the rich, the poor—only it takes us a longer time. Quite a series of attempts, different approaches and much patience are necessary to feel, for instance, how the other sex may see the world, and we shall never understand it entirely. However the nearer we come to see the feminine viewpoint, if we are men, and vice versa, the more we are capable of understanding our mother and the Original-We, which included us once, and the Breach-of-the-We, which pushed us out of the paradise of our first years.

Sometimes the more general conception of the human mother may be the approach to our personal mother with her special attitude and temperament. Sometimes our concrete mother and certain remembrances, revealing the relationship between our mother and her children, may lead us to understand in a deeper sense what human motherhood means. Pictures like Raphael's Sistine Madonna, or well-known characters in literature may come to our mind helping us to understand certain sides or traits of motherhood. On the other hand this meditation may help us to understand some works of art, which we have known but not yet appreciated.

One of the students of We-Psychology who had had rather serious difficulties with his mother was inclined to deem her as "not a mother at all," until in the course of such meditation the powerful and gloomy "Queen of the Night" in Mozart's "Magic Flute" came to his mind. Suddenly he understood that the "idea of the mother" may not only include protection and love but also the deep and natural instinct which wants to avert all danger and risk from the child. In such a case the slightest admixture of egocentricity transforms the loving protection into rigid jealousy or wilful possession. Now he understood the pressure which had spoiled his whole childhood was the expression of a certain kind of immaturity in his mother's personality, and he felt within her dominating attitude the natural and almost mysterious power of maternity. Even the distorted egocentric personality seemed to conceal deep within it the original perfume of mother love.

The Egocentric Emotions

The pressure reaction, which we must understand if we are to make the basic changes in our behavior necessary for the development of character, involves some egocentric emotion and expression of it. In the pressure situation we feel depressed, indignant, or terrified. Perhaps we may be angry, and we do all sorts of foolish and unwise things.

Looking at our behavior critically, we may realize that we should not have these emotions much less let them take command of the situation. It is one thing, however, to know that we ought not to do so and quite another to know how to keep from feeling, say, depressed, terrified, or angry, or from giving undesirable expressions to such feelings. Most of us are idealists enough to know when these emotions are "undesirable reactions" and what expressions may be unwise under any circumstances, yet we have not learned what to do. No mere determination or strength of will is sufficient to keep us from experiencing some negative emotions under pressure. Such qualities may be useful in holding them in check and in determining what expression, if any, we shall permit ourselves to give them. When it comes to keeping from feeling these emotions—when it comes to eliminating the pressure discomfort itself—we are forced to go much beyond determination and will-power into a search for the psychological source of our reactions. We turn to this search from the viewpoint of We-Psychology.

Let us recognize first that there are sound negative reactions which are suitable to the occasion which evokes them. They are the objective answer to negative situations of which disappointment, frustration, and a feeling of danger are examples.

Suppose you expect a good friend for dinner. At the last moment he calls up to say that for reasons beyond his control he cannot come. Should you react with disappointment? Certainly, you should. Yet for how long a time? In what degree, and in which form? If your whole evening is spoiled, your reaction is too strong. If you break with your friend because of his refusal, you are too touchy. If you quarrel with your wife, you simply transfer your emotion from its real cause to an innocent yet convenient (because present) victim.

In these situations we see that there are two different mistakes to be distinguished. The first is the unwarranted strength of the emotion, and the second is its misdirection—the venting of itself upon an object which is really no proper object of its expressions. We shall explain the second case first because it is the simpler situation. Practically, however, we deal in most instances with intermixtures of these two mistakes.

Let us approach our explanation by taking an imaginary situation. Suppose a businessman coming home from the office quarrels with his wife. Dinner is not ready. The evening suit is not laid out. His tie is missing! She thinks: "He is irritable today, business is going wrong." She feels innocent, knowing that the real cause of her husband's mood is to be found in his office. He, perhaps, admits it, but nevertheless he cannot bear his wife's indulgent smile. "Do not look at me condescendingly like that," he rages as he slams a door behind him. Then he thinks: "She is wiser than I am and with better character. That's what drives me mad."

What should you do if you were in the place of this businessman? The formula supplied by We-Psychology is short and clear but it is sometimes very difficult to make it work. The formula reads: "Deeds instead of moods! Replace emotions by objective actions."

Egocentric emotions are involved in attempts to attain the

point +100—that is, the striving for superiority or fighting against −100 (inferiority feelings). Actions as well as emotions can be egocentric or objective, and the more actions are objective, the more they open the way out of the egocentric mood. The objective action, of course, presupposes an objective look at the object with which it is dealing. Our businessman, let us imagine, steps out on his balcony, where he has some flowers. Being angry, he looks at them at first somewhat casually. Then he notices insects upon them and begins to pick them off, working angrily, maybe still explosively sputtering to himself. Even so he is much more objective than before, and his objectivity in the next half hour increases considerably.

The decisive point is that he begins anew to see things as they really are and spends his energy in a useful way. Thus emotion seems to be transferred into physical activity or sensible, workable ideas and adequate thoughts. Looking back from this state to what one did or felt before, one is ashamed and can scarcely understand one's own behavior. Now our businessman is able to see himself and his wife at least somewhat objectively, and his moodiness and irritability diminish or disappear.

In terms of We-Psychology, the connection here can be understood better and stated more exactly. It is not that a blind psychic energy (anger) is transformed into a more useful sort of energy (helpful action). The egocentric attitude of the person has been replaced by a more We-feeling one. Insofar as our businessman felt offended, his goal was to protect his endangered Ego, which seems to be himself. His attention was focused on his own significance, his self-esteem and his self-defense. Therefore, he was alarmed by the slightest danger, feeling seriously attacked by the mere shadow of a casual inconvenience. He was not able to be objective.

Afterward the searchlight of his attention is directed to his flowers or other things in the outer world. He is occupied impersonally with the outer world. The egocentric question: "Who is superior (+100), who is inferior (−100)?" is not involved in what he is doing. The tension of self-esteem (+ or −100) is eased. It is more or less replaced by calm indifference as to his own value, and by adequate interest as to the real problems of the outer world. He finds a sounder position nearer to zero, and at once he understands better his own situation, his wife and his environment. He is more objective and in being so, is more We-feeling. To be completely objective means to be entirely We-feeling at the same time.

Out of this analysis we come to a second formula which may be stated several ways. Do not fix your attention on your own wound; observe as interestedly as possible your surroundings. Or: turn your searchlight on what happens in the outer world; do not focus it upon the problem of your own egocentric self-esteem. Or: remember that your offended Ego is not the center of reality—it is an error, a dream, a mere self-deception, only your Seeming-Self. It should not matter.

Very often the second formula helps to realize the first one. Both are right. Nevertheless there are many cases where they fail the user in spite of all serious endeavor and all pressure and all psychological insight.

The more we have to deal with ordinary egocentric emotion merely transferred to someone or something, the easier it is to overcome it with the help of our formulae in somewhat the way we have described. It is a simple transference and change in the direction of the emotion and can be controlled as indicated above. The more the emotion, transferred or not, is excessive (too strong for its apparent cause) the less it is possible to master it and to replace it by useful deeds.

In the cases of such failure, in spite of a proper application of these formulae, it is evident that they do not help us to get at the very source of the difficulty constituting the pressure. Another attempt and another method of self-education must be applied in order to deal with such an egocentric emotion. A more careful research and a deeper self-understanding must be developed. If fear, for example, is rooted in the deeper layers of the shell (an old fear experienced for the first time in childhood) we must dig deeper to uproot it.

We come now to the most difficult technique in character development insofar as a change in the egocentric reactions to pressure is concerned. Again we turn in imagination to our businessman for a description of the situations and processes to be considered.

Suppose now that our businessman understands that he is unjust to his wife, but he cannot help bearing her a grudge. Seeking to understand the situation better, we discover that his irritation began in his office when his senior associate patted him on the shoulder and said he should not work too hard. It sounded somewhat condescending as if he were a schoolboy and his associate the teacher. He always felt depressed in such a situation, and, without knowing it, he tried to bully the next person he met.

Thus he came to speak harshly to his wife, but she smiled. This again seemed to show that sort of condescension which he felt he could not stand at any price. Now he knows that neither his associate nor his wife is supercilious, yet he feels inferior to them. The more he sees that he is wrong, the more his inferiority feeling increases and the more he behaves like the offended Star or the helpless, injured Clinging Vine.

This is not only a momentary emotion. It is a comparatively permanent readiness to react in the same way. He may have controlled himself successfully a hundred times. He may have regretted many outbursts of his mood, yet in spite of all his good purposes, his emotional reaction remains the same and there is always the same tendency toward undesirable behavior under pressure. The difficulty is that his emotional reaction is greater than it should be and in such cases its direction is independent of logical reasons. Self-education seems to fail and all prayers seem to be in vain.

How should we proceed if we were this unhappy person? The first and most decisive rule we have to obey here has been mentioned already. It runs: Do not fight against your vice. If you do, you cannot find its roots. Observe it curiously, without judging it, and try to trace it back to its origin. For instance, the resentfulness we have been describing shows some important characteristics upon more careful examination. From a study of them we may surmise that the touchiness in question grew out of a certain childish tragedy. The chief trait of this person's "symptom" is a certain peculiar color, so to speak, of his inferiority feeling. His opponent is believed to be superior, condescending, kind, benevolent, and right while he feels that he himself is wrong, guilty, powerless, wretched, lonely and lost. How did such a feeling arise?

Of course, the colors and shades of such "symptoms" are different in different people and also in different periods of the same life. However, their style and their conditions show enough common traits to reduce them to one typical and unfortunate childhood situation. It cannot be one experience or an accident. Usually it is a permanent position in which the child finds itself (let us say, between the child and one of its parents) out of which innumerable bad experiences arose. To understand this childhood situation, it is desirable to look for a concrete experience—a scene, as it were, in the child's life—which represents the whole pedagogical problem of the child and covers at the same time the present symptoms.

To make it as easy as possible to grasp the principles and processes involved, we come back again to the illustration we have been using, which, we hope, may suggest how the reader may replace the circumstances of the example by the details of his own life. Our businessman now seeks to remember when in his childhood he experienced the reactions he has now. At length he may recollect that his older sister always had to look after him. She was well meaning but a little awkward, bursting with kindness, but behind this nice-looking mask, quite egocentric—she was a moral Star with a little touch of the Clinging Vine. His best weapon was to grumble, to slam doors and to suffer conspicuously. These we recognize as the weapons of the Clinging Vine combined with some qualities of the Star or even of an unsuccessful Nero. Suddenly (while we imagine ourselves in the businessman's place), as we are thinking at random about all these things, a very concrete scene, forgotten for many years, may come back to our mind. And at once we know that this picture represents the very essence of our difficulty.*

The boy of four or five was playing with a small boat on the bank of a little stream near his parents' house. He was forbidden to put the toy into the water, yet he did so, and the beautiful ship

---

*One does not always clearly recall one single typical scene. There are cases in which it is sufficient to know the "atmosphere" of the typical event, to recover the feeling tone of some vaguely recalled scene. One cannot even be sure that his scene is not an invention of his imagination. Even so, it is better to imagine or invent *one* concrete scene. It may illustrate very nicely the origin of the symptoms; and the *picture,* whether memory or imagination affects our unconscious more than the mere thought.

floated away. The boy cried and his sister came. Instead of running after the ship (as he expected her to do) she tried to comfort him, saying that it was only because of her forbearance and kindness that she did not scold him as he deserved for disobedience.

He felt neither comforted nor edified by her sermon but only betrayed. The ship was lost. The We-relationship with his sister seemed broken because she did not do as he wished, and—worst of all—he felt unable to stand alone as a single Ego amid this bad and treasonable world. Being a Clinging Vine, his earlier experiences had prevented him from acquiring his own armament against the outer world. Thus, he was forced to cling for protection to his traitress, who remained his guardian, and to be cautious and watchful and indignant, and pretending friendliness at the same time. Only the Sham-We with his guardian-traitress could help him. He had to get her kindness without trusting her. This was the only policy possible for him in his situation. The result was suspicion, resentfulness, irritability.

With the help of this recollection, one understands now the problem which up to the present moment could not be solved—the reconciliation with the sister. As a grown man he loved her, it is true, and thought he had loved her all the time and that he had also excused and forgiven all her pedagogical shortcomings and mistakes, knowing well that she did for him all she was able to do. Now he comes to realize that the viewpoint of his boyhood was still operative within his unconscious life and had been all these years notwithstanding what he had thought. Then it was necessary to forgive her once more—as a boy and as a grown-up person at one and the same time.

Here he faced the problem of forgiveness. Since all of us must face it in one situation or another, we should analyze it here quite carefully. Usually the problem involves the difficulty of understanding the situation. The better we can comprehend it, the more likely we are to forgive. The first step is to seek understanding.

To that end one should endeavor to put himself in imagination into the other's position, to feel how he felt and to understand better than he, the conscious and especially the unconscious reasons why he acted as he did. The undertaking to do this often leads at length to certain highly significant conclusions.

For one thing one may realize that the acts of another are again and again the expression of an Ego which was in a sense forced upon the individual. The circumstances of the Nero's childhood, over which he had no control, all unwittingly brought about a mistaken way of thinking and feeling about himself which seemed sound to him. To the extent that he remains unconscious of these errors, he is much like the color-blind person who simply does not see, and never has seen, things as they really are. Thus, the tyrannical, unjust deeds of an angry Nero may sometimes be understood as the outgrowth of a development in early childhood for which he was not responsible. In the last analysis, taking all the psychological factors into account, it may be possible to feel that these unjust acts are more the deeds of an immature child, or the products of a situation than the deliberate acts of an adult with full insight into all that was involved.*

In some cases it seems impossible to look thus upon the deed and the doer, since it seems that the individual cannot be viewed as the immature child. Perhaps one feels that somehow the Nero ought to have grown up enough to understand the nature of his act and its consequences. Legalistically speaking, we say ignorance is no excuse for a violation of the law. Now one looks at the Nero and his deed from somewhat the same viewpoint, or perhaps one faces a different situation. Let us assume that the Nero has come to the point where he understands his tendencies to be ruthless and to find satisfaction in them. Maybe he even accepts them, seeking to justify himself by saying that it is his nature to act thus. In one sense of the word he cannot be said to have acted unconsciously. He was aware, in a way, of what he was doing.

Even in these cases one must still recognize the fact that egocentricity is back of the deed. It must have been the act of a person who is yet misled by egoistic thinking, unconscious in its origin and still not recognized as the erroneous thing it is. Otherwise the deed never would have been done. A person simply

---

*This argument may in some cases properly be used by the egocentric person himself in seeking forgiveness for the past but he must not rely upon it to excuse future acts.

cannot be objective and act other than in a We-feeling way. The very fact that the Nero acted as he did is proof that he is not yet delivered from his egocentricity. By some such analysis, perhaps more incisive yet, one may come to feel that the Nero did not act with clear vision; that the more malicious his intent was, the less he has really known the full inner meaning of his motives and his deed.

If one can come to look upon the situation from any of these viewpoints, he has, as we say, taken the poison out of the deed. It may sting and hurt and promise death itself, but it has no power to poison one's attitude, and so one can forgive the injury. The reaction of Jesus on the cross seems to be a perfect illustration of what we are talking about. He could say, "Father, forgive them for they know not what they do," because he understood that those who crucified him did not indeed know what they were doing.

Over such a highway of thinking, we may come to the place where we, too, can forgive. If we do not or cannot travel it, there is still another path to the forgiving attitude. It is the realization that we, too, are in need of forgiveness. Somewhere, somehow, we too have worked an injustice on others. Perhaps it was someone near and dear to us. Maybe we have already discovered how great the injury was. Looking back, we may see the past in a new light and with regret realize that we need forgiveness. Sometimes the new viewpoint brings bitter regrets indeed and gives new meaning to the familiar prayer, "Forgive us our debts. . . ."

Even if we have not discovered as yet the specific act of omission or commission which makes us feel, maybe very keenly indeed, the necessity of forgiveness, we must nevertheless realize that we are in need of it. All men are egocentric, all have pursued false goals, all have sometimes achieved $+100$ at the expense of reducing others to -100 perchance with great harm as yet not realized. All are humanly frail. We are no exception. "There is none perfect, no, not one." So, we too must need forgiveness for deeds possibly more grievous than those we are called upon to forgive. Some day our eyes may be opened to see some now wholly unsensed wrong which will cause us to cry out, "Oh, if I had only known," and to seek forgiveness in anguish of spirit.

By some such processes we must come to be able to forgive.

Thus the businessman had to recall memories of his sister's attitude, her features, her eyes, and many other things. For the first time in his life, he came to understand how unhappy and dejected she must have been when he was four or five and she was about twelve. For the first time, too, he was able to look at their—his and his sister's—childhood as a unit. "*Our* childhood was not happy," he thought. "*We* suffered, both of us, and we made each other suffer." It was clear that he had fought against his sister, as it were, even in defending his "independence" against his associate and his wife. He reacted against all these "guardians" in a similar way, as if he were still the four-year-old boy. Sometimes he had felt that he behaved like a boy, yet he had not seen before that he had imputed to the others the hated role of his guardian sister.

This was the reason, too, for his excessive emotional reaction. It was due to an inner state of constant apprehension and quick readiness for self-defense developed by the years of experiences with his sister. Now a trifle could be the external cause of a violent reaction just as a lighted cigarette carelessly thrown aside might set off a terrific explosion of gunpowder. All the old anger, like a store of powder, explodes violently. Thus, it is clear why in his case such a small thing precipitated such undue emotional disturbance.

Then he began to laugh, and he realized that he would not be able to resent this guardianship anymore, now that he saw it not from the viewpoint of the child but as an adult. Yet he was too optimistic. In the next few weeks he relapsed many times into his old reactions, but every time the thought soon came to his mind: "It is not this real person whom I rebuke. It is my twelve-year-old sister, and I am four." The more he felt that this was true, the more it helped him and the more he succeeded in replacing his egocentric emotions by objective deeds.

Here we should say something about prayer. Suppose, in our example, that the businessman had prayed many times that God would deliver him from his irritability. Yet his petition was not granted. Now we see that his demand was too superficial and its fulfillment would have been a pedagogical error, so to speak. The unconscious conflict with his sister, which persisted in the deeper layers of his personality, would never have been settled and his full independence would never have been developed, if his "symptoms" had disappeared before the deeper problem of his maturity had been disclosed. Character cannot be developed in any such evasive superficial way. In such a case, therefore, one's prayer should be: "Help me to solve the problem which lies hidden beneath my shortcomings. Do not deliver me from these symptoms before I see what they mean."

Now, having gone through these experiences of depth psychology—which is possible of course without any knowledge of psychological terms—he was able and ready to take the whole responsibility for his present behavior even though it was caused by old inhibitions and sore spots acquired in childhood. In a certain sense, he even had to take the responsibility for mistakes which his educators had committed. He understands, for instance, that the situation between his sister and himself was unsatisfactory because of a certain bad relationship in childhood between her and her mother which distorted the personality of the sister. This again was caused by the fact that the father, disappointed by his married life, withdrew from his wife and transferred his tenderness to his daughter. The marital frustration, again, was the outcome of certain educational mistakes, very frequent at the time, which had distorted to some extent the personalities of both his parents.

He had to outgrow the stage when he blamed his parents as the guilty ones, then his grandparents, then the wrong attitude of the whole century—until at last he perceived that he had to deal with our general human imperfection and weakness. He found himself to be caught up in the human struggle against the darkness of human ignorance and error. He understood, then, that he could not run away from the battlefield. He had to accept his human destiny, and he did.

Of course it took him a long time to achieve this new degree of maturity, yet there was no other way out. He had to think about his childhood and his family, as if he wanted to write its history, had to go through old fears, reproaches, and mistakes, not only intellectually but also emotionally, by remembering scenes, dreams, feelings, and old family gossip. After such an attempt at inner understanding, life confronted him anew with his Black Giants in the actual everyday experiences and he had to test whether or not he had overcome his tendency to transfer his old fears to the new situations. The ups and downs of success and failure, and the alternation of inner research and meditation with outer trial in everyday life lasted until the old grudge against his sister and the momentary slight disappointment by his wife or his associate became quite different experiences, both conscious now and both controlled by his new insight. Only when this was done could the real We of his marital life develop, freed from the unconscious handicap of the transferred, old and unforgiven struggles with, and injuries by, his sister.

The way described above may be helpful in eighty to ninety percent of our everyday difficulties under pressure. In the average life the realm of the transferred emotions is very large. Both faults, the under- and the over-development of emotional reactions to the original stimulus, usually arise from the same cause. Their true causes are not to be found in the present situation but in the deeper—and mostly unconscious—layers of life where the results of old experiences are like gears which have grown so rusty that they cannot be shifted and therefore the individual is unable to change his speed or to reverse the engine.

It is impossible to change one's behavior by will-power or mere attention as we are so often adjured to do in the name of an older concept of character development. We must discover and correct the trouble in the motor itself, not in the actual handling by the driver—by our conscious self-control. The injunction to control ourselves is a futile appeal to this driver. To repair the engine or perhaps to clean out the rust means to correct old errors, to settle old enmities, to forgive old forgotten injuries, and to attain forgiveness for them. Changing the figure, it means to clean out the cellar of our lives whose door we have kept shut or whose very existence we have ignored.

Now there is no doubt that a good productive development in the Maturing-We group is possible only if one's We-feeling attitude is thoroughly effective in all parts of our life. However, the Breach-of-the-Original-We and its results (egocentricity, rigid inner laws, compulsory fighting against inferiority and striving for superiority—in short, all that we have described as the shell) has taken root in these unconscious parts of our personality which correspond to (and have been formed in) the years of our early childhood.

In order to become really mature, and that means effectively We-feeling in the sense of the Maturing-We unit, we should relive our childhood and solve the problems which were too difficult for us then. They are not, or should not be, too difficult for the adult now. The result is a restoration of the We-unit, yet not of the old, obsolete, outgrown, Original-We, but of the new Maturing-We of grown-up people.

As a formula we say: The obstacles of the Maturing-We group (such as irritability, moodiness, unsound emotions) disappear the more readily, the more our old (and mostly unconscious) wounds, the results of the Breach-of-the-Original-We, are nursed and cured. Egocentricity cannot be overcome by fighting against itself, but by making it superfluous, useless, and senseless—in realizing that the We-group is the deeper and stronger and higher reality.

Genuine character development in the sense of the achievement of wholesome reactions involves something much deeper psychologically than the former theories of self-control by willpower and high ideals, valuable as they may be at times. Character development as we understand it includes this difficult self-education by which one's egocentric emotions are indeed mastered but not by being bound by some strong chain of self-restraint against which they rage in inner fury. Rather are they dissolved by understanding and forgiveness and replaced by love and creativeness. The way to overcome darkness is not to fight or to inveigh against it but to introduce the light—not to suppress the negative, but to develop the positive. This we must do by going courageously downstairs into the cellar of our life—into the unconscious, the dark region where the forgotten remnants (experiences) of the past dwell like specters haunting the present. Then, when we turn on the light of that understanding which includes forgiveness, the specters vanish. We find they are not real but only illusions. Thus anguish and fear and harshness are banished from life with a consequent peace that passeth all understanding—the calm and poise and joy that is objective, We-feeling living—the abundant life of the Master.

Our way of self-education is not something different from

the usual way of human life. All of us are led this way, more or less successfully. It is, we are convinced, the way of Christianity and therefore the way of human history. However the more we understand this way and its goal, the Maturing-We group, and its different steps—pressure and character development by self-exploration and the reconciliation of former unconscious conflicts—the more we are able to avoid the harsher and more painful experiences of maturing into which our egocentric mistakes may plunge us.

There is a certain percentage of people, however—let us say ten or fifteen per cent—who are unable to go this way of self-education—not because of laziness or indifference but because of the inner structure of their difficulties. They are the more serious cases, from the psychological viewpoint; and they have the more difficult task. Here we find that we have come to the limits of the possibilities of self-education.

Seen from the medical viewpoint, in these cases a feeble, too delicate constitution prevails, either conditioned by hereditary weakness or by infirmity acquired very early. The more serious part of the manifold realm of neuroses, the slighter part of the psychoses and certain diseases on the border line between psychic and physical disturbances are to be mentioned here. They include compulsory neuroses, milder manias, certain so-called psychopathics, and some glandular disturbances. However, the symptoms are not necessarily striking or alarming. They may be the same as we have described in our illustrations, yet they are rooted in conditions that we cannot reach by self-education.

Seen from the psychological viewpoint, in these cases, the Breach-of-the-We was so early and violent that the child reacted not only with his psychic means of defense—his Ego construction—but with his whole inheritance, as it were. The strongest glandular reactions, on the physical side, and the deepest human dread on the psychic side came into action. The shell, therefore, and the whole egocentric system was made so strong and rigid that only a major crisis can break it down. Nevertheless the more we are able to do for ourselves through self-education, the more we may reduce the rigidity of the shell. Then there is less necessity for life to bring great pressure to bear upon it.

Gradually we may reach by self-education even the highest

levels by what may be said to be a more or less lengthy series of
relatively small steps—self-taught. When the development is
through crisis and with the aid of a psychotherapist or other
helper, one may reach the same levels, but by one or more very
large steps taken with great pain and suffering.

Inhibitions

Strong emotions, even if they are egocentric, have one advantage from the viewpoint of self-education. They may lead our
opponents to criticize us or fight us perhaps with stronger emotions. Therefore, we may discover either that we are wrong or, at
least, that people think we are. The opposite fault, the complete
or partial lack of emotion, where a sound reaction in the realm of
the feelings should be expected, is a more difficult problem in
self-education, and it is harder to trace the inhibition back to its
origin and to correct it. Yet in the last analysis, the inner psychological situation is about the same as in the other cases.

The lack of feeling may show itself in different ways, the
visible symptoms diverging greatly. A lack of initiative, of tenacity, of energy, or a weakness and suggestibility may be found here
as well as apathy, indifference, inability to love, or pity, blindness
to beauty in nature and art, and many other defects. That the
Turtle is the very representative of this category has already been
said. The Nero, too, is largely incapable of love and of pity, yet
less completely so. However, this does not mean that the Nero
and the Turtle are unable to feel pressure. They are relatively
insensitive or calloused and limited in their emotional reactions,
sometimes to the point of seeming to be almost devoid of them.
One might say they have too few emotions or are emotionless.
Sometimes they even pride themselves on this quality which they
interpret as poise or calmness or even self-control. But sooner or
later they realize pressure as a certain sense of danger, or they feel
uncomfortable and uneasy. Rather often they also experience a
certain resentment of the pressure, and then suddenly dread and
anguish—the emotions of the relatively emotionless type—show
up in their consciousness.

The first mentioned symptoms—suggestibility, weakness,

and lack of initiative, tenacity, and energy—are usually part of the Clinging-Vine type. Yet the way out is the same, and the first obstacle which must be overcome is the same, too.

This lack of feeling often seems to be the result of so-called self-control, as high inner culture, or even as virtue. Clinging Vine seems to be, unconsciously tries to be, or, in some cases, consciously pretends to be, modest and unpretentious. It is really cowardly and helpless. Turtle and Nero display a certain countenance, which people may deem to be philosophic or heroic, whereas it is really a mask. Therefore, it is difficult in these cases to understand the inner connection and to trace back the pressure to its real roots.

Let us speak of lack of initiative, tenacity, and energy, first, and of lack of love and pity afterwards. Imagine yourself now in the place of a man (we shall call him John) whose employer was a gruff old man. John must ask his employer for something, not a favor, but his right—a few days of vacation time or part of his salary past due. The employer has no right to decline to give what is wanted, only he may frown, or grumble, or at the most, if John is compliant enough, may tell him to come back later. That is sufficient to make John hesitate, to turn on the threshold before he knocks, and to postpone again and again making this request which, as he sees the situation, is right yet dangerous.

John knows that something is wrong with him. He has scolded himself and fought against this kind of weakness, without any success worth mentioning, for many years. Sometimes he invented good excuses and believed them, saying that his superior was busy, that he had to save his employer's time, that he must not be egocentric—not stress too much his private interest. Moreover, he thought, didn't Jesus say that one should not be troubled about tomorrow and that one should not resist the evil?

At any rate, passing over the theological problem which turns up here, John should try to admit that besides his good Christian readiness for suffering there could be in his behavior a certain—at least very little—admixture of fear of man. Indeed, he would have been more courageous if he were demanding the leave or the money for his friend instead of himself. However, this trait is not so objective as it seems to be, for if one faces his superior, asking him for what is right, one is not acting egocentrically at all. If one dodges this dangerous encounter, depriving himself or another person by his cowardice of his good right, he is nothing but egocentric. He simply endures the loss of what is due him to avoid a right but disagreeable step. Therefore, let us adopt the hypothesis that there is in John's personality a certain egocentric fear, or lack of courage.

What was he afraid of? What was the danger? The fear—the more he dared to feel and to recognize it—was an exaggerated emotion similar to those discussed in the previous chapter. We have seen that in dealing with such situations it is necessary for one to go back to his childhood, where he can dig out the oldest form of his inhibition. So we assume that John undertakes to do so, and he finds that its cause was a certain kind of fear having its origin in childhood. He was afraid that his father (or another adult) might reject his We-feeling but childish suggestions; therefore, he did not dare to show his heart. He did not appeal to the We-feeling in others which he felt in his own heart. This appeal as it seemed to him was just what the adults reproached in him. His best emotion, his self-evident We-feeling, was the sin! He remembered his father's eyes, strict and threatening, or scornful and cold, which to his childish way of thinking well-nigh condemned him to death. Now John transfers fear of the condemning eyes to everybody who is his superior or who could make himself (as he feels) his judge. If he could stand these looks, he would be free from his inhibition.

The first step toward the mastery in such a situation is to understand this transference; to see that it is not only an error or a mistake, but an unsound, transferred, and very rigid mechanism. The difficulty is that one reacts, as he would say, quite against his will, "as if ..." There is a double "as if" which one cannot correct at once. First, he behaves as if the other one were his "father"—were that very malevolent person, strict and scornful, which existed only in his childish fantasy, since his father was not as malevolent as he thought him to be. That is the first error. The second is, that one is not a child, even though he reacts as if he were. He should learn that as a grown man he is not so helpless and lost as he felt as a child and as his sense of inferiority feeling now makes him feel.

In We-Psychology we describe this "transferred" relationship by saying that one makes the other his Black Giant, and himself the Dwarf, either the white one, if one is the good child seeking merited protection as a Clinging Vine, or a black one, if one is the "bad child," resigned to his fate more like a Turtle. Here the black color of the Giant signifies what seems to be the threatening, forbidding aspect of the other, and white symbolizes the kindly, benign, helpful nature which one felt the adult had.

The first step correcting this defect is to be found in the field of the intellect. John had to understand the situation. The second step takes place in the emotional realm. It was necessary to face the threatening eyes and feel: "They are not as dangerous as I supposed; and even if they were, I could endure them now, for I am no longer a child but grown up." If John could succeed, it would be all right; if not, he would have to go on in the double way, thinking, meditating, dreaming about his childhood and facing the tasks of everyday life with the help of his new psychological insight.

Just here John remembered that he was not only afraid of his Black Giant, but that he wanted it to be White. Were not there a few days that his father smiled on him? Didn't he feel happy and secure in this approval? The fact is that John would not have been startled so much by this frowning if he had not longed even more for the smile. He wanted to be the White Dwarf indulged, protected, spoiled, by the White Giant, because he felt helpless and afraid in the presence of the Black Giant. This feeling of fear is very obstinate, and very inaccessible to one's willpower and self-control, because it is only the outcome in reverse of another feeling, namely, the original love and longing for his father. Before the Breach-of-the-We, there was nothing but love between the child and his parents. Afterward, when the irritated father judges the child unfavorably—scolds or threatens him—the child feels helpless and is afraid, and now the father is the Black Giant. There are times when the child longs for the approval of the father, when he once again wishes to be caught up in his arms literally or figuratively and protected and cared for. In this longing there are painful memories of the Lost Paradise of the original unbroken We-relationship. The father, when thus longed for, appears not as the forbidding, dangerous Black Giant but as the kindly, helpful White Giant.

The child cannot get rid of the Black Giant because he cannot renounce the White Giant. He is unable to do so because he cannot cease being the child which actually needs a guardian. Grown now to manhood, John is actually no longer a child needing a guardian, yet he still unconsciously feels as he did in childhood. He has not yet become mature enough emotionally to feel that he can bear the unfavorable judgment of another. He still needs the White Giant, and thus his fear is, as it were, We-feeling with inverted signs. It is love turned into the negative.

If one really grasps this truth, he will not only know it intellectually, but he will realize it emotionally. Thus John not only recollected many scenes and facts, but the whole atmosphere of these early days. He felt the fear once more, as he felt then, and behind the fear, his longing for love. Behind his yearning he felt touched by love itself, and he smiled, cried and laughed and wept as a child.

The process illustrated here is not mere suggestion, nor mere psychoanalysis. It is real life. It involves facing the very essence of life, tackling the task, enduring the danger, which you, being a child, could not do then. In some cases it means almost going through hell to heaven, for you need all your maturity if you try to redo and to relive your not-lived childhood, and you will find yourself quite another person than you believed, and perhaps were, outwardly hitherto.

However, all this inquiry into early experiences, important as it may be, is only the first half of the whole way out. This delving back into the childhood and into our unconscious—the introspective part of self-education—has to be completed, controlled, tested and justified by the second half—the part that involves turning away from introspection to the world of actions designed to change one's life. The new experience that you are afraid of is fearful in part because, childlike, you still feel you must have the approval of some White Giant. In your helplessness as a child, you did indeed need the good-will and love of some White Giant—without it you could scarcely have existed, but now the situation is different. As the older and adult person you should be able to live, to work, to fight if necessary without the approval of others, and moreover to love without being loved. You should have become able to renounce having a White Giant. If you did so, you would no longer have any Black Giant to fear because being able to go on without this approval means that you do not fear being judged disapprovingly.

Your task then is to go, face your superior, renounce his approval, recognize your loneliness and your being adult; live, work, fight if necessary, and first of all, love without being loved again. That is the attitude of the mature person. He is rich enough to give without pay. The deeper you have delved into your childhood and the better you have worked out the old emotional problems which referred to the Breach-of-the-We, the more and the richer you will display your adult and mature We-feeling.

Our next rule is: Take small steps. That means we cannot solve the whole problem at once. We should face our Black Giant at first in his least dangerous incarnation. Perhaps you are embarrassed to call a restaurant waiter who keeps you waiting. You feel that your attitude is not kindness but egocentric timidity, and you dare not to trouble him because you want him to smile at you. You wish his good-will. Call him naturally, but determinedly, risk his frowning, prepare to endure the consequences.

This step appears very small. Seen from the outside it means almost nothing in comparison with the task of encountering your superior. Yet, seen from the inside it is a very large step and a dangerous one; it contains the decisive factor: the projection of the Black Giant was there; you have challenged him—and he did not crush you. This little experience means a certain change in your inner life. The mechanism of transference has proved useless, and therefore its influence has decreased.

According to this principle of the small steps, dare one day to oppose your subordinate, then the next day your coordinate, and at last your superior. You will collect many new experiences, good ones and bad ones. You should relate them—particularly the frustrations, which cannot be avoided—to the not yet solved problems of your childhood. Behind all of them you will find this one central and chief problem of human life: the courage of heart.

If you do not succeed in everyday life, you should go back into deeper layers of your past. If you fail in going back, you should turn anew to everyday life in order to find new experiences, new observations and new tasks, which may show you new doors leading back into the past. Gradually you should find the clear and creative attitude which experience proves to be valid. It enables you to remain calm and confident in a situation from which you would have withdrawn in former times. Out of this calmness the creative answer, the solution of the problem, arises. You realize that you master the situation, your fear and your timidity disappear, and your initiative develops in accordance with your maturity.

It may be useful to insert here the record given by one of the younger We-Psychologists about his own cure through self-education. He was a sound man, entangled only in a few inhibitions which did not handicap him too much in everyday life. He was highly interested in psychotherapy from the general religious viewpoint as well as with regard to his personal development, and he had read and thought a great deal, had observed his own dreams, and inspected his recollections.

Thus he knew that most of his difficulties had their roots in his relationship to his father. When he was a boy—somewhat of a Clinging Vine—his father, who ran a large farm, was always the Giant for him; mostly the black one, the thunderer or a kind of a "Godlike Policeman" (these were his, the son's, own words). Moreover, he understood that he, being this discouraged boy, always had felt a longing to have his father be kind to him, protecting and indulgent. In adult years he had transferred this role of the Black Giant, whom he wanted to be a white one, to all the authorities and to every superior he had to deal with. He knew that it was nothing but transference; this knowledge, however, did not help him enough, and he tried to overcome it by fighting it and by scolding himself without any success.

At this stage in his self-education he was obliged to go to the office of the mayor of a very small town where he was then living where he had to make some statement, as required in that country, about his moving from one street to another one. He postponed this visit until the time for making his statement was past. Then he postponed it anew because the thing became a little more troublesome after the time had passed. At last his wife urged him to go so earnestly that it was more inconvenient for him to stay than to face the Black Giant.

Thus he went. In the office he met the mayor's first assistant, a friendly little man who apparently was glad to include some conversation in his dull official work. He smiled and bowed to the visitor asking him to wait a minute until he had finished his letter. The visitor understood—in his intellect—that the situation was favorable, but in his feeling, however, his inhibition increased. The alarm bell, as it were, rang in his chest. His glandular system, like soldiers, became mobilized, as if the enemy were approaching the doors of the fortress. He told himself repeatedly the obvious truth, that this official had no right and, as it seemed, no intention to hurt him. A few words would be enough to apologize for the delay, and there was no reason for worrying. On the other hand, in the other half of his personality, the excitement grew. His heart beat more rapidly, his breath became short and he had a strong sensation of being choked. The contradiction between reason and emotion was evident.

Here the visitor invented a new step, very simple and very creative at the same time. He asked himself: "What is my emotion like? To what is it related?" Instead of fighting *against* the emotion, he began a new search for a way out. He faced the emotion curiously and kindly instead of striving to suppress it, and thus he opened the channel through which his emotion could be led in order to become productive.

What kind of emotion was it? What was its adequate reason? Since everything has its adequate cause, this extraordinary excitement must have been once the normal, reasonable reaction to a real situation. What was this situation? What was this reaction? What was its background? Its aim? This little man writing on the desk? No. Not at all. A very great man, tall, powerful, and gloomy looking—the father. He almost believed he saw his father as he used to see him when he was a child. It was not a real vision, but a very strong impression of his personality, and he realized at once that this father had become an old and helpless man in these last years. The most amazing thing, however, was his sensation of size. The man at the desk seemed to be extraordinarily small and the image or the shadow of the father tall as a giant. This fact surprised our visitor and so amused him that he could scarcely restrain himself from laughing. When the assistant turned to him, he told him—the first time in his life without any embarrassment—what the matter was. Now he was as able as anybody else to settle his business even with authorities and all kinds of father-substitutes. The transference of the Black Giant was gone.

It may be useful after the description of this concrete case to outline in a few words the rules which are involved in it and which are related to what has been said before. In the former chapter, dealing with too strong emotions, the problem was not how to suppress them, but how to change them and to lead them into a useful direction. Now we have the more difficult cases where the emotional reactions are lacking, and that means where life itself seems to be too weak, since life without emotion would not be life at all.

There may be people whose emotional life is poor by constitution or inheritance, such as the feeble-minded. They do not suffer because of unexpressed possibilities, since they have very limited resources and few potentialities that might be developed. Our present problem does not include them, but all the others who feel that they are not really alive and who suffer from their own dullness.

For all these the first step is to face their pressure. Maybe they only miss certain reactions which they know as useful or delightful in the life of their companions, like musical understanding or enjoying art or nature; or they have no compassion or they are not able to love. They should examine themselves to see whether this was always the same, or when it began; under which conditions it increased or when there were exceptions. Thus one should try to describe the inhibition in a formula; for example, like the inscription on a danger sign: "It is not allowed to overstep this point in showing one's love. . . ." Or: "It is dangerous to face the Black Giant!" or: "Attention: Two miles yonder is your enemy!" or even: "Keep quiet! Don't stir! The fiend is watching you!" Not only the expression of any emotion, but the incipient arousal of the emotion itself, may have been inhibited by such a "law." We have "learned" this attitude by innumerable bad experiences and frustrations in our childhood. At last it became part of our shell, and that means of our "second nature"—of our egocentric behavior. The hound learns, contrary to his first nature, to watch partridges without stirring them up. The child learns—when his first nature has been "broken"—to see the sweets without wanting them. He is a Turtle.

It is important to know this but it is not enough. All these inner laws are enforced by threats. Behind every sentence we can and should find the addition: "lest you are sent to everlasting damnation!" or: "lest you are excluded from our society!" Both versions indicate the same danger and have the same result: dire fear. Even their symbol in dreams and fantasy is very often the same—the threatening eye of the judge. This threat is usually unconscious, yet it serves as a reminder and inhibits the transgression of the "law." As soon as you try to overstep your inhibition, you defy the Black Giant—and that means the old fear awakes. You feel anxious, excited, agitated, without knowing the reason, until you give up and resign your independent attitude. The threat, as it were, is the lifted forefinger or the scolding voice of the Black Giant. At first you cannot yet distinguish any symbol or recollection; you only realize the dim yet terrible shadow of the Giant. In order to overcome this barrier you have to discriminate what your giant is like. Is he the father? or the teacher? or the terrible policeman?—and you cannot recognize him without observing him. In order to observe him, you must evoke him and look at him carefully, and you evoke him just by doing what he forbids you to do. Challenge, defy him by transgressing his laws, and observe his reaction (*i.e.,* the reaction of your own unconscious) and you will be able to overcome your inhibition. As far as you are afraid of a specter, you cannot observe it, and it remains powerful. As soon as you dare to watch it, it loses its power, and you discover that it never had existed.

Now, we should know two things. First, out of what situation in childhood this special law or "sanction" may have emerged. Then, what mythological or superstitious material coming from outside (fairy tales or folklore) may have been mixed up with the individual discouragement. Then, having learned this, we have to face the Black Giant himself.

Suppose that what comes to your mind when you try to face this dim and indistinct fear, and when you remember what has threatened you most in your early years, takes the shape, more and more distinctly, of an eye—a threatening eye. This watching eye, now, becomes a symbol. It represents at the same time the expression and the cause of your fear. Here it is not enough to think intellectually, and to find out that this teacher and that policeman in your old town had the same expression in their eyes or that a picture in your mother's Bible had it.

You should actually dwell upon all that the "eye" signified in both your thinking and feeling. Look at it from the viewpoint of your childhood. Recall again and again all that you thought and felt about it. Reconstruct all your reactions in your fear of it. Dare again to feel the childish fear of the past, then try to imagine or find the person or the situation which now is nearest to this old and fearsome experience. You will find that there is something somewhat horrible, dreadful or weird in your reaction, or in the image which causes your reaction, and it exceeds the natural, reasonable amount of emotion caused by the real situation in childhood.

This has to be replaced by faith. We-feeling has to be renewed. The mere passivity and terror has to be replaced by the new confidence and creativeness, which naturally tends to well up into the personality when the Self is released from the mistakes of the Ego.

Lack of Sensitivity

Many people, as we have pointed out, are partial Turtles. Even the most sensitive and—what means almost the same—the most gifted people show very often a degree of callousness or blindness in certain areas of their life which is surprising to the layman who does not understand the nature of this deficiency. There are musicians, scholars, experts with great talent who do not see that their wives suffer cruelly, or that their children starve for want of paternal interest. They are "absorbed" in their chief or only interest or they seem to be diverted or absentminded not for a certain time but chronically. On the other hand, their reactions are extremely sensitive in the field of their own interest. Very often they are Stars in their professional life and Turtles in their family relationships. The reverse seems to occur more rarely.

The combination of partial Turtle and Nero is very frequent. Indeed, it is almost impossible to be a Nero, without being blind and deaf to the suffering of one's victims.

This callousness may be described as the "law" which prohibits compassion, sharing, and even understanding, because otherwise an enormous amount of suffering would be the result. The warning, the so-called "sanction" of the inner law, opens the way out, here as well as in many other cases. One has to face the impending danger, to evoke the Black Giant—here it would be better to say the black situation—and to realize that the consequence may have been very dangerous in early childhood, but is not dangerous at all for the adult.

Theoretically, it is not difficult to describe the way out, yet the practical accomplishment needs more careful instruction. In the last analysis, the reason for this lack of sensitivity has been the Breach-of-the-Original-We. To develop, therefore, the sensitive attitude means to go back and dig out the old, forgotten We-feeling reactions and to make them grow and become more varied and ripen until they reach the level and the maturity of the other parts of the personality. Yet, where may we find the living remainders of this old and, so to speak, prehistoric We? It seems that we cannot remember them.

Two reactions, however, which are noticeable in almost everyone's personality, mark just the transition from Original We-feeling to egocentric behavior. Usually we call these reactions already egocentric and try to avoid them. We should do the opposite; we should acknowlege and cultivate them.

The first reaction is our so-called feeling of identification with people who undergo a certain kind of unfavorable treatment. One of us cannot bear any injustice done to anyone else. Another one becomes raging when he sees courtesy and kindness misunderstood or neglected by the person to whom it was shown. One identifies oneself with every speaker and trembles that he may stop short; or one becomes excited when he sees some very capable actor on the stage display his power and meet some tragic destiny. When you read Shakespeare, do you side with Caesar or Marc Anthony, with Hamlet or with Fortinbras? Wherever this sympathy turns up, we feel genuine emotion. It is *our* emotion; not only my own, not only his, the victim's of injustice, or the hero's in history or literature; it is the common emotion of several people; it is the last remainder of We-feeling in the Original-We and it may be the first new step of mature We-feeling reaction. We should pay attention to it, and try to display it more and more.

The further way, then, shows the same alternation between inner discovery and outer experience which we have described above. Look at the scene which moves you in the street or at the movies. Dare to react as you feel, in spite of all your clumsiness or shyness. React, show your heart! Do not be afraid that your reaction may contain a high amount of egocentricity. The non-reaction is doubtlessly more egocentric. Then go home and meditate. Find out what situation in your childhood may correspond to the scene which touched you so much. Which inner string in your past experience vibrates in sympathy with the tone coming from outside? Go back into your past dreams and feel what has happened until you hear the pure and strong tone of that emotional string. The better you hear the sound, the nearer you come to yourself. Then go ahead in the outer world and expose yourself to new kindred experiences.

The second reaction we mentioned before may be understood as the counterpart of these attitudes. We have described above only negative reactions, sympathetic emotions raised by unfavorable, unjust, or tragic situations. Indeed, it is easier to discover negative We-feeling emotions than positive ones. Everybody, however, has positive ones, too; it is only more difficult to find them, since they are more carefully concealed because of their more serious interference with the egocentric law.

Remember the murderer who kills the whole family and spares the little child. Why does he act in this dangerous way? Did his heart, his We-feeling emotion, his Self compel him to pity the baby? Was his reckless, callous, egocentric shell broken here in this moment, or was there a crack in it all the time?

You will not maintain that your lack of We-feeling reaction is comparable to the cool unfeelingness of the criminal, but there are more and larger cracks in your armor than you know. What sort of events touches you, besides the unjust, sad, or tragic scenes we discussed before? Did you never weep in the movies? (Even the Neros are rather strongly touched by certain scenes.) In other cases it may be almost pure egocentric sentimentality. The Nero, however, and the Turtle in the service of their egocentric goal, cannot develop sentimental reactions. If they feel moved, and even in a very childlike manner, this usually means a crack in the egocentric armor. The significant content of the scenes that move them is usually as simple as it is characteristic: it is the restoration of the Original-We. Mother and child come together again, after they were separated for a long time. Loyal love is rewarded at last by happy marriage.

The primitiveness of the fact seems to be necessary. More sophisticated stories fall flat (without regard to artistic values, speaking of the mere action or plot). The reason is that the We-feeling here in question belongs to the system (or set) of reactions which was in operation when the Breach-of-the-We occurred.

We should face these emotions and enjoy them. Then we should proceed in the well-known alternating way, scrutinizing our childhood, understanding the causes of our so-called sentimentality, exposing ourselves to similar experiences, finding new hints and clues, and going on with our research. Moreover, we need patience. It may take us months and perhaps years until we become as sensitive and able to love as we should. It is easier to change and improve an excess of emotion than to develop enough emotion where none was.

There are other cases where not a general inhibition of emotional response, not the complete deficiency of understanding, sharing, or love is the characteristic symptom, but only a certain part or sort of response for a certain type of person seems to be missing, while the same reaction toward another person may be developed sufficiently. It is natural that a man responds, physically as well as mentally, to a certain "type" of woman, and vice versa. Rather often, however, his physical response answers the appeal of one type, while his mental inclination is occupied by the opposite type. A girl marries a man to whom she feels a strong attraction physically but her psychic tenderness is not connected with her erotic desire; it remains turned toward her father or her mother. Or a man adores his wife, only he offends her unintentionally by neglecting her simplest feminine wishes. He never shows his tenderness, never praises or acknowledges her, never brings her little gifts, no flowers, no sweets, and nevertheless, he loves her profoundly. When his wife's doctor tells him that she suffers, he cannot understand, he cannot believe that something could be wrong in his married life. What a curious kind of colorblindness there is in his eyes! How may he cure himself, supposing that he acknowledges, at least theoretically, the necessity of such a cure?

Let us take as an instance the last case. The doctor convinces the husband that his wife suffers. He explains his feeling that a certain kind of attention, yet not all attention, is missing—a certain kind of warmth, yet not all warmth. Then he mentions the old Chinese proverb, that the love of the husband may be seen in the sound color of his wife's face. That's all he knows. The lady is unhappy, there is no doubt. The husband asks her why directly. She weeps, but she cannot explain what it is. She does not know, herself, and thinks that perhaps it is her own fault.

The sorrowful husband is deeply stirred by the fact that his wife indeed looks ten years older than his friend's wife who is her senior. He begins to observe and he discovers that his friend seems to woo his wife as if they were not yet even engaged. There are flowers, sweets, tender jokes, and mutual banter every day. "That may be nice for them," he thinks; "it is not my temperament. It would be ridiculous for me." Going on in his reflection, he wonders why the whole atmosphere in his home may be so different from his friend's home. Then he remembers: his parents were earnest and severe people. There was no laughter, no art, no music, no gaiety. They loved one another—only a certain tone was missing, as in his own life: there was no courage for play.

He tried to imagine how he could be joyous together with his wife. Oh, he could, when he was alone, or with a few very good friends, without her. Was she the obstacle? No, she liked to be gay, she could be radiant in society. Why couldn't he come simply to kiss her ears and caress her hair, jokingly, as he occasionally saw other men treat their wives?

Now he knew: there was a distinct obstacle. The look of her eyes. No, not her eyes, his mother's eyes. They seemed to condemn him. Her judgment was clear and simple: "You are wanton!" It was impossible to overcome this obstacle. His mother was right. But was she right thoroughly? He began to ponder. She was a wise woman, she was right in many fields of life, but her relationship to his father had been a problem for him. Perhaps she was frigid, almost asexual.

For the first time in his life he understood that there was a tragedy in his parents' life, too, and his love for his mother, who had died many years ago, increased and became more mature. He never had dared, so far, to look at her from the viewpoint of the mature man. Now he did, and he discovered her anew and in a deeper sense than before. He understood, but he could not help her. He would not have been able to help her, if she had been alive, but he had to help his wife, otherwise the tragedy would be repeated. Why was it so difficult to be tender with her? To show her his heart? Was it forbidden to do that? Was he afraid of being misunderstood? Or even blamed? She would not blame him. He knew she would be happy, for she was not like his mother. Now he saw: he expected her to react just as his mother would have reacted, because he supposed her to be like his mother. At least his emotional attitude was like that, while intellectually he understood that she had quite another type of temperament than her mother-in-law.

However there was another obstacle. He felt like a very small boy as often as he tried or imagined to be kind and tender with his wife. He supposed her to be much more experienced, more adult, more mature. He knew this was an error, again, but it was sufficient to deter him. Actually he was as little sophisticated as she. She was not the strict and almost Puritan lady. She was longing for affection, and suddenly he remembered that she had told him that a few years ago. So it was his duty to overstep the borderline, which his mother had created in his personality—and it was possible.

One day he brought her a rose. She was extremely surprised and her reaction was almost clumsy. For a few moments he felt disappointed, and his heart seemed to withdraw. Yet his attention was directed toward her and he kept it there. He saw her helplessness and felt the more secure. Two awkward children had to learn how to be happy, and gradually they learned, in spite of many failures and mistakes. The husband's "mother-projection" or his "mother-fixation," as it is sometimes called, disappeared. It is probable that on her side, too, there was a certain kind of projection or inhibition to overcome, yet the way out was the same for both of them. As we see now, it was the same as in the case of "lack of initiative."

The explanation of this curious fact is rather simple. The way out has to be *traveled;* one has to make steps, to be active. Sensitivity, however, represents more or less a passive quality; it means reaction more than action. So the problem is how we may become more aware of our surroundings—by doing something since it is not enough just to open one's eyes. Our "blind spots" are not removed by such a mere passive kind of endeavor. We have to take a risk, by showing our heart. The gift, the tenderly offered present, exposes us to the danger of refusal and criticism. The heart we show is not protected. Only by observing our mate and by understanding his needs may we succeed. Therefore, the remedy of callousness and insensitiveness is simply: to give our attention, our time, our thoughts, our experiments, our gifts, and, at last, to give ourselves as completely as possible to our neighbor—in short, to find ways of cultivating We-feeling.

Part III:
Idolatry and the Attempt to Escape from the Crisis
Idolatry

The psychological development during the first half of the crisis can be described as *regression.* The rigid prejudices of the Ego are melting away under the increasing pressure of perilous circumstances, and earlier, more childlike valuations are revitalized. A wealthy lady, for instance, may have been convinced for many years that she could never drive to a bridge party in an old, jolting Ford car. Unless she had a new Packard every year she preferred to stay at home. After her husband's bankruptcy she was actually sick and in bed for a year; two years later, however, she had learned to enjoy the shaky old Ford, and she felt better than in the days of the new Packards.

The Ego becomes more modest, more insecure, more primitive, though not more reasonable. The lady with the old Ford is now crazy about housekeeping. She dismisses her maid, wants to do everything herself, and spends hours figuring out whether it is more economical to send the sheets to the laundry or to buy a washing machine on the installment plan. The Ego-image of the sophisticated society lady has been replaced by the earlier image of the good housewife; but it still carries much egocentricity and is still threatened by a Shadow. For the society lady the unbearable situation had been: old clothes, imitation jewelry, and an unfashionable car. She had been forced to accept all this. And now her "abyss," the new Shadow, is exactly the opposite: to fail as a housewife, to spend a dime in vain, to increase the financial burden of the family. Her former social life now appears to her as an abomination.

The new Ego-image, which is historically a very old one, may be more useful for the time being. It may even represent a rather satisfactory adjustment to the new situation. Yet it remains rigid and based on fear rather than on genuine creative power. To bring about real reintegration, a further step in the direction of regression is needed. The lady has to become more definitely like a little child; and that means helpless, confident, and ready to do whatever life wants her to do. That is the second and more painful step on her way through the crisis; but it is still part of the first half of the journey.

Her friends warn her that she neglects her husband, as she neglects her make-up and clothes. He does not like housekeepers anyhow, so he may have an affair, one day, with a society girl. And suddenly she remembers that several times he did not come home for dinner, on some futile pretext. Here she sacrifices her youth and her beauty, doing all the hard work, and he betrays her! Or does she exaggerate? Maybe she sees specters? Sleeplessness, restlessness, distrust ensue. She feels forsaken, left alone in a hostile world. Nobody can understand her, nor does she understand herself. She is afraid she may go insane.

Her present Shadow, her former Ego-image, the spendthrift, the society lady, turns up again, but now it is projected into the outer world; it becomes the rival, her husband's sweetheart. And she does not know whether this beautiful girl exists in outer reality or in her own fantasy only. In any case, it represents her own unlived life, her twin sister, who has to be accepted and loved. Now her crisis is at its climax. She is completely unequal to the tasks of everyday life, neither a housewife nor a society lady—nothing but a desperate child.

As if by chance, in one of her hopeless moods, she listens to a sermon or a lecture or a radio address. Someone says: "All your fears and sorrows only indicate lack of love. If you could love you could forget yourself; you would live for the benefit of other people; and you would be happy." She knows this is true. She does not remember that she has heard and read similar ideas a hundred times—they come now as "the good news," the gospel, strikingly fresh and powerful. She feels an immediate relief, a vague dawn of new possibilities, new vistas of life, new security. And she writes a letter to the lecturer, giving herself completely to the new cause.

She is honestly ready to renounce her Ego, or better: her egocentricity is breaking down through its own failure and she begins to feel dimly that she herself may be different from her Ego. The real Self is about to emerge. The rigid structure of her imagery and the system of values as established in her early years, after the breach of the original We, disappear. And reality, freed from the dictatorship of egocentric evaluation, seems to whirl around in a dizzying chaos of destruction and new creativity. She does not know what is good and what is bad. Anything is possible. She is a child, she needs a leader, a teacher, an adult.

Then the answer to her letter arrives. She is accepted. The "master" signs her membership card. She is one of his many disciples. She is at home. He tells her what is good and what is bad. He knows everything. He protects her. Wherever he is, there chaos is replaced by peace and harmony. She readily gives up her Ego. She understands that all her egocentric valuations, desires and fears were erroneous. But she had not known better because she did not yet know *him.* Now he takes away all her doubts. She is happy, healthy, efficient and ready for every sacrifice. She is thoroughly reborn.

She meets others who have gone through the same experience: they are reborn, converted, saved, too. And she enjoys enormously the new fellowship. There are drunkards who stopped drinking three years ago, epileptics who got over their fits, professors whose blood pressure went down from 200 to normal, and truck drivers who can easily drive eighteen hours, now, though a year ago they were fatigued after a half day's work. And she discovers with amazement that she no longer asks whether her husband has an affair with another woman or whether she spends a dollar too much for her laundry—if only all three of them, her husband, his sweetheart, and the laundryman, would join the movement and be reborn like herself.

The process of regression has reached the point where in early childhood the breach of the original We took place. All egocentric traits have gone. The Ego and the Shadow have lost their importance, and therefore both fear of inferiority and striving for superiority disappear. Even the demarcation line between consciousness and unconsciousness is strangely slackened. The individual feels dreamy in bright daylight, and creative visions as well as forgotten memories loom in the twilight of consciousness.

But certainly not all those who turn and regress to the inner situation of early childhood will enter the Realm. In such a moment more than ever we are exposed to the "blind guides of blind people" who "traverse sea and land to make a single proselyte" and then "make him a son of Gehenna twice as bad" as they are themselves (Mt 23:15–16).

What happens in such a case may be described psychologically in the following manner: Regression clears away all the barriers between the images and the real Self. Creativity flows once more through all the channels of the collective imagery. And the whole process of development and education, of groping for a way and of learning from failure and success, would virtually begin anew—were it not for the "blind leader" who, like the parents in early childhood, seeks to impose his will and his judgment as infallible truth. He is there. We always find someone who gladly assumes this role; and we are more than glad to project on him the collective and powerful image of the Great Prophet.*

---

*The reader who is accustomed to Freudian language should keep in mind that the phenomenon which we describe as idolatry must not be confused with simple transference in the Freudian sense of the word. In the case of transference the Ego remains in control of the individual's life; only one image from the unconscious emerges, is projected into the outer world and influences the individual's behavior—which, however, remains egocentric. Idolatry is the abolition of the Ego and the enthronement of a projected image in place of the real Center.

In most cases he is objectively somewhat nearer than we to the real center, which means that he wields more knowledge and power than we have been able to muster during our egocentric past. Thus, to a certain extent, he is fitted to be our teacher or guide. But we are not satisfied (nor is he himself) with his role as a temporary advisor. We find ourselves for the first time in our adult life in the immediate presence of our own creative center. We sense the burning fire of life and we do not yet know whether it will enlighten us or destroy us. And he interprets it, he explains our situation. He knows—at least we think he knows—the central fire, and how to deal with it. Through him we hope to find it when we need it, and he protects us if it threatens to burn us. He steps in between our real center and our bewildered conscious-ness (which has not yet found a new point of crystallization since the breakdown of the Ego-image). Instead of discovering that the real center is our own real Self, and that its nature and name are not "I" but "We" and even more than "We"—we replace this dangerous development with something simpler and, as it were, more reliable: we confuse the person who apparently masters the central power with the real center itself. He who seems to be the channel, or who at least seems to open the channel of power, now is looked upon as the power itself. He is the Great Magician, the Medicine Man of primitive tribes, the inspired Founder of mod-ern spiritual movements.

Objectively the primordial images, such as the Great Prophet or Leader, the Great Mother or Priestess, and their negative counterparts, the Ogre and the Sorceress, are so close to the center that, during the first half of our individual life as well as during the first half of our racial history, we can scarcely hope to distinguish them sufficiently. By relapsing into a childlike state of mind during our individual crisis we are again exposed to the same danger: the danger of confusing inwardly the real center with a primordial image, and accordingly, of projecting not only the image but, as it were, the image together with the real center, on a person in the outer world.

This person then becomes our "projected Self." We pivot around him like a satellite around its sun. He is "our life"; without him we are nothing; we accept his valuation, his goal, his taste, and, of course, his philosophy. His word is the unquestionable truth, his judgment is absolute, and his will is the will of the universe. He becomes our god.

When we discussed the problems of egocentricity, we had to say that the Ego finally supersedes the real Self in pretended assumption of all the functions of the latter: the Ego replaces the We-group (therefore it cannot love any one else); and it takes the place of God (therefore it has no ethical scruples). Now we find that a similar process takes place if the second half of our Ego-crisis is replaced by a pseudo-conversion. One of the images becomes the representative of the real Self and therefore of the We-group and of God. But this image is not identified with the individual's own personality, it is not called "I"; it is projected into the outer world and identified with a human being who is consequently considered as a super-human entity. This is the psychological essence of idolatry.

The subjective experience of the person who idolizes some one else is "fascination." He is awake and conscious, of course, he can reason and judge—but his viewpoint is completely different from the viewpoint of all other people except of those who are fascinated by the same idol. And it is extremely important to add that the idolater is not egocentric at all. He is idol-centered, but not Ego-centered; and he is, therefore, capable of sacrifice and service. This is why idolaters can be organized into powerful groups, while egocentric people doom every organization to inefficiency. Both, however, the idolater and the Ego-worshiper, serve the wrong center. They represent two different kinds of eccentricity, and therefore both will perish finally from the same disease: their lack of central power which means lack of creativity.

With regard to human history idolatry is even more important than egocentricity. The latter may account for a large part of the evil and suffering in our world; but it is related to individuals, and we know that during the second half of the individual life the power of the Ego decreases. It may do much harm but it will die before it reaches its destructive goals. Idolatry, on the other hand, is related to larger groups (except for the "great love" which is often mutual idolatry between one man and one woman). And idolatrous groups live longer and are more influential than egocentric individuals. They are able to form pressure groups, religious movements and political parties of considerable importance.

And the lifetime of more than one generation may pass before the lack of creativity, which idolatry has in common with egocentricity, finally brings about their collapse.

In a superficial estimate we can assume that every individual with an average life-span of sixty years may spend at least one year in a state of critical or even catastrophic inner disturbance. This may be one entire year filled with serious emergencies, dangerous experiences and difficult decisions; or there may be many, let us say six or twelve, such periods spread out irregularly over the sixty years, each lasting a month or two.

In a city of a hundred thousand inhabitants there are at any given moment at least fifteen hundred people (we repeat: normal people, not neurotics) who have lost their inner equilibrium. Their egocentricity is breaking down and they would be able to discover their real center—or better: the power and the glory of the real center would break through the debris of the collapsing Ego like the sun through the clouds—if it were not for the false prophets, the blind leaders of blind men, who create idolatry instead of faith, and advertise a cheap pseudo-center instead of the real treasure which can be bought only by giving up everything else.

During public emergencies such as earthquakes, floods, epidemics, economic depressions, revolutions and wars, the number of individual crises is multiplied considerably. And in a period of rapid social change as, for instance, when an agricultural country is suddenly industrialized, practically nobody can avoid the inner crisis precipitated by the change of outer circumstances. Then real religion as well as all pseudo-religions have their great opportunity. These are the hotbeds where the decisive historical movements start, where progress or destruction, health or sickness for the coming generation are prepared, and where each individual decides, consciously or unconsciously, whether he will worship an idol and increase darkness, or serve the real center and contribute to the power of light. But none of us can escape entirely the errors of our century. We can only endeavor to be swayed by them as little as possible.

Ministers, doctors, psychologists, counselors, teachers, writers, artists, actors, politicians, newspaper men and movie-producers—all of us, knowingly or unknowingly, participate in the collective guilt of our time: we produce idolatry instead of faith. We exploit the crises of our fellow men, the breakdown of their egocentricity, their suffering and their opportunity for further development, for our own egocentric or idolatrous goals. We loudly proclaim our philosophy, our art, our policy as the general remedy, and by doing so we—silently—offer ourselves as idols. For most of us, to be a success means to be idolized.

Consciously there may exist a strong antipathy against hero worship. But much stronger, though less conscious, is our general antipathy against responsible, independent, creative personal development. We like equality, but we confuse it—as long as we are egocentric—with conformity. Our Ego misuses the fact of our human imperfection in order to level or to deny the different degrees of maturity and integration. And when we become idolaters, or idols, the only difference in values which we admit, of course, is based on idolatry: the idol being the only absolute value. In other words, most of us want to remain either egocentric "rugged individualists" and, if possible, idols for others, or enthusiastic idolaters, or peculiar mixtures of both—as long as life allows us to be so. But finally life destroys all eccentricity.

For a certain time, however, the group of idolaters seems to be more immune from the crucial tests of history than the egocentric individual who cannot meet the requirements of creative development. First of all, the members of this group have a good conscience, they are not haunted by feelings of inferiority or insecurity. Their leader knows all the answers, he has solved all the problems, no doubt is left; even if here and there an individual member fails, the group as a whole is perfectly right.

The Ego-center has been dissolved. This is a real advantage, because it effects simultaneously the removal of the Shadow. No fear, no tension, no anxiety spoil the inner welfare of the group members. They are individually happy, carefree and relaxed. They have no personal sorrows. The group will take care of everything. The paradise, indeed the lost paradise of the "Original We-group" which had been destroyed by the "Breach of the We," is re-established. The nostalgia of these many years has been fulfilled—and for the moment at least it seems irrelevant whether this wonderful success represents progress or regression; whether the happy group is living in a medieval state of mind or exploring possibilities of the future—they do not care, they are happy.

Moreover, they are unanimous, and that gives them a special sense of security. One person could be mistaken. But fifty—or five hundred—cannot be wrong. And then they have realized, all of them, a certain kind of growth. What used to be impossible is done now without difficulty. A man with a serious speech-inhibition has learned to talk; a lady who could not refrain from talking now seems to be the incarnation of modesty. There is some real reintegration, since the Shadow has disappeared and the general consent of the group prevents all malevolent criticism. The new experience of brotherhood brings many buried talents to light. The group seems to be supported by creative power, and the leader seems to be a real prophet.

The Shadow and its disastrous results—tension, inhibition and fear—have been eliminated; but the real center has not been reached. It remains hidden in the unconscious, its creativity stalled and its mask, its outer appearance, projected on the Idol who now represents the center of many individuals and of the group as a whole. This projection is the sham-We-center of a sham-We-group, and it displays an amazing amount of sham-creativity. Finally it creates its own counterpart, the Anti-Idol, and its own destruction.

The individual member of the group has no sorrows, but the group as a whole has many. The member fears nothing; his philosophy is right, his conscience is clear, his cause will and must succeed in history. The group as such, however, and its leader or its board of executives, face a different picture. There are competitive groups, propagating terrible heresies, and they are extremely successful. They have to be fought, conquered, exterminated—or they will annihilate this group which alone is in possession of the full truth.

The Shadow has been removed from the inner structure of the individual; now it emerges anew, multiplied, reinforced and projected into the outer world. Just as the individual Shadow used to be the enemy and the abomination of the Ego, now the rival group, the worshipers of the competitive idol, become the enemies and the abomination of the idolatrous group. The Ego used to transfer the role of the adversary, for instance the negative father-image, on different people who subsequently became the substitutes for the original "enemy." Now the group as a whole projects the image of the arch-enemy, that is, a kind of super-enemy or devil, or another group of idolaters and especially, of course, on the other Idol.

The parallelism between the egocentric individual and the idolatrous group can be carried still a step further. The Ego through its one-sidedness originates the Shadow, the center of the repressed functions within the individual's own unconscious structure. Then the same functions and qualities appear in the outer world; the role of the enemy is unconsciously transferred to someone else. The "evil" is first located outside the individual; later it is recognized as a part of our inner life; the transference is traced to its source; and this discovery usually initiates the crisis, the breakdown of the Ego, and the start of a new life, either real faith or idolatry.

Exactly the same process can be observed in the development of the idolatrous group. The group first discovers the outer enemy, the rival group and the competitive Idol. This engenders outer danger, fight, discipline and aggressiveness, which constitutes the belligerent or heroic period of the group's history. Rather soon, however, the next step follows, leading in the opposite direction. Consciously the idolater cannot understand how a normal person could possibly worship another Idol than his. His Idol appears (to him) to be the real Self and the center of reality; the others claim the same for their Idol and their vision of life. And the two Idols contradict each other completely. One group, let us say, idolizes the austere, ascetic rules of misunderstood monasticism, their leader wearing a black monk's hood and a long beard; while the other group tries to live in the complete anarchy, promiscuity and irresponsibility of misunderstood "return to nature," its leader wearing nothing but the green vines of Dionysius. To the majority of mankind both groups are equally ridiculous; but in their own eyes they are the only "righteous" people in the world; and to each other they are the arch-enemy and abomination. From the psychological point of view the very fact that they exist together and that they are not able to redeem each other, means that both of them are doomed. Indeed, history often destroys one idolatrous group through another one; but not so much by outer warfare as by an inner process of fermentation.

Consciously the ascetics in our example despise and pity the Dionysians; and vice versa. Both of them enjoy the superiority of having the right insight and the mission with which to convert their opponents. As long as a member of the ascetic group meets the Dionysians officially, nothing will happen. He will preach, arouse resistance, and go away with the deep satisfaction of a martyr for his cause. As soon, however, as he meets them privately he will make the strange and dangerous discovery that, after all, those horrible Dionysians are not quite as bad as they are pictured in the pamphlets of the asceticists. There is some understanding possible; some inner response, some "yes" arises within the visitor's mind where his group loyalty would demand a reckless and blind "No!" The unlived life of the ascetic is experienced in the Dionysian group; and vice versa.

This discovery prompts a new inner crisis in the visitor. The value of his group, the truth of his idolatry, the identity of his Idol with the real center, are questioned—and all the birth-pangs of the maturing personality begin once more. The second half of his crisis cannot now again be blocked. He relapses out of the sham security of the idolatrous group into the unbearable uncertainty and loneliness of his private doubts and errors and experiments. Thus he learns the bitter lesson that each individual has to find the way alone, by himself, and that no ready-made formula, no group conviction, no Idol can spare us the hardship of our own development. And by going the way which he is forced to go, he finally finds himself, and the real center, and the real "We."

This individual member is lost to his former group, and his case becomes a temptation and danger to many of his fellow idolaters. He has lost his faith in the Idol, he has left the group; and the fact that his infidelity, painful as it might have been, did not destroy him, but on the contrary gave him increasing health and creativity—this fact imperils the group and the power of its Idol more seriously than any outer enemy could do.

The spell of the Idol has to be defended by every means. Persuasion and force, praise and punishment, lies and calumnies are used, indeed must be used, with reckless cruelty. Their "highest values of life" are at stake, and since their Idol to them is God, or at least first cousin to God, no bad conscience or feeling of guilt can arise, and "anyone who kills you will imagine that he is performing a service to God" (Jn 16:2). This is the source of all fanaticism.

Every idolatrous group is prone to project its unlived group life, its unconscious Anti-Idol or Devil, on its inner enemies, the rebels within its own ranks, even more than on the outer enemy, the rival group or the competitive Idol. Each idolater is imperiled by the potential collapse of the group. Each one is afraid that he may have to face the second half of his private crisis; therefore, in defending his Idol he defends his own immaturity; and in cursing the rebellious infidel he tries to prevent his own relapse into the process of development. Therefore he is as ruthless as a drowning man fighting for his last chance of life.

If the idolater is forced to admit that the idol does not solve all the problems, and that there is therefore "unlived life" in the idolatrous group, he will instantly discover that the group has not solved all his private problems either, and the responsibility for the "unlived life" will shift from a collective to an individual one. He will discover that each member is accountable for the collective debts which the group has accumulated. Consequently the relapse from idolatry into individualism originates terrible feelings of guilt. And the lack of any center or pseudo-center—the Ego having already failed earlier, the Idol failing now, and the real center not yet being available—throws all the members of the collapsing idolatrous group into a state of utmost confusion, and confusion results in anxiety.

The psychological situation at such a moment seems to be rather close to the appalling description of the great tribulations in Matthew 24, when Jesus foretold the destruction of the temple and what great calamities would precede it. Many scholars have thought that these descriptions were nothing but "old Jewish traditions" which did not fit in with Jesus' teachings nor with reality. Depth-psychology has now rediscovered this phenomenon in the life of individuals as well as of groups and nations. And the microscope of psychology is not even necessary, for wherever we look in history—present and past—we find tribulation; and we begin to understand that this is a way—the more painful of two possible ways—which may lead us upward to a new plane of development. These crises, therefore, have to come; "but the end is not yet."

The most tragic example of an idolatrous group is a family in which one member is idolized by all the others. Imagine a young mother who loses her husband or feels betrayed by him. Her egocentric hopes break down, her Ego resigns; life would be meaningless to her were it not for her only child. For him, however, she continues her toils; he becomes the center and the justification of her further existence. She has overcome her Ego, her whole life is one of sacrifice and service; but she has not found the real center: she serves an Idol. She gives herself to her son, but she cannot give her son to a cause, or to God. The boy to her is more valuable than anything or any one in the universe, and if God should threaten to take him away she would say: "You cannot do this, for it would be immoral, and you must remain moral. If the boy dies, then I will see, God, that you do not really exist." God has to serve the boy, not the boy, God.

All idolized family members are gradually depraved by the superhuman values which are ascribed to them. They can never measure up to the expectations of their environment and they do not even try to do so. They simply pretend to be, not by endeavor and achievement but by their very birthright, the superhuman being which their worshipers want to see in them. The Idol, in this case, accepts his idolization, he believes in his own godliness. And the result is not—as his mother may hope—a new Christ, but a cruel, reckless oriental despot, who cold-bloodedly annihilates his opponents.

The mother who believes that her child is an angel by this error forces him to become a devil. The husband who idolizes his wife brings about her moral and physical decay. We destroy what we want to preserve most eagerly. The unconscious suicide of the Ego, which we mentioned earlier, is paralleled by the unconscious murder of our idols. But in idolatry the secret crime is more efficient and more far reaching: the idolaters kill their Idol and the Idol kills its worshipers. All evil is busy destroying itself.

In larger groups we often find the same development as in the idolatrous family. "Caesarean madness" is the typical fate of the human being who confuses himself with God. And the larger the number of worshipers the more people are suddenly faced with the "inner tribulation," namely the second half of their individual crises, when at last the Idol is unmasked as a poor lunatic or a morbid fool. And so strong is our fear of the "inner tribulation" that when our Idols begin to collapse some of us succeed in whitewashing, in repairing them time and again. Or we worship a notorious fool rather than live without our Idol.

If the idolized person honestly believes in his own absolute value and power, he may perform miracles and wield an uncanny spiritual influence over thousands of people, until the unavoidable Caesarean madness destroys him and turns the enthusiasm of his followers into anxiety and "gnashing of teeth." If the idolized person is aware of his predicament, however, two opposite attitudes are possible. He may be an egocentric and exploit the illusions of his admirers, laughing at their gullibility, as is the case, unfortunately, with many artists, actors and lecturers. Or he may be more or less objective and eager to serve the real center. Then he will strive gradually to open the eyes of his followers and to make them independent of himself as soon as he can. They might do their best to prevent this progress; but, if he really lives out of his center, he will finally force them through darkness and loneliness into maturity. That is what Jesus did. His is one of the very few examples in history which show (in the three temptations) that not only egocentricity but idolatry can be avoided, and that when it arises among the disciples it can be overcome and corrected. It was this he meant, when he said: "My going is for your good. If I do not depart, the Helper will not come to you" (Jn 16:7). And then by his death he forced them, against their will, to face the last phase of their own crises, to grow fearless and independent and mature, and to be initiated into the life of the Spirit.

Yet there is another tragedy which threatens all idolatrous groups and which can postpone the final collapse of the Idol and the new beginning of spiritual life for an indefinite time. That is the egocentric deviation of idolatry.

The idolaters have to defend their Idols not only against outer enemies (competitive groups) and inner enemies (possible renegades in their midst) but also against their own inner doubts. When they joined the group, as we said before, all problems seemed to be solved, apparently no aspect of life remained un-lived, and the Ego together with the Shadow was reintegrated into the new—though eccentric—We-experience. Ten years later, however, the situation is different. The inner life of the individual has grown, and this growth should have been, but was not, a conscious development. The real center has continued to be creative. But the Idol is separated from the real center, denying its existence and pretending to be the center itself. Therefore, the Idol is not creative. Its new contributions to group life are meager and similar to the pseudo-productivity of the Ego: the remnant of power, great or small, but no longer increasing, is spread out thinly; living thoughts are replaced by empty analogies or artifi-cial definitions, and questions which cannot be answered are discarded as being "against the law."

The further growth of the individual member cannot take place inside the conscious life of the group, nor inside his own consciousness, which must not differ from the life of the group. Thus the new development is confined to the unconscious, which means a primitive and elementary awakening of images and this, according to the creed of the group, should not exist at all. Imagine a boy who is "converted" at the age of twelve and becomes a member of the ascetic group which we mentioned before. Good people, he is taught, have no sex life. At the age of twenty-two he still has no conscious sex life; he still is a loyal member of the group. But unconsciously he indulges in wild and sadistic fantasies, and his dreams reveal the sexual level of a caveman. In the opposite case, a girl has joined in the exuberance of her teens the Dionysian group which boasts of its promiscuity. Sexual restrictions, she assumes, are silly; modern people laugh at them. At twenty-five, however, she begins to feel a peculiar longing for husband and child; and to stifle her natural growth, her taste for monogamy, she has to proclaim loudly, in words and actions, that modern man is polygamous—and shallow—and dis-gusted with his shallowness.

In both cases the desperate war against real life is waged for the sake of a certain kind of sham-life which may be properly described as the Group-Ego. Its relation to the real center is similar to the relation of the individual Ego to the same center. The difference, however, is that the Group-Ego is a collective mask, expressed in terms of "We" (*we* are asexual; or, *we* are polygamous); and, therefore, has more tenacity than the individual Ego. The relationship between the Group-Ego and the Idol itself can best be described in terms of development. The Idol at first is a person. Later he may be superseded by a place, like a palace or a temple, or by some insignia, like a crown or a garment. All this, however, does not sufficiently protect the idolatrous group against the danger of accruing unlived life. Therefore around the Idol a fortress is built in the form of habits, rules, laws, theories, and especially an elaborate educational system.

The philosophers prove, the teachers teach, the lawyers proclaim and the policemen show by physical force that the Idol is right. And all this together creates an impersonal style of life which more and more obliterates the original Idol. The latter, at least, was a person, and deviated as he may have been, he lived a tragic life, deserved our human interest, and aroused psychological curiosity. Group-egocentricity, however, is a dead, mechanical apparatus, unconsciously designed to protect the group against its own creativity. If the Idol is the mask of the real center, the Group-Ego can be described as the coffin of this mask, a beautiful whitewashed sepulcher. In literature it appears as a rigid system of ideas, an "Ism."

The characteristics of the "Ism" are the same as those of egocentricity. The first is the assumed completeness of the vision of reality. The "Ists" know, or at least they say, "one day we will know" everything. And facts which disturb their views are boldly denied. The physicist, for instance, if he is an idolatrous Ist, cannot discover any meaning in dreams; nor can the Christian Scientist, if he is an idolatrous Ist, discover the reality of matter. Every Ism in this sense is absolutism; even the relativist believes that his relativism is absolutely right.

Second, the Ism includes, visibly or invisibly, a rigid valuation. He who subscribes to the Ism is good. All others are bad, or at least stupid; they have to be instructed or changed, and if necessary forced to acknowledge the truth. In this sense every Ism is moralism.

Third, the real center is excluded, because the Ism is based on idolatry and the Idol replaces the center. Continuing creation, the essentially new, therefore, cannot be acknowledged (lest it overthrow the Idol and his Ism). It is instructive to see how the opposite Isms have solved this problem in similar ways. Natural "scientism" says that by means of cause and effect the future is determined, nothing really new can happen, the parts of every new whole have been present from the beginning. And the "theologist" says God once created the universe; now he supports it; but there is no new creation any more. In both cases the Group-Ego is protected against dangerous surprises—theoretically. Practically, however, the growing though repressed life will rebel against its imprisonment. It will bring about one explosion after another until the Isms themselves are exploded.

The Ism defends itself, asserting eagerly how and why all other Isms are wrong. But it has no adequate weapons against real growth. And one day life will present it with undeniable facts which simply show that the Ism is insufficient. (Thus the telescope proved that the Ptolemaic view of the world was wrong; and hypnotism proved that materialism was inadequate.) But, curiously enough, for large numbers of people the authority of the Ism, or the Idol which supports it, is strong enough to outweigh the most obvious facts—until the breakdown of the corresponding social patterns prompts the inner crisis by outer disaster.

This process is hastened by the fact that more and more egocentric individuals misuse the same Ism together with the idolaters. The Idol is inaccessible for egocentric people, but the Group-Ego can be exploited by them. Many Ists therefore have not only to face the second half of their crisis but the first half too. That means that all their private egocentric blunders, tricks and even crimes are committed "in the name of the Ism." And this, fortunately, though unjustly, promotes the catastrophe.

All great religions are eruptions of truth. Christianity in particular shows an inexhaustible power, which time and again has exploded the Group-Egos of deviated communities as often as they became too rigid. And its dynamics seem to increase rather than to diminish. Idolatry and group-egocentricity can throw their poisonous cloak over everything; all sciences and arts, philosophies and religions can be misused in the service of the Group-Ego as well as of the private Ego. And every prophet can be misunderstood as an Idol. If they lose their power, smothered by the Ego-love of their followers, they will disappear. It is the most encouraging fact in history that Christianity, however often and deeply it has been misused and misunderstood, has never been quenched nor lost its spiritual power.

Part IV:
The Creative Way Through the Crisis
Conscious Growth

Our feud against egocentricity is sometimes misinterpreted as a disparagement of individualism. However, it is a fact we observe everywhere that people who try to live for their own sake, considering the satisfaction of their private desires as their highest goal, are disowned by life in an unmistakable way. They are doomed to tension, frustration, irritability and fear, though the latter may remain unconscious for a long time. Therefore, we want to avoid or decrease as much as we can this deviation which we have carefully investigated and labeled "egocentricity." It is similar to, but more refined than, egoism and almost identical with what is usually called "rugged individualism." But we do not condemn individualism as such.

All human life begins in a peculiar state of instinctive collectivity, which psychologically may be described as "the original We-experience." The little child, like the primitive savage, has no consciousness of being different from other members of the group. Subjectively he is not aware of any conflict between his own interest and the interest of the others. And objectively he shows no difference between the conscious and unconscious strata of his mind. We describe his psychological state as "tribal consciousness." The individual knows, feels, thinks and wants only what the group knows, feels, thinks and wants. All mental and emotional forces, courage and fear, joy and sorrow, belong to the group and not to the individual. The little child has to share his life with others, or it cannot develop. This organic unity of the original We-group is beautiful, but not enviable.

The way of history has been, and, as far as we know, the goal of history still is, the unfolding of human life and especially the gradual evolution from tribal to individual consciousness, and from collective to personal responsibility. Unfolding, "differentiation," however, has to be balanced by unification or "integration": the individual should become conscious not only of his unique personality (for everyone is unique and cannot be replaced by anyone else) but he should become conscious also of his own membership in the group and of his responsibility for the other members and for the group as a whole. His consciousness should become personal, he should discover that he is different, with special qualities and rights and duties of his own, but his consciousness should not be narrowed down to the interests of one single individual. It should not even remain tribal, in the sense of understanding the qualities, needs and interests of the group. It should grow, include and integrate the qualities, needs and interests of other groups: it should become universal. Our consciousness becomes more personal, different from other consciousnesses, and at the same time more universal: we become alive to our participation in the development of mankind, we become world-conscious. But each individual should find and maintain his own viewpoint, his own individual kind of world-consciousness. There should be no uniformity; nor should there be indistinctness, nor indulgence in vague generalities.

The word consciousness, however, denotes only one important aspect of our human problems. The other aspect, equally important, and inseparable from the first, may be characterized by the word "power." Growing consciousness without growing power is a miserable deformity. The clairvoyant who does not know what to do with his insight is a frequent example. If his consciousness were really clear he would know that he has to dig up and develop his power, courage and aggressiveness until they equal his clairvoyance. Then he would become what he was meant to be: one of the superior strategists of human evolution. And in the opposite case, the person who wields more power than consciousness is a dangerous maniac. He is almost bound to become an idol. People will admire him and expect him to be as wise as he is strong, and soon he will break down under the responsibilities which life bestows on him far beyond his conscious horizon.

Thus we may say: The equilibrium of consciousness and power constitutes the desirable type of character which history, as far as we know, wants us and almost compels us to develop. We call this type the mature personality, and the process of maturing which leads up to this goal, individuation. In order to understand the latter term more clearly, however, two questions must be answered which necessarily arise from the foregoing discussion.

The first question is a very old one: How can the individual, becoming more and more conscious of his individual needs, possibilities, and desires, at the same time serve the group and its interest? Is there not a fundamental conflict between social duties and personal enjoyment? Were not the moralists right in decreeing that the individual must be compelled by laws, praise and punishment to fulfill his duties towards society, and that otherwise there would be anarchy and social chaos?

The second question is a new one. Fifty years ago it could not yet have been asked, because it presupposes the knowledge and acknowledgment of conscious and unconscious psychological functions. The question is twofold, related to consciousness and power: If individuation means that the individual emerges out of the tribal consciousness, is it not then advisable for the individual to separate himself from his tribe as much as possible? How can he feel responsible for the group, and how can he maintain his membership in the group though he seeks to free himself from it more and more? And if the power at first is concomitant with tribal consciousness, must not the individual consciousness lose all power? Or, how can the power be shifted from the tribe to the individual? How can tribal power be transformed into personal power?

The answer to both questions is one. Based on our theory concerning the structure of the human mind, it represents a working hypothesis, scientifically neither better nor worse than other hypotheses. It has the advantage of being largely in accordance with the experiences of many centuries as recorded in religious literature, and it can be used and tested by anyone who wishes to do so.

The answer is this: Our duties toward ourselves and toward our social environment coincide. Indeed there is only one duty—namely, to grow mature. To find ourselves our center, our highest value, means to find our group, our spiritual home and our positive relationship to God. It means unlimited growth, both of individual creativity and of expanding brotherhood. The pessimist objects: This is a beautiful fairy tale, well suited to win acquiescence, but it does not solve our problems because it is not true.

Answer: It holds good in practical life. Only our egocentric goals are in conflict with our social duties—and with our duties toward ourselves—and ultimately with our egocentric interests. Even from the viewpoint of the Ego it would be better to be less egocentric. But the real interest, the natural goal and the ethical duty of the individual, is to become aware of his real nature so that by expanding his consciousness he discovers his inner imagery, representing his fellow men.

Both his inner images and his companions in outer life are reciprocal factors in his development; in hurting them he hurts himself. He has membership in many groups; and the more richly his inner imagery unfolds itself the larger grows the number of individuals, and groups, and groups of groups whom he understands and loves. His responsibility for other people is the same as his responsibility for his eye or his hand; what happens to them happens to his inner image, and that means to the organs of his mental organism. If he does not develop his capacity to love his fellow men, the inner images will atrophy, the buried talents will degenerate and grow like cancer; he will hate his brothers; and his unlived life, the psychic cancer, will torture him until he stops and turns to face his crisis—or until he dies.

The egocentric person, the immature individual, disappears. He perishes or he outgrows his handicaps. And the same is true for idolaters and egocentric groups. In the long run human history is an endless series of inexorable ultimata, always handing down the same verdict: grow up or perish. To grow up, however, means to become oneself and that means to become an epitome of mankind, namely to become conscious of human nature—through the images. Or in other words: mankind, through these images, becomes conscious reality within the individual.

Here we reach the point where the deepest riddle of psychology has to be faced. It is the mystery which is indicated in our central equation: the real center, the Self of the individual, is identical with the center of the group and with our relationship to God; or in a simplified formula:

$$\text{The Self} = \text{the We} = \text{He}$$

The Gospel of St. John expresses the same idea in the words ". . . that they may be one, even as we are one—I in them and you in me—that they may be made perfectly one" (Jn 17:22–23). Thus the mature personality is on the one hand free, independent and self-responsible; he represents his group and the whole of humanity in his own unique way, and makes his special contribution in his own manner—that is individualism. And on the other hand he remains and indeed becomes more and more an essential part of the whole. The more his maturity develops the more he sees how dependent he is. His interests and endeavor are concerned with the whole which supports him; the growing brotherhood conditions his inner life; and last but not least, his creative power is the power of the group—it is a super-individual power.

In the mature personality mankind reaches a higher level of consciousness; creation continues, the race, as it were, awakens; deeper and more powerful layers of the collective unconscious are brought to light. They become individualized and remain universal at the same time. Thousands of people find their own problems expressed, lived and solved in the lives and works of these men. The consciousness and the power of the integrated person are at the same time individual and collective. We can find this in variant degrees wherever there are mature people; and it becomes evident beyond doubt when the great names of mankind are mentioned: Dante, Shakespeare, Dostoievsky, Goethe, Beethoven, Lincoln—they are symbols, not idols, of human evolution. (The better we know their deficiencies the less we can idolize them.)

Thus we may say: individuation is the way of human development which leads from tribal power and consciousness to individual power and consciousness by way of growing integration. The collective problems, possibilities and responsibilities become parts of our individual consciousness and tasks for our individual creative power. The sorrows of humanity become our personal sorrows and the creative power of the race is entrusted to us in individual forms.

But the riddle remains. Just how the original center, the tribal or group center, which evidently is one, can be multiplied into innumerable individual centers, and how the different consciousnesses of several individuals are able to preserve their original oneness, or regain it after having lost it through differentiation—this problem cannot be solved by philosophical discussions. And it is useless to make lofty metaphysical statements to the effect that beyond space and time there is neither oneness nor multiplicity nor number. We ourselves simply have to live, to grow, and to mature. Only in this way can we come nearer to the truth.

One consideration, however, concerning the relationship of consciousness and power, may throw some additional light on the course we must follow. There are two kinds of consciousness. You can be conscious of your hand as you are conscious of a tree: the object exists in the outer world and you can study it from outside. Now close your eyes and be conscious of your hand from inside, and you will discover that you are within your hand. The hand is you. If someone hits it you say, "You hit *me.*" Then, look at your wife, first from the outside: she is an object, like the tree; second from inside: try to feel her existence as you felt your hand. If someone hurts her you will feel, "He hurts *me*"; and the more so the more your contact image, the Eve image, is alive. If you don't feel it then do something to overcome your egocentricity or idolatry.

The inner kind of consciousness—we may call it subjective consciousness—is identical with power. If someone steps on your toes you will react vigorously, and if he hurts your wife, your Eve-image will tell you immediately what has to be done. No lack of courage, no alibi, no "reasonable scruples" will stop you; your power will be aroused and will act. Otherwise you are cut off from your Eve-image by egocentricity or by idolatry.

Expanding consciousness includes both the subjective and the objective attitudes. We develop our objective consciousness by seeing and understanding the outer world more completely. Here the inner imagery provides the organs of perception. You cannot perceive what happens to an underprivileged child unless you harbor a responsive image of boy or girl. Yet if you do so you cannot limit yourself to objective observation. You cannot help being involved emotionally, subjectively, centrally, and that means religiously. Here again the inner images function as channels of power. What happens to the underprivileged children happens to you. They are hurt, your inner images suffer with them, your creative power is challenged. You will react vigorously, provided you are not petrified by egocentricity or idolatry.

The relationship between power and consciousness is dynamic. It forces us to grow or to suffer. We may describe it in the following way: "I am hurt because the underprivileged child is hurt. I am furious, I am a channel of subjective power. At the same time I look more objectively at the one who hurts the child. And I feel with him, too. I become subjectively conscious of him; he, too, is represented in my inner imagery. I understand him, he is part of myself. I hurt the child when he does it. I hurt myself. My reaction against him becomes reaction against myself. If I hurt him, I hurt myself anew. The outer conflict becomes an inner one. I have to create a new way of dealing with both of them, or they will destroy my life. I must be, and will be, creative."

Expanding consciousness is identical with expanding creative power, or it is not expanding at all. And if it expands it brings about a deeper individual responsibility, higher capacities and increasing courage. The creative center is alive, the collective images grow; and both the central power and the images through which it functions become more conscious every day. Thus the mature personality through his own development shows his fellowmen the path to the future. He is the pioneer exploring the next step in evolution. By doing so he furthers creation; and that means he is a servant of God.

The way of individuation is painful. We can avoid some, but not all, of its suffering by way of prevention through better education, re-education and self-education. And it is here more than anywhere else, in the field of "watching and praying" that religion, psychology and medicine should cooperate. But there will still be crises and catastrophes, with bewilderment, fear and anxiety, even for the best prepared and wisest men. Our own death or the death of our beloved ones may be the crucial test. And if we are able to face this, perhaps we will have to go through the breakdown of the cultural values in our group and our nation. Would we under such circumstances still retain our faith and creativity? Would we be able to go the way of Job?

Theoretically we may say that all suffering is due to deviation. If mankind had never gone astray, if neither Egos nor Idols had replaced the real center, the whole way from tribal to individual consciousness and from the tribe's responsibility for the tribe to the individual's responsibility for the world, would have taken place without fear or suffering. But this is a purely theoretical idea. As a matter of fact every step forward in the development of individuals and groups is hampered by fears and sorrows, prejudices and inhibitions, consciously as well as unconsciously, and individually as well as collectively.

Our inner evil, the disease which thwarts our development and confuses our history is simple in its direction: it is rebellion against time, as we have stated above, and therefore is resistance against evolution, or, if we prefer the religious term, against creation itself. Yet is is complicated in its inner structure and cannot be overcome by the simple and childlike resolve "not to sin any more." We must study it carefully and overcome it gradually by wise and long-range religious strategy. It is in this area that depth-psychology can and will make its contribution.

Our general aversion against time and what time does to us results in the conviction that we are completely conditioned by the past. The past, we think, is certain, we can rely on it, while the future is insecure and dangerous. We try to build dams and canals to control the floods of the future. We "take thought," we trouble about what we are to eat or drink, applying our experiences, conscious and unconscious, to the future, as if circumstances ten years from now would still be the same as they were ten years ago. That is why we "store up treasures where moth and rust corrode" and cherish our egocentric prejudices as if they were truths.

In the realm of mental life a false conviction becomes a mock-truth, an illusion. It bears fruit as a psychic reality; it causes reactions of infinite consequence. And as an error it leads finally to catastrophe. Thus the conviction that the past is more important and more real than the future influences our thinking in science and philosophy to the effect that causality and its correlative ideas, determinism and irresponsibility, are considered as the exclusive scientific truth. The opposite view, creativity, freedom and responsibility, is deemed poetical dreaming and idealistic superstition.

This false conviction about the past, however, does not originate in the lofty realm of thought and theory. Its foundations are not to be found in the conscious mind (otherwise philosophical discussion would lead us nearer to truth, which it never does). A wrong philosophy is always based on some distortion in the unconscious structure of the philosopher's mind. Discouragement of little children engenders unconscious fears and inhibitions which later produce, unconsciously, the wrong kind of thinking, thinking based on real experiences and true facts but wrongly interpreted.

It is not our conscious philosophy, our "reasonable caution," it is our unconscious discouragement and its result, our inner "eccentricity," which force us to rely on the past and to forestall the future. There are in the first line, of course, our individual experiences, some of them still in our memory, most of them forgotten or repressed. We have learned that we must not do certain things and that certain other things must be done; we have learned to pigeonhole people and situations: "this is good, that is bad; this man is kind, the other one is dangerous." The world has become a rigid pattern of categories. And worst of all, we think we know ourselves; we mistake our capacities and limitations in such a way that actually we are limited by our belief in our limitations, and yet are incapable in spite of the confidence in our capacities. Egocentric confidence does not help us, and objective confidence is not available as long as we trust only the past. In this sense we are determined, unfree, conditioned; we are slaves of the past; we are discouraged, limited, inhibited; and the best thing that the future could bring us is a terrible crisis. And as you know, old slaves prefer to remain slaves.

Are we not right in smiling condescendingly at our children's undaunted hope for a golden time to come? "They are not yet disillusioned, not yet sobered down by reality," we think. And most of us cannot imagine that there could be a third point of view, fusing the confidence of the child and the disillusionment of the adult into real courage and real faith.

But the discovery of a third point is a complicated task. Not only do our individual negative experiences have to be overcome; we are not only liable for our own mistakes; we have to pay, as it were, the debts of our parents, our century and our whole race. The "breach of the original We" and all the ensuing discouragements of our childhood were possible only because our parents and educators were not creative enough. Their love lacked either wisdom or warmth. And this was so because they themselves had not been brought up in the right way. Their faults were the results of the faults of their educators; and so back to Adam's fall. We are saturated with the results of the egocentricity or idolatry of all our ancestors. The transmission of evil from one generation to the other has been described earlier; we may call this method of transmission the outer or educational way. Yet there is an inner means too by which negativity is transferred from one generation to the other: this may be called the biological way. And here is the point at which we need the collaboration of natural scientists, physicians, and especially endocrinologists.

The genes, as we know, carry the human inheritance, physical as well as psychological, and transmit all kinds of destructive and degenerative factors as well as positive ones. Concerning the inheritance of inner images very little is known. A certain difference between the imagery of far distant races seems to exist, constituting at the same time the cause and effect of the cultural background. Within the deeper layers of the minds of half-castes our psychological research reveals not two different sets of images, but two styles or atmospheres which make the images much richer, more varied and less distinct (but not less rigid) than in the case of pure racial stock. The son of a Slavic father and a French mother after having sufficiently analyzed his "unconscious of the past" was able to distinguish rather exactly the two possibilities or styles of life equally at his disposal. He amused himself by preferring one year what he called his "Tolstoi-soul" and the next year his "Anatole-France-soul." Thus far he was not a slave of his past.

More important for us is the psychological inheritance which is concomitant with the slighter degrees of "blastophthoria," that is, the damage done to the genes by alcoholism, syphilis or psychotic tendencies. If one of your four great-grandfathers was a drinker, to a slightly greater degree than the average of his contemporaries, or if one of your ancestors was a great musician or a very secluded misanthrope—you will surely have to pay the price for what they did or omitted to do. Is it your glandular system which influences your imagery? Or do the inner images cause the glands to work the wrong way? In any case, your inheritance prompts you to react more violently to all negative experiences which challenge your nervous equilibrium. If the teacher blames you, you feel hellfire and brimstone raining down upon your head, while your classmate in the same situation can scarcely refrain from laughing. Later you are driven to write novels or to found a new denomination, while he lives comfortably by selling insurance. The "sins of our fathers" are alive within us; we have to redeem our ancestry or we cannot live at all.

Another chain of cause and effect must be mentioned here, too. It is not necessarily "unconscious" in the proper sense of the word; it may be recorded in documents, letters and family tradition. You may know it, yet you have to pay for it, to accept it as part of your personal fate, and to forgive your ancestors for having acted as they did. This is the fact that one of them, let us say, about 1700, migrated to Russia, or to America. Another one married the wealthiest girl in Boston; or he could have done so and married a gypsy instead. The third one held many shares of a deserted gold mine and sold them the day before the mine turned out to be the richest one in the country.—Our financial and social situation is largely conditioned by our forefathers' decisions and actions; and we have to accept them as though we had made them ourselves.

Our responsibilities, debts and liabilities are collective and cover the whole of human history. Our nightmares and our sleeplessness, our fear of the future and our hatred of competitiors may well be induced or intensified by the gloomy tragedies which our ancestors endured for thousands of years. How can we, discouraged and loaded with negativity as we are, make up for all the accumulated evil of the past? Are we not truly in a debtor's jail?

For twenty or thirty years it looked as though depth-psychology would find the way out. Freudianism and Adlerianism proclaimed the remission of all debts. Bad conscience, feelings of guilt, fear and anxiety were "nothing but" errors acquired in early childhood, and individual repressions resulting from these errors. Two bloody world wars were needed to prove that this was only half of the truth.

Now we know better: Jung discovered the collective beneath the individual unconscious; and the darkness that we have to face grew to super-human proportions. The more the "unconscious of the past," the storehouse of racial memories, was investigated, the more it seemed to determine our future. We became more and more enslaved by the past. There was no doubt: depth-psychology, medicine, mental hygiene and eugenics were not sufficient. Strong as they were they were not strong enough to pay our debts, to free us from our obligations and to open the way to the future. Then we understood that only religion was able to do this.

And there were religious voices—or were they pseudo-religious ones? Indeed they had been heard already for some time, saying: "There is no evil! Look for the positive value which is to be found within everyone and everything. Do not countenance negative thoughts or feelings, they are wrong. Everything is beautiful. We are not fettered by the past, nor by sin, nor by diseases, nor by wrong social orders. There is no darkness; just believe in the light." It was a powerful message; and it seemed to work. Many people became much happier.

But—cities were raided, thousands of women and children were maimed. "Everything is beautiful, there is no darkness." Millions of soldiers were killed in action, nations reduced nations to starvation. "We are not fettered by sin," Are we not? Is there no evil in our world? Should we not do something about it?

Religion without a thorough study of sin, religion without awareness of conscious and unconscious, individual and collective darkness, evil and deviation, is not religion but blind idolatry. Let us be aware, as honestly and objectively as we can, of our dangers and negativities. Let us bring to consciousness this terrible "unconscious of the past," let us face the task as depth-psychology reveals it. Let us acknowledge our individual and collective debts. And, knowing that there is no other possibility, let us look for the really religious way out. This is what we know about the way out:

During the second half of the crisis both idolatry and egocentricity disappear. Our method of thinking changes completely, not because some one convinces us of a new truth, but because the underlying structure of our mind breaks down and is replaced by a new one which is at the same time old and original. Life once more pivots around the real center as it used to do at the time of tribal consciousness. But during the period of egocentricity our consciousness has been individualized, and now it remains individual. Thus the result is individual consciousness of the real, and that means universal, center. This new-old structure produces a new-old kind of thinking. Gradually our whole vision of life is revised; our emotional attitude towards people and circumstances is transformed; the scope of our consciousness is enlarged; and our responsibility is felt in a new and more comprehensive way.

The change is neither sudden nor complete. It covers several years as a process of organic growth; otherwise the human mind could not stand it. But in a psychological description it is advisable to omit the factor of slow development and to contrast the attitudes and especially the methods of thinking before and after a person's crisis—let us say, for example, at the ages of thirty-five and forty-five, assuming that the crisis reached its climax at the age of forty. And still another preliminary remark is necessary before we enter into this decisive aspect of our psychology. People who have gone through their crises will recognize the facts immediately, even though they may prefer another terminology or even another viewpoint for the description. Those who have made at least a few successful steps through the first stages of the crisis will understand without too much difficulty. But all those who have not yet faced their crises or who have withdrawn from them into idolatry or more sophisticated egocentricity, will not be able to find the slightest degree of meaning in all this. They will say, "Why should we read this stuff? After all, we are not morons!" And they will be right, they should not read it.

Here our psychology is in the same predicament as the preaching of St. Paul because we have to speak about the same paradoxical truth. It is and must be "sheer folly" to most psychologists (1 Cor 1:21–23). But if there are people who have—more or less—gone through this inner change which we call the crisis; and if their experiences and reactions are different from the experiences and reactions of people who have not yet gone so far, then there must be a psychology of "post-critical" life, though "pre-critical" readers will be deaf to its language. Youngsters before they go through puberty cannot appreciate the psychology of married life. The materialist must deem St. Francis a fool. This fact, however, should not prevent our writing on the psychology of St. Francis, provided we can find a viewpoint which allows us to understand his experience.

The change, as we said, expressed itself most clearly in our ways of thinking, in philosophical and scientific reflections as well as in practical considerations. The connection of cause and effect, resulting in concepts of necessity and lack of freedom, is not forgotten, but is embraced in the larger scheme of means and goals. Causality becomes a servant of creative freedom.

The new viewpoint, however, is quite different from the cheap anthropomorphic "teleology" of the year 1600. It is based on carefully observed psychological facts. And it shows in many practical experiences that we are conditioned by the past only insofar as our inheritance provides certain means, limitations and tasks. Our goals and possibilities, our incentive, power and creativity come to us from the future. The past, we may say, limits some of our means, though not all of them; but the future creates new possibilities. We have no wings because our ancestors, millions of years ago, became mammals rather than birds; yet we may build airplanes and fly nevertheless.

The chain of cause and effect is infinite, and so is the pyramid of means and goals. There is no "first cause" and no "final goal." Every goal becomes a means in the service of a still higher goal. And every means can be replaced by another one. This dizzying view should set us free from fear and enable us to play our part in the work of creation in spite of all our handicaps and all our sense of guilt—if only we could find the faith which reveals within ourselves the creative force of the Center. But in the beginning this force is unconscious, unknown, unbelievable, even though it makes us grow and think and act, and sometimes gives us creative ideas long before we overcome egocentricity and idolatry.

Everyone, of course acknowledges that children are conditioned by their own future insofar as they are under the necessity of growing up. In due course they will be adolescents, adults, and finally old people; this much we can foresee. And therefore this development seems to bear out the argument for causality and determinism. The determinist says: "The seed is determined by the parental plant, and likewise the child by his race. He has to grow and to die; his so-called goals are merely biological causes projected into the future; the real causes are to be found in the genes." Are they, really? Or is all this only an artificial argument, a roundabout way of forcing future-conditioned creatures back into the pattern of past-conditioned dead things?

Determinism and egocentricity are inseparable. As soon as an egocentric person tries to imagine that human evolution may be conditioned by the future he instantly thinks: "Then we are determined by Providence—or by Platonic Ideas, which control reality as lifeless everlasting patterns." Wherever he looks he sees determinism. His Ego needs this view and will defend it to the last, and believe it even when it cannot be defended anymore. The following argument, therefore, is not meant as an attempt to convert opponents. It may, however, be an important aid to those who are close to or are already in their crises and who try to free themselves from their own deterministic prejudices.

Children, we said, may be bound to develop in certain ways and patterns, insofar as they have to repeat—not exactly but more or less—the development of their race. Yet they reach one day the end of the road which, as it were, has been built by their ancestry. They enter the firing line of civilization and have to go ahead alone into the unknown. To what extent are they still determined by the past when they enter the no-man's-land of the future?

As an example think of the problems of marriage. A hundred years ago marriage was a conventional thing; people knew what they were expected to do and they did it. Marriage, then, was a pattern almost entirely conditioned by the past. Now it is different. Every married couple nowadays has to grope its way through a pathless primeval forest. Marriage at this moment is beyond the frontiers of traditional civilization. We know that our children will marry but we do not know how they will do it; and we cannot teach them what they should do. There are books and maps and even agencies pretending to know all about the new country. But at best all they know is the past. They draw conclusions honestly and scientifically, and their conclusions would be right—if life were not changing every day and calling for real creativity, which means traveling without a map and without security.

Every individual in our time has to face situations where not only the outer tradition but even the inner equipment, habits, patterns, instincts and reflexes, fail him completely. What will his answer be if life asks him a new, and hitherto unheard of, question? If he were determined by the past, his inner pattern would produce the answer, but it does not. He is at a loss, forsaken, and he will perish unless something new, unexpected and creative turns up and solves the problem. Where does the new idea come from? Is it a mechanical and necessary result of existing conditions? Then: Why all the birth-pangs of the creative action? And why must some people fail while others succeed and shape the future with their new discoveries?

Fortunately, we have now the means to explore to a certain extent what happens in our unconscious mind during the time of crisis and the ensuing period of creativity. The animal instinct, as we have seen, is in human life largely replaced by collective imagery. The more a given predicament develops into a crisis the more we see the images "regress" to earlier stages. That means the influence of egocentricity and idolatry is undone: the images lose their distortions and their rigidity, they become more primitive and more powerful; or, we may say, they free themselves from the tyranny of idol or Ego and reestablish their original relation to the real center. Then a new development of differentiation and integration begins, the new growth leading to a new kind of life at a higher level of consciousness.

As an example, the case of a young married couple, probably one of the typical cases of our time, may be described in fuller detail. In the interest of discretion, however, it has to be slightly altered, and in order to be clear it will be somewhat simplified.

When the young man fell in love with his prospective wife he went through the first part of his crisis quickly and courageously. Not understanding what happened to him, he nevertheless sensed that some positive development had taken place, changing him "from a boy into a man"; and he knew that he owed this painful and beautiful experience to his bride. Neither Tristan nor Romeo, he felt, could have realized a deeper or more powerful love.

The girl was somewhat less enthusiastic and probably more

mature than the boy. She went into the adventure with thoughtful honesty and overcame the resistance of her family without too much trouble. She wanted him to be the father of her children, and her determination gave her courage and—as her aunts and uncles observed—a new kind of beauty. Thus, on their wedding day everyone was convinced that they would be a happy household, far above the average.

Three years later, at the climax of their difficulties, they tried to understand the situation psychologically. And what they finally discovered was this: he had developed very early two opposite Eve images, one being an almost exact portrait of his mother (as he saw her, and as she tried to be, hiding all her human deficiencies and all negative emotions). This mother ideal did not know the word "no." She pampered and spoiled the boy, her only child, and handed over all problems of discipline and authority to her husband. The opposite type was represented by an old, though extremely vital, Mexican woman who lived in the neighborhood and who was apparently fond of music and alcohol. This image, which may be called "the gypsy-mother," was despised, forgotten, almost repressed, and recurred only in some strangely exciting anxiety dreams.

Later on the image of the good mother was developed into two new opposites: first a radiant madonna, aloof, blameless, and beautiful like a statue on a golden pedestal; and, second, a kind of motherly nurse who carried all the tenderness and warmth of the earlier "ideal mother." This pre-puberty development resulted from sexual fantasies and daydreams which could not be applied to the former good mother. In the daydreams the nurse then developed into a good-natured sensual creature, half priestess, half prostitute, who without doubt had inherited some traits from the bad Mexican woman. She was well suited to fulfill all the changing desires of the growing boy, but she was so far removed from reality that she caused much feeling of embarrassment and almost of guilt. She was in danger of being condemned and repressed into the unconscious, together with her older sister, the Mexican.

Then the boy met his future wife. Up to this point all girls had been to him either madonnas or nurses. He had either adored them or had enticed them to indulge his insatiable thirst for caresses. Now he found a madonna who was a nurse. She knew how to caress without losing her heavenly dignity. She was motherly, kind, gay and not at all prudish. Thus the two images, madonna and nurse, coincided in the boy's half-conscious mind, and their fusion brought about the change in his character which we have mentioned. This was the first half of his crisis; and he mistook the half for the whole, and increasing strength for increasing maturity. The earlier "good mother" image had been restored, and he did not know that the gypsy-mother was still imprisoned in his unconscious and that her powerful image absorbed the better part of his masculinity.

His wife had learned in earlier childhood to defend herself against two older brothers and had become a tomboy. But from a few good experiences with her father, who died rather early, she sensed vaguely that one day a man would be able to help her overcome her tomboy attitude and to become her feminine self. During her teens she dominated the boys of her own age and revered some older gentlemen. But the boys left her alone and the older men were of no help to her. She experienced many disappointments and her rigid Ego-pattern was considerably softened. Then she met her future husband and instantly fell in love with him.

He was of her own age but she felt little inclination to dominate him. Instead of the brother image she transferred on him the father image, and for the first time in her life she was docile and tender toward a man who was not twenty years her senior. This new experience made her happy and convinced her that this boy could help her to become a real woman. He expected her to be his "good mother," at once nurse and madonna, and to spoil him without reward. She expected him to take care of her inner development and to overcome her childish tomboy resistance. Thus both of them were conditioned by "the unconscious of the past." Their ideas about the future, their goals and hopes were necessary results of former experiences. They were in the debtor's jail and had to pay for their own and their ancestors' deviations.

The two transferences clashed. Both were bitterly disappointed. Their hopes broke down and their confidence in life and in each other was replaced by dreary pessimism. He developed temper tantrums because she did not caress him as the mother image prescribed; and she became the tomboy again, and a furious one, because he could not awaken the gentle Sleeping Beauty who waited day and night for the daring Prince. Finally they separated; and that was the beginning of the decisive crisis for both of them.

The husband's Ego was identified with the image of "the little one who has to be nursed." Now the nurse failed him; and the breach of the egocentric sham-We was as tragic as the breach of the original We. The Ego, unable to exist without its counterpart, broke down. Sleeplessness, despair and plans of suicide followed. He behaved like a newborn baby without his mother, complaining senselessly, accusing everything and everybody, and doing nothing to change the situation. The regression to earlier attitudes was evident.

The older images turned up; older both individually and racially. The "Mexican woman," the representative of reckless Dionysian power, came to life again. The young man began to drink and to rave. Then he had an accident and was for three days in a hospital. And during this time he realized the state of complete loneliness and darkness which is significant for the climax of our crisis. Forsaken by men, not aware of God, deprived of all values of his former life and of all hopes for the future, he had to face the fact that human life has no right, no claim and no power of its own. And he accepted the fact because it was reality, and reality was nothing but this.

After a long time, presumably several hours, of dullness and vague sensations (at least vague in recollection), of anxiety and nothingness, extreme cold and extreme heat, he awoke to a new and astonishing experience of objectivity. He still felt weak and exhausted, but quite comfortable. Everything seemed to have more vivid color; people were more "real" to him than they used to be; and he realized a peculiar kind of relationship to everything and everybody. He described it as "a sincere interest but at the same time a serene detachment."

Psychologically we understand that from the viewpoint of his Ego he used to consider everything only with regard to its usefulness or injuriousness to his personal goals. Thus we may say, objects showed him only two colors: white if they pleased his Ego,

and black if they offended it. When his egocentricity was replaced, more or less, by objectivity he discovered that they had
colors of their own, regardless of their values for him. For the
first time, as it were, he saw red and blue and green—the beauty
of life. Music could be beautiful though it disturbed his sleep.
The nurse was an interesting person, though she did not spoil him
at all.

Then the young man thought of his wife. For the first time he
discovered her beauty and her personality, apart from her relationship with him. He understood that she had problems, needs
and conditions of her own; he saw that he could and should help
her; and he remembered some happy moments when, by chance,
he had done something important for her development, though
he had meant it in the interest of his Ego. Thus he knew that he
had the power to make her happy. And suddenly he discovered
that he was in love with this "lonely and disappointed creature
who looked so desperate and weak, but who was as beautiful and
powerful as nature herself."

This latter expression seems to indicate that his inner Eve-
image was no longer projected on his wife (which would have
meant idolatry) but was used as a means of contact and understanding, directing his own central power, his love, in the right
direction. He considered her deficiencies and needs as they actually were instead of imposing on her his arbitrary ideas; and
therefore he knew what he had to do. He wrote her a letter
which, as she later confessed, was altogether unusual and at once
convinced her that he had changed. She felt that he loved her and
that she could now trust him. Her Ego and her pride still advised
her to be cautious, but she could not help calling him up. Eve
responded because Adam was wooing in the right way. The result
was a new beginning, new love, and the attempt to develop a new
form of marital life with more mutual consideration, understanding and consciousness.

Before his crisis the young man had been largely conditioned
by "the unconscious of the past." The first half of his crisis had
replaced the more differentiated images (madonna and nurse) by
the more primitive image of the ideal mother. This regression
however was not sufficient. The egocentric rigidity of the mother
image did not allow a practical adjustment to the given situation.

He was still unconsciously conditioned by the past. He was still kept, because of his collective debts, in the prison of his egocentricity. His poor wife, whom he expected to play the role of the ideal mother, preferred to run away. He broke down and his regression continued; the counterpart of the ideal mother, the gypsy-mother, usurped control of his consciousness. He reintegrated her power, but did not yet begin the difficult process of redifferentiation. He behaved like a caveman, until the discrepancy between his conduct and the requirements of our civilization stalled him completely.

Even then, regression continued. The earliest, most primitive images lost their specific forms; the "unconscious of the past" was gone; the debts of history were canceled; the crisis reached its apex; the door to the real center was unlocked; and the future with its unknown values and formative forces drew him in a new direction. The "unconscious of the future" began like the dawn of morning to filter into his consciousness. And his first discovery in this new way of life was the experience that objective consciousness is We-consciousness, that our most genuine interest is the welfare of our fellow men rather than our individual welfare. When he went down and hit the rock bottom of life he found love.

The crisis, as we see, is the point where we are forsaken by the "unconscious of the past." The chains of cause and effect, all the things which are determined and may determine us, are of no avail. Not even our oldest images, representing all the inheritance of the race, can show us the way out. In such a trial we need something more, beyond the stored-up wisdom of the race, beyond the past, beyond time and space. We need creation, or we perish.

The intensity and depth of our crises vary from a few moments of utmost despair to several months of complete melancholy or a vague sense of depression which may last many years. A good many steps of the way can evidently be worked out in the unconscious, and sometimes the mature results enter our consciousness after some weeks of preparation; yet we may have been unaware of this preparation except perhaps for an incomprehensible sleepiness, tiredness or general restlessness.

The more we can observe the details of the process the more we discover the well known features of the "Great Turn," or the "Great Way," as it has been described by spiritual leaders all through the history of religion. Seen from the viewpoint of depth-psychology the essential stages of the journey are three.

The first stage is regression and reintegration. It corresponds to the "purgation" of medieval mysticism. The Ego or the idol, the rigid structure of the former life, collapses, together with all its valuations, prejudices, resentments, desires and fears. The "censorship," the screen between consciousness and the unconscious, breaks down. Old images, forgotten emotions, repressed functions, come to life again; primitive obsessions and projections, visions and nightmares endanger the equilibrium of the good citizen. Without adequate inner or outer help, religious and psychological, he will be in an evil predicament.

This is the situation which the psalmists have described with amazing exactitude: "The sorrows of death compassed me, and the floods of ungodly men made me afraid. The sorrows of hell compassed me about: the snares of death prevented me" (Ps 18:4-5). And again: "Many bulls have compassed me: strong bulls of Bashan have beset me round" (Ps 22:12). The outer and the inner evils fuse; death or insanity seems to be certain; all the negativity of the universe seems to be arrayed against us. There is only one way out: the religious way: "Yea, though I walk through the valley of the shadow of death, I will fear no evil: for thou art with me" (Ps 23:4).

The power of the images, terrifying as it may be, is borrowed power. It appears to be genuine and invincible only as long as we do not know the real center. The appeal to the center, therefore, is the only thing left for the person who is "beset by the bulls" of the collective unconscious. Even the atheist, if anything disagreeable takes him by surprise, reacts with a superficial turn to the center. He says "O God!" or "For goodness' sake!" If the believer can do the same thing in a more serious way, even though in the moment of fear or pain his concept of God may be vague or childish, it will help him more than anything else.

The turning toward the center is the second stage of the journey. But the center itself, the aspect of God which can be experienced in such a situation, is quite different from what most people expect it to be. Either we project some learned or emotional ideas into the universe; or, knowing we must have no image of God, we use an empty frame, three feet square, and according to our creed we think God will fit the frame. Yet, he does not. His appearance, if he appears at all, crushes our beautiful frame. We are frightened and offended and decree that the power which destroyed our convictions must be the devil.

The nearer we come to the center, the more we leave the images behind, the more are our fears turned into anxiety. And anxiety, if we face it, is turned into awe. What seemed to be the power of darkness now manifests itself as the power of light. After the great and strong wind comes the earthquake, then the fire, and then the still small voice (1 Kgs 19:11–13).

The terrible and destructive aspect of the godhead—the "tremendum" in theological language—originates as a subjective human experience, though an unavoidable one if our religious convictions and our rigid theology are smashed by the grace of God. We live in a jail which we call our castle; a foreign soldier breaks through the doors, come to free us by blasting the walls of our castle—and we fight him with the last might of our broken Ego, calling him scoundrel, knave and devil, until we are exhausted, overwhelmed and disarmed. Then looking at the victor with disinterested objectivity we recognize him: St. Michael smilingly sheathes his sword.

The power which brought about the fight was grace. The "evil" which caused our anxiety was, in the last analysis, grace. And even the real scoundrels, our competitors in egocentricity who betrayed us and wounded us so unjustly, even they, as we discover now, were already working unknowingly and unwillingly in the service of the super-human strategy of grace. This fact is no excuse for their evil-doing; but it shows the transcendent power and wisdom of the coming kingdom of heaven. And above all it shows that the kingdom is there already and is working in spite of and even through the errors and felonies of its prospective citizens.

Here begins the third stage of the journey, identical with the "illumination" of the old mystics. It is not only an intellectual insight but is at the same time an emotional experience of utmost reality and a volitional change which overthrows the whole system of our values, goals and means. It gives us a new viewpoint, or rather a double viewpoint, which enables us to see people at the same time as rascals and as children of God. Evil reveals its creative implications, and what we deemed to be good now shows its fiendish danger as the devil's bait. Deeper insight, more power, increasing responsibility, and above all a higher kind of love, more detached and more comprehensive—these are the characteristics of the new life, as far as we are able to describe them in the language of our empirical, and that means humanly limited, psychology.

The "unconscious of the past," we may say, was conditioned by our images and their historical forms. The "unconscious of the future" is conditioned only by the center itself. It is creative power, using the images, now cleansed and timeless, according to its creative plans, which are our own unconscious goals. The crisis then is the transition from an eccentric, less conscious and less powerful life—pivoting around the Ego-image or an idolized image—to a well-centered, more conscious and more powerful life—pivoting around the real Self. This Self proves to be the center both of the individual and of the group, and therefore transforms the individual into a servant of the group—that is love; and proves to be also our relation to God, and therefore transforms individuals and groups into servants of God—that is faith. The crisis, if it is complete, means conversion.

Our concept of "crisis" coincides with the meaning of the Greek word *metanoia* (Mt 3:2, 8; Mk 1:4), which is rather inadequately translated as "repentance." The imperative "repent!" should not be interpreted, as some modern commentators do, as "change your mind!" No one can change his mind purposefully except for the replacement of one eccentric view by another equally eccentric view. No one can voluntarily decrease his egocentricity or idolatry. The only thing we can do, and the only useful interpretation of the central Christian imperative is: do not run away from your crises; try to stand the impact of reality and to discover the light behind darkness; do not resist evil. Then evil will be found to be grace.

We have seen and can see every day how people are forced into their crises by the consequences of their deviations, and how skillfully they try to escape. Some are caught and ground in the mills of grace, which appear to be cruel and almost sadistic if looked upon from the viewpoint of Egos and idols. Some escape time and again, postponing their crises and increasing the sum total of their debts. And some seem to need not an earthly crisis but a metaphysical one: they have to go through "the eonian fire," the fire between the eons or world-ages. (The translation "everlasting fire" is incorrect; something which is beyond time cannot last.) And some, as Jesus said, "will never see death" if they obey his teaching (Jn 8:51).

There is evidently a way which leads us through the crisis without the great tribulation or the eonian fire. And Christianity is certainly the way, or at least a way, of achieving this. If our psychology is truly religious it must enable us to do what humanly can be done to find this better way, and to become a servant of God, cooperating with his will in his creation. Such religious self-education will therefore be the test stone of our psychology.

Part V:
Practical Aids on the Way Through Problems

The human predicament is obvious. We misunderstand, misuse and repress the creative powers which are entrusted to us. They turn into the negative and destroy us, unless we find a way out. This has been seen more or less clearly for at least three thousand years. Accordingly innumerable remedies have been recommended and tried. But the result has been deplorable: except for a few great leaders, a few individual saints, and some small groups which experimented with a new kind of community, the rest is mediocrity—merely conscious goodwill based on a foundation of unconscious negativity.

If we try to help others, forgetting our own worries, we are told: "Why do you note the splinter in your brother's eye and fail to see the plank in your own eye?" (Mt 7:3). And if we try to work out our own salvation we discover that we are interested only in our private welfare and in the immortality of our dear Ego. What is the way out?

The way out is clearly described in the words of the New Testament: "Your light is to shine before men, that they may see the good you do and glorify your Father in heaven" (Mt 5:16). Our positive power, if only we could develop it, would help others without our "taking splinters out of their eyes." Thus we have to go back, after all, to the plank in our own eye. How can we remove it? What are the ways and means of religious self-education?

Let us keep in mind that the endeavor of self-education will be thwarted by the egocentricity of its motives, unless the process of development brings about a thorough revision of its own motivation. We should try, therefore, from the beginning, to eliminate egocentric motives as much as possible. Especially dangerous is the egocentric admixture in our social, moral and religious goals. "I want to go this way, and I am ready to pay the highest price for the training, because I want to be a better social worker, psychologist, teacher or preacher, in order to lead others on the right way." This motive is wrong unless it is completed by the thought: "and I would go this way even if I should have to give up all preaching, teaching, consulting and social work."

Even immaculate goals such as scientific research, or the simple conviction that it is our moral duty to improve our characters, cannot provide an adequate motive. A high-ranking scholar of theology has tried hard to go through the experiences of depth-psychology, in order to investigate its values for Christian life in general and for his denomination in particular. His unconscious remained completely blocked, giving him not one single dream. Now he is convinced that there is no such thing as depth in psychology at all, and that the whole related literature is "mere fantasy." In these cases the goal is impersonal; some idea, cause or value is at stake, and the person is only a means in the service of this goal. Experience, however, has shown that religious self-education bears fruit only if the motive is exclusively personal. The motive must be personal, though not egocentric. The mature, unegoistic personality should be the goal.

God wants the person rather than the cause. He creates men, not books, or organizations; actions rather than ideas are his concern. That seems to be the unanimous teaching not only of Jesus and the Jewish prophets, but also of Buddha and Lao-Tse.

The ideal motive, then, would be God's own command, the voice which told Jonah to go to Nineveh and Jesus to go to the desert in order to be tempted. But we are rather deaf, nowadays, or we mistake the stirring of some unconscious egocentric desire for the voice of the Lord. We should make provision, therefore, for a huge dose of skepticism with regard to all the impulses which arise during our silent worship and meditation and prayer. The devil, especially in his role of the lawyer of our Egos, imitates perfectly the appearance of an angel, using for his own purposes the power of our unconscious imagery, which we frequently mistake for the power of the Lord.

Fortunately God uses many languages. If we do not listen to the "still small voice" he may express himself more urgently in storms and floods, and if we misunderstand him again he may try to help us by unleashing the earthquake. The language which we understand best is suffering. That is why the mourners are blessed; and that is why suffering, either our own or our friends' suffering of which we may be a cause, is the best and most efficient goad toward self-education.

But the aim should not be just removal of suffering, or as the physicians' aim is, restoration of health as it used to be. Suffering should make us aware of the fact that there is a higher goal, and that more suffering is in store if we fail to reach this goal. The dynamics of our situation which provide the motive, the power, and the direction of the whole process is this: we have to grow, to develop our mature personalities, or we shall perish.

The goal may now be defined as expanding consciousness (Gerald Heard); integration of the personality (C. G. Jung); the growing We-experience, as we would call it; or membership in the mystical body of Christ, as St. Paul has described it. The decisive point is that the goal of our self-education must not be an arbitrary idea about what we want to be like. It has to be the very goal of human history, the will of God; and its ways and means have to be the ways and means of human development. We can only bring about what reality would produce anyhow: but it is possible to do it with less waste of time and effort, avoiding detours, errors and, above all, our usual egocentric escapes.

This presupposes, of course, a method of finding out what may be the desirable step, the creative reaction, in every given situation. The general direction of development—expanding consciousness, the integrated personality, the We-experience—is known, as is the general religious command "Love your neighbor." The question remains however, what can we do to develop all this, if so far we only feel distrust and competition? Here depth-psychology can make a decisive contribution which, together with the traditional experience of Christianity, may be able to solve this problem for a large number of believers and seekers.

Such cooperation with life, or, to put it religiously, with creation, looks rather satisfactory, at first sight. Soon however we come to face three serious obstacles.

The first is a moralistic one. By analyzing ourselves, it is said, we shall grow even more egocentric. Introspection leads us into all kinds of vanity, until finally our main occupation will consist in writing a diary, and our chief interest will lie in becoming a more exceptional case. Answer: This is true, if the original motive was too egocentric. But if sleeplessness or marital troubles gave the incentive, be sure your pains and sorrows will prevent your becoming an interesting case. Therefore it would be better to wait until the situation is disagreeable enough.

The second objection is a religious one. Self-education, it says, is self-salvation. We cannot work out our own salvation. We are saved "by grace alone"; therefore we should wait until the grace of God makes us see that we have already been saved two thousand years ago. If you believe in the blood of the lamb no self-education is needed, and if you do not believe, no self-education can help you. Answer: It is true, many of the imperatives of the New Testament, especially such as the one in the letters of Paul "let us cleanse ourselves" (2 Cor. 7:1), are addressed to people who have already received the Holy Spirit. Therefore they apply, nowadays, to almost no one. But there are other imperatives and admonitions for beginners and seekers who are not yet saved: "ask . . . seek . . . knock!" (Mt 7:7); "make terms with your opponent!" (Mt 5:25); then, time and again: "forgive!" (Mt 6:14–15); and above all the very essence of Christian self-education—or, as we may say more exactly, of self-education toward Christianity: *metanoeite!* And remember, it means not only "repent!" (Mt 3:2). It means "go through your crises, whether it takes you one year or ten!"

All these imperatives, summed up in the paradoxical command "love your enemy," imply self-education. And they need careful psychological explanation and application. Otherwise our "education" will take place without our knowledge, against our will, and in the negative direction. The result will be what we see everywhere in so-called Christian communities: repression, unconscious vices, hatred and envy in the disguise of love, and cowardice hidden behind big empty words.

The third and most serious objection is a psychological one. Our purpose includes, among other difficult things, the integration of our conscious personality. That means the acceptance and assimilation of unconscious contents, such as repressed desires and undeveloped capacities, into our conscious mind. How can we do this? Our Ego does not want to see the things which would destroy it. Its resistance against the conquest of the unconscious is a struggle for survival. Only an objective helper, a psychologist, a modern father-confessor, can overcome this resistance.

Answer: This would be true if there were only one evil, one Shadow, one darkness. But evil is always manifold; and its different forms are contradictory and antagonistic. In time the Shadow, for instance irritability, will increase to the point where you identify yourself with its tendencies: "I am furious!" and then you will disown and condemn your former Ego, the softness and smugness of the pseudo-Christian. The Ego and its Shadow are equally evil; blaming each other they bring to light hidden hideousness. All our unconscious deviations and possibilities will become conscious if we go on raging against ourselves—which is the very meaning of the word "crisis." All we need, in addition to suffering, courage and patience, is a good, simple and clear psychology of the unconscious; a zoology, as it were, which teaches us how to deal with the beasts of our unconscious Zoo. Then our courage will grow into faith, and finally we will be able to face the lions in Daniel's den. Your unconscious resistance is the stronger the less faith you have; and vice versa.

The discoveries of depth-psychology enable us to revitalize most of the treasures hidden in Christian and other religious traditions. Meditation and prayer, art, music, dancing and dramatics, auto-suggestion, and even fasting and the practice of alms appear in a thoroughly new light. The arsenal of Christian tools, which had been reduced to mere intellectualism by the iconoclasts of the last four centuries, will be restored in an entirely new sense (which means a very old sense). The saints reappear from the limbo of the unconscious; but now they are not heavenly officials beyond space and time, they are inner realities, collective images and powers which have to be cultivated, revered and used. And they must be carefully distinguished from the real center; they must not become idols.

No one should be lured without urgent necessity to enter his turmoil of creativity and spirituality. If you are allowed to stay where you are, you had better stay. No curiosity, no scientific purpose, no moral duty give you the right or even the possibility of going through the purgatory of depth-psychology. The only ticket of admission is personal suffering. And the reason, one of the reasons, is this: dozens of collective and personal convictions, opinions and prejudices have to be burned or melted away; much criticism, indignation and fear, a host of emotional restrictions veiled in intellectual "knowledge," have to disappear before the doors of depth-psychology open up. And since religious self-education, at least this special way of religous self-education, is based on depth-psychology, the conditions of failure and success are both religious and psychological.

For whom then is this way possible? What are the minimum requirements for those who want to make this attempt? From the religious side two things are needed. First, the belief, or at least the suspicion, that there is or may be—as William James puts it—"an unseen order, and that our supreme good lies in harmoniously adjusting ourselves thereto." And, second, a certain tolerance toward God, which means our readiness to allow God to be as he wants to be and not as we expect him to be according to our own conceptions, theologies and creeds (and our interpretation of the Bible which we think is the only right interpretation). We should give him the chance to teach us something new about himself. On the psychological side we need a certain amount of personal suffering, as we have pointed out, and a certain readiness to admit that something may be wrong in our own inner structure. If these four requirements have not yet been met we should wait. There is no hurry, for the inner situation will be better prepared when we begin some years later. And it is never too late.

Principles

From the foregoing considerations we can easily derive the main principles which should govern our religious self-education. Three of them apply to self-education because they are general principles of human life, and self-education is part of our human life, focalized and concentrated; the other three furnish the practical basis of our endeavor.

1. *Creativity*

The first principle has been mentioned already; it is the simple fact that we can and should achieve only what the tendency of evolution (if you prefer the secular expression) or the will of God (if you choose the religious term) wants us to do and will finally force us to do. This principle, of course, includes the decisive presupposition that there is a will of God and that God is creative; or that there is a tendency of evolution; and that both the will of God and the tendency of evolution can either be obeyed or disregarded. If you do not believe this, or if, at a minimum, you cannot assume this at least as a working hypothesis, you cannot undertake religious self-education, and must try to live without it as long as you can.

2. *Freedom*

The second principle concerns the relation between the human being and the aims of his development (whether they are termed evolution or the will of God). We are not only free to neglect these aims purposefully for a long time, committing conscious sins; we are free also, and indeed much more inclined. to miss them by mistake, forgetting, confusing, misinterpreting them. Thus we commit unconscious sins and produce biological deviations (for example, through the wrong diet, alcohol, wrong marriage, wrong vocation, etc.) as well as philosophical errors (for example, wrong theologies, morals, laws, etc.) and psychological blunders (for example, repression of useful capacities or transmutation of virtues into vices).

Being subject to deviations, we cannot know for sure what our next step has to be. Neither science nor theology nor ethics can teach us what is right or wrong in a given situation. Otherwise there would be no decision, responsibility or creativity on our part. If you think all "commandments" are written in the Bible, just watch your child: he desperately wants, let us say, more ice cream. If you give it to him you will spoil him, and he will hate you later when he finds out. If you do not give it to him, you will disappoint him, and he will hate you now and later too. The will of God requires us, as far as we can see, to be creative. He has created the world; could not you, his child, at least create a satisfactory solution of the ice cream problem? You cannot find it in books: you must be creative yourself. And you cannot be sure about the result: you must take the risk. You may be wrong; you may do harm to your child; both you and he will bear the consequences. The principle is: be creative, at the risk of failure; and if you fail, do not give up; be creative again.

3. *Faith*

Our freedom to choose the right or the wrong way should fill us with enthusiasm because it enables us to be creative, to find the new way, the unheard of solution. On the other hand it should make us humble because it means that many of our decisions may be wrong. The third principle, therefore, is that all our decisions, judgments and convictions should be temporary, open to criticism, and adjustable to further development. In particular, "Do not judge," do not condemn anybody; you can be certain that you do not know him thoroughly.

On the other hand we have to act. We must give ourselves entirely to a cause, a vocation, a love, for instance, when choosing a wife or husband, a profession, a creed. Those decisions should be final. The ensuing actions cannot be undone; and yet they have to be based on judgments which are admittedly imperfect, immature and subject to further development. How can we put at stake our lives and what is more, the lives of our friends and relatives, in the service of a goal which ten years from now may appear in a quite different light? The answer is: faith.

We cannot act and therefore we cannot live unless we believe that life is creative and that even our errors—though they may engender infinite suffering—will finally be stepping stones of evolution. Evolution, consequently, has to be understood as transcending space and time. It has to be the religious, not the biological concept of evolution.

If you kill yourself and some friends in an automobile accident the damage may be enormous. The redemption may presuppose other worlds and future lives; at least the compensation cannot be found on our earth—and still there will be redemption. If you do not believe this, you have to renounce religious self-education as it is discussed here. So you had better ask and seek and knock in order to find that faith, that confidence in the creative will of God (which now turns out to be the basis of evolution) who will help us to pay all our debts or to cancel them instantly if we dare to trust his grace.

For the purposes of religious self-education the three principles, creativity, freedom and faith should be combined in the following way: We should learn to cooperate with the creative will of God, which means we should develop our own creativity. God has created us as creative beings and therefore given us freedom to err; we have erred for thousands of years, we are deeply deviated, we shall err again; but we must take the risk, bear the consequences, pay the price; otherwise we can never find the way out. And we can take the terrible responsibility for our future errors only if we can find, gradually or suddenly, the trust in God's creativity which time and again restores us as his children.

The practical steps which can and should be made in this direction will be discussed in the following chapter. These steps are psychological because they influence the structure of our character, changing vices into virtues and replacing inhibitions by capacities; and they are religious because their final goal is faith, receptivity to grace, and the very entrance into the kingdom of heaven.

Grace given from above and faith found within oneself are

identical for the one who has them; yet they seem to be separate
entities as long as we cannot reach them. Many people feel: I am
unworthy of grace because I have no faith; and I have no faith as
long as grace is missing. The solution of this seemingly insoluble
problem, and therefore the all-powerful center of religious life
and religious self-education, can be easily recognized by those
who have experienced its might: it is the Spirit. If we need a more
exact expression, to distinguish this Spirit from its egocentric
caricature, human intellect, we may call it with St. Paul: "the
Spirit of God" which makes us "sons of God" (Rom 8:14) or
"the Spirit of Christ" (Rom 8:9); they are one and the same. We
may call it the eternal spirit which appears to us as "the unconscious of the future." It is the principle of principles in human
life.

However, many people, serious seekers after faith and truth,
tell you honestly that they have never seen a really religious
person and especially never a Christian. They have always been
disappointed, betrayed and cheated by wolves in sheep's clothing,
false prophets, idolaters and hypocrites. Moreover, they know
history; they remember the thousands of heretics and witches
burnt in the name of Christ. And they know that no dogma or
creed or interpretation of texts stands uncontradicted. Therefore
the word "Christ" makes them suspicious; they shrug their shoulders and turn away.

If a genuine Christian has to deal with these victims of
pseudo-religion he should not preach or discuss, but live Christianity. Only his creative life can undo the results of irreligious
and therefore destructive lives. And if the reader of this book
happens to be himself such a victim of false prophets he should
not worry about names. He should ask and knock and seek; when
the door opens he will know where he is. He has not even to
believe firmly in the three principles of creativity, freedom and
faith. It is enough, at the beginning, if he can accept them as
working hypotheses.

4. *Polarity*

The other three principles refer to our practical work. Its
basis is the principle of polarity. "Differentiation" unfolds life in

innumerable pairs of opposites, such as young and old, masculine and feminine, expansion and contraction, tension and relaxation, etc. "Integration" keeps them in balance and enables the creative center to use them alternatively without preference. "Disintegration" disturbs the balance: one extreme is favored and developed, the opposite is repressed, stunted and turned into the negative; and the center is superseded by a pseudo-center, namely the Ego or an idol.

Self-education, therefore, and all psychotherapy, tries to re-establish the sovereignty of the center by reintegrating the pairs of opposites. Our way is the discovery of hidden talents and the rehabilitation of possibilities which have been in disgrace for many years. We are looking for the virtues within or behind the vices. Our goal is the redemption of that which was lost. If education is the straightforward development of interests and capacities which are consciously acknowledged, our work should be called re-education. We constitute a rescue squad rather than guides. Our endeavor is a search for unknown treasures, a mining in the depth of the unconscious. We want to change the negative into positive power, and destruction into creation. And therefore we have to learn how to face, and if necessary to provoke and to unmask, the powers of hell.

5. *Tolerance*

The next principle follows logically: tolerance. We must not fight against the negative powers which we hope to transform into positive values. This refers to outer as well as inner evils. Distrust, competition, calumny, betrayal, persecution, hatred—arising against us in the outer world—provide good opportunities for self-education. Distrust, aversion, disgust, fear, greed, passion, compulsion, anxiety—arising within our own mind—are even better. They force us to deal with the negative powers and to discover their true location within ourselves.

The great imperative "Do not resist evil" should not be misunderstood as ethical advice. A moralist who says "you must not resist evil" could just as well say that water ought to run uphill. Not resisting evil is an art which requires practice, wisdom, discipline and above all, faith. It does not mean, of course, to submit to evil, to yield or to connive at it. It means acceptance without cooperation; tolerance, sympathy, and confidence in the final positive outcome. To learn this art of not resisting evil is already a decisive part of our self-education.

The first application of the principle of tolerance may be described in some detail because of its practical importance. It is tolerance toward our own inner life, or psychological honesty. In watching our emotional reactions, remembrances, blunders, "distractions" and dreams we may discover, and indeed we want to discover, our own hidden vices, our unconscious and repressed ugliness, in the hope that finally it may turn into beauty. These discoveries are painful and sometimes unbearable. Sometimes we may be frightened by our own passions, revengefulness or hatred; at other times we may be ashamed of the complete emptiness and dryness of our inner life; or we may be convinced that we will lose our minds.

Not to resist our inner evil, to be tolerant toward our own wickedness, wretchedness, or stupidity is more difficult than to be the martyr of outer enemies. Fortunately we are not alone on this frightful road. The writer of the Twenty-Third Psalm has gone through the same experience. And the great religious self-educator, St. Paul, has left us the compass of his inner journey: "I am certain neither death nor life, neither angels nor principalities, neither the present nor the future, no powers of the height or of the depth, nor anything else in all creation will be able to part us from God's love in Christ Jesus our Lord" (Rom 8:38–39).

The cowardice of later centuries, however, has found a new escape for Egos and Idols: the wrong use of a valuable tool, namely of meditation. "Concentrate on good thoughts. Meditate on the words 'God is love.' Do not permit any distraction. Do not indulge in personal sorrows. And especially, do not hate or condemn or despise anyone or anything." This mental discipline is good if it is balanced by the opposite discipline, namely the discipline of reckless honesty: tell yourself and tell God what you are really like. If wisely guided the meditator can solve a large part of his problems by meditating on negative symbols. If this "negative" part of his practice is omitted he is in danger of producing an additional repression. He deprives himself of his creative forces, shuts them up in the unconscious and becomes paler, softer, and weaker every day.

Our way is this: pour out all your fears and anxieties, malicious joy and greed and hatred, and you will be astonished at the terrific amount of power which is pent up in your unconscious mind. We can release this power and transform it from negative into positive power, only by bringing it into the open, into the light of consciousness, and by accepting ourselves as we are, even though the mountain of debts seems to crush us. This is the principle of honesty. And it is clear that it can be applied only if connected with the principle of faith which we described above. The two together constitute the next principle: forgiveness.

6. *Forgiveness*

The principle of forgiveness in its psychological application embodies the same mutuality as in its original formulation (Mt 6:14–15). "If you forgive men their trespasses, then your heavenly Father will forgive you; but if you do not forgive men, your Father will not forgive your trespasses either." But we have to add an important fact which in the New Testament is little stressed though not missing: the dead men's bones within the whitewashed tombs—the fact that many evils persist in our unconscious unforgiven; and they cannot be forgiven as long as they are repressed.

We harbor unconscious hatred of forgotten origin, perhaps an early betrayal by mother or aunt. We may discover that unconscious anxiety absorbs all our creative power, because we felt, when two years old, that our father did not love us enough. To bring to light the buried skeletons of our early tragedies, to understand that the evildoers who almost killed us were the victims of other evildoers, and that those again did not know how to love, because they were betrayed by their own parents—that means to acknowledge the wickedness of mankind and to forgive full-heartedly because we ourselves are badly in need of forgiveness for the ugly things which we have done.

Even before we feel that we are forgiven, and that the whole debt is canceled, we may realize the amazing change from darkness to light and from hatred to love. We may have hated the one who spanked us or spoiled us and thus made our lives miserable for thirty or forty years. In the next moment we may see as clearly as in a dramatic vision this person, forty years earlier, being himself spanked or spoiled by someone else who was supposed to love him dearly. There is only one possibility left: love and compassion and the ardent impulse to help mankind to get rid of this tragedy. And we join the army of love.

The same power which was hatred, revengefulness, resentfulness or bitterness, now flows through us as love, courage and initiative. Suddenly we know what we have to do. The negative image, the channel of negative power, is now changed into a positive symbol, charged with the creative might of the real center. Forgiveness, if it is genuine, immediately releases the creative and spiritual power which we have called the unconscious of the future. If this sign is missing we may be certain that we have not yet been forgiven because we ourselves have not yet forgiven.

Methods

How can we find our real center? How can we get rid of the Ego or of the Idol? The first answer that arises in individual life as well as in the life of the race is the imperative: "Thou shalt not . . ." Not to steal, not to tell lies, and so on—these "negative" commandments are necessary wherever individuals have to grope their way from the original tribal consciousness to the mature universal consciousness. They are much-needed implements of social security until we grow mature enough to realize our individual responsibility for all human life. Then we will no longer need general, prohibitive commandments; and the positive creative order, the Will of God, will be understood and obeyed immediately.

The "law"—its morality, and especially its application in bringing up children—is a temporary though unavoidable stopgap which is easily misused and which then produces the opposite of the expected result. If we were saints we could tell our children "you must not . . ." without poisoning them. Yet in such a case they would need no law, not being thrown into egocentricity by egocentric parents. As it is, we are not saints, and we unknowingly misuse the commands (which are God's) in the service of our own purposes (which are egocentric). We say: "You must not disturb your father's nap," as if it were God's nap, because we are not creative enough to give the children a creative occupation which would make them grow and would keep them quite naturally from disturbing their father's rest.

Moral commandments usually arouse egocentricity, either egocentric resistance or egocentric obedience (the "good child" and the "bad child" being equally egocentric), because even the best moral laws are enforced by egocentric authorities, and unconscious egocentric implications cannot be avoided even in their most careful applications. This is our psychological contribution to St. Paul's philosophy of the law (Rom 7).

Later, when the victims of our misused morality reach the age of self-responsibility and self-education, the only viewpoint they are able to apply to their inner lives is the moralistic command. Yet now the negative imperative "I must not . . ."—the cause of repression—is completed by the positive imperative "I must . . ." which tries to overcome the result of repression without however repealing repression itself. For twenty years a man may have thought sexuality evil; then, in order to be a good husband, he wants to be potent, affectionate, passionate, although sexuality in general still remains an evil to him. He kills his horse and then blames it for not pulling the wagon. We make this mistake not only in the field of sexual life but also in the fields of courage, initiative, self-confidence, emotional honesty, and so on.

The pale-blooded, nervous person, sickly and irritable, suffers from repressed—that is, unlived—life. The moralistic method, which is always the conservative method, cannot help him at all. Thus history makes its counterthrust with the liberal idea of "letting go." Relax! do not worry about what people will say! show yourself as you are! be confident! trust your instinct! nature is good! you are all right if you are free! In ethics, theology, mysticism, psychology (Sigmund Freud), education (Alfred Adler) and social life we find the unanimous conviction that everything would be fine if only we could replace repression by its opposite: honest and unrestricted expression.

In some cases, to a certain extent, this "expressionism" is a useful method of self-education; and in education it is at least better than repression. If you have to write a letter it is better to wait until a creative mood moves you to write. If you force yourself, without the creative urge, your letter will be poor and shallow. In many cases, however, your creativity may never move you; or what you think to be creativity may turn out to be a superficial egocentric illusion.

On the whole, the method of unrestricted self-expression has not borne the fruit which its prophets expected. There is not less unlived life nowadays than there was one hundred years ago: it is only that other functions are repressed. Our liberal life now allows all kinds of sexual satisfactions—but real love is almost forbidden. Loyalty is deemed to be stupid, promiscuity is "natural"; one hundred years ago the opposite was the case. From the psychological viewpoint both valuations are equally wrong, and the corresponding methods of education and self-education, namely repression and expression, have equally failed. Repression can neither be avoided nor undone by expression.

The trouble is that even under the most liberal system of life we do not dare to express what we really are. Repression is the result of early fear; and it began long before any educational principles became efficient. Its cause is not lack of pedagogical insight but lack of creativity, which indicates lack of faith on the part of the adults. The child was afraid, for instance, to show his childish heart to the older brother who ridiculed him so successfully. And the parents did not know how to help him. So he decided, unconsciously, that love and loyalty were not permissible. And he learned to repress his tender emotions and to express the opposite: scorn and malice. Thirty years later he tries to express freely all that he can find within himself. What does he find? No great love, no passion, nothing of all the things which he wants to develop. But if he is honest enough, not resisting his inner evil, he may discover a vague tendency to torture his brother who had tortured him. If he would dare now to express himself recklessly—would he go and kill his brother? Perhaps. Or he may write a furious letter, hateful, silly, and completely out of place.

Thus, we see that it is certainly better not to act upon all the tendencies and urges which we may discover in the deeper layers of our unconscious mind. Revengefulness, hatred, envy, greed and anxiety would upset our family life and our social position. If all repressions were released at once in a big city, the city would be an insane asylum with insane wardens. It happens partially during riots and revolutions; and to a slighter degree it is officially permitted (and controlled) as a kind of safety valve, in the carnivals of the southern countries, the countries with less rigid repression.

If you repress what you harbor, you will be stifled by your own unlived life. If you express the repressed tendencies, you may destroy and kill. You must find another way to "make terms with your opponent, so long as you and he are on the way to court" (Mt 5:25). The way out, indeed the only way out, as far as we know, is the way of confession. But the word confession must be understood, and the method must be used in the right way, according to the structure of the human mind and the special problems of our time. Otherwise the result will be the opposite of what it should be.

Originally there were two people involved, the confessing initiate and the priest, the father confessor; or, since the ministry has lost the knowledge and the power of the confessional way, the psychologist. But the latter is often as poorly equipped for this dangerous work as is the minister.

Imagine the confessional process in all its crudity and ruthlessness. It is a powerful and dangerous discharge of high voltage; and if you are not an expert in this field you had better stay away—or defend yourself by assuming the role of a judge. If you judge, you turn confession into new repression. Where there is judgment, there is no truth. And absolution is judgment, too. If someone confesses in order to be absolved he is unable to confess the "hidden sins," namely the darkness of his unconscious mind.

The superficial deeds which he remembers can be easily told and are easily plucked, but these are only the poisonous flowers blossoming above the earth. The roots remain in the unconscious, and they will thrive again and again—new flowers, new sins to be confessed daily. And both the sinner and the absolver live in an unconscious agreement never to touch the poisonous roots, because the same explosion, the same revolution would upset the whole outer and inner lives of father confessor and parishioner alike. "Keep off! High Voltage!" That is one of the reasons why two thousand years of confessional practice have failed to discover the unconscious. The result of this wrong practice is that scarcely anything can be more boring and more useless psychologically than the usual routine of confession.

We have to revitalize, indeed to recreate, the meaning of the old and colorful word, if we can use it at all. And we try to do so by stressing two aspects of its meaning: one being known, but too much neglected so far, the other being quite new and, as far as we can see, included only vaguely in some old descriptions.

The first aspect is that the nearer mankind draws to real Christianity the more the Christian can and should confess to the One who was always supposed to be represented by, or present in, the father confessor, namely God. A trustworthy friend, a father confessor, if possible an expert in depth-psychology, should be available in case of emergency. But the main part of the task has to be solved by the individual alone by himself in confessional meditation; and that means "in the presence of God." Try to pour out before him whatever comes to your mind. Be not embarrassed by his presence. Do not refrain from strong words—say "swine" if you mean swine; God knows what you say and what you do not say anyhow. He knows your conscious and your unconscious mind equally. Therefore his presence will help you discover your "secret sins" and unearth your "buried talents."

Here we reach the second point: our confession has to bring to light the unknown, the unconscious darkness, and the undeveloped creativity of our deeper layers. Confession then becomes research, investigation, discovery. We discover our individual as well as collective drives, too much and too little power, emotional drought and emotional floods, destructive and constructive urges, our animal nature and our vegetal nature. If we can spread out before him all the hidden roots of our virtues and vices, if we are honest and courageous enough to release before him the high voltage of our unconscious hatred and love, we may discover that

all our power is in the last analysis his power, and that our
darkness turns into light because he is both darkness and light.

Expression of what we find within ourselves, honest and
reckless expression before the face of the Eternal, assuming responsibility for what we are, even if we are unaware of it, and
asking God to help us to master the wild horses, or to revive the
skeletons of horses which we dig out during the long hours of our
confessions—this is the psychological method of religious self-
education. It is a way of bringing to consciousness our unconscious contents, and of establishing control over our hidden
powers. It is the way to mature responsibility. It is the old way of
the psalmist: "Yet who can detect his lapses? Absolve me from my
faults unknown! And hold thy servant back from willful sins, from
giving way to them" (Ps 19:12–13).

Not in the presence of a minister or a psychologist, but in the
presence of God, things change completely. If you hate your
brother, and you pour out all your hatred, remembering at the
same time, as much as you can, the presence of God—and your
hatred does not change, then you are not sufficiently aware either
of the presence of God or of your hatred, and probably of neither.
Be more honest, give vent to your emotions. You hate your
brother: imagine his presence, before God tell him how you feel,
kick him, scratch him. You are ten years old now—get up from
your chair, don't pretend to be a wise, old Buddha, pace the floor,
yell, scream, punch the furniture, express yourself. Rant and rage
until you are exhausted, or until you laugh at yourself.

You hate your brother: God is there, tell him the truth, be as
honest as those old Hebrews: "Routed, dishonoured, be they who
delight in harm to me" (Ps 40:14). Pray God he should punish
your brother, torture him, help you to defeat him. Try to be one
with God, the old God of vengeance. He will help you, if not in
killing your enemy, then otherwise. Look: during all your rage,
listening to your furious prayer, God was there, his presence
encompassed you like the calm, creative smile of a father who
knows that his child will spend his fury and then discover the
truth and find the right way. Certainly you will find the right way,
but only when you have spent your force, honestly and thoroughly, in rage and fury or complaint and despair. It will take weeks or

months; you may have to travel the long way through the whole Old Testament, not just through a few Psalms of hatred and vengeance. And finally you will meet the God of the inner storms: "smoke fumed from his nostrils, and scorching fire from his lips, that kindled blazing coals, as down he came on the bending sky, the storm-cloud at his feet" (Ps 18:8–9). It is a nightmare more real than anything you have ever seen in the outer world. But it is not yet real enough. The highest reality emerges out of the fire in complete calm. We may realize it for a moment beyond space and time: the center itself. And at last "What is old has gone, the new has come" (2 Cor 5:17). The new is "God's peace that surpasses all our dreams" (Phil 4:7).

Thus we combine the old practice of "the presence of God," well known in the tradition of meditation and prayer, with the new practice of depth-psychology, well known in modern literature. The result is "confessional meditation."

Much unconscious, unexpected material will come to light; facts, tendencies, emotions, capacities, and power. It may take time, weeks and perhaps months, but it will happen. Forgotten scenes will be recalled, people and relations will appear in a different light. More important, of course, than the accumulation of material is its new evaluation and its application to our future. Grudge will change into compassion and hatred into love. Destructive tendencies will give way to newly discovered creative capacities. Our unlived life, thus released from its prison, wants to be lived. We are dimly aware, during this time, of the primitiveness and immaturity of our new desires and ideas; yet the same regression which enabled us to unearth the unconscious power now makes it difficult to refrain from its immediate use. No mistake, however, would be worse than this. Confessional meditation without continence, fasting, voluntary privation, is doomed to failure. Express your hatred or love, your greed or envy, before the face of God; but do not express them to the people whom you hate or love. This is the best way to discover more or deeper hatred or love, and to draw nearer to the real center.

You may find that your passionate love for Miss A turns a week later into more primitive passion for Aunt B, then into a dizzying longing for your mother, and finally into awe and adoration for the terrifying Great Mother whom you did not know until you met her in your meditation. If in the meantime you had married Miss A you would have deceived her, because your love was merely projected; and you would have stopped your own inner development. Not even your unconscious tie with Aunt B would have come to light, unless you had divorced your pseudo-wife, A.

Our repressed drives, when they come to consciousness, are primitive, undifferentiated and powerful, like young hippopotami. Not to satisfy them is a heroic task, presupposing some training in the old and almost forgotten art of fasting. Therefore, when you set out on the road of self-education learn how to fast—not only with regard to eating too much (any good dietician can help you to learn that) but also with regard to some of your other bad habits. We not only eat and drink and smoke too much: we also talk too much, read too much, write too much; we are too busy satisfying our petty needs. If you like to smoke, stop it, and you will meet with "the beasts in the desert." And when you have the first great dream, and, stunned by its appalling colors, would like to tell your friends or husband or wife about it—stop! Fast! Refrain from gossip! If you betray the secrets of the soul no further secret will be entrusted to you. "Men will have to account on the day of judgment for every light word they utter" (Mt 12:36).

Sometimes, however, the urge is so strong that the happiness of our whole life seems to depend on the fulfillment of this new and passionate desire. And still it is a merely transferred or projected desire. We are still far from the real center. We are shaken by the earthquake or the storm; we do not yet hear the still small voice. Then we need all the faith and all the courage we can muster. Because here we are at the point where we may understand one of the deepest truths of Christianity: "If your right eye is a hindrance to you, pluck it out and throw it away" (Mt 5:29). Conscious sacrifice is required instead of unconscious repression, expressing all the anguish of unsatisfied vital needs before God, but not before our fellow men. The childlike imperative "you must not . . ." is replaced by the mature insight "I will not . . ." Thus we may learn to leave "brothers or sisters or father or mother or wife or children or lands or houses" (Mt 19:29). This conscious sacrifice is what is meant by fasting and plucking out our eye. It is an integral part of confessional meditation.

On the other hand the necessity of self-control is not limited to the phenomenon of transference and projection. There is no demarcation line between projected and real love. We must take the risk of deceiving ourselves and our beloved ones. And this danger is much greater during the period of intense confessional work than at any other time in human life. But the long and winding road of self-education cannot be traveled in seclusion and solitude. It has to be a part of our normal activity. We have to live in the world, and its demands, satisfactions and disappointments are an integral contribution to our psychological research. We should refrain—at least during periods of crisis—from important decisions and from strong emotional reactions toward the outer world. But we should study this world and study our reactions toward it, and even sometimes try, in the sense of an experiment, to do something against our habit-patterns or beyond our usual self-control.

This experimental method has been used in a rather superficial way by Alfred Adler, and termed "positive training." It provides a practical possibility of utmost importance if we combine it with confessional meditation and apply to it the "practice of the presence of God." The method then becomes an unerring test for what we mean by "presence"; it becomes at once stimulus and technique for further training in outer life, and a source of valuable material for the exploration of our unconscious mind. The psychological question which determines the method is this: is the entity whose presence controls our behavior really God, or is it something else, another value, an idol, or just our Ego? The method therefore may be called: "the practice of the presence of whom?"

Imagine you discover during your psychological morning confession that you are a sheep in a wolf's skin. You behave like a wild beast; your friends are afraid of your irritability. But deep down in your heart you are kind and mild, and you want peace and harmony, you want to be a Christian, and if someone should strike you on the right cheek you would like to turn the other one. Nevertheless, all attempts in this direction have failed so far.

And you understand: they failed because you forgot the presence of God. You are often aware of his presence at eight o'clock during your meditation. At nine o'clock, when you enter the office, you see only the girl who forgot to mail the letters; and you howl like a wolf.

This time you try to do a better job. The presence of God should exclude the wolf. You try your best to keep his presence in mind. The girl, of course, forgot the letters. You smile. The telephone rings twice; it is the wrong number. Then you are out of cigarettes. Your fountain pen breaks. And finally the girl wants a day off. You need all the strength of your inner wolf to maintain the sheep's smile. You look like the most self-conscious sheep that ever bleated. And the girl suddenly needs two days off and you give her three—remembering, spasmodically, the presence—of whom?

When you come home you should analyze this experience as carefully as possible. You may consider it as a complete failure. Very soon, however, you will find out that it is one of the most valuable contributions to your self-understanding. Who was present? Which power or entity was in control of your reactions? There was the conscious purpose not to grow impatient, and to smile at any cost. Did this imply that you wanted to be dishonest, to hide your true emotion, to disguise the wolf in the sheep's skin? No. You wanted to *be* the sheep, and you failed, because the shepherd was not there to protect you.

Now you remember: it was always like this during your childhood, and later too. If there was a protector you felt secure, you enjoyed peace and harmony, completely in the role of the good boy. And as soon as you felt left alone, without protection, you were on the defensive, firmly convinced that everybody was your enemy; and you had to be the howling wolf. This time, however, it was different. You knew: God is present. It was more than the theoretical insight into his omnipresence. It was a real experience, during your meditation, at eight o'clock. But why had you to fight the wolf all the time? Why did you not feel at ten as free as you had felt at eight?

You analyze further. Do you remember the vague presence, the shadowy figure in the background of your mind, at eight o'clock as well as ten o'clock? Try to visualize him. He was something like a good great father, watching you and protecting you. And you wanted to please him. You wanted to be his good boy. So you tried very hard to be patient and kind, checking, as it were, every minute: "I am a good boy, am I not, 'daddy' God?"

He was a childish substitute of a God, the idolized image of a commonplace father. And still you could not deceive him. You knew that he knew that you were not as good as you pretended to be. So you had to exaggerate your goodness. Your pretense was bad; you were afraid; he was angry; the whole thing became a stupid farce. You acted in the presence of an infantile idol and not in the presence of God. But now you know that even in your best meditation you are still far removed from the real center; and that you have to work through many more weeks or months until you can really "turn the other cheek" creatively and victoriously. But without this experiment you would never have known that you had been an idolater for so many years.

Without the verification in outer life all our inner progress remains questionable. And without the inner experience of new understanding, power and creativity, all our outer improvements would remain a shallow masquerade. The pendulum of religious self-education has to swing back and forth between introvert and extravert experiences, confessional meditation and positive training: this is the best way to avoid the one-sidedness and self-deceptions which always threaten our spiritual development.

Confessional Meditation

The methods described in the last chapter have to be applied in each case differently. The way which leads us to maturity and the special task we have to face in a given moment have to be explored almost every day anew. Our dreams, if we know how to use them, are a great help; but even if we have no dreams at all we can find our way. We should first try to locate our Ego-image, to determine whether it occupies the place of father, mother, son or daughter. (See Diagram I.) Often it may be an interesting mixture; and sometimes we may discover, for instance, that the Ego is basically "daughter" but that under certain circumstances it assumes the role of mother or even of father. This, then, constitutes a secondary line of Ego defenses and requires additional attention in self-education.

Since we usually transfer the repressed images onto our fellow men we can often locate the Ego by inference from our transferences. If we are always afraid of powerful authorities our Ego must dwell in the passive (lower) half of the character chart. (See Diagram II.) If we are angered by the inefficiency of our employees we live our Ego-life in the active (upper) half of the chart. If we loathe tenderness and intimacies we are too masculine: the Ego is on the right side. And if we are afraid of disharmony and misunderstanding we have developed a feminine form of egocentricity: our Ego is on the left side.

The task of self-education, however, is always a double one. If the "feminine qualities" (tenderness, understanding, longing for harmony, the so-called "anima functions") are repressed and underdeveloped, the feminine images, mother and girl, will be transferred onto several people (usually but not necessarily women). One lady may appear as a mild protective mother, though in reality she is an egocentric go-getter; and another may be seen as a sensual and greedy vampire though objectively she is an average person. These transferences present serious tasks for our self-education and it will be difficult enough to get rid of our egocentric eyeglasses.

On the other hand we can be certain that in such a case of repressed femininity the masculine functions, corresponding to the images of father and boy, will be disturbed, too. They will probably be overdeveloped, in order to compensate for the deficiency of the opposite side. If the person is a man he may be unaware, for a long time, of his exaggerated "masculinity." Indeed he may consider it a virtue; but many of his mistakes and frustrations will be due to his onesidedness. If the person is a woman this form of egocentricity will be more evident—and vice versa.

Looking at Diagrams III-VI we may decide first that one of them, let us say No. III, applies to our special problem: we have to face our "Giants." Then, however, it is very likely that one day we will discover the opposite problem as well: half-consciously and furtively we may bully and maltreat those who are weaker than we. Thus while applying one of the diagrams practically we should at least theoretically ask ourselves how far the opposite diagram could be applied, too.

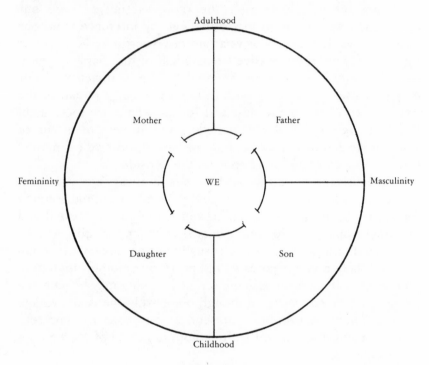

DIAGRAM I
The Original We-Experience

The following diagrams serve a double purpose. They illustrate the psychological facts described in this book, and they provide some assistance for those who try to practice confessional meditation. The commentary which accompanies them is therefore divided into two sections. The first part may be read when the diagrams are studied as illustrations of the theoretical explanations. The second part should be carefully considered when they are used as charts for the "journey through the seething seas of the unconscious." However, the reader should never forget that the human mind does not exist in space. Its element is time. No picture or diagram, no configuration in space, can therefore be more than a poor crutch. It helps us somewhat if we are able to move along anyhow; but it fails us if we rely too much upon it.

The Original We-Experience (Diagram I)

1. Diagram I represents first the "ideal family," four people, two adults and two children, two males and two females, related to each other as indicated by the four sections of the outer circle as father, mother, son and daughter. The typical attitudes of the four people, and their experiences of fatherhood, motherhood, boyhood, and girlhood, provide the basis of all collective images. The inmost circle, labelled "We," denotes the "tribal consciousness" as expressed in myths, habits, collective ideas, judgments, sympathies and antipathies. The contents of this tribal consciousness may or may not remain individually unconscious; the individual will act according to them anyhow, which means that he will serve the interest of the group rather than his personal interest.

At the same time the same diagram represents the inner structure, the imagery, of each of the four members of the group. The We-Psychology maintains that the inner life of the group and the inner life of each one of its members can be represented by the same diagram. The child finds already in his half-conscious mind the images of the "wise old man" and the "great mother." He does not yet understand them, but he trusts and loves their representatives in the outer world; and he knows that one day he will be one of them himself. Therefore the healthy child feels neither insecurity nor inferiority. He is a well balanced but largely unconscious organ of a well balanced but only vaguely conscious social organism: the family. This is the "Orginal We-experience."

Each member of the group accepts one of the four images as his leading image (which after the "breach of the We" would become his Ego-image), and uses the other three as "contact-images." They enable him to understand and love the three other members of the group. The father, for instance, should feel responsible for the whole group, the group being his central value, as represented by the "We-center" of the diagram. The Father image, upper right section, should be his leading image, representing masculinity and leadership. He should not forget, however, what childhood means, nor should femininity be missing in his inner structure.

2. Try to find out how much or how little of the "Original We-experience" has survived in your own case. Consciously you may be a non-conformist or even a rebel, and still you may discover some family pride ("we, the Smiths, do not do that") or some dependence on your cultural background ("we Southerners are different"). Many collective likes and dislikes and ready-made patterns of reactions control our behavior; they remain unconscious though operative until some outer criticism or inner self-observation raises them into consciousness. They are "remainders of the "Original We.""

Their contents may be right or wrong, questionable or plainly obsolete (for instance, our aversion toward a certain smell, our preference for a special landscape, a racial prejudice, etc.). It may or may not be misused in the service of later egocentric goals. Our task here is neither to judge nor to change them. We should only find out how far they are based on collective images and racial instincts rather than on conscious teaching and individual experience. And we should raise them into consciousness, rendering them flexible means in the service of higher goals.

The Egocentric Group (Diagram II)

1. The group of four squares has superseded the circle (squares symbolizing egocentric rigidity). The central circle, the We-experience, has disappeared: the "Breach of the original We" has occurred. The image of the daughter (lower left hand corner) has become the Ego image, though the person in question may be a boy, an adult woman, or even an old man. The other three images have been repressed into the unconscuous as far as they represented functions and qualities of the person himself: he cannot take responsibility (adulthood is missing) nor can he stand disharmony (masculinity is missing). The three dotted squares represent unconscious images, which consequently have turned negative.

The repressed images are then transferred onto the other members of the group, not in their original and natural form, but

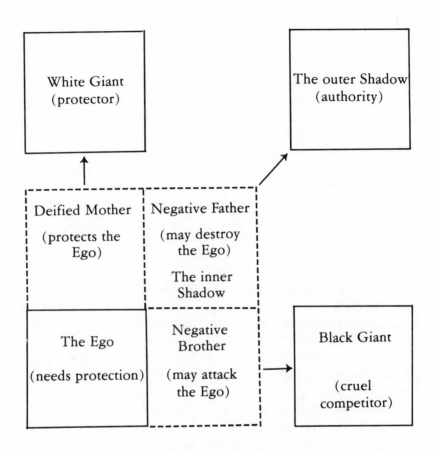

DIAGRAM II

The Egocentric Group

This diagram showing the Ego in the lower left-hand corner represents only one of the four possible cases. The others, with the Ego in the other three corners, may easily be constructed according to the given example. (The four possible positions of the Ego constitute the four forms of egocentricity, described as Star, Nero, Turtle and Clinging Vine in the author's *How Character Develops.*)

rather in an exaggerated and primitive shape. One person (whether man or woman) is honored with the task of protecting the Ego: he has to play the role of the "White Giant." Another one is pushed into the place of an angry and unjust father: he becomes the "Ego's Shadow." A third is considered the inimical brother, a cruel and dangerous competitor. We call him the "Black Giant."

Imagine four egocentric people, each one representing one corner of the original square and transferring the other rigid and distorted images on the other members of the group. The result is a ghostly "dance macabre" of four people who pretend to love each other, but who do not know who they are.

2. Find out where your Ego and your Shadow are. Our basic pattern of egocentricity is determined by our goal, the Ego-image, and its opposite: the thing that we are most afraid of, the Ego's Shadow, the "abyss," the unbearable situation. It is represented by the egocentric caricature of the opposite image (the "egocentric daughter" would rather die than assume responsibility and make sacrifices). The Ego-image is often quite conscious, while the Shadow remains unknown; in other cases the Shadow is well known and the Ego-image remains unconscious. But we should not forget that most of us have developed a rather intricate policy of life with interwoven features of all four images. The question then is which Ego-pattern is the basic one: it is always the one that conditions the opposite image to be the Shadow.

The next task is the discovery of the virtues behind our vices. As far as you happen to be an egocentric "step-mother," whether your are man or woman, you will find that behind your egocentric vanity and striving for recognition you have developed some good objective qualities which are characteristic of an ideal mother. You like harmony, you understand the needs of your fellow men and you know how to satisfy them.

We should not throw away the baby with the bath. We should not fight against our Ego-pattern indiscriminately. If our Ego is located in the place of the "Son," we enjoy our long training in renunciation and our successful discipline in asceticism. But we should learn to use it or not to use it, freely and according to circumstances. The father, and even the egocentric one, likes responsibility; the egocentric sissy has developed the most subtle ways of diplomacy. They should use these "virtues" for the sake of the We-group rather than in the service of the Ego.

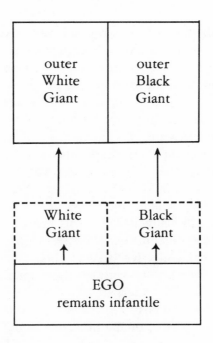

Conquering the Giants (Diagram III)

1. The two foregoing diagrams (I and II) refer to the problems of diagnosis; the four following ones are related to the way out as we may achieve it by means of confessional meditation. We describe the "journey" in four significant directions, leaving it to the imagination of the reader to work out the special combinations and complications which may be needed in his own case. Since the Ego usually represents a mixture of several images it is advisable to begin our practical training in terms of attitudes and functions rather than in terms of images. The word "childhood" here covers the common attitudes of boy and girl; "adulthood" those of man and woman; "masculinity" those of the two male and "femininity" those of the two female members of the group. The exact diagnosis of the location of the Ego will then be

worked out gradually while the egocentric attitudes are already dwindling away under the impact of a good-humored self-analysis. (Do not moralize: by condemning yourself you keep the Ego alive!)

The inner Shadow will then be a mixture of the two opposite images; and the "outer Shadows," the transferences of the inner Shadow onto people in the outer world, will be a mixture too. The transferences of the Shadow (in the proper sense), and of the Black Giant, which appear as two different figures on Diagram II, are in practice so frequently blended that the two words can be used almost synonymously.

The lower rectangle represents the Ego of a person who remained infantile. The dotted squares are his repressed and therefore degenerated images of adults, the "White Giant" being too white, the "Black Giant" too black, and both being superhumanly big, almost like angels and devils. This unfortunate inner structure is based on painful experiences in early childhood and connected with old collective dreams about the terrible Great Mother or the father Saturn, who eat their children. This image has provoked its own counterpart, the "White Giant," because life would have been impossible without this remedy. The more the child fears the doctor, or the dog, or the dark, the more he needs the mother or the aunt to protect him. The outer experience of being spoiled is always connected with some collective image of a great protector.

Both images are transferred, later, onto all kinds of authorities: boss, teacher, minister, government, church, God, or even husband or wife. Sometimes one person carries both images. That person may be the White Giant while he praises us, but turns black as soon as he frowns. In this case it is a matter of life and death to keep him white. In reality he may be green or red, and rather small; we see him black or white and always gigantic, according to our distorted and colored eyeglasses.

2. We should write out and meditate on a list of all our black and white giants, with all their good and bad qualities, as we see them. The changes of color and size and especially the double transference, the same giant being alternately white and black, will convince us that the source of this evil is to be found in our

own unlived life. We should be what we think they are. Moreover, we are unconsciously what our consciousness erroneously ascribes to them. And we cannot get rid of the Black Giant and the fear which his image creates, unless we give up our claim to protection and our longing for the White Giant.

The White Giant, especially if we project this image on God, is very bad: it prevents us from growing up, becoming independent and assuming our own responsibility. The Black Giant, even if we do not project this image, makes us suffer and therefore is extremely helpful, forcing us into our own crisis. What we deem evil is really good, and what we call good is very bad. This insight is an important milestone on the road of our inner journey: the Ego valuation is replaced by a more objective, more central understanding of the relativity of all inner values.

Thus we realize that we have to integrate the images of the Black as well as of the White Giant. The inner way is to go back in our imagination to the earliest scenes with them which we can find, either in memory or in mere fantasy. Be the child once more, frightened to death by your father's severity, or spoiled by the sentimentality of your aunt. And at the same time be there as the adult that you are, or even wiser than you are in reality. You will feel the child's anguish and fear, or, when spoiled, his shallow smugness. At the same time the adult's resentment will rise in angry waves. You will realize an anger, unknown so far, because it was carefully repressed. Now be honest. Tell your father or your aunt who is there without being there how you feel. They have poisoned your life, murdered your creativity. The terrific power of revenge will surge up from the unconscious and flood your consciousness. You may be carried away by your "sacred wrath"; but remember: God is still there, too.

Drag your father or your aunt before God's tribunal. Listen to what he may tell you. He certainly will not be the White Giant that you want him to be. He will disappoint you. And still you may sense his smile. Then, bewildered by rage and shame, you will recognize that you are obsessed by an image, playing a role, convinced of your own righteousness, exactly as your father and your aunt were playing a role, serving an image, being convinced of their moral right. You are certainly as weak and blind as your aunt and your father have been. You are equally human, obsessed by the same collective images, caught in the same collective misery. So you may shake hands and forgive one another.

Then prepare the next step, the extravert part of the way. But keep in mind where you are on the road. The destructive power, fury, and revenge have given you a new experience of strength and almost of joy. All cowardice, all inferiority feeling were gone; you realized for a moment what your ancestors would have called the sacred rage of the battlefield. Your buried talent, your unlived life, arose from the dead; you were integrated for a minute, though on a primitive level of consciousness. This regression brought you close to the center, and its creative power can catapult you wherever you want to go. You can use your new strength for constructive development. You have unearthed your buried sword: try to reforge it into a plough. And you will see that God has forgiven you as you have forgiven your aunt or your father.

At the next opportunity face the person on whom you transfer the image of the Black Giant. Remember that you are not afraid of *him* but of your inner image which you transfer on him, and that you can be (and indeed have been) this image yourself. If necessary go fast, within ten seconds, through the whole gamut of emotions and insights: fear, fury, sacred wrath, bewilderment and mutual forgiveness. Then tell him as kindly and objectively as possible what you have to say; talk business with him; and keep your inner secrets for yourself.

The task is very similar if you have to meet the black situation, the abyss, instead of the Black Giant. (For instance, in the case of a speech inhibition: try to speak, but not before you have unearthed the roots of the evil.) Do the impossible thing, assume responsibility, make your decision, become the leader, expose yourself to criticism and failure. But choose only small steps. Do not expect too much. And if you fail, as you probably will do nine times out of ten, go back to your confessional meditation, face once more your Black and White Giants, try to unearth more fear or hatred or revengefulness, and try to realize a deeper degree of forgiveness.

Exploring the Doghouse (Diagram IV)

1. Here the situation is the opposite of that in Diagram III. The Ego-image is high up in the air; the Shadow is consequently represented by a situation rather than by a person: it is helplessness, withdrawal, failure, defeat. Consciously this person may say he has never experienced defeat, that he has been a splendid success all through his life. In early childhood, however, he must have had this experience and found it so unbearable that he repressed even the slightest reminder of it. His unconscious policy of life now is: to do everything to forestall defeat.

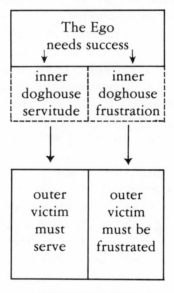

DIAGRAM IV

Exploring the Doghouse

The Journey of Those
Who Have Been Spoiled
(partly or completely)
by Outer Success

His abyss may be symbolized by a doghouse. But the only way in which it appears outwardly is its transference on other people. His inner doghouse, repressed and abhorred, provides the refined and almost fiendish skill of putting others into their own doghouse. He needs victims. That seems to be the only thing which makes him feel that he is not a victim himself. He teases, blames, ridicules, but does not allow anybody to pay back in kind. He wants to be served, but does not serve himself. He cannot even apologize or say "thanks," so much is he afraid of any possible humiliation.

2. If such is your case, little can be done as long as you are satisfied with your life. You are using only half of your possibilities, but you cannot change this situation unless you suffer. Life, however, will draw you closer and closer to your own doghouse; your good luck will fail you, and then your better luck may begin, with nightmares and nervous jitters.

Try to discover your early experience of the doghouse. Gather all the evidence and draw conclusions, like Sherlock Holmes. The crime has happened; reconstruct its circumstances as carefully as you can. Go in your imagination through the presumable hell of that childhood experience, and try to anticipate the possible hell of tomorrow. The two series of pictures will help each other. Imagine that some one does to you what you like to do to your victims. And always look for the most disagreeable situation: this is probably what has been done to you.

If you have found your abyss, go through it in your meditation, feeling as you did in childhood that something "impossible" happens, and realizing at the same time as an adult that there is no real loss. You are ridiculed, exploited, defeated; it is true, you may lose your "face," your reputation, your glamor—indeed you lose your mask, and your real face, your human nature appears. You are miserable but honest, now, without pretense and without claim; frank, plain and naked; completely alone, forsaken, enslaved; but all your humiliation exists only as long as you fight against it. Accept it—and finally you cannot help accepting it, and it is gone. Then you discover the essential secret of the doghouse: there is no doghouse at all.

Meanwhile everday life will give you many a chance to check your inner progress by outer experiences. Do not shun the humiliating situations; face them, exploit them for your inner development. Allow yourself to be teased, ridiculed, exploited; learn that you can survive without losing your human dignity, and that you can serve without feeling enslaved. Learn that failure and defeat are part of human life as well as success and victory. And the rhythm of contraction and expansion will encourage you, foreshadowing death and resurrection. Thus, in complete loneliness you may discover that most people, knowingly or unknowingly, are as alone as you are. You will discover their real faces behind their masks; you will love them; and finally you will find the great brotherhood of suffering mankind.

If you succeed in breaking the spell of the Giants and of the doghouse you will be able to say with St. Paul that you are "initiated into the secret for all sorts and conditions of life, for plenty and for hunger, for prosperity and for privations" (Phil 4:12). If it is not so, go back to your confessional meditation and begin anew.

Awakening "Sleeping Beauty" (Diagram V)

1. The person represented in Diagram V has developed the egocentric caricature of masculinity as his Ego-image. It can express itself in terms of pure intellectualism and moralism, or as super-orderliness, pedantry, and fastidiousness, or as coarseness, cruelty and brutality. Women are despised, misused and sometimes dreaded. All this is bad enough if the person is a man. If it happens to be a woman, her Ego is doubly deviated; she is an "animus-ridden" lady. The typical dream of these people who do not dare to expose themselves emotionally is nakedness.

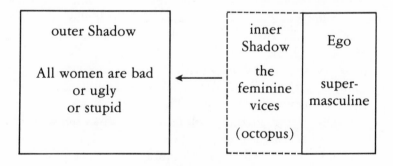

DIAGRAM V
Awakening "Sleeping Beauty"

The Journey of Those Who Reject Tenderness and Neglect Harmony

The "anima," the feminine image, is repressed into the unconscious and degenerated into some dreadful and loathsome collective symbol such as the serpent, the vampire, the octopus. These images are later transferred onto almost every woman in the outer world, so that they appear to be "ugly, mean, base, treacherous, shallow, stupid, or enigmatical, incomprehensible, unfathomable." All "womanish" reactions are denounced; and one half of human life is sacrificed. The basis of this unfortunate one-sidedness is always of course an early tragedy between the child and the first representative of femininity, his mother.

The way out cannot be found by loving or trying to love a woman in outer reality. This must fail unless it is accompanied by the discovery of the repressed anima-image within the individual's own unconscious. The negative symbol, the octopus, has to be faced, and its virtue, the loving Eve, has to be discovered behind its vice. Thus the inner defense mechanism of the Ego becomes useless. Its fear of the octopus, its loathing and disgust are recognized as the disguised creative power of the real center: even Eve is a child of God, and a beautiful one. Then the rigid Ego disappears; its counterpart, the Shadow, is integrated; loathing is superseded by love, and the new life can develop.

2. The way through confessional meditation is in this case characterized by the word relaxation. Give up your self-control. All your discipline and concentration are mere Ego-defense and therefore self-deception. Try to be honest: let come to consciousness what lurks and lures in your unconscious depths, though it be as ugly and obscene as the witch Baubo or as beautiful and pernicious as Lilith.

The symbols may be indistinct and changing: Eve, Venus, Sleeping Beauty, Cinderella, witches, queens and madonnas may visit you in dreams and fantasies. The emotional gamut will prove to be rather simple: loathing will be replaced by lure; we will feel our loneliness, not yet being courageous enough to woo, because that would mean to admit our longing, our unhappiness, weakness and helplessness. Then we may recognize that just this is human life, and suddenly the power of love will push us ahead like a tempest. We are servants of the real center. We have to obey. And the unspeakable joy and courage of a super-individual passion will make us humble and strong at the same time.

The way is the same for men and women. Men will find that the Eve-image teaches them the values, the beauty and the dignity of womanhood. The more they develop Eve, the more they have to become Adam, and to replace their Ego-image by true masculinity. The woman, discovering her inner Eve-image, suddenly learns what it means to be feminine. She renounces her former Ego-image which was too masculine, and finds that the male qualities are useful to her if they remain secondary, and that they help her to understand and to enjoy her newly found counterpart in the outer world, the real Adam.

The introvert way should be paralleled by outer experiences. The steps usually are three: first we should learn to reveal and to express appropriately our tender emotions, without too much modesty or shame. Second we should learn to woo, even if there is no or almost no chance of success. This includes the art of giving gifts which meet the partner's taste, exploring his real needs and capacities, especially those which he does not know himself, and helping him to live a fuller, and more creative kind of life. The third step is the final test of love: where there is love there can be no disgust. The mother does not mind her babe's dirty diapers. Two lovers like to eat with one spoon. The good nurse, the real physician, are not deterred by the odor of rotting

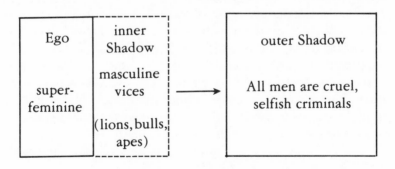

DIAGRAM VI

Organizing the Organizer

The Journey of Those Who Are Afraid of Disharmony,
Disapproval and Privation

pus. And, at the Lord's Supper, do you like to share the communion cup with your Christian brothers? Hygiene, of course, forces us to disinfect the cup; but behind hygiene hides our lack of love.

Organizing the Organizer (Diagram VI)

1. Diagram VI represents a person whose Ego-image shows merely feminine qualities, though it may have a masculine name. The individual, whether man or woman, is a sissy, not balanced by masculine traits. All masculinity has been repressed into the unconscious and has degenerated into primitive collective symbols such as lions, tigers, dogs, bulls, horses, apes, criminals and especially burglars. To be chased by a beast or frightened by an intruder is a common dream of all effeminate people.

The unconscious image of the intruder is then transferred onto friends and enemies alike. The "anima"-character is therefore soft and kind, but suspicious and cowardly. And his repressed aggressiveness often finds an outlet in unconscious cruelty (corresponding to the unconscious sentimentality of the animus-character). The lack of animus-qualities is most obvious in the person's incapacity to organize time and energy, his carelessness with regard to money, his lack of discrimination, and his tendency to indulge in all kinds of weakness.

What these people need is discipline and organization, but they cannot develop them as long as they are afraid of sacrifice. The power of organization is the capacity to say "no," to face disapproval and disharmony, and to overcome them by an effort at conscious creativity. This power, however, has been transformed into destructive and primitive tendencies. The task, therefore, is to integrate these tendencies, to raise them into consciousness and to transform them into positive "virtues."

2. The origin of this repression is always connected with a father problem. The confessional meditation should therefore begin with remembrances concerning the father (or the mother, if she was the more masculine type). What did we learn about masculinity? How much tenacity and fortitude, how many Spartan and Stoic virtues did we develop? Now we must make up for what we skipped in early childhood. Now we have to face first the inner burglars, bulls and lions and later the outer opponents. This

is similar to, but not identical with, the task of facing the Black Giants (Diagram III). The giant is our superior, and stronger than we are; the burglar is cruel and malicious, but he may be rather small and limited in his strength. It is his inhuman recklessness which renders him terrible. Often, however, the two images are combined as a giant intruder.

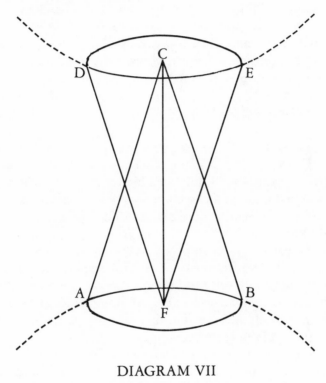

DIAGRAM VII

The Natural and the Spiritual We-Experience

(The Way to Maturity)

The emotional aspect of our reeducation begins with fright or horror, leads through hatred and cruelty—now our own primitive cruelty, taken over from the checked and astonished opponent—and it ends in a completely new attitude toward suffering, our own as well as that of other people. What seemed to be unbearable is now easily sustained, and even death has lost its repulsiveness. The development is from horror via hatred to herosim.

The extravert part of the way may begin with modest experiments in "Spartanism." Fasting, saying "no" to ourselves first, later on to friends and even to superiors. Renouncing our favorite distractions; refraining from caresses and (very important!) from gossiping and telling lies. Thus we may train ourselves to make sacrifices; we may prepare the sacrifice of our time, strength, health and lives; and finally we may meet the great test of maturity: if necessary, to inflict, consciously and conscientiously, pain and sacrifice upon our most beloved friends.

The Natural and the Spiritual We-Experience (Diagram VII)

1. Diagrams III to VI deal with the reintegration of the one-sided and eccentric personality. There is no doubt that the new equilibrium can be found only on a higher level of consciousness, the person being individually conscious of and responsible for the whole group to which he belongs. This progress is usually reached through the failure of our eccentric deviations; but it would take place, and even more markedly, if no deviation had occurred at all. The first task, correcting our eccentricity, corresponds to the medieval idea of "purgation"; the second task, achieving the higher consciousness, is "illumination." Both, as we said, are practically interwoven; theoretically, however, it is useful time and again to separate them.

Moreover, Diagrams III to VI refer to egocentricity; they are of no—or almost no—use in cases of idolatry. The development described in Diagram VII, on the other hand, applies to all kinds of sham religion. Our Idols, high as they may be, are still deviated nature; their spirituality is spurious. And the true Spirit, the Spirit of the living God, will put us to a test and destroy all such delusions. The Idols will fail us when we need them most urgently, just as health and money and friends and all other natural values will fail.

Consider the cone ABC: it represents the natural life of the human being, including the lower or tribal consciousness as well as the Ego-consciousness of the civilized individual. Its goal is self-preservation. Time, however, symbolized by the line FC, leading upward, brings about the gradual decrease of the cone's perimeter and finally its end at C. Human life does not last. Individuals and groups, institutions and cultures, decay and disappear. Hence the melancholy of so many poets and philosophers. Even the best kind of life, the deepest We-feeling and the highest courage, do not alter the fact that life is doomed to die—because it is meant to change, and to rise again.

The circle AB is identical with the larger circle of Diagram I, representing the original We-group (or the member of the group who lives the group-life). The inner circle of Diagram I, the "We-center," here is the point F, the beginning of the spiritual life as represented by the cone DEF. This "spiritual cone" increases to the same degree as the "natural cone" decreases—if the development is not disturbed by eccentric deviations which may engender the decrease of both cones at the same time.

The cone DEF represents the higher consciousness, the "maturing We-experience," the "inner light" which is given to us as a seed (point F) and is supposed to engross our earthly life increasingly until the latter vanishes completely and the former alone survives (point C). Notice that the spiritual center of the original We-group during the second half of the development encompasses the narrowing "natural cone," so that center and perimeter are exchanged. The mature personality should lead an all-embracing spiritual life which permeates and surpasses his physical existence rather than remaining its hidden center, as it used to be during the first half of his life.

2. The practical implication is that every loss in the realm of natural life could and should be an adequate gain in the realm of the spirit. Loss of money or reputation, accidents, diseases, death of our friends or relatives, and finally the visible approach of our own death—all these losses should become spiritual gains.

The progress may be achieved when the loss occurs in reality—this is the most painful way; or it may be prepared in imagination, replacing the outer event by inner growth. This psychological preparation not only decreases the pain of the actual loss but sometimes supersedes it entirely and thus helps to avoid it ("some will not taste death"). The way for the beginner, however, should be a third one: remember losses that you have not yet assimilated. Do not acquiesce, do not repress your emotional reactions. If you feel resentment, bitterness, rebellion against God or man, express it thoroughly through confessional meditation. This is the reaction of the natural cone. Then remember the spiritual world. Look for the center and its possible growth. What does the natural loss mean? What does God want you to discover, or to understand, or to do? This question is the first beginning of your spiritual reaction.

Did the wolf chase you? Be sure he acted—without knowing it—as the shepherd's dog. You are in the hands of the living God, and all who know agree that this is terrible. If you could help him to help you it would be less painful for both of you. Indeed, all evil would cease to be evil in the very moment that you could understand and accept and forgive. This does not mean acquiescence. Stop the evil-doers; they do harm to many people; and, if you cannot stop them, exploit what they have done for your own growth. Then it ceases to be evil to you, though it remains evil for them.

This inner growth, the transformation of the collective powers from the original We-structure into the structure of the maturing We-experience, is not an action of our conscious will, though the will must cooperate; nor is it a merely emotional process, though emotional changes are important; nor is it an intellectual event, though the higher understanding is usually its most significant symptom. It is a central development, including willing and thinking and feeling alike. It is spiritual growth. It is continuing creation and therefore worth every sacrifice.

KUNKEL'S WORK AND CONTEMPORARY ISSUES IN PSYCHOLOGY AND RELIGION

I
The Creative Ego Response

Life continually confronts us with a variety of difficult situations. Because of this the Ego is frequently called upon to respond to situations that are perplexing, frustrating, overwhelming, or threatening. The difficulties that confront us may be outer situations or inner situations or both. Examples of outer situations might include a parent who has to deal with a difficult child, a student who must take an important examination, a boy or girl who fears rejection, a soldier in a combat situation, a man at his work who has a tyrannical boss, and someone facing an illness, old age, or death. Obviously there are a myriad of such examples. Inner difficulties would spring from anxiety, boredom, overwhelming emotion, a great disappointment, difficulty in sleeping, etc.

Two kinds of Ego responses are possible. One is rigid and unproductive; the other I call "The Creative Ego Response." In the former, the response is characterized by inflexibility, panic, defensiveness, rage, and sterility. In the latter, a response occurs that is exactly appropriate to the kind of situation with which the person is faced. It cannot be stylized or characterized because the creative Ego response is always unique and one-of-a-kind. For this reason we cannot describe it by adjectives the way we can describe the rigid Ego response. Of course the rigid response comes from the egocentric Ego. It is the nature of egocentricity that it can only respond to difficult situations in unproductive ways. The creative Ego response, on the other hand, has its inspiration from the Real Self. This is why it is unique and effective. The following are some examples of creative and uncreative Ego responses drawn from contemporary situations, biblical examples, and literature. These examples are only a sampling of the hundreds of thousands of examples that could be given. Let's begin with examples of the rigid Ego response.

The first is based upon a real life situation. A man in his thirties, whom we will call Joe Brown, is divorced. His three year old son is staying with him over the weekend and Joe has taken the boy with him when he goes to visit friends. There are several couples, all married with small children, and while the children are playing in the backyard the adults are talking and enjoying themselves in the house. All goes well until the son of one of the other couples comes into the house in tears complaining loudly that Joe Brown's son has hit him. No one is very upset except Joe. He goes out to the backyard where the children are playing and sternly admonishes his son. The other boy, satisfied that justice has been done, returns to the backyard and resumes his play.

But a short while later he is back with the same story: Joe Brown's little boy has hit him again. This time Joe is really upset. He goes out to the yard again and shouts at his son that he isn't to hit the other boy anymore.

For ten minutes all goes well, and then the little boy comes into the room a third time and amid his tears complains bitterly about Joe Brown's boy fighting with him. Joe doesn't try to find out what really happened; he doesn't ask his son for his version of the story. Enraged, he goes to the back yard, finds his boy, who cringes now at his father's approach, and gives him a beating.

When Joe returns to his friends he feels dreadful. He can't forget how his son cringed at his approach. He is ashamed of himself for losing his temper. He knows that things have gone wrong, and though he accused his son of being a bad boy, he senses that somehow it is he who has failed.

Joe goes to see a therapist and begins to understand what happened. He concludes, "I felt as though my son was making me look bad in front of my friends. I was certain that they would all think I was a bad parent, that I couldn't bring up my son right or control him. Besides, I didn't know what to do about it. When I scolded my son and his bad behavior didn't stop, I was at the end of my rope."

The matter of the other boy came up. It occurred to Joe that maybe the other boy was as much at fault as his son. Was the other boy the completely innocent victim that he pretended to be? What if the other boy had done someting to make Joe's son want to hit him, and then used this as a way to get him into trouble? Joe reflected, "I didn't like this boy. I didn't like the way he was a tattle-tale, but I didn't want to bring it up for fear of offending his parents. Obviously he was getting a lot of satisfaction from getting my son in trouble. But I never gave my son a chance to tell his side of the story because I was so concerned with how he was making me look."

There is nothing unusual about this story. In one form or another it has been repeated a billion times throughout history. Where is the parent who hasn't been driven by his child into a frustrated rage? The fact remains that Mr. Brown wasn't able to find a creative way to deal with his rage and frustration.

His rage came because he was afraid of how his son was making him look to the others. Mr. Brown was a Star. It was extremely important to him that he be thought of highly, and he couldn't bear it when his son's bad behavior might turn into critics the people whom he wanted to be his admirers. We are even justified in wondering if some of his son's behavior came from an unconscious need on the part of the boy to defeat his father's egocentricity, for it's a fact that children are unconsciously impelled to touch upon the parents' weak spots until the parents have worked them out.

Mr. Brown's frustration came because he couldn't think of any way to deal with the situation. When a parent feels he can't cope with a child, that parent is especially likely to respond in an uncreative way.

When his father went into a rage and beat him it was for the boy a "Breach-of-the-We." The brutality the boy then experienced was a negative influence driving the boy into his own Turtle or Nero egocentric pattern. When the boy becomes a father himself the danger will be that he will pass on to his son the kind of egocentric fathering he received.

What happened between Mr. Brown and his son was dark, but light came out of it. Joe was upset, and this was good, because this drove him to examine himself and what happened. With the help of the therapist he faced his own darkness, and went through the crisis that the incident had plunged him into. From his Real Self came the insights that he needed in order to understand himself better and, hopefully, prepare himself to deal more creatively when another similar situation occurred. He was even able to go to his small son and tell him that he was sorry the way things had turned out. When he explained to his son that he lost his temper because he didn't know how to deal with the situation it relieved him of some of his anguish, and made his son feel more secure. In this way some of the Breach-of-the-We was healed.

Our next example comes from the Bible. King Saul is desperate. Some time ago the prophet Samuel had told Saul that Yahweh had forsaken him and chosen someone else to sit upon his throne. Saul tried everything he knew to forestall this prophecy of doom. He singled out David as the chosen one of God and tried to kill him, but all efforts failed. Now David is safely in exile. Samuel has died, and Saul's kingdom is being invaded by a superior army of the Philistines, his ancient enemies.

Saul tries to get guidance from Yahweh by dreams, by casting the sacred oracle, and by consulting prophets, but Yahweh will not answer him. Finally he goes to a necromancer, a woman who is able to summon up the spirits of the departed from Sheol. He wants her to bring back the ghost of Samuel. This is a desperate step, for Saul had persecuted the wizards and necromancers, killing them or driving them away because they belonged to the old Canaanite religion and did not worship Yahweh. But now he himself has to resort to such a woman.

Saul arrives at night at the cave, which is the refuge of the necromancer, with a few of his closest courtiers, and persuades the frightened woman to conjure up Samuel. When Samuel's stern apparition appears, Saul explains his plight to his old tormentor and begs for some word from God, but Samuel can only repeat his unrelenting prophecy of doom and rejection. Completely undone Saul collapses on the floor of the cave. Destroyed by fear and hopelessness, he is reduced to a quivering, abject coward.

Saul is certainly faced with a desperate situation. No one can blame Saul for his fear, and while we might wish he would show more courage we can understand why he is afraid. But the fact is that Saul's response to his difficulty is uncreative. He is so concerned with saving himself that he is unable to find any positive response to his plight. The only response possible for him as long as he comes from this egocentric posture is total collapse. His last several years have been one long attempt to defend and preserve his ego; now that there is nowhere else to turn, he can only collapse. In Kunkel's language, he has become a craven Turtle.

My third and last example of the rigid Ego response is taken from Shakespeare's play *Hamlet.* It has been revealed to Hamlet by the ghost of his father, that his father has been murdered by his father's brother Claudius, who has now taken over Hamlet's father's throne and married Hamlet's mother. Claudius does not realize that Hamlet knows about the murder, but he has an uneasy conscience about what he has done. Claudius wants to repent and cleanse his soul, for his offense "smells to heaven." But, Claudius asks himself, how can he ask for forgiveness when he still possesses all those benefits for which he murdered? He has the throne, the queen, the power, the fulfillment of all his ambitions, and he is not willing to give them up. Claudius wants to keep what he has, yet agonizes because he feels that his bosom is "black as death." So he prays:

> Help, angels! Make assay!
> Bow, stubborn knees; and, heart with strings of steel,
> Be soft as sinews of the new-born babe!
> All may be well. (Act III, Scene 3)

Claudius is a man who wants power, and will use any brutality necessary in order to get it. In Kunkel's language, he is a first-class Nero who has achieved his egocentric goal. But when we reach our egocentric goal and should be happy and content, we are instead afflicted with uneasiness and a bad conscience. Claudius is intelligent enough to realize this, and in his prayer he tries to overcome his egocentricity, asking his stubborn knees to bow, and his steely heart to become soft like a child's. The stubborn knees and steely heart depict his egocentric state which defeats the sincerity of his prayer and are an obstacle to his attempt to reach God. If Claudius had been willing to relinquish his throne, give up his power, and go through the crisis this would have brought upon him, there might have been hope. But he is not willing to do this and he knows that for this reason his prayer is futile. At last he gives up the attempt:

My words fly up, my thoughts remain below:
Words without thoughts never to heaven go.

Claudius is faced with an inner difficulty: his bad conscience and the resulting anxiety and misery this brings upon him. Outwardly everything is going just as he wanted, and there is no threat that he knows about in his outer life, but inwardly he is confronted by a challenging problem to which he cannot respond creatively because he cannot give up his egocentricity. His attempt at prayer is not sincere; it is in the service of his egocentric purposes, and for this reason it fails.

As Kunkel has pointed out, however, we are seldom entirely egocentric. In most of us there is an admixture of the Real Self and egocentricity. We can see Claudius' genuine personality coming through in his capacity to be honest with himself. Claudius knows that he can't expect forgiveness if he is unwilling to relinquish his ill-gotten gains. He is unable to free himself from his egocentric desires, but at least he is honest enough to know it, and this honesty comes from the Real Self. So does his misery. Claudius is not so completely evil that he is able to do evil without experiencing remorse; he has gone beyond the boundaries of what his Real Self allows and he suffers accordingly.

Perhaps it was this genuine quality in Claudius that brought about one positive, though unsuspected, benefit from his prayer. For while Claudius was praying, Hamlet had crept up behind him with the intention of avenging his father's death, but when he saw that Claudius was praying he changed his mind. He didn't want to kill him then for fear that the dead man's soul would go to heaven if he were killed in what appeared to be an act of repentance.

We could give many more examples, but these three illustrations drawn from diverse sources are enough to enable us to see what it means to speak of rigid and defeating Ego responses.

The following are examples of a creative response.

The first example comes from a man who—like Joe Brown—was also in his mid-thirties. Bill Baylor, as we will call him, was married and had two children. He had a job as a low-level administrator in a government agency. He hated his work because he hated both his supervisors and many of the agency's clients. His supervisors appeared to him to be bullies who made his life miserable and were out to get him. If he made the slightest mistake he feared his bosses would be on his back about it, and perhaps even use it as a pretext for having him dismissed. Though he didn't make a great deal of money he was afraid that if he lost this job he wouldn't be able to get another one. His work called for him to enforce the terms of government contracts with private contractors. Many of these private contractors, he felt, were also out to get him. They seemed to despise him, and he saw them as powerful people who wanted to do him in. Bill's world was populated with Black Giants who made him feel like a helpless little dwarf.

To compensate for his insecurity Bill overdid his job. To be sure he didn't make any mistakes and couldn't be criticized, he took his work home every night. This alienated him from his family. Besides, when he was home he was fearful, moody, and generally unpleasant to be around. His wife didn't like this, and was resentful because he worked so much. Bill liked his wife, and her rejection of him made him more anxious. When he became impotent with her this only made everything worse.

Bill had been reduced to a frightened, dreary, hopeless man. His egocentric posture was that of a Clinging Vine who tried to cling to an unrewarding job and to the strength of his wife only to be terrified with the realization that they weren't going to hold him up. He also had patterns of the Turtle who runs and hides in the face of real or supposed difficulties, only now there was nowhere to hide. Small wonder he was now in an egocentric crisis: depressed, anxious, exhausted, and unable to sleep at night.

One day Bill was driving alone in his car and felt so despondent he found himself contemplating suicide. He thought: "I could drive my car fast and then run into a tree along this highway. That way I can kill myself but my family and everyone else will think it was an accident." Bill wanted out of his misery, but there was enough We-feeling left so he didn't want his family to be burdened with the pain of having a suicide to live through. He was thinking about ending his life this way when it occurred to him that he might not die. What if he only injured himself? Then life would be even worse. He couldn't bear that. In his despair he began to talk to God and the conversation went something like this:

> God, you're no help to me. You know my awful state and you do nothing about it. I can't even kill myself. I'm a failure at everything I try. I fail at work. My wife doesn't like me. I'm failing my children. Everything I've turned to has turned to nothing. All right, God, I'll tell you what. I can't make myself run into that tree but I'm a dead man already. As far as I'm concerned, I'm dead to everything. And since I'm dead it doesn't matter what happens at my job. Nothing can hurt me—I'm dead.

Bill's fantasy that he was a dead man lasted for several days. Of course he knew he was walking around alive—he wasn't crazy—yet the image that he held of himself was that he really was dead now. In this state of mind he went to work as usual but, to his surprise, he found that he had lost his fear. After all, if you're already dead what is there to be afraid of? Not even his bully bosses could threaten him with anything now that he was dead, and the crassest of his clients couldn't touch him either. Without his fear, of course he found he was much more effective at his job.

When he went home he wasn't moody as he had been before, and since he was dead he didn't bother to bring his work home. To his pleasant surprise he found that he was now potent again with his wife. After all, what's the point in being afraid of your wife's rejection when you're dead? Miraculously Bill found his life was suddenly going extremely well. He had a lot less fear and a lot more energy now that he was living life as a dead man.

Of course we can see what happened. When Bill declared that he was a dead man, what died was his egocentricity. In going to his death Bill went through the darkness of the Crisis. He no longer tried to avoid it. Since his Ego was dead he no longer had to defend it, and since his energy was not absorbed in propping up his weak Clinging Vine Ego he operated out of the Real Self. That meant that his life became full of surprising power.

When we hear such stories we wonder if the change lasted.

Of course it didn't. After Bill felt better for several days he began to try to hang on to his improved state. As soon as he did this his "dead" Ego came back to life and his old egocentricity returned. I'm afraid this is the way it is with egocentricity. We go through the Crisis and some of our egocentricity does indeed vanish, but once through the darkness we regroup on the other side and become egocentric again. If we use an imaginary scale of 0 to 10, we could say that when a person's egocentricity hits 9 or 10 he is threatened with collapse. If you go through the Crisis as Bill did, you wind up on the other side with an egocentric rating of about 2. When things begin to go better again your Ego regroups and starts to defend itself again in the old way, but it's not as bad this time, and you wind up at about 6 instead of 9 or 10 where you were when the Crisis started.

So even though Bill didn't stay on this high level, he had changed. He remained less fearful, more effective, and better able to relate to his family. Who knows how many more times Bill will have to "die" before he is completely cured?

For our second example of the creative Ego response I would like to return to the story of King Saul. When we left Saul he was prostrate on the floor of the cave, a hopeless and defeated man, but that's not where the story ends, for now something unexpected happens. The so-called "Witch of Endor," the woman who conjured up Samuel's ghost, and who, according to Hebrew tradition, must have been an evil person, now becomes a heroine because of the compassion she feels for her erstwhile enemy. Perhaps she realizes that there is a noble heart in this beaten man who cringes on the floor of her cave. At any rate, in order to help him she speaks to him encouragingly, trying to rouse in him once more his manly spirit, and offers to make a hot and strengthening meal for him. At first Saul refuses to budge from his prostrate position, but at last, enticed by the woman and his courtiers, he gets up and eats the fatted calf the woman has cooked. Strengthened both in body and soul, Saul takes up his armor and weapons and rejoins his army. The next day the Philistines attack and the final battle is on. Saul knows that his cause is hopeless, that his army will lose the battle and that he will die. Still he fights on until his army is destroyed and he himself is severely wounded. Then, rather than subject himself and his people to humiliation by allowing himself to be captured, he falls on his own sword and dies.

At the end Saul was transformed from the craven, defeated man who lay on the floor of the cave to a hero. The Saul who lay prostrate on the ground was an egocentric man whose last desperate attempt to protect his Ego had failed. There loomed before him only the dark, inescapable crisis of death and destruction. Kunkel has told us that the only way through the Crisis is to accept and go through its darkness and not try to escape from it. With the help of the woman this is what Saul does. He gets to his feet, goes into battle, and embraces his death. This means that he stops trying to protect his Ego and gives his Ego up to the inevitable death. In this way his egocentricity is destroyed. At the end he lived from the Real Self, for which his memory is treasured to this day.

The story of Saul is an important illustration of the creative Ego response because it tells us that such a creative response does not guarantee that the Ego will find a way through its difficult outer situation. In most of the examples of a creative Ego response we will see that this response leads to the resolution of an otherwise overwhelming problem. In Saul's case this was not possible. There was no escape from his death. We need to understand that the creative Ego response is to be made regardless of its outcome. As soon as we say, "If I always make a creative Ego response, things will turn out the way I want them to," we have fallen into egocentricity again. Saul knew things were not going to turn out the way he wanted them to, but he embraced the darkness that he feared anyway. He walked through the wall of fear and found his own true Self on the other side.

Very often the creative Ego response requires that we embrace exactly that which we fear the most. Let's go back to Joe Brown. What might Joe have done in his particular situation? It's always dangerous to be an armchair quarterback and try to second-guess a situation. We must remember that the creative Ego response comes out of a certain situation; it comes spontaneously and can't be programmed in advance, nor can it be second-guessed. Just the same, we can let our minds muse on the possibilities open to Joe. One of them would have been to make a frank admission to his friends of his difficulties. He might have said,

"Look, I feel bad over this situation. I've spoken to my boy twice and he still is hitting this other boy. Frankly, I don't know what to do about it, and I'm terribly afraid you will think I'm a bad parent." Loss of face is what Joe feared the most. If he had acted this way he would have embraced exactly this loss of face, but the chances are that the reaction of the others would not have been criticism but friendship and helpfulness. Such an open admission of his difficulties might well have constellated among the adults a creative "We" situation out of which the proper response to his boy might have sprung.

My next example of a creative Ego response comes from a story in the New Testament which is found in many ancient manuscripts in the first part of Chapter 8 of the Gospel according to St. John. The scribes and Pharisees bring a woman to Jesus who was caught committing adultery. While everyone is looking on they say to Jesus:

> Master, this woman was caught in the very act of committing adultery, and Moses has ordered us in the Law to condemn women like this to death by stoning. What have you to say?

Jesus is in a bad position. His enemies want to trap him and it looks as though the trap is inescapable. If he says that the woman should not be stoned, the scribes and Pharisees can say, "Look, this man tells us to go against the law of Moses." If he says that she should be stoned, he might be accused of brutality, and the woman's death could be blamed on him. Besides, there is the fate of the woman involved. If he argues for mercy this might be understood as approval of her actions. In any event, it is not likely to be of much avail. If he doesn't argue for mercy, the woman is almost certain to be killed. In short, it looks as though Jesus is up against an insoluble difficulty.

The story tells us that Jesus wrote on the ground with a stick for a few moments. We don't know why he did this. Perhaps he was allowing time for his creative process to work. At any rate, he comes up with a jewel of a response. Looking up at his questioners and the crowd he says:

> If there is one of you who has not sinned, let him be the first to throw a stone at her.

Or, in the more familiar King James version:

> He that is without sin among you, let him first cast a stone at
> her.

Then we are told that his detractors and the threatening
crowd, upon hearing what Jesus said, silently went away one by
one.

Jesus' response was perfect. No one could accuse him of
denying the law of Moses; neither could the woman interpret
what he said as his approval of what she had done. But at the same
time he saved her life and showed that mercy was, in this case,
better than judgment. Moreover, he had done so in such a way
that no arguments had been created. When the people left it was
with a creative realization of their own darkness and Shadow, not
with resentful thoughts toward Jesus.

But notice also that what Jesus did and said, while entirely
and uniquely correct for this situation, is inapplicable to future
situations. If he tried the same thing in a future similar situation it
wouldn't work. We can't formulate "rules" for the creative Ego
response to guarantee that we will always come up with one. Nor
can we decide in advance of a situation what our response will be.
There is no way the Ego can control the creative power from
which the creative Ego response comes, and any attempt to do so
would be self-defeating because it would in itself be an egocentric
effort. The creative Ego response has a certain spontaneous,
unpredictable quality. Only our egocentric responses are predictable, not our creative ones. When we hear people say of us "Oh, I
know just what he'll say," then we can surmise that our egocentricity is so strong that our responses in life have become stereotyped, rigid, and therefore predictable. It's not that way with the
creative Ego response which is, as Kunkel has said, free and
incalculable precisely because it is creative.

So far we have considered examples of the creative Ego
response that would give the impression that it always leads to
some kind of direct action, but this is not always the case, for
sometimes we find ourselves in a life situation in which no action
is possible. In these cases, however, it is always possible to find
the correct attitude, and this too is a creative Ego response. Let us

suppose, for example, that we are faced with illness, old age, or death, and that there is nothing to be done about it. Or suppose that someone whom we love a great deal is suffering in some way and there is nothing we can do to change the situation. Or suppose we have suffered a great financial loss and the matter cannot be changed. In such circumstances there may be no action we can take to rectify the situation, but no matter how grievous the circumstances of life there is always a creative attitude that can be found with which to face it. Our next example illustrates this. It is given to us by Jung, who quotes from a woman who wrote him a letter about how she learned to face her difficulty. She writes:

> Out of evil, much good has come to me. By keeping quiet, repressing nothing, remaining attentive, and by accepting reality—taking things as they are, and not as I wanted them to be—by doing all this, unusual knowledge has come to me, and unusual powers as well, such as I could never have imagined before. I always thought that when we accepted things they overpowered us in some way or other. This turns out not to be true at all, and it is only by accepting them that one can assume an attitude towards them. So now I intend to play the game of life, being receptive to whatever comes to me, good and bad, sun and shadow that are forever alternating, and, in this way, also accepting my own nature with its positive and negative sides. Thus everything becomes more alive to me. What a fool I was! How I tried to force everything to go according to the way I thought it ought to!*

We don't know the difficult situation this woman was facing that impelled her to find the creative attitude she describes in her letter. One suspects it was an illness, perhaps made more difficult by advancing old age. However this woman does make clear that the creative Ego response does not necessarily remove the outer difficulties we are facing. It may or it may not. As we have seen, when we demand that the outer difficulties are removed, that is in itself an egocentric act. Forms of psychology and religion that tell

---

*The Secret of the Golden Flower, tr. Richard Wilhelm, com. C. G. Jung. New York: Harcourt Brace, 1931, 1962, p. 126.

us they have a method for ridding life of its problems and having everything turn out the way we want lead us down a false path. Even though it is a path that the egocentric Ego wants, in the long run it is against our best interests, for in pursuing our egocentric goal we fail to find the source of truly positive living.

Naturally, if we can overcome a difficulty we do so, but there are some hard facts and problems in life that will not go away, and we need to know that even then there is a positive way through. Kunkel put it well when he wrote:

> Part of the process of facing −100 involved the realization that one can be creative, that even though one cannot clearly foresee what he could do in the feared situation, he can, when the time comes, find a way out. . . . The Self is endowed with the capacity to endure courageously even the grimmest trage-dies of life. It has the God-given power to look back of the −100 and find the courage to live cheerfully and peacefully even when improvement of one's circumstances proves impos-sible as it sometimes does.*

When we imagine some of the dreadful things that could happen to us, it is hard to have faith that there could still be a positive way through the difficulty. Only a fool or some kind of a saint would invite a disaster upon himself because he is so confi-dent he could overcome it. Not for nothing did Jesus include in the Lord's Prayer the petition, "Do not put us to the test."

But sometimes we are put to the test, and when we are we can only survive if we are able to get beyond our egocentricity and find the creative response. This happened to Vice Admiral James Bond Stockdale who was shot down over North Vietnam. For eight years he was the senior naval officer held prisoner by the North Vietnamese. He was tortured fifteen times, held in leg irons for two years, and kept in solitary confinement for four years. This is the sort of situation that makes most of us shudder and think to ourselves, "I could never have stood that." Many of the prisoners couldn't stand it, but others did, including the

---

*Fritz Kunkel, *How Character Develops.* New York: Charles Scribner's Sons, 1940, p. 267.

admiral, and in an article in *National Review* entitled "The Melting Experience" James Stockdale tells us how they did it.*

Stockdale was under tremendous stress. He notes that when a person is under stress he naturally scrambles for some way to stop the stress, but when there is no way to stop the stress, one can only undergo what he calls a "melting" experience. He writes of such an experience:

> Some of your inhibitions, some of your feelings, fears, and biases melt as you come to realize that under the gun, you must grow or fall—in some cases, grow or die. A sort of transformation takes place under pressure—under what the alchemists of the Middle Ages called the "hermetic."

It's not hard to see that the "melting" to which Stockdale refers is the melting of our rigid egocentricity. It is also interesting that Stockdale refers to the experience of being under a stress from which one cannot escape as akin to the alchemical experience in which base substances were kept confined in a heated retort until they were transformed into precious metals. Stockdale goes on to elaborate the analogy between alchemy and his personal experience in prison in a way reminiscent of Jung, who saw in alchemy a symbolic representation of the individuation process.

The admiral goes on to tell how he endured the long periods in solitary confinement:

> A fellow prisoner, a math scholar, once did me the tremendous favor of passing to me (and I mean by that putting it through the concrete wall between us with our tap code, as I memorized it) an arithmetic formula of expansion that, in a remarkably few iterations of such simple form that they could be performed with a stick in the dust, would yield natural logarithms to three or four decimal places. After weeks of thought, I reconstructed the process of going from natural logarithms to logs of base ten. I slowly became the world's greatest expert on the exponential curve; I dusted off the construction of a log-log duplex deci-trig slide rule in my head. (No paper or pencils were allowed in the cell; my log

---

*James Stockdale, "The Melting Experience." *National Review*, December 25, 1981.

tables had to be etched with a nail on the concealed side of a
bedboard.) I became one of the few men alive to truly understand why any number raised to the zero power necessarily
had to be unity. I spent months and months in deep concentration and, at one point, could have written a pretty good
advanced mathematics test.

But the difficulty of solitary confinement was nothing compared with the stress of torture. The goal of torture was not only
to compel the prisoner to sign propaganda statements, but to
bring about an increased isolation among the prisoners. This was
done in two ways. First, any attempt by a prisoner in isolation to
communicate with fellow prisoners by wall tap, whisper, or any
other kind of signal would, if discovered, result in torture. Second, the prisoner who was being tortured would be compelled
not only to make statements for propaganda purposes, but to
betray his fellow prisoners with whom he had tried to communicate. Stockdale writes:

> Their system was designed to produce the propaganda and
> information they wanted no matter which the American chose
> of the two obvious ways to go: to stay off the prisoner tap-
> code communication network and eventually become so de-
> pressed after a couple of years that he would presumably be
> willing to buy human contact at the price of collaboration with
> the enemy; or to join the American communication network,
> that is, to join the American covert civilization, get caught
> communicating, as one did from time to time, and then be put
> through the standard chain of events. That chain went from
> torture to submission to confession to apology to atonement.
> The atonement was of course to consist of giving away prison-
> er secrets—being an informer, in other words—plus writing
> the old propaganda statement about how we had been guilty
> of bombing "churches, schools, and pagodas." In theory at
> least, we were in a no-win situation.

Stockdale tells us that he was able to survive even under
these dreadful conditions because he eventually distilled one
major idea by which he lived: He was his brother's keeper. He
writes:

It soon became clear that the only way to go—for peace of mind, for mental health if you will, as well as for practicality— was to forget that business about lying low and staying out of trouble by not communicating. Everybody had to get on the line and take the torture when he was caught because we had a civilization of Americans behind walls, a civilization of political autonomy that would have the courage to rule itself responsibly, with its own laws, with no contact for eight years with the parent country or its government in Washington.

And he adds:

To ignore a fellow captive in the pressure chamber is to betray him. Anybody who has been there knows that a neighbor in the cell block becomes the most precious thing on earth, a soul who deserves your care and cooperation no matter what the risk.

Stockdale also tells us that eventually everyone who was being tortured would be compelled to betray his fellows. What then? He gives us a surprising answer:

The sting of guilt was taken out of the program by the common-sense expedient of never keeping secrets from other Americans. No matter what we said or were forced to say under torture in the privacy of the interrogation room, we routinely put out the details on our tap-code net. This started as a matter of tactical defense and expediency, but its fallout in terms of expiation of guilt feelings was golden. We learned that the virtues of truthfulness and straightforwardness have their own reward.

In Kunkel's language, we could say that the prisoners experienced the "We." "We-psychology" replaced egocentricity, and this gave the prisoners the amazing strength to endure the worst physical isolation and torture imaginable. This is why Stockdale answered the question "What kept you going?" with the reply, "The man next door."

The situation of the prisoners was certainly a crisis situation. It seems that the ones who survived the best were the ones who didn't attempt to escape the threat of torture, but did what they felt they had to do even though it meant torture was the consequence. Oddly enough, those who failed to make it through their ordeal were those who clung to hope for a quick and optimistic outcome to their difficulties. It was not, of course, hope that was the negative influence, but hope based on illusions. Stockdale tells us:

> I saw the unintentional cruelty of disillusionment kill a rare sort of depressed and thoughtful man. You would never guess how. It was not messages of gloom, but cheery messages of hope, persistently drummed into him month after month, that eventually did him in. He internalized and took seriously those upcoming surefire release dates. After a number had eventually passed, his mind drifted away, he couldn't hold his rice down, and he died of a broken heart.

We have seen that there is something spontaneous and unpredictable about the creative Ego response. It comes from the innermost Self, which is always alive and intact even when we are not aware of it. The question naturally arises whether the Self operates more effectively in us when we are "working on ourselves," or if we don't need to do anything to raise our level of awareness and can just trust to the Self to save us when the situation comes. In a later chapter we will deal with this question in some detail.

II
Kunkel's Psychology
and the Bible

We have called Kunkel's psychology religious because it shows how the Ego must become centered around the Real Self if a person is to become whole. We have seen that when we are egocentric we are alienated from the Real Self, and noted that Kunkel didn't hesitate to call this state of alienation the psychological equivalent of sin. He said this because he understood the Real Self to express God's creative purpose and power within the individual. If this is so, it is likely that there would be evidence of Kunkel's psychology in the Bible. It is also likely that the contemporary reader would find it helpful to read biblical passages with Kunkel's psychology in mind.

As already noted, Kunkel wrote a psychological commentary on the Gospel According to Saint Matthew, *Creation Continues.* In my book, *The Man Who Wrestled With God,* I used insights from the psychology of Kunkel and Jung to show that the Old Testament stories of Jacob, Joseph, and Moses are the first documented case histories of the individuation process. These stories from the Book of Genesis give us all the essential information about the way egocentricity is transformed as people go through their crises and learn to follow the greater Will within themselves. In *The Kingdom Within, A Psychological Study of the Sayings of Jesus,* I wrote about the depth of psychological understanding in the teachings of the Lord, an understanding that is especially clear in the light of the work of Kunkel and Jung.

Kunkel's and my books only scratch the surface; the entire biblical narrative could be profitably surveyed from such a psychological viewpoint, just as it can be studied from an historical or theological viewpoint. If this were done, it would not simply be an exercise in applying psychology to a sacred text. The biblical narrative comes alive to us when its inner, psychological depth is revealed, and the Bible in its turn enriches our psychological understanding.

It should not be surprising that the Bible is such a rich psychological document. Since it claims to be the sacred narrative of the interaction of God and man, it is natural that a great deal of psychology should be involved and revealed in the narrative. In what follows, I illustrate further the applicability of Kunkel's psychology to biblical exegesis. No attempt is made to be complete, only to explore the possibilities for biblical studies that include Kunkel's psychological viewpoint.

Herod Kills the Innocent Children

In this story we see an example of the collision between the Ego and the Self. When the Christ Child was born, magi from the East came to worship him. They had seen his star as it rose, and recognized from their celestial observations that the appearance of this star signaled the birth of someone with an unusual destiny. Following the star they arrived in Jerusalem and inquired where they could find the newborn king of the Jews, as they now believed the child to be. The appearance of the magi with their remarkable question disturbed all of Jerusalem, and especially the king, Herod, who became especially alarmed when he learned from the scribes and priests that tradition said a great leader would come from nearby Bethlehem. Pretending that he wished to worship the child himself, Herod sent the magi on their way to Bethlehem, with instructions that when they located the child they should return to him and tell him where the child was. Actually, of course, he wanted to kill this child whom he perceived as a threat to his power and throne.

After the magi had found the Christ Child, worshiped him, and given him gifts, they were instructed in a dream not to go back to Herod but to return home another way. Shortly after,

Joseph was also warned in a dream and told to take Mary and Jesus and escape to Egypt. Our biblical text tells us:

> Herod was furious when he realized that he had been outwitted by the wise men, and in Bethlehem and its surrounding district he had all the male children killed who were two years old or under, reckoning by the date he had been careful to ask the wise men (Mt 2:16–17).

When Jesus was born it was the beginning of a new life for Israel and for the world. Jung has offered the suggestion that Christ is a representation of the Self. Whatever we may think of this hypothesis, it is clear that the Christ Child is an expression of God's creative energy at work in the world. Later St. Paul, as we have observed, would say that Christ dwelt within the soul of everyone. The Christ Within and the creative Center or Real Self are analogous terms and can be understood psychologically to refer to the same reality.

One might think that the emergence of this creative life would be welcomed, but Herod did not welcome it because it threatened his power. Herod could only see the Christ Child as a threat to himself and his throne. Clearly Herod was caught in and blinded by his egocentric stance. When he killed the innocent children of Bethlehem it was an attempt to maintain his security and protect his Ego.

The story of the murder of the innocents is a tale of the collision between the creative Center and one man's egocentricity. In terms of Kunkel's four types of egocentricity, Herod was a Nero. As such he had to be in control, and he became anxious when he felt his position of power was in danger. This egocentric stance, with its resulting anxiety, blinded him to the beautiful truth of the birth of the Christ Child. In his paranoia, which was the consequence of his egocentricity, he committed a great crime.

The Temptations in the Wilderness

Just before Jesus began his ministry he was baptized by John the Baptist. As he came up from the waters he saw the heavens open, and the Spirit of God descend upon him like a dove and a voice proclaim,

> This is my Son, the Beloved; my favour rests on him (Mt 3:17).

Immediately after this electrifying experience Jesus went into the wilderness, led by the Spirit. We are told that the purpose of this solitary time was so that he could be tempted by the devil. Evidently a crucial time of testing was necessary before Jesus could begin his ministry.

It is important for the modern reader to realize that the story of Jesus' baptism and the story of his temptations by the devil are one story. This might be overlooked since the first story concludes Chapter 3, and the second story begins Chapter 4. However, in the ancient manuscripts, before chapter divisions were devised by the Church, the baptism-temptations narrative was one story. This makes psychological sense, for the experience Jesus had at his baptism could have been highly inflating. As soon as a person has a truth revealed to him, or a personal visitation by the Spirit of God, inflation is a danger. Inflation is an egocentric state that causes us to make more (or less!) of ourselves than is correct. Had Jesus succumbed to inflation his mission would have been destroyed.

It is clear that Satan tempts Jesus to exactly such an inflation. There are three temptations. In the first one Satan says:

> If you are the Son of God, tell these stones to turn into loaves.

But Jesus replies,

> Man does not live on bread alone
> but on every word that comes from the mouth of God.

If Jesus had turned stones into bread he would have become extremely popular and famous, especially since he lived in a land in which starvation was a likely possibility for many people. Moreover, he would have been doing a "good" thing, for isn't it good to feed starving people? In short, to put the situation in Kunkel's terms, the temptation was to become a Star.

In the second temptation Satan says:

> If you are the Son of God throw yourself down; for Scripture says: "He will put you in his angels' charge, and they will support you on their hands in case you hurt your foot against a stone."

But Jesus quotes Scripture in reply,

> You must not put the Lord your God to the test.

Had Jesus cast himself off a cliff and been swept up by the angels he would again have become famous; a great marvel, and the object of enormous admiration and wonder. Many people would no doubt have wanted to make him an Idol. In Kunkel's language, we can again see that the temptation is to become a Star.

The third temptation is for Jesus to worship Satan and in return receive all the kingdoms of the world as his own to rule over. Jesus replies,

> Be off, Satan! For Scripture says: "You must worship the Lord your God, and serve him alone" (Mt 4:3–10).

If Jesus had acquired dominion of all the kingdoms of the earth he would not necessarily have been praised, loved, and adulated, but he would have been feared. The aim would be to acquire power, not praise. In Kunkel's language, the temptation was to become a Nero.

It's interesting that only two of the four egocentric types are represented in the story of the temptations of Christ. Kunkel says that the more vital, gifted child is more likely to gravitate toward being a Star or Nero, and the less vital, or overly sensitive child tends to become a Clinging Vine or Turtle. We may surmise that as a child Jesus was the former and that is why the temptations that came to him were for adulation or power.

When we look at this story from the viewpoint of Kunkel's psychology we also gain an important insight into the nature of Satan. Traditional theology views Satan as a kind of metaphysical being, a lesser divinity than God himself, as it were. Sophisticated biblical scholarship might see Satan as an example of biblical mythology that was alive for the people of biblical times but must be disregarded today. Jungian psychology has seen Satan as the dark side of God, the positive side of God in the baptism part of the story being represented by the dove. But looked at in terms of Kunkel's psychology Satan personifies the self-serving motives of the egocentric Ego. With most of us, our Ego-serving motives are unconscious to us and this makes up our truly dark side. In the case of Jesus, according to the story of the temptations, he was able to make this dark side of his Ego conscious and in this way could keep it from destroying his ministry. When we look at the story in this way we can understand why Kunkel said that the secret is that the Ego itself is the devil.

Jesus and the Woman Who Loved a Great Deal

We have noted that the story of Herod and the story of the temptations, while they mainly concerned the interaction between egocentricity and the creative Self, also illustrated two of Kunkel's egocentric types, the Star and the Nero. There are many other stories in which Kunkel's egocentric types are exemplified.

In Luke 7:36–50 is perhaps the most remarkable story in the Synoptic Gospels, apart from the passion narrative. In this story Jesus is dining with Simon, one of the Pharisees, when a woman comes in who has a bad reputation. She is so grateful for something that Jesus did for her that she covers Jesus' feet with her tears and wipes them with her hair. Then she covers his feet with kisses and anoints them with ointments. In those days, when people walked everywhere, feet became sore and dirty, and it was a gracious act for a person to minister to the feet of a friend or guest, but this woman has gone to extraordinary lengths in her attention to Jesus.

When the Pharisee sees what is happening, he is critical and says to himself that if this Jesus was truly a prophet he would know what a bad person this woman is and would have nothing to do with her. Jesus perceives what Simon is thinking and says to him,

> There was once a creditor who had two men in his debt; one owed him five hundred denarii, the other fifty. They were

unable to pay, so he pardoned them both. Which of them will
love him more?

And Simon replies,

The one who was pardoned more, I suppose.

Jesus says,

You are right. Simon, you see this woman? I came into your
house, and you poured no water over my feet, but she has
poured out her tears over my feet and wiped them away with
her hair. You gave me no kiss, but she has been covering my
feet with kisses ever since I came in. You did not anoint my
head with oil, but she has anointed my feet with ointment. For
this reason I tell you that her sins, her many sins, must have
been forgiven her, or she would not have shown such great
love.

Then he adds the startling statement,

It is the man who is forgiven little who shows little love.

The woman's love is an outpouring of the life of her Real
Self. She has transcended her Ego personality and includes herself
and Jesus in a mature "We" relationship. She wears no false mask,
puts on no front, but is absolutely genuine in her actions. Jesus
recognizes that her emotions and actions proceed from her innermost Center. She reached this state of development not because
she led an exemplary life, in the usual sense of the word, but
because she went through a time of darkness and suffering as she
was forced to confront a number of sins, the nature of which the
story does not specify. In Kunkel's language we would say that
here was a woman who went through the Crisis, to emerge on the
other side with her egocentricity stripped away from her; so she
was able to live from the Real Self, out of which came her
extraordinary love.

Simon, on the other hand, is stuck in an egocentric posture.
As a successful Pharisee, who led an exemplary life in the eyes of

the people of his time, he "starred" at being good. No doubt the
Pharisee from time to time was confronted by minor crises of his
own, but he was evidently too well defended to suffer from them
very much. His very success made it difficult for him to truly love,
because his success shored up his egocentricity and prevented him
from being plunged into the kind of Ego-crisis that might have led
him into his own creative Center, and hence his own capacity to
love.

This story gives us the clue to understanding the mystery of
the Beatitudes. Here they are as we find them Matthew 5:

> How happy are the poor in spirit:
> theirs is the kingdom of heaven.
> Happy the gentle:
> they shall have the earth for their heritage.
> Happy those who mourn:
> they shall be comforted.
> Happy those who hunger and thirst for what is right:
> they shall be satisfied.
> Happy the merciful:
> they shall have mercy shown them.
> Happy the pure in heart:
> they shall see God.
> Happy the peacemakers:
> they shall be called sons of God.
> Happy those who are persecuted in the cause of right:
> theirs is the kingdom of heaven.

In almost every instance, the state that Jesus refers to in the
Beatitudes as a blessed state is a state that is undesirable from our
usual Ego point of view. Who wants to be poor in spirit? Who
seeks to be gentle? Who wants to mourn? Who wants to suffer
hunger and thirst? Even the "pure in heart" do not represent a
desirable state since the Greek word for pure is "katharos," from
which we derive our word catharsis. It means, therefore, being
purified by great suffering. And, of course, no one *wants* to be
abused and crucified.

From Kunkel's point of view, however, we can see why these
are blessed states and experiences, for in the experiences that
Jesus cites, the Ego has been defeated, and with the defeat of the

Ego there can emerge the life of the Self. By going through the experiences of the Beatitudes we go through crises in which our egocentricity is stripped away from us, and the result is a blessed state of consciousness that can't be reached in any other way.

The Wealthy Young Ruler

There are as many ways of being egocentric as there are different individuals, but they all have a common denominator: all are rigid states that prevent us from entering into the creative life. In Luke 18:18–23 we have a striking illustration of this. The Gospel tells us about a wealthy person from one of the leading families of the country who asks Jesus,

> Good Master, what have I to do to inherit eternal life?

Jesus answers him,

> Why do you call me good? No one is good but God alone.

He goes on to recommend the Ten Commandments to him, but the wealthy aristocrat replies,

> I have kept all these from my earliest days until now.

When Jesus hears this he replies,

> There is still one thing you lack. Sell all that you own and distribute the money to the poor, and you will have treasure in heaven; then come, follow me.

But we are told that when the rich aristocrat heard this,

> he was filled with sadness, for he was very rich.

Matthew, who has a similar version of the story, adds that he went away "sadly."

It is interesting that when the rich aristocrat called Jesus "good Master" Jesus rebuked him and refused to accept the title "good." We can assume that Jesus recognized the man's approach to him as flattery. Jesus, as we saw in the story of the temptations, had faced his own egocentricity. He did not want to Star at being good and immediately handed that temptation back to the man.

We get the feeling in the story that if this man had followed the Commandments and led a decent life it might have counted for something in God's eyes, but when the man insisted that he had done all this, and was still hungry for something more, then Jesus instructed him to give up all his money and follow him.

There is no reason to suppose that this urge on the man's part to go the whole way was not genuine, a true expression of his Real Self. Jesus perceived, however, that if the Real Self was to be realized the man would have to give up his wealth, to which he was egocentrically attached. For a wealthy man such as this to accept poverty would have been a great crisis, and the man wasn't up to it. Sadly, he walked away. The difficulty with wealth apparently is that it is too great a temptation for the Ego, which incorporates wealth into its position as a Star or Nero, for wealth makes us feel admired or powerful.

In this case it is likely that the young man was a Nero, whose wealth meant power to him. He was a different kind of Nero than Herod. Herod was an openly brutal man, but this wealthy aristocrat followed the Commandments and no doubt people regarded him as an exemplary person. Since in that time wealth was often regarded as a sign of God's favor, it is even likely that his money increased the esteem in which he was held in the eyes of the people. To this extent, his wealth might also have fortified a Star egocentric position. However, as mentioned, Jesus perceived that the man was egocentric and had to go through the crisis of poverty and give up his egocentric needs and attitudes if he wished to progress further spiritually. There are all sorts of ways to be egocentric. Some are obvious, some cleverly concealed. Herod was obviously egocentric; this man's egocentricity was more subtle but also injurious to him.

There is an interesting finale to the story: Jesus does not run down the street after him begging him to change his mind and trying to persuade him that he is making a mistake. If Jesus had done this it would have been an infringement on the man's free will. Evidently only our free choice can lead us out of our egocentricity. If Jesus had begged the man to return, and if the man had agreed, we may surmise that his motive for doing so would have been in itself egocentric. He might have thought, "I must be awfully important to this important man. I can be more important with him than with all of my wealth."

In the context of this story we can understand more clearly several other sayings of Jesus, for example, Matthew 16:26:

> What, then, will a man gain if he wins the whole world and ruins his life? Or what has a man to offer in exchange for his life?

In the King James Version this reads:

> For what is a man profited, if he shall gain the whole world, and lose his own soul?

We can understand Matthew 10:39 in a similar way:

> Anyone who finds his life will lose it; anyone who loses his life for my sake will find it.

To win the world is to fulfill our egocentric ambitions. In the very act of egocentric success we are in danger of losing our soul, that is, our innermost Self. On the other hand, if we are defeated and lose our life, then we can gain it. This is why Kunkel urges us not to resist evil when it comes, but to go through the darkness even if it seems like death. It will be the egocentric Ego that dies, and then the genuine Center can emerge.

The Man Who Did Not Want To Be Cured

In John 5 we have a marvelous example of a Turtle. The story concerns a man who had lain beside the pool of Bethzatha for thirty-eight years without being cured. The belief was that from time to time an angel troubled the waters of this pool, and that the first person who then entered the waters would be healed. Lots of people had apparently been healed in this way, but even though this man had been there all those years he had never reached the waters first.

Now Jesus passes by and sees the situation and asks the man,

Do you want to be well again?

The man gives an evasive answer,

Sir, I have no one to put me into the pool when the water is disturbed; and while I am still on the way, someone else gets there before me.

It's not hard to surmise that this man doesn't want to get well; for an egocentric reason he wants to be sick. That's why Jesus asked him the question, "Do you want to be well again?" If the man had answered that question honestly he would have gained insight into himself, but our egocentricity resists insights that reveal our egocentric posture and so the man comes up with an excuse instead. Jesus now does a dreadful thing to this man: he cures him on the spot, saying,

Get up, pick up your sleeping mat and walk.

The story doesn't end here, however, for one thing doesn't happen that we might expect would happen, and something unexpected takes place instead. We might expect that the man would be grateful and thank Jesus, but no expression of gratitude is forthcoming. Instead the man goes to Jesus' enemies and tries to get him into trouble by telling them that Jesus cured him on the sabbath. Healing was a form of work, and work was not to be done on the sabbath. As a direct result of what the man said, Jesus was persecuted by his detractors. In fact, our story tells us that as a result of the altercation Jesus had with his enemies after this incident, a plot was born to kill him which ultimately resulted in his crucifixion.

The man by the pool had made his illness part of his egocentric defense. His vindictive attitude toward Jesus came from his egocentricity, and his lack of gratitude showed how far he was from his Real Self.

Sometimes it's hard to tell the difference between a Star and a Nero, as we have seen, and similarly it is often difficult to tell the difference between a Clinging Vine and a Turtle. Generally we can say that the Clinging Vine is more active in seeking out someone to lean on. The Turtle seeks out a more passive position in which he will not be called upon to face life's difficulties; his posture is: just leave me alone. Bearing this in mind we would have to say that the man by the pool was a Turtle who had found the perfect protected niche where he would not be exposed to life's hardships. While illness for a healthy person is a great hardship, it is different for someone who has incorporated the illness into an egocentric defense system. Hence his anger when Jesus stripped him of his protective illness, thereby forcing him into the world.

The Man Who Buried His Talent

It was hard to be sympathetic to the man by the pool of Bethzatha, but often the Turtle is a person who does win our sympathy. This is the case in the parable of the talents. In this story, which we find in Matthew 25:14–30, we are told of a man who was going abroad, and entrusted his three servants with his money. To one man he gave five talents, to another two, and to a third, one talent. Then he left. When he returned he asked each person to tell him what he had done with the money and to return the money to him. The man who had received five talents had traded with it and made five more talents. The man who had received two talents had likewise doubled his money, but the man with one talent had buried it in the ground. We are told that he was afraid of his master, whom he knew to be a hard man, and that is why he had hidden it in the ground.

The man who buried the talent is a good example of the Turtle. That's just what the Turtle does—hides—and the Turtle's motivation, as the story makes clear, is fear. What the man needed to do was to walk through his wall of fear and invest the money. Even if he had lost it his master would have respected his action. As it was, his one talent is taken from him and given to the man with the ten talents, and the offending person is called a good-for-nothing servant and is thrown out,

When we read this parable we may think that the man with the one talent was punished too severely. We can understand why he played it safe, and why he was reluctant to risk his talent and possibly have to confess a loss to his master. But life does not sympathize, and the Turtle betrays life just as much as any of the other egocentric types. It is for this reason that he is punished so severely in the parable.

Carrying the Cross

Curiously enough, I have not been able to find good examples of the Clinging Vine, but there is one saying of Jesus that makes it quite clear that there is no room in the Gospel of Christ for this egocentric type either. We find it in Luke 9:23 and 14:27, with parallels in Matthew and Mark; since it occurs so often it must have been an important statement. Luke 9:23 reads:

> If anyone wants to be a follower of mine, let him renounce himself and take up his cross every day and follow me.

Luke 14:27 reads:

> Anyone who does not carry his cross and come after me cannot be my disciple.

Some biblical scholars dispute the authenticity of this saying. They argue that it cannot be from Jesus since Jesus had not yet gone to his cross, so how could he refer to taking up the cross? However, in the above quotations, the cross is clearly a symbol of a psychological/spiritual burden to be carried. Everyone must have been familiar with this symbolism since it was the custom for a person who was to be crucified to carry his own cross to the place of execution. Actually, it makes little difference whether Jesus actually said this or not. The fact that the Gospel authors are at pains to have Jesus say it shows that this saying, and the attitude that goes with it, are close to Jesus' message. As James M. Robinson put it,

A saying which Jesus never spoke may well reflect accurately his historical significance, and in this sense be more "historical" than many irrelevant things Jesus actually said.*

The saying is especially important now, for there is an attitude in Christianity today to let Christ carry our burdens for us. *He* was the one who was crucified for us, and *we* don't have to worry about all that. All we have to do is be good, deserving sheep who accept the benefits of what he has done for us. This childish attitude is clearly in conflict with the statement that we are to take up our own cross and carry it every day *all by ourselves.*

As Jung has often pointed out, carrying our own cross is a symbol for carrying our own psyche, hence for individuation. Individuation requires us to carry the burden of our personalities and our lives consciously and courageously. The Clinging Vine tries his hardest to avoid carrying his cross. He wants to find someone else to carry it for him, someone to whom he can cling for support. Judging from Jesus' saying, this egocentric position has no place in a genuine Christian attitude.

The Shadow

Over the years I have had occasion several times to write about Jesus' view of the problem of the Shadow. The first treatment of the problem appeared in *The Kingdom Within.* This was followed by an article published in various places entitled "Jesus, Paul and the Shadow"; this article is now a chapter in my book *Evil: The Shadow Side of Reality.* So the subject of the Shadow as perceived through the Synoptic Gospels has been given a fair amount of attention. However, as we have seen, Kunkel had some original thoughts with regard to the Shadow, and these thoughts are exemplified in many places in the Gospels. I will present just one example: the so-called "woes" against the Pharisees, such as we find in Matthew 23:27–28:

Alas for you, scribes and Pharisees, you hypocrites! You who are like whitewashed tombs that look handsome on the out-

---

*James M. Robinson, *A New Quest of the Historical Jesus.* London: SCM Press, 1959, p. 99 footnote.

side, but inside are full of dead men's bones and every kind of
corruption. In the same way you appear to people from the
outside like good honest men, but inside you are full of
hypocrisy and lawlessness.

Looked at from the point of view of Jungian psychology,
Jesus is accusing the Pharisees of having a clean, polished persona
on the outside, but having a shadowy, corrupt life on the inside.
Jungian psychology would point out that here is a person who
appears to others (and himself) as a clean, honest, upright person,
but in the unconscious is his unrecognized dark side.

This is good as far as it goes, but actually there are two
problems with these Pharisees: *first,* they are hypocrites; *second*
they have within themselves "dead men's bones" and "every kind
of corruption." The Greek word that is translated "hypocrite"
means an actor or pretender. So the Pharisees are people who act
as though they are a certain kind of person when in reality they
are quite different. It's not hard to see that their hypocrisy is a
product of their egocentricity. They are Stars, who act as though
they are righteous in order to be admired when this is not really
the way they are. Clearly Jesus condemns this egocentric, hypo-
critical posture.

But the dead men's bones and corruption, and the lawlessness that comes from it, represent a different problem than the
hypocrisy: they symbolize everything the Pharisees had to kill in
themselves in order to maintain their egocentric stance.

Egocentricity creates two dark psychological problems. The
first is the false front the Ego has to put on in order to maintain its
egocentricity. The second problem is the inner darkness that
accumulates because of the need to deny everything in oneself
that would contradict the egocentric posture. Both of these problems are pointed out by Jesus in his scathing denunciation of these
people who posture egocentrically at being good when they are
really killing their creative life, so that it turns dead within them.
This distinction is an important one for psychology and we will go
into it in more detail in a later chapter.

The Crisis

There are many biblical examples of the Crisis. The crucifixion itself is a symbol par excellence of the Crisis the Ego must endure as it goes to the creative and victorious life of the Self. But the example I have chosen is the story of Peter's denial of the Lord.

At the Last Supper, Simon Peter, foremost among the disciples, had sworn to Jesus,

> Lord, I would be ready to go to prison with you, and to death (Lk 22:34).

In Matthew's version Peter says,

> Though all lose faith in you, I will never lose faith. . . . Even if I have to die with you, I will never disown you (Mt 26:33–35).

But when Jesus has been seized by his enemies and taken away for trial and crucifixion, Peter hides himself among others in the courtyard. When a servant girl recognizes him and says to the people around that Peter was one of Jesus' followers, he denied it vehemently, saying,

> Woman, I do not know him (Lk 22:57).

Three times he is accused, and three times he denies that he ever knew Jesus. After the third denial the cock crowed. Peter then remembered that the Lord had predicted that before the cock crowed he would have denied him three times. Overwhelmed with guilt and grief because of his betrayal of Jesus, Peter leaves, weeping bitterly.

It's always a dangerous thing to make promises about the future; perhaps this is why Jesus warned us against taking oaths (Mt 5:34–37). We can only promise what we will do on some future occasion if we have total self-knowledge; otherwise what we don't know about ourselves may come up to make our former promises empty. This is the case with Peter. His affirmation of his undying loyalty to Jesus was sincere at the time. This means that the part of Peter that was conscious was able to sincerely affirm his loyalty. But Peter was not yet sufficiently conscious of his egocentricity. Egocentricity, as we have seen, always means that the Ego seeks to protect itself and further its goals—survival in this case. Peter is so unaware of his egocentricity that when Jesus is taken prisoner he denies him three times without apparent conflict. But when the cock crowed, he remembered what he had promised out of love for Jesus, and realized he had just denied him in order to save himself. Then Peter was plunged into his terrible Crisis and wept bitterly.

It is interesting that he wept "bitterly." The mother of bitterness, Jung once pointed out, is disappointment. We are even more likely to feel bitter if we have contributed to the cause of our disappointment. People can suffer all kinds of tragic fates, Jung observed, without being bitter, but when we have brought our disappointment upon ourselves, bitterness may take over. This is the way it is with Peter. He weeps bitterly because he is so deeply disappointed in himself and because he alone is to blame for his behavior.

Peter is particularly torn apart because his promise of undying loyalty to Jesus was based on his deep and profound love for Jesus. This love for the Lord came from Peter's deepest Self, while his denial of the Lord came from his hitherto unrecognized egocentricity. The conflict between the two was extreme and tore Peter apart.

But Peter went through his Crisis. We can assume from Peter's later life that he did not rationalize his actions or make excuses for his behavior. In facing up to himself and going through the darkness, Peter underwent a crucifixion at the same time as his Lord. In a sense Peter was right after all when he told Jesus that he would go to death with him.

The Creative Life

Kunkel cannot emphasize enough the creative and victorious life that comes from the Real Self. This makes us think of the resurrection of Christ. Whatever else the resurrection is, it certainly is a symbol for the indestructibility of the Real Self. It shows us that when the Ego is grafted onto the Self the Ego also participates in something that is enduring and cannot be destroyed by death or evil. The victorious and creative life that proceeds from the Real Self is a life that can be lived in the here and now, on this earth, as we saw in our chapter on the Creative Ego Response. However, the resurrection story also seems to point to metaphysical implications, that is, it suggests that the life that proceeds from the Real Self may endure in some way beyond our physical death.

The fact that the resurrection is preceded by the story of the crucifixion makes perfect psychological sense. We saw with Peter that his Ego had to go through a crucifixion and death. When we go through the Crisis or Crises that strip away our egocentricity it is always like a death. That's what it feels like as we go through the darkness. Only later do we realize that real life is on the other side.

In this light we can understand Jung's statement that the emergence of the Self is always a defeat for the Ego—except, of course, it is our egocentricity that is defeated, because our real Ego shares in the victory of the Self. In this same light we can understand certain sayings of Jesus as well. For instance, in Matthew 6:25–34 Jesus says:

> That is why I am telling you not to worry about your life and what you are to eat, nor about your body and how you are to clothe it. Surely life means more than food, and the body more than clothing! Look at the birds in the sky. They do not sow or reap or gather into barns; yet your heavenly Father feeds them. Are you not worth much more than they are? Can any of you, for all his worrying, add one single cubit to his span of life? And why worry about clothing? Think of the flowers growing in the fields; they never have to work or spin; yet I assure you that not even Solomon in all his regalia was robed like one of these. Now if that is how God clothes the grass in the field which is there today and thrown into the furnace tomorrow, will he not much more look after you, you men of little faith? So do not worry; do not say, "What are we to eat? What are we to drink? How are we to be clothed?" It is the pagans who set their hearts on all these things. Your heavenly Father knows you need them all. Set your hearts on

his kingdom first, and on his righteousness, and all these other things will be given you as well. So do not worry about tomorrow: tomorrow will take care of itself. Each day has enough trouble of its own.

If we take the words of Jesus concretely they don't make very good advice; certainly we need to work and lay aside provisions for the future. But when we understand what he is saying as a dramatic way of representing the psychological attitude of trust that comes when the Ego is firmly rooted in the life of the Real Self, then it helps us understand that the Self holds up the Ego and that is what makes us secure. Then we are also in a position to recognize how egocentric most of our worries are. The important thing, Jesus says, is to concentrate on finding and living the creative life. Then the other things that we need will find their proper place.

But what if they don't find their proper place? What if things continue to go badly for us? We must remember again that the creative life from the Self does not necessarily mean that things will go well for us. But even if they don't work out, the energy of the Self will find a way through, for this is the way it is with the creative life. In New Testament language, this is the nature of the resurrected life with Christ. This is what Paul has to tell us in the Epistle to the Philippians:

I have learnt to manage on whatever I have. I know how to be poor and I know how to be rich too. I have been through my initiation and now I am ready for anything anywhere: full stomach or empty stomach, poverty or plenty. There is nothing I cannot master with the help of the One who gives me strength (Phil 4:11–13).

III
Jung, Kunkel and the
Problem of Evil

For the atheist the existence of evil poses no philosophical problem. Good and evil are purely human judgments. No explanation for evil needs to be given. That's just the way the world is. A polytheistic religion, such as Greek mythology, also has no problem with evil. In Greek mythology the gods and goddesses sometimes help people and sometimes are vengeful and capricious. In any case, the deities are not bothered by their actions because they are basically unconcerned with human beings and their welfare. But in an ethical and monotheistic religion, such as Judaism or Christianity, which believes there is only one Divine Being, and that this Divine Being is just, and has loving intentions toward mankind, the problem of evil looms large. For if God is just and loving why is there so much evil in the world?

The situation is much the same in psychology. A secular psychology need not concern itself philosophically with the problem of evil. For a secular psychology, evil is only a practical problem. It can content itself with the matter of how best to face and cope with evil and need not be concerned with its origin or place in the total scheme of things since there isn't any total scheme of things. Or, if there is, it can leave that matter to theology since, from the point of view of a secular psychology, whatever God there may be plays no part in the psychology of a human being.

But a religious psychology cannot avoid the problem of evil,

for a religious psychology asserts that there is a certain meaningful process that unfolds in the developmental process which takes
place in the individual. It cannot hold this position, or make sense
of the developmental process, without trying to come to terms
with the existence of evil in the world.

If a religious psychology believes in a transcendent God, it
runs into the same problem as theology. Unlike the secular
psychologist, the religious psychologist believes that the Divine
Being interacts with the human soul. Even if the religious psychologist only speaks of the Self, and says he can't go beyond this
to speak of a transcendent God, he still must try to account for the
relationship of the Self to evil. Does moral evil come from the
Self? If not, what is its origin?

This is not the place to make an intensive study of the
problem of evil. To the best of my ability I have already done this
in my book *Evil: The Shadow Side of Reality*. But since Jung and
Kunkel both make important contributions to a psychology of
evil, I do wish to compare the two psychologists in this chapter.
However, first we will have to summarize how Christianity has
approached the problem, since both Jung and Kunkel come from
a Christian background, and their viewpoints regarding evil are
partly a reaction to it.

First a comment on the problem of evil as it is dealt with in
the Gospels. Here it is clear that there is an evil power at work.
This evil power, personified as the devil or Satan, goes about the
world inciting people to sin, spreading mental and physical illness,
and generally trying to lead people away from God. Jesus knows
about the devil. He talks with him in the wilderness, and frequently encounters his agents, the demons, as he goes about his
ministry. What is striking is that Jesus never questions the existence of Satan and the evil he creates. At the same time he never
doubts the basic love of God for his creation. We have to assume
that in Jesus' view God knows about Satan and allows him to do
what he is doing for some ultimate purpose. Therefore Satan goes
about doing his thing, and while human beings are in great peril if
they become servants of evil, the necessity, or at least inevitabil-
ity, of evil is not questioned.

Theologically the early Church never resolved the problem
of evil. In fact, there is no Christian dogmatic position with regard

to evil. We don't find any statements about the problem in the Creed, and beyond the baptismal admonition that the Christian should put aside the ways of the devil, no dogmatic statement of faith is required from the Christian. The closest we come to an official Christian position with regard to evil is the so-called *Doctrine of the Privatio Boni*. The seeds of this doctrine can be found as far back as Aristotle. In the Church it was first expressed by Origen. St. Augustine developed it more completely to help him in his theological struggles with the Manichaeans. Since Augustine it was espoused by various theologians up to Thomas Aquinas.

The Doctrine of the Privatio Boni says that God created the world good and perfect, but when the world fell away from its original perfection evil arose. The basic notion here is that evil has no essential substance. Only the good exists on its own power; evil exists only insofar as there is a departure from the good. Criticisms notwithstanding, it should be noted that the Doctrine of the Privatio Boni does not deny the existence of evil. It merely tries to show how it came into being, and note what kind of existence it has.

We can roughly compare the existence evil has, according to this view, with the existence of a disease. Let's say that a person is ill with an infectious disease such as cholera. Cholera exists as a disease as long as there is a more or less healthy organism for it to infect. But when a person dies from cholera then the disease no longer exists. The cholera bacillus continues to exist, but it's not a disease until it spreads in a living host.

This is rougly the way it is with evil, according to the Doctrine of the Privatio Boni. Evil exists as long as there is something more or less whole that it can destroy, but it cannot exist on its own. In philosophical terms, evil derives its substance from something else, and has no substance of its own. This is why the philosophy of the ancient Chinese book of wisdom, the *I Ching,* says,

Evil is not destructive to the good alone but inevitably destroys itself as well. For evil, which lives solely by negation, cannot continue to exist on its own strength alone.

And elsewhere:

> ... for evil must itself fall at the very moment when it has
> wholly overcome the good, and thus consumed the energy to
> which it owed its duration.*

St. Augustine, in defending the Doctrine of the Privatio
Boni, says much the same thing:

> Evil ... can have no existence anywhere except in some good
> thing. ... So there can be things which are good without any
> evil in them, such as God himself, and the higher celestial
> beings, but there can be no evil things without good. For if
> evils cause no damage to anything, they are not evils; if they
> do damage something, they diminish its goodness; and if they
> damage it still more, it is because it still has some goodness
> which they diminish; and if they swallow it up altogether,
> nothing of its nature is left to be damaged. And so there will
> be no evil by which it can be damaged, since there is then no
> nature left whose goodness any damage can diminish.**

Now let's see what Jung had to say. We have already seen
that Jung inferred from his psychological studies that there is a
regulating center within each person that he called the Self and
which represents that individual's totality. But what is the nature
of this Self? Jung answered this question by saying that the Self is
a paradoxical unity of all the otherwise opposing and conflicting
tendencies within a person. Thus the Self unites masculine and
feminine qualities, the conscious and unconscious dimensions to
personality, dark and light, above and below, the spiritual and the
sensual, and good and evil into one whole being. His favorite
expression for the Self was that it was a "complexio oppositorum," and his last major scientific work he called *Mysterium
Coniunctionis* because it concerns the mysterious and wonderful
union of disparate parts of the personality in the unity of the Self.

Jung was critical of Christianity because his perception of the

---

*The *I Ching,* tr. Richard Wilhelm, New York: Pantheon Books, 1955, pp. 103 and
153.

**St. Augustine, *Contra adversarium legis et prophetarum* I 4f.

Self differed from the Christian image of God. He particularly disliked the Doctrine of the Privatio Boni because he believed (misguidedly, I think) that it denied the reality of evil, and he was critical of the image of Christ that the Church presented because he believed Christ lacked the dark, shadow side and therefore cannot represent human totality. He writes:

> The Self is a union of opposites *par excellence,* and this is where it differs essentially from the Christ-symbol. The androgyny of Christ is the utmost concession the Church has made to the problem of opposites. The opposition between light and good on the one hand and darkness and evil on the other is left in a state of open conflict, since Christ simply represents good, and his counterpart the devil, evil.

And elsewhere he says:

> For in the Self good and evil are indeed closer than identical twins.*

Unfortunately, Jung doesn't tell us what he means by evil. For instance, in the Bible, God has a dark and wrathful side that can be destructive, but it only destroys what is not fit to exist. God's dark side is not identical with a power of evil that is bent on sheer destruction of what is good for no ultimate purpose. If Jung means by evil the dark side of God in the biblical sense, then Jung's statement that the Self contains good and evil doesn't depart from the biblical position. But if Jung means that the evil in the Self is that which is inherently destructive, a power that destroys that which is good and fine, then the matter is different. It is hard to see how such an evil could ever be included in a totality when it represents a power that can only destroy, unless, of course, the evil, in the process of its integration into the totality of the Self, is itself transformed. But evil transformed or redeemed is no longer evil. Furthermore, if evil is included in a paradoxical whole, being transformed into the process as it takes its proper place in the total scheme of things, it is hard to see why

---

*C. G. Jung, *Psychology and Alchemy,* CW 12. Princeton, N.J.: Princeton University Press, 1953, 1968, pp. 19, 21.

this whole is not in itself a great good—the Summum Bonum of the theologians.

On the other hand, if evil is not transformed or redeemed in the process of integration, but remains inherently demonic and destructive, the notion that evil is a part of the Self is hard to digest. Not only does it seem like a logical impossibility, but it appears to be offensive to our human feelings and moral values. For if the Self is evil, what hope can there be? And if the Self is evil, what possibility is there that human nature can ever be anything but evil, or at least half evil, as it vacillates between goodness and evil?

When Jung discusses evil he uses an ambiguous language. For instance, he seems to casually identify light with good and dark with evil. Jung is fond of saying that light and dark combine in the Self into a remarkable totality. Who would want to quarrel with him? Doesn't night go with day, and wouldn't it be unbearable if the world was always light, and the sun always high overhead? If this were so how we would yearn for the shelter of darkness to alternate with the brightness of the light of day. And in human personality too, we value the dark qualities as well as the light, for this lends variety, depth, and flexibility to personality. But why identify light with the good and darkness with evil? Both light and dark are good; neither is evil. By letting the notion of evil tag along with the notion of darkness a person can find himself saying, "Oh yes, of course that's the way it must be," without really thinking about the matter. Darkness? Yes. But evil? That's another matter.

To make the matter more complicated, Jung at times seems to reverse his position with regard to evil. For instance, in his autobiographical *Memories, Dreams, Reflections,* in a chapter entitled "Late Thoughts"—so we can assume that what he says here expresses his mature reflections—Jung seems to forget what he said about the Self's being good and evil, and to disregard what he said in *Answer to Job* about man's moral superiority to God, and to espouse a thoroughly Christian attitude. In the chapter "Late Thoughts," Jung finds himself faltering before the task of finding the words with which to express "the incalculable paradoxes of love." He concludes that "God is love" and that this is what his idea of the Self as a *complexio oppositorum* means.* He says nothing about this remarkable and wonderful Love being combined with Hate, or requiring Hate as its opposite in order to exist. Clearly this Love of God transcends all the opposites and is their principle of unity in a most marvelous way. He even winds up quoting St. Paul from 1 Corinthians 13 and saying that there is nothing more to be added to these words. One could hardly hope for a more Christian position in the matter, for clearly this Love of God that Jung perceives is a "Summum Bonum" in the highest sense of the word.

For the most part, however, Jung argued that the Self combines good and evil equally, and nothing is said about a higher Love under which both are subsumed. For the rest of our discussion we will assume that the inclusion of evil in the Self represents Jung's more official position in the matter.

Kunkel, unlike Jung, never to my knowledge used the terms good and evil to describe the Self. Nor was he fascinated, as Jung was, by the idea of the Self as a *complexio oppositorum,* though he certainly would not have been opposed to the idea. Kunkel emphasized the creativity of the Self. For him the Self is a creative power, constantly available to us, that expresses itself in new forms of life, and propels mankind on to higher spiritual evolution and psychological development. To be sure, when the energies of the Self are thwarted or dammed up they turn destructive, but, like the dark side of God in the Bible, they are only destructive of what stands in their way, and therefore isn't fit to exist.

The Self for Kunkel is an intrinsically positive energy. Although Kunkel never says so explicitly, for him the Self can't contain evil because evil is, by definition, only destructive while the Self is creative. If he doesn't call the Self "good" it's because the Self is beyond goodness as we human beings reckon it.

It would seem that Jung and Kunkel disagree on the nature of the Self with respect to the relationship of the Self to evil. Kunkel's view is the more optimistic one as far as human nature is

---

*C. G. Jung, *Memories, Dreams, Reflections.* New York: Pantheon Books, Random House, 1961, p. 353.

concerned since he sees the Self, which is at the core of human nature, as such a positive force.

But if moral evil doesn't come from the Self, then where does it come from? Kunkel's answer is that moral evil comes into existence when the Ego deviates from the Self. This deviation occurs because of the egocentricity of the Ego. If the Ego lived a life that perfectly expressed the Self, a creative life would be the result, and there would be no room in it for evil. Kunkel wouldn't say that it was a "good" life because that would confuse such a life with a purely human idea of what a good person was like. For Kunkel, to be creative was higher and more godlike than to be "good."

Once again the I Ching is instructive. Hexagram 25 is called Wu Wang—Innocence. The image is of Heaven, the Creative, above, and Thunder, the Arousing, below. Out of this comes the hexagram "Innocence," and the Judgment which reads:

> Innocence. Supreme success.
> Perseverance furthers.
> If someone is not as he should be,
> He has misfortune,
> And it does not further him
> To undertake anything.

In his commentary, Richard Wilhelm says of this hexagram: "Man has received from heaven a nature innately good, to guide him in all his movements. By devotion to this divine spirit within himself, he attains an unsullied innocence that leads him to do right with instinctive sureness and without any ulterior thought of reward and personal advantage."

Kunkel would say that his "innately good" nature comes from the Self. He would also say that one can act without any ulterior thought of reward when one is free of egocentricity; then right action can proceed virtually instinctively from the Self.

Elsewhere in the commentary Wilhelm says, "When ... movement follows the law of heaven, man is innocent and without guile. His mind is natural and true, unshadowed by reflection or ulterior designs. For wherever conscious purpose is to be seen, there the truth and innocence of nature have been lost."

Again we can compare this with Kunkel. The "law of heaven" springs from the Self, which Kunkel has compared to the creativity of God within us. When "conscious purpose," that is, an egocentric attitude, intrudes, then the truth and innocence that proceed from the Self are lost, but when we are free of egocentric desires, our basically true and innocent nature manifests itself. It would seem that the *I Ching* is closer to Kunkel's understanding of the Self than Jung's.

Kunkel's position also appears to be closer to the Christian position than Jung's. It can even be argued that Kunkel's position is a psychological version of the Doctrine of the Privatio Boni. In the theological doctrine, as we have seen, evil comes into existence when the creation falls away from God. In Kunkel's view, it comes into existence when the Ego departs from the Self. The similarity of the two positions is apparent. So from the Christian point of view Kunkel's position is quite satisfactory, but it doesn't answer all of the questions.

First we must remember that as far as psychology is concerned, the matter can't be decided by theology, nor by our personal preference, but only by the facts. So we are confronted with the factual question: Is the Self, the core of human personality, inherently evil and destructive? Or is the Self inherently creative and purposeful? Jung seems to have adopted the first position, but uses confusing language. Kunkel has adopted the latter position, but he doesn't furnish us with the kind of empirical data that would be necessary to settle the matter.

Probably it will always be impossible to produce such empirical data. The existence of the Self is asserted for two reasons. First, it is a mental construct, a hypothesis, invoked as the best possible explanation for a variety of psychological facts and experiences (such as evidence that there is a centering function in the human psyche, and symbols from the unconscious such as the mandala). Second, it results from dynamic, personal experiences that certain people have had at certain times. In neither case are we likely to find the kind of psychological data that would enable us to settle the matter definitively since none of us can claim to have experienced the Self in all of its entirety, or, if we have, we cannot find words with which to convince others.

Two things should be noted, however. First, Kunkel's idea that egocentricity produces evil behavior is sufficient to account for a wide range of moral evil. Manifestations of evil, such as the death camps in Nazi Germany and all the way to the most hideous crimes in our day, can be explained on this basis. It is no small matter to be egocentric. In theological language, to be egocentric is to go against the Will of God, and what could be a worse evil than that? To the extent that we are egocentric, everything about us is wrong and goes wrong, and we can only perpetuate evil.

One suspects that both Jung and Kunkel arrived at their conclusions about the relationship of evil to the Self via their personal experiences. Jung, for instance, in *Answer to Job,* argued for man's moral superiority to God. He also tells us in the introduction, and in his Letters, that *Answer to Job* was written as the result of a personal crisis. However, he doesn't tell us what that personal experience was, and the emotional tenor of *Answer to Job* tends to obscure the scientific issues and to create more heat than light.

While Kunkel never says so, one gets the impression that he must also have arrived at his conclusions about the nature of the Self from his personal experiences. Like Jung, he doesn't tell us what they were. Perhaps the experience on the battlefield that was told in the introduction to this book, in which he felt an immense sense of the love of God flowing over the tragic battlefield, was one of a number of experiences that led him to believe that at the core of things was a Power that was creative and indestructible. All of this is impressive, but it doesn't make for an exact science. Perhaps everyone will have to decide about evil for himself on the basis of his own experiences with that underlying reality that both Jung and Kunkel called the Self.

Second, there remains the question of how egocentricity originates. Kunkel says that the egocentricity of the parents and other significant adults disrupts the Original-We of the child and precipitates the child into his own egocentric pattern. Thus egocentricity creates more egocentricity. As the Bible puts it,

> The fathers have eaten unripe grapes;
> the children's teeth are set on edge (Jer 31:20; Ez 18:2).

According to Kunkel, the process is apparently inevitable and unavoidable. It *must* happen that people will be egocentric in their dealings with children and so produce egocentric tendencies in a child whose natural disposition is to be in harmony with other people. Only theoretically can we imagine that a child might grow up under such favorable circumstances that he has not been forced into egocentricity and is therefore naturally and perfectly free of egocentricity.

We can't help but wonder if this is all there is to the matter. The Self, as we have seen, is the foundation for the life of the Ego; the Ego, in fact, is created by the Self to represent it in life. In view of the fact that egocentricity is so universal and unavoidable, it is possible that the Self *intends* it that way. Perhaps the Ego *must* first become egocentric if certain higher developments are to take place. If this is so, then we are left with the paradoxical position that the Self, which is by nature creative and urges the Ego to follow its will, also intends that the Ego shall deviate from it at a certain point in life.

This paradoxical position resembles certain early Christian theologians, such as Irenaeus, who believed that God intended humanity's fall in the Garden of Eden, and who regarded the original sin as a "felix culpa"—a happy sin—because without it the redemption through Christ would not have been possible. On a psychological level this would be a way of saying that an Ego that has passed through egocentricity into a state of reunion with the Self is more developed and creative than an Ego that never left the Self in the first place.

However this may be, it seems clear that our attitude toward the origin of psychological evil will depend on our understanding of the relationship of Ego and Self. We will return to this point one more time at the end of the following chapter, after our exploration of the role of the Ego in individuation according to Jung and Kunkel has been made more explicit.

IV
Kunkel, Jung, and the Ego in Individuation

Both Kunkel and Jung agree that the individuation process requires that the Ego become the medium through which the Self is lived and in which the Self reaches consciousness. Kunkel, as we have seen, points out the egocentric nature of the Ego that must be overcome if individuation is to take place. In Jungian psychology, however, the word "egocentricity" rarely occurs. This is because the concept of egocentricity does not exist in Jungian psychology in any explicit form. Our task now is to see how Jung does describe the Ego in its relationship to the individuation process, and then contrast Jung's description with Kunkel's.

There are at least three ways in which Jung and his colleagues describe the Ego in its relationship to individuation. In the first way, the Ego is said to be one-sided; it is said to have an unbalanced development that must be corrected if a person is to become whole. This lack of balance is not due to any egocentric qualities in the Ego, but to certain inevitable circumstances. Even though its lack of balance must be corrected by the Self, the Ego is represented as a more or less innocent victim of the inevitable circumstances that surround its developmental process.

Second, the Ego is said to have a value system against which the Self rebels. The Ego is here portrayed as the unwitting victim of its own misguided idealism, good intentions, or ignorance.

Third, certain moral or character deficiencies are said to exist in the Ego, and these obstruct the process of individuation. Kunkel would identify these deficiences as the result of egocentricity. Jung doesn't do so because he seems to lack the concept. Because Jung doesn't clearly identify egocentricity, Jung's descriptions of these Ego deficiences lack the force and clarity of Kunkel's descriptions.

Following are some examples of these three ways of describing the relationship of the Ego to the individuation process. They will be taken from the writings of Jung, Marie-Louise von Franz, and others. The chapter will conclude with a brief additional point about the problem of evil which we can see more clearly in the light of the chapter.

I

In Jung's *The Visions Seminars,* he says:

Inasmuch as it is not distorted by consciousness, the primitive has a nature-like *naiveté.* But as soon as there is consciousness, the conscious chooses, it is the beginning of differentiation, and differentiation is one-sidedness necessarily. But when such a one-sidedness of development reaches a certain culmination, then comes a break, then comes a sort of collapse, what you call in America a break-down.*

Kunkel spoke of the Ego-crisis. Although Jung doesn't use this expression he seems to be referring to the same thing when he refers to "a sort of collapse" and "what you call in America a break-down." However, Jung says this Ego collapse is due to a one-sided Ego development; no mention is made of egocentricity. Kunkel would not for a moment deny that the Ego is one-sided, but would point out that this one-sidedness is in the service of the Ego's egocentricity. Egocentricity, for Kunkel, is the fundamental disorder, and one-sidedness is secondary to it, while Jung speaks of one-sidedness as something that just happens to the Ego.

Part of the reason Jung emphasizes one-sidedness is his theory of the four functions of the psyche: thinking, feeling, sensation, and intuition. Jung says that a person will develop one of

*C.G. Jung, *The Visions Seminars.* Zurich, Switzerland: Spring Publications, 1976, Book One, p. 16.

these four functions, and will partially or totally neglect the development of the other functions. Whichever function is most natural to him will be the function that is most developed. The result is an unbalanced Ego development.

Kunkel doesn't mention Jung's theory of types, although he certainly would have had no quarrel with it. If he had considered it, he would no doubt have pointed out that the Ego's development of one function at the expense of the other functions is partially dictated by the Ego's desire to protect itself and further its ambitions, that is, by its egocentricity.

Jung seems to recognize this tacitly when he says elsewhere in *The Visions Seminars:*

> When the plant grows up it is wise enough to develop leaves on each side, but we are in the unhappy position that if we develop one side, we do not develop the others; we cannot develop everything at the same time. This differentiation of a function is one of the miracles of culture, of consciousness. Consciousness says, this is very useful, now use your clever mind and you will have power.*

The desire for power is an egocentric desire. The more power the Ego feels it has the more secure it feels, and the more it can realize its ambitions. Jung has the Ego say, "this is very useful, now use your clever mind and you will have power." In Kunkel's language this means that the egocentric goals of the Ego distort the superior function to its own purpose, deny those functions that are less developed, and so make the Ego feel inadequate and powerless.

Later Jung writes of a woman patient whom he earlier described in *The Visions Seminars* as one-sided:

> Her inherited Christian attitude is responsible for the standstill in which this woman found herself, when her development came to an end. She simply could not solve her problems with the typical Protestant point of view. In natural conditions there would be no standstill and life would simply flow on,

---

Ibid.

and only if consciousness interfered by imposing a certain attitude would life be stopped. So naturally it is our most developed attitude that accounts for our breakdowns.*

Notice how innocent the Ego is made to appear. Because this woman inherits a certain Christian attitude and has a certain superior function she is fated to a breakdown. No mention is made of her egocentricity. Instead "it is our most developed attitude that accounts for our breakdowns." This quotation shows that the concept of egocentricity seems to be lacking in Jung. Even when he speaks of it implicitly he doesn't seem to have a conscious grasp of its meaning.

Kunkel wouldn't deny that there is such a thing as an inherited Christian attitude, but would argue that this attitude has been incorporated into the woman's egocentric pattern and that is why it is uncreative, rigid, and incapable of change.

II

Let's go on and discuss Jung's idea that the Ego has a certain value system that obstructs the individuation process.

In his introduction to *The Secret of the Golden Flower* Jung discusses the fact that even though conscious willing may have a high moral value it may still lead to a personality breakdown. He writes:

> . . . It is a fact that consciousness heightened by a necessary one-sidedness gets so far out of touch with the archetypes that a breakdown follows. Long before the actual catastrophe, the signs of error announce themselves as absence of instinct, nervousness, disorientation, and entanglement in impossible situations and problems. When the physician comes to investigate, he finds an unconscious which is in complete rebellion against the values of the conscious, and which therefore cannot possibly be assimilated to the conscious, while the reverse, of course, is altogether out of the question.**

Ibid. pp. 23–24.
**The Secret of the Golden Flower,* tr. Richard Wilhelm, N.Y., N.Y., Harcourt, Brace 1931, p. 89.

Notice the similarities between Jung and Kunkel in this quotation. Jung's list of symptoms reminds us of Kunkel's analysis of depression, anxiety, and lonelinesss as the consequences of egocentric separation from the Self. Notice also that Jung refers to a breakdown, and a catastrophe happening to the Ego; this is analogous to Kunkel's idea of the Ego-crisis. However, notice how innocent the Ego is made to sound in the above quotation. Poor Ego is the victim of its own high value system! To be sure, its value system is out of balance and must be corrected by the unconscious, but one gets the feeling that the Ego is only guilty of a kind of noble error.

The same attitude can be felt in Edward C. Whitmont's definition of the Shadow, which we will discuss more completely in the next chapter. Whitmont writes:

> The term *shadow* refers to that part of the personality which
> has been repressed for the sake of the ego ideal.*

An "ego ideal" sounds noble. It may be misguided, but who can be blamed too much for having ideals? But Kunkel would say that there is nothing noble about the Ego as long as it is egocentric. As for the Ego's ideals, Kunkel would emphasize that as long as we are egocentric our real goals are self-serving, and the ideals we may purport to have are a sham, a cloak under which our egocentricity can remain hidden.

III

In certain places, however, Jung and others do identify certain negative traits in the Ego, and when they do they appear to be closer to Kunkel's point of view. For example, the ego may be referred to as narrow-minded, or lazy, and especially, as prone to becoming identified with an archetype and therefore becoming inflated about itself. The Ego may also be described as too weak to stand up to the pressures of an experience with the Self. However, they are not explicit about the origin of these negative,

---

*Edward C. Whitmont, *The Symbolic Quest*. Princeton, N.J., Princeton University Press, 1969, 1978, p. 160.

undesirable Ego traits, and this leads to a certain amount of obscurity. Consider the following quotation from Marie-Louise von Franz:

> Very often the reason for schizophrenia is not so much the invasion of the unconscious, but that it happens to someone who is too narrow for the experience, either mentally or emotionally. People who are not broad-minded and have not enough generosity and heart to open to what comes are exploded by the invasion.*

When a person is weak, narrow-minded, lazy, or inflated, Kunkel would say that this is because of the Ego's egocentric condition. When people are too narrow, and lack generosity and heart to be open to what comes from within, it would again be an egocentric state. In no way would these traits come from the Self. We can see that in the writing of Jung and others negative Ego traits are sometimes identified as obstacles to the Self, but the conclusion is not drawn that the individuation process is being thwarted by egocentricity.

Next consider this statement from Marie-Louise von Franz:

> Clearly there are two possibilities of consciousness, namely a rigid one and one which has a *paradoxical attitude* and therefore does justice to the paradoxical factor of the unconscious. The latter would be what you could call a consciously open system, an open *Weltanschauung* which is always ready to accept its opposite, or meet the opposite and accept its contradictions. If you have a conscious attitude which is ready to accept the opposite, to accept the conflict and the contradiction, then you can connect with the unconscious. This is what we try to achieve. We try to bring about a conscious attitude with which the person can keep the door to the unconscious open, which means that one must never be too sure of oneself, never be sure that what one says is the only possibility, never be too sure about a decision.**

---

*Marie-Louise von Franz, *Alchemy.* Toronto, Canada: Inner City Books, 1980, p. 217.
**Ibid.*, pp. 144–145 (italics hers).

In this passage, von Franz notes that there are two possible conscious attitudes; one is rigid and prevents the integration of unconscious material, and the other is open to the unconscious. We have seen that Kunkel identifies rigidity as the result of egocentricity. Since von Franz sees rigidity as one of the two possible attitudes of consciousness, it is evident that she is describing egocentricity without, however, naming it as such. It may seem irrelevant whether it is named or not, except that failure to identify egocentricity as a fundamental problem leaves the impression that the negative ego traits just happen, and lends a certain air of innocence to the Ego. This von Franz does when she speaks of conscious attitudes that must be adopted, as though it were all a matter of attitude and education.

In another place, however, von Franz sounds more like Kunkel:

> The ego is identical with the Self to the extent that it is the instrument of self-realization for the Self. Only an egotistical inflated ego is in opposition to the Self.*

Here von Franz notes that an egotistical (read "egocentric") Ego must be in opposition to the Self. What she fails to note, however, is that we all have an egotistical Ego that is necessarily in opposition to the Self—until such a time as life's crises and sufferings have changed us. The extent to which the egocentric nature of the Ego is missed is shown on the very next page:

> A tendency to deviate and to become one-sided is inborn in consciousness, it is linked with its need for clarity and preciseness.**

Clearly, von Franz, like Jung, says that the Ego's problem is due to its tendency to become one-sided, and that this is because the Ego strives for clarity and precision. Kunkel would agree that the Ego tends to become one-sided but would argue that this becomes a real problem when the Ego becomes egocentric. So the

---

*Ibid., p. 155.
**Ibid., p. 156.

notion of egocentricity seems to be missing in Jung. Here is
another example from von Franz:

> Jung said that to be in a situation where there is no way out or
> to be in a conflict where there is no solution is the classical
> beginning to the process of individuation. It is *meant* to be a
> situation without solution: the unconscious wants the hopeless
> conflict in order to put egoconsciousness up against the wall,
> so that the man has to realize that whatever he does is wrong,
> whichever way he decides will be wrong. This is meant to
> knock out the superiority of the ego. . . . In religious language
> you could say that the situation without issue is meant to force
> the man to rely on an act of God. In psychological language
> the situation without issue, which the anima arranges with
> great skill in a man's life, is meant to drive him into a
> condition in which he is capable of experiencing the Self.*

Jung speaks of a situation in which there is no solution.
Kunkel puts it more strongly when he speaks of the Ego-crisis.
Von Franz says the intention of the Self is to knock the superiority
out of the Ego. Kunkel says the Self precipitates an Ego-crisis in
order to get the Ego out of its egocentricity. Von Franz speaks of
the anima who arranges a situation with great skill that is meant to
drive a person into a situation in which he must experience the
Self. Kunkel would say that such a situation must destroy the
egocentric posture or it will not be effective. The language of von
Franz and Kunkel is not far apart, but Kunkel's language is
stronger because he sees the egocentricity of the Ego as something demonic, while von Franz regards it as an error. Jung and
von Franz are more like Gnostics, who saw the great human
failing in terms of error and ignorance. Kunkel stands more in the
biblical tradition because he sees the great human failing in terms
of egocentricity, which is the psychological equivalent of sin.

IV

Our final example is taken from *Jungian Analysis,* which is a
collection of essays written by contemporary Jungian analysts.

---

*Marie-Louis von Franz, *The Interpretation of Fairy Tales.* New York: Spring Publications, 1970, VI-4.

The purpose of the book is to give a comprehensive and up-to-date presentation of the process of Jungian analysis, so we can consider the following point of view presented by Murray Stein in an article entitled "The Aim and Goal of Jungian Analysis" as representative of a current Jungian viewpoint.

Stein gives us a general statement of the goal of Jungian analysis. He writes:

> Jungian analysis takes place within a dialectical relationship between two persons, analyst and analysand, and has for its goal the analysand's coming to terms with the unconscious: the analysand is meant to gain insight into the specific unconscious structures and dynamics that emerge during analysis, and the structures underlying ego-consciousness are meant to change in their dynamic relation to other, more unconscious structures and dynamics.*

The part of this statement that concerns us is the part that refers to the Ego: ". . . and the structures underlying ego-consciousness are meant to change in their dynamic relation to other, more unconscious structures and dynamics."

Murray Stein says that he is now speaking of "deep changes" that take place in analysis, changes that take place in the Ego as it undergoes the analytical process. The aim, Stein says, quoting Jung, "is to bring about a psychic state in which (the) patient begins to experiment with his own nature—a state of fluidity, change, and growth where nothing is eternally fixed and hopelessly petrified.** So far it sounds as though it could be a description of the change that takes place in the Ego when its rigid egocentricity is destroyed, and the creative life from the Self begins to emerge.

But the picture changes somewhat when Stein describes the Ego more completely. He writes:

> The ego ("I") exists in a field of associated psychological contents, such as memories and familiar thoughts, feelings,

---

*Jungian Analysis, ed. Murray Stein. La Salle, Ill.: Open Court Publishing Company, 1982, p. 29.
**Ibid., p. 39.

and fantasies (earlier "I's"); together they make up ego-consciousness. This ego-consciousness is a structured psychological entity—a "character structure" made up of habitual
tendencies of thought, impulse management, and so on. . . .
Ego-consciousness, in turn, is in the orbit of the central organizing agency of the personality, the Self. The dominant pattern of organization shown by ego-consciousness is made up of
both innate, instinctual/archetypal trends, which are parts of
the Self, and social/cultural influences and introjects; this
pattern is the result of the foregoing developmental history. . . . The core of the dominant pattern underlying ego-
consciousness is made up of a selected number of the many
potentialities for psychological development within the Self,
and therefore it exhibits the property of "one-sidedness" relative to the psyche as a whole.*

Notice that in this otherwise splended description of the
origin of egoconsciouness there is no mention of egocentricity.
Stein now goes on to a clear statement of what happens to the Ego
in the analytic process:

In the analytic process, the ego's attachment to an earlier,
underlying dominant pattern of organization is dissolved as it
is brought into an intensely conscious relationship with other,
more unconscious parts of the Self. This experience is emotionally painful and the ego usually resists it. A person's ego
prefers to maintain its familiar psychological identifications
and arrangements of inner objects, even after these have been
recognized as outmoded, one-sided, and Self-defeating patterns. This is resistance to individuation, and in analysis, as
our statement of the goal implies, one faces such resistance
and seeks to diminish its inhibiting effects. The ego resists
transformation for a reason: it is threatened with the erasure
of a former construction of identity. This process is perceived
as the threat of regression to earlier, more helpless, psychological states, and ultimately to extinction of a conscious standpoint.**

---

*Ibid., pp. 39–40.
**Ibid., pp. 40–41.

Here Stein comes within an inch of saying what Kunkel is saying. When he speaks of the Ego's "former construction of identity," of its perception of the analytic process as a "threat," of its fear of "extinction," and of the Ego's "resistance" to change, we are certainly reminded of Kunkel's analysis of the egocentricity of the Ego and its consequent resistance to the Self. But the fact is that egocentricity is *not* identified as the central problem of the Ego, and because it isn't the arrow it doesn't quite hit the center of the target. This is where Kunkel's analysis of the Ego could dot the "i's" and cross the "t's" of Jungian thought, and make for a more complete picture of the Ego than is now available in Jungian writing.

V

Now we are in a position to look once more at the problem of evil. The question introduced before was whether moral or psychological evil comes from the Ego or the Self. Kunkel, we noted, saw evil as a psychological condition that arises when the ego is egocentric and so deviates from the Self. Jung, on the other hand, seemed to imply that the Self was partly evil and thus the origin of psychological evil, although, as we noted, it wasn't clear whether the Self was *really* evil (that is, inherently destructive) or only had a "dark side" that the Ego encountered when it deviated too far from the Center.

I would like to suggest that some of the murkiness of Jungian thinking about the origin of evil comes because Jungian psychology is murky about the psychology of the Ego. Because it does not see egocentricity clearly, there is a temptation to see the Ego as the unwitting, even innocent victim of a dark and rapacious Self. Since the evil side of the Ego is not clearly demarcated, evil is imputed to the Self when it really belongs to the Ego in its egocentric condition. That the Self isn't really regarded as intrinsically evil is suggested in the following description that von Franz gives us of the philosopher's stone, the alchemical goal that is, according to Jung, the optimum symbol of the Self. She writes of the qualities of the stone:

> The qualities are not only ethical but include all sorts of suppositions as to what a human being should have: health,

humility, holiness (from a description that apparently means, "wholeness" or purity), chastity, virtue (effectiveness or effi- ciency), victoriousness (to be able to overcome, a faith which has the capacity to trust, or to understand spiritual qualities which cannot be seen), faith, hope . . . charity, compassion, goodness (a kind of benevolence), patience (which is very important), temperateness (a balance between the opposites), discipline or insight, and obedience.*

This list of the qualities that alchemy ascribes to the philoso- pher's stone is like the qualities that Kunkel says belong to the Real Self. There is no mention made of anything evil in von Franz's description. To the contrary, the philosopher's stone, that is, the Self, is described by her as the source of positive, healing, and creative life-energy.

Conclusion

I have gone into the subject of the relationship of the Ego to the individuation process in Jung and Kunkel in some detail because I believe it to be of importance to Jungian psychology. As mentioned, Kunkel's psychology in no way replaces Jung's, but it does fill in a lacuna. That lacuna is the failure of Jungian psycholo- gy to study in sufficient detail the Ego and the way its egocentric formations defeat individuation. As I hope I have shown, in many places Jung and others imply that there is an egocentricity to the Ego that gets in the way, but they failed to make this clear. Because they failed to see clearly the egocentric nature of the Ego, there is a tendency in Jungian psychology to see the Ego in too innocent a light. This results in a projection of the evil side of the Ego into the Self, and perhaps from this comes Jung's state- ments that the Self is partly evil. Jung persisted in this kind of statement even though he himself sometimes contradicted it, and even though the various texts he used for the symbolism of the Self clearly stated otherwise. I think he did this because evil must be located somewhere. If you don't see that it resides in the egocentric deviation of the Ego, you are bound to project it into the Self instead.

---

*von Franz, *Alchemy,* pp. 264–265.

V
Kunkel's Psychology and Other Jungian Concepts

We have already briefly compared the concepts of the Self held by Jung and Kunkel. Now we will examine in more detail their diverging viewpoints on the Self, and also relate Kunkel's psychology to other Jungian concepts such as the persona, the anima, the psychological types, and, especially, the Shadow.

We have seen that Kunkel differed from Jung because Kunkel saw the Self in a positive light, while Jung sometimes says that the Self contains good and evil equally. In addition to this difference, there is a difference of opinion about how the Self originates.

Jung describes the Self as a reality that must be slowly and painstakingly built up through the process of individuation. Jung's favorite model of the Self, as we noted, is the alchemical image of the philosopher's stone, and the philosopher's stone is the end product of the laborious art of the alchemist. For Kunkel, however, the Self exists as a complete entity in the individual from the beginning. It is a reality that is always there, even though sometimes it seems to hide itself, and even though it can't always be experienced because of the egocentricity of the Ego. As we have seen, when the Self does manifest itself it gives to the Ego the capacity for a creative Ego response to difficult situations, and endows the Ego with the capacity for a creative life. For Kunkel, what needs to be built up is not the Self, since it is always there,

376

but a relationship to the Self, and this always entails the elimination of egocentricity.

Kunkel was aware of the differecences between his view and Jung's in this regard. He writes:

> The "Self" for us is a metaphysical reality which exists not only all through the individual life but also beyond space and time. Jung thinks of the Self as an entity which comes into existence only through the process of integration. We would say it awakes, or should awake; he would say it should be brought into existence through our personal development.*

Different representations of the Self are found in religion as well as in psychology. Consider, for instance, the contrast between the personified representation of the Self in Christianity, and the impersonal representation of the Self in Eastern religious thought. In Christianity the Self appears as Christ, who is the Son of Man incarnated in the personal human figure of Jesus of Nazareth. Even after the death and resurrection of Jesus, the Christ continues to be available for a personal relationship with individual human beings. In Eastern religious thought the Self is remote from human affairs and there is nothing like a personal relationship. Contact with the timeless Absolute can only be reached as a person denies the desires that attach him to this world, and through yogic practices achieves immersion in God. Jung describes this difference in these words:

> . . . we must emphasize the difference between East and West in their treatment of the 'jewel,' that is, the central symbol. The West emphasizes the human incarnation, and even the personality and historicity of Christ, while the East says: 'Without beginning, without end, without past, without future.' In accordance with his conception, the Christian subordinates himself to the superior, divine person in expectation of His grace; but the Eastern man knows that redemption depends on the 'work' the individual does upon himself.**

---

*Kunkel, *In Search of Maturity,* p. 118 fn.
**Jung, *The Secret of the Golden Flower,* p. 133.

Jung's view seems closer to the Eastern one, Kunkel's to the Christian. For Jung, the Self is the product of hard inner work. Just as the Yogi works hard for Nirvana, and the alchemist labors to produce the philosopher's stone, so individuation is an *opus,* a psychological work requiring the greatest effort and diligence. For Kunkel, the Self may "awake" and come into expression at any time, but it has always been there. When it is active the Self acts like the grace of God, rescuing the Ego from its dilemma and endowing it with the power to live effectively.

It looks as though the two viewpoints are in conflict, and that we must choose one or the other, but perhaps the paradoxical reality of the Self can only be expressed by both viewpoints. Looked at in this way, the Self is personal and impersonal, something to be laboriously developed and something that can operate spontaneously at any time. According to this view, both Jung's and Kunkel's models are necessary in order to express the way the Self operates and is experienced.

The situation can be compared to the predicament of the physicist who tries to make a mental model of light that includes all of the phenomena. Light, the physicist assures us, is like a series of particles, because many light phenomena can only be explained if we think of light in this way. For instance, it is known that a beam of light bends in a gravitational field, and this requires us to think of light as a beam of particles emanating from a light source. On the other hand, the physicist says that light must be thought of as a wave, for other phenomena, such as refraction, can only be explained in this way. It seems that something can't be both particles and a wave, but this apparent contradiction doesn't keep the physicist from thinking of light first in one way and then in another way depending on which model best fits the phenomena that are under consideration.

So perhaps both Jung and Kunkel are right. We must remember that the Self is a reality that escapes our rational comprehension. As St. Paul would say, "now we see through a glass darkly." With our incomplete state of knowledge, and our difficulty in comprehending rationally a reality that is irrational and paradoxical, we may have to content ourselves with apparently conflicting descriptions. The important thing will then be to take into consideration both descriptions at the same time, and not feel compelled, for misplaced reasons of logic, to discard one in favor of the other.

One thing is certain, that even though the Self, as Kunkel says, is a reality that is always there, the capacity of the Self to be spontaneously expressed may be the result of hard psychological and spiritual work. When a person acts spontaneously, that person can either act erroneously from an egocentric position, or accurately and creatively from the Self. When the latter kind of spontaneous action takes place it may seem so spontaneous, and even effortless, that we forget it is only possible because of a great labor of personal development that the individual has undergone. As Coleridge put it, in a quotation my friend Al Kreinheder of Los Angeles called to my attention:

> It's always better to do the spontaneous thing, but you should have so developed yourself that the spontaneous act is the correct act.

The Persona

The word "persona" is a Latin word that originally meant the mask worn by an actor to depict the character he was assuming on the stage. Jung used the word persona in a specific psychological way. He writes:

> The persona . . . is the individual's system of adaptation to, or the manner he assumes in dealing with, the world. Every calling or profession, for example, has its own characteristic persona. . . . Only, the danger is that (people) become identical with their personas—the professor with his text-book, the tenor with his voice. . . . One could say, with a little exaggeration, that the persona is that which in reality one is not, but which oneself as well as others think one is.*

---

*C.G. Jung, *The Archetypes and the Collective Unconscious*, CW 9 i, pp. 122f, as quoted in the glossary of *Memories, Dreams, Reflections*.

When Jung says that the persona doesn't show others what a person is really like but only what a person thinks himself to be, and when he points out the danger of becoming identical with the persona, he is putting the persona in a negative light. The best one could say about the persona, looked at in this way, is that it is a kind of necessary evil. Jungian psychology in general has perpetuated this negative attitude toward the persona that began with Jung.

Thayer Greene, however, a Jungian analyst from New York, in an article entitled "Confessions of an Extravert" (*Quadrant*, Winter 1975), points out that the ancient actor didn't wear a mask to conceal his identity, but to project out into the audience in an effective way the true identity of the character he was portraying. Greene argues that the person is a positive asset to the personality, and properly employed becomes the psychic organ through which the Self is expressed in the world. He claims that the usual negative view toward the persona many Jungians have is due to their introverted prejudice against extraversion. He tries to correct this prejudice by showing the importance of the expression of the Self in extraverted (outer) life, and the usefulness of the persona in accomplishing this.

Kunkel's psychology suggests that while Jung is often correct in pointing out the negative qualities of the persona, nevertheless Greene is basically correct. Viewed in the light of Kunkel's psychology the persona is a front masking a person's true identity only when it is used egocentrically by the Ego. However, when the Ego functions properly, then the persona performs its intended purpose as the proper vehicle for the expression of the Self in human relationships and outer life.

For instance, a Star will use the persona for the egocentric purpose of winning admiration. The personality she expresses through the persona will not be her genuine personality but the personality she wants other people to believe is hers. Similarly, the Clinging Vine will adopt the kind of persona that will make him appear to others as a needy, deserving person worthy of help. In this way he uses the persona for an egocentric purpose. But when the Ego functions as the instrument of the Self, the persona becomes the means through which others can see our true reality. Jesus expresses this well when he says:

> In the same way your light must shine in the sight of men, so
> that, seeing your good works, they may give the praise to your
> Father in heaven (Mt 5:16).

The Anima

Jung has said that the anima is compensatory to the persona.
For instance, let us say that a man's persona is one of power in the
world. He is perhaps a successful and tyrannical businessman, a
Nero who strives to dominate the lives of others and control his
outer environment. The anima in such a case will compensate this
attitude by ruling the man from within. He may then be a prey to
compulsive sexual fantasies that dominate him as completely as he
dominates other people. Or perhaps he is the slave of obsessive
paranoid fantasies, or is plagued by phobias over which he has no
power but which have power over him.

The Roman emperor Caligula is an example. Caligula was so
ruthless that he is said to have told guests at his banquets that it
was in his power to kill them at any time. But Suetonius, the
ancient historian, says that "he hid under the bed when it thun-
dered, and fled in terror from the sight of Aetna's flames," and
that at night "He found it hard to sleep and would wander
through his enormous palace at night crying for the dawn."*

In the light of Kunkel's psychology, I would like to suggest a
slight alteration of Jung's theory that the anima compensates the
persona. We have seen that the persona can be misused by the
egocentric Ego. What the anima compensates, therefore, is not
the persona, but the egocentric stance of the Ego.

In the case of Caligula, the egocentric attitude is clearly that
of a Nero. He only feels secure when he is in control of others,
and his egocentric ambition is to dominate his situation completely. It is this attitude that the anima compensates by inspiring in
him phobias and dark fantasies. It is possible to see how the anima
might compensate everyone of the four egocentric types that
Kunkel describes. Let's see how this would look.

We have already spoken of the Nero type. Since the Nero
opts for power over the outer environment, the compensation the

---

*Will Durant, *Caesar and Christ*. New York: Simon and Schuster, 1944, p. 265.

anima brings about is to make the person helpless in the face of a frightening inner environment. Such a person would then be the prey of sexual compulsions, phobias, or dark fantasies in the manner we have described.

The Turtle tries to hide from life situations with which he feels he can't cope. The compensation would be for the anima to create difficulties that can't be avoided because the man carries them around inside of himself. This is in fact the case, for Turtles are the victims of inner moods that assail them with a sense of inferiority and incompetence. They may find a way to escape and hide from life, but they can't find a way to escape and hide from the anima and the accusations and depressions she brings upon them.

The Star, like the Nero, is a prey for uncontrollable fantasies—but of disgrace. An example can be found in the Legend of the Holy Grail, in the story of Parsifal and the Hideous Maiden that Robert Johnson explains so well in his book *He!* Parsifal is a Star; he is the most renowned of all the renowned knights. He is celebrating his exploits with the other "Star" knights one day at a great banquet that the knights have given to celebrate their prowess, when in walks the Hideous Maiden. She is a woman who is so horrible to look at that the mere sight of her throws every man into a depression. She proceeds to go from knight to knight reading a list of that man's sins and omissions, and when she comes to Parsifal the list is the longest of all. The celebration collapses, and each knight slinks out of the banquet. The Stars have not found an admirer in the anima figure of the Hideous Maiden! To the contrary, she ruthlessly criticizes them. This is the way the anima may compensate the Star, who seeks adulation from others, but falls victim to the doubting thoughts the anima brings upon him from within.

The compensation the anima brings about may be experienced outwardly or inwardly. So far our examples have been of inner ways the anima compensates, but in the case of the Clinging Vine the compensation may be felt in the outer situation. The Clinging Vine feels dependent on other people for security. The anima, however, behaves so badly that she drives people away. The Clinging Vine's anima becomes moody, demanding, and manipulative, and sooner or later makes the person unbearable to others until they desert him in disgust. In this way the anima brings about exactly the situation the Clinging Vine least desires.

If the anima compensates a man's egocentric Ego stance, then does the animus compensate a woman's egocentric Ego? Those of us who like nicely balanced ideas would like to think that this is so, but in fact I've not been able to find comparable examples. Neither did Jung, to the best of my knowledge, come up with examples of how the animus compensated a woman's persona. The fact is that a woman's psychology may be so different from a man's that such comparisons are not always possible.

The Psychological Functions

We have already commented on some aspects of the relationship between egocentricity and the four functions of the psyche when we noted that the egocentric Ego attaches itself to the main function, and denies the inferior functions, because the main function helps it to feel secure and fulfill its egocentric ambitions. This brings us to an interesting question: Is the "choice" of an egocentric type partly determined by the principal psychological function?

For instance, our contemporary American culture favors people who are extraverted and have thinking or sensation as their superior function because it is an extraverted sensation-thinking culture. Introversion is often looked down upon, and the need of the introvert for a certain amount of time alone is regarded in some circles as perverse. Feeling is especially devalued in our culture. While a thinking or sensation type may find his primary function financially rewarded, the feeling type is less likely to find financially rewarding employment that uses his principal feeling function. Under such conditions an introverted feeling type of person may find life more overwhelming than a person with a different function. This might tend to push that type of person into a Turtle or Clinging Vine posture. It's hard to be a Star when your primary function is not well adapted to the values of the culture, and difficult to be a Nero when your primary function tends to inculcate a feeling of inferiority. On the other hand, let us say a person has thinking or sensation as a main function. That person might find it considerably easier to achieve recognition or power, and this would tend to create the Nero or Star type of egocentricity.

This would account for the main egocentric orientation, but we must remember that there is seldom one single egocentric pattern; rather we are egocentric in one way in one situation, and in another way in a different situation. A person whose successful extraverted thinking function may have pushed him to become a Star or Nero in the outer world of achievement might turn up as a first-rate Turtle in the face of personal relationships that call for intimacy, since these situations require the feeling function. Similarly, the confident Nero or Star extravert may be a first-rate Turtle when it comes to dealing with the inner world, just as the introvert may turn Turtle when it comes to dealing with the outer world.

Of course it is not the main function that is to blame. Properly speaking, the main function is a means for expressing and experiencing the Self. The inferior functions are also means of expressing and experiencing the Self, but are less at the disposal of the Ego. The problem comes because the egocentric Ego is always seeking to further and protect itself. When this is the case, the main function is distorted into the service of egocentricity, and the inferior function, because of this same egocentric cowardice, is feared and avoided because it involves the Ego in situations in which it is less likely to succeed.

The Shadow

Kunkel's contribution to the idea of the Shadow is especially important; he helps us to revise our understanding of the Shadow from both a Jungian and a Christian perspective. Let's begin by considering again Whitmont's definition of the Shadow:

> The term *shadow* refers to that part of the personality which has been repressed for the sake of the ego ideal.

We have already noted that what is repressed is not repressed for the sake of any "ego ideal," but because the repressed parts of the personality would interfere with our egocentric posture if they were released and expressed. Kunkel himself suggests this when he writes:

> Our basic pattern of egocentricity is determined by our goal,
> the Ego-image, and its opposite: the thing that we are most
> afraid of, the Ego's Shadow, the "abyss," the unbearable
> situation. . . . The Ego-image is often quite conscious, while
> the Shadow remains unknown. . . . The question then is which
> Ego-pattern is the basic one: it is always the one that condi-
> tions the opposite image to be the Shadow.*

For example, a Clinging Vine's goal is to remain a dependent
person. In order to do this he must naturally repress his urges
toward independence. A little boy (or girl) has a certain amount
of natural inclination toward independence. He may walk to
school by himself, and becomes angry when mother insists on
escorting him across the street. These early urges toward independence will later be helpful in leading the boy into mature manhood, but they must be denied and pushed out of sight if he is to
be a "successful" Clinging Vine. The repressed urges toward
independence then become part of the dark secondary personality
that we call the Shadow.

The Star's goal is to be admired. You can only be admired if
you are an unusual person. In order to maintain her posture as a
Star a woman must accordingly repress and deny all of her
inferior and ordinary side. It is hard for Stars to admit that they
are also ordinary people, with the same human needs and urges
that other people have. Accordingly the Shadow of the Star is the
ordinary person.

The Nero must dominate other people. What must be repressed if he is to be successful in this is his urge and need to give
and receive affection. Accordingly, the Nero's Shadow embodies
his loving, tender, receptive side.

The Turtle feels compelled to hide from life's difficulties. In
order to do this she must deny her courageous side. Her instincts
for healthy self-assertion thus become part of her Shadow.

It is clear from this analysis of the situation that the Shadow
includes some positive aspects of the personality. The urge to
become independent, our capacity to be an ordinary person with
human qualities and failings, our need to give and receive affec-

---

*Kunkel, *In Search of Maturity*, p. 269.

tion, and our courage and resourcefulness are clearly desirable qualities. This explains why Jung once remarked that the Shadow is ninety percent pure gold, and why the integration of the Shadow is so valued in Jungian analysis and has such positive effects.

If the Shadow is such a positive figure, why is it that recognition of the Shadow is so resisted? Of course the answer is that we resist recognizing our Shadow because if we recognized it we would have to give up our egocentricity. Thus we deny the best part of ourself, in order to maintain the worst.

Furthermore, when we first look at the figure of the Shadow it looks frightening precisely because it has been repressed into the dark regions of the unconscious. Something that has lived in a cave all its life may not look so great when it is finally brought into the light. In our dreams, for instance, the courage we have repressed may appear at first as a desperate man thrashing about angrily. Or our urge toward independence may first be seen as a reckless motorcycle rider. Or our ordinary man or woman may appear as a person who is seemingly inferior.

Finally, there is the fact that the Shadow as well as the Ego is an incomplete figure. Even though the Shadow contains positive attributes, he or she remains a partial-personality. By itself, the Shadow can't represent the Self because of this incompleteness, and therefore the Shadow, like the Ego, must be redeemed from its present condition.

The Shadow doesn't always appear as such a bad figure, however. A man in therapy who had never achieved his proper place in life because he was so fearful (i.e., a Turtle) dreamed of encountering John Wayne. In the dream he was fearful of Wayne, drew his revolver on him, and considered shooting him. When asked what he thought about John Wayne, the dreamer replied that he thought he was a fine man and a heroic figure and he couldn't understand why he was so hostile to him in the dream. From Kunkel's perspective we can understand: John Wayne embodied exactly those courageous masculine energies in the dreamer that he feared because their integration would mean the destruction of his Turtle egocentricity.

Confrontation with the Shadow is feared because it leads to an identity crisis. Once we see our Shadow, we no longer know who we are. This identity crisis is often mirrored in our dreams, for instance, in the familiar motif of losing our purse or wallet. The Ego fears this loss of identity, but in fact what is lost is only our egocentric identity. In losing this, we may discover our true identity (that is, the identity of the Self). On the other hand, if we don't go through the Crisis that contact with the Shadow brings about, we may be destroyed. Looked at from this point of view it is clear why there is such resistance on the part of the egocentric Ego to the Shadow.

Now we are in a position to see that there are really two "Shadows." To put it a better way, the Ego has two dark sides, not one.

One of these dark sides is truly evil, and the other, while feared, is not. The Shadow, in the sense in which we have been discussing it, is one of these two. Its "evil," as we have seen, is a judgment made upon the Shadow by the egocentric Ego. Far from being intrinsically evil, the Shadow contains positive qualities that need to be integrated.

The darkness that *is* truly evil is the Ego's egocentricity. This egocentricity can't be integrated; it can only be outgrown, left behind, or destroyed. The really evil Shadow that we cast is the unrecognized dark side of our egocentricity, i.e., the sum total of all our unconscious, egocentric, self-serving motivations. It is this that we must recognize and be purged of through our suffering. This is why Kunkel wrote,

> The Ego without knowing it is always fighting on the side of evil and darkness, although it pretends to be a servant of light.*

In our chapter on biblical examples of Kunkel's psychology we discussed the story of the temptations in the wilderness. There we saw that Jesus was tempted by Satan to pursue egocentric goals—of power and stardom. This story identifies what is truly evil: the Ego's egocentric urge. It is this, according to the example

Ibid., p. 104

of Jesus, which must be admitted, faced, and resolutely put away. The Shadow, on the other hand, according to Jesus, is like an inner adversary who must be accepted, and with whom we must come to terms. Jesus says:

> Come to terms with your opponent in good time while you are still on the way to the court with him, or he may hand you over to the judge and the judge to the officer, and you will be thrown into prison. I tell you solemnly, you will not get out till you have paid the last penny (Mt 5:25).

If all this is so, then Jungian psychology must revise its conception of the Shadow, but Christianity must also revise its conception of what is good and evil. While Jesus called for reconciliation with the Shadow, and identified egocentricity as the real spiritual danger, the early Church didn't see this distinction and heaped all the evil onto the Shadow. I have argued this point in detail in my book *Evil: The Shadow Side of Reality* in a chapter entitled "Jesus, Paul and the Shadow." What happened was that the early Church set up a set of "ego ideals" for Christians to fulfill: the Christian should be loving, kind, faithful, not subject to sexual passion or anger, etc. However, the Church failed to see the hidden egocentricity in its attempt to fulfill these ideals. Instead of encouraging the integration of the personality it fell into moralizing, and moralizing, as Kunkel reminds us, always creates egocentricity. Moreover, as the Church heaped all the blame for evil onto the Shadow it became less and less conscious of the Ego's truly evil side, i.e., its egocentricity.

The Church has tended to favor the Ego, in spite of its egocentricity, over the Shadow. Of course, this is just what the Ego wants, for this reinforces the notion of the Ego that, after all, in spite of a few failings, it is innocent.

However, our dreams say otherwise. For instance, in our dreams the dream-Ego often encounters figures that it identifies as evil, but our dream figures are just as likely to regard the Ego as evil. The situation may get so bad that a dream may even call for the execution of the Ego, as though saying, "This Ego isn't any good; it doesn't represent us properly and must be done away with." This is why Kunkel says:

> The Ego and its Shadow are equally evil; blaming each other
> they bring to light hidden hideousness.*

Elsewhere Kunkel makes a statement that is certain to shock
conventional Christian consciousness:

> The startling fact is that the real Self favors the Shadow in
> opposition to the Ego, in spite of the Shadow's destructive-
> ness.**

This is like saying that in a showdown God actually is on the side
of the Shadow and is against the Ego. He prefers Mr. Hyde to Dr.
Jekyll! This is the opposite of what the Church has been preaching
for a long time, but from the psychological point of view we can
understand it because the Shadow only destroys what isn't fit to
live, and even in its destructiveness it is genuine, while the
egocentric Ego is a sham.

The following charts will illustrate what Kunkel means:

Figure 1
Creative Center

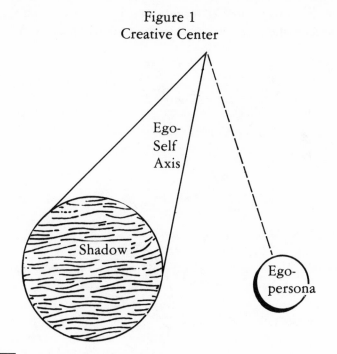

---

*Kunkel, *In Search of Maturity,* p. 233.
**Ibid.,* p. 158.

In this figure the Ego is represented by the small circle because it is not in touch with the creative energy of the Self and so has become increasingly constricted. The dark "new moon" on the lower side of the Ego's circle represents the hidden evil that the Ego always engenders when it is in this egocentric state. The small Ego circle is labeled "Ego-persona" because the persona has been twisted to serve the Ego's egocentric needs. The line from the Ego-persona circle to the Center is a dotted line; this represents the broken relationship between the two of them. Since the Ego-Self relationship is so tenuous the Ego loses more and more of its energy as life goes on. For this reason the Ego becomes increasingly weak and ineffective, and must resort to more and more egocentric devices in order to keep going.

As the Ego becomes weaker its energy accumulates in the Shadow. The Shadow therefore becomes larger and stronger than the Ego and this condition is represented in the diagram by the larger circle denoted as the Shadow. The relationship between the Shadow and the Center is represented by the open, strong line that connects the Shadow-circle to the Creative Center. The rela-

Figure 2

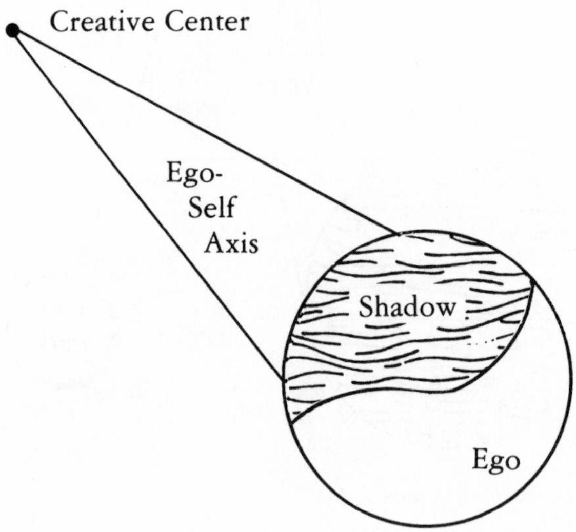

tionship between the Shadow and the Self is intact because, however destructive the Shadow can be, it is genuine and, as we have seen, the Self always favors what is real (the egocentric Ego, in contrast, is a sham).

This figure shows how the situation might look if the Ego lost its egocentricity. The Shadow still forms a somewhat distinct personality. We are always two, never one, but the two now have a relationship. Together Ego and Shadow make up the total Ego structure. They have a talking relationship, as it were, and are now more like comrades than enemies. As a result both are enclosed in one circle, and both enjoy a solid connection to the Self, represented by the line entitled the "Ego-Self Axis." The dark "half-moon" line that was under the Ego in the previous figure is no longer there. This is because the Ego's egocentricity has now been dissolved.

If this analysis of the Ego and its dark sides is accurate, we might expect some evidence of it to appear in dreams. The fact is that if the Ego is too convinced of its innocence, and therefore unaware of its egocentricity, a dream may occur in which the Ego is arrested, imprisoned, or tried for some crime it didn't commit. In such dreams the dreamer typically awakens feeling frightened but with a feeling of baffled innocence. Dreams also sometimes occur that show the creative life that it is possible for the Ego to have under more favorable conditions. In the next chapter we will look at examples in dreams of these and other psychological phenomena.

VI
The Egocentric Ego
in Our Dreams

In most dreams, the dreamer is directly in the dream. When we report such a dream we use the first person singular, and say something like, "I had a dream last night. I was walking down the street when suddenly this man jumped out in front of me from behind a building and ..." We call this "I" in the dream the "dream-Ego," and this dream-Ego seems closely related to our waking Ego. Because the Ego appears so often in our dreams, usually with a central role in the drama, dreams can give us a certain amount of information about the Ego: what state it is in, and its relationship to the Self as reflected in the Ego's relationship to the various dream figures.

All kinds of things can happen to the Ego in our dreams. It may meet with disaster or good fortune, encounter friends or enemies, get lost or find the way. The Ego may also react in various ways. We may run away when a threatening figure appears, or we may choose to stand our ground and fight, or we may try to make friends. In our dreams we exercise a certain amount of choice, and when we awake we may ask ourselves such questions as: "Why did I run away from that person? . . . Did I do the right thing when I killed that dog that seemed to be threatening me? . . . When the woman told me there was a gold coin hidden in the forest why didn't I go to look for it instead of turning back toward home?"

Jungian psychology, in its absorption in the figures and sym-

392

bols of the unconscious, sometimes overlooks what is happening to the Ego. But dreams enable us to analyze the Ego by scrutinizing the actions, choices, and condition of the Ego in dreams. Our task now will be to look at some dreams and see what instruction dreams can give us about the Ego, and especially about the egocentric condition the Ego may be in.

In these dreams we will be looking only at the posture of the Ego in the dream. The symbolism in most of the dream examples is complex and we could spend a long time exploring it, but this is not our present purpose. It will suffice us to see how the Ego is faring in the dreams, what the Ego's posture is, and what are its choices and actions.

Let's begin with a biblical example. In the Book of Daniel we are told about the mighty King Nebuchadnezzar who had a big dream and sent for the holy man Daniel for an interpretation. Nebuchadnezzar says,

> The visions that passed through my head as I lay in bed
>   were these:
> I saw a tree
> in the middle of the world;
> it was very tall.
> The tree grew taller and stronger,
> until its top reached the sky,
> and it could be seen from the ends of the earth.
> Its foliage was beautiful, its fruit abundant,
> in it was food for all.
> For the wild animals it provided shade,
> the birds of heaven nested in its branches,
> all living creatures found their food in it.
> I watched the visions passing through my head as I lay in
>   bed.
> Next a watcher, a holy one came down from heaven.
> At the top of his voice he shouted,
> "Cut the tree down, lop off its branches,
> strip off its leaves, throw away its fruit;
> let the animals flee from its shelter
> and the birds from its branches.
> But leave stump and roots in the ground
> bound with hoops of iron and bronze

in the grass of the field.
Let him be drenched with the dew of heaven,
let him share the grass of the earth with the animals.
Let his heart turn from mankind,
let a beast's heart be given him
and seven times pass over him!
Such is the sentence proclaimed by the watchers,
the verdict announced by the holy ones,
that every living thing may learn
that the Most High rules over the kingship of men,
he confers it on whom he pleases,
and raises the lowest of mankind" (Dn 4:7–14).

Daniel is uncomfortable with his task of interpreting the
king's dream because he knows the dream is aimed at Nebuchadnezzar's egocentricity. So Daniel says,

> My lord, may the dream apply to your enemies, and its
> meaning to your foes.

Having made this tactful statement he then proceeds with the
analysis of the dream. Daniel tells the king that the great tree
symbolizes the power of Nebuchadnezzar that stretches over all
the earth. But the "watcher" is a holy one from heaven who will
cut down Nebuchadnezzar's power and destroy it, and will force
Nebuchadnezzar to live like an animal for seven years sharing a
humble lot with the beasts. The fact that the roots and stump are
left in the ground means that there is the possibility that Nebuchadnezzar and his strength may grow again. Daniel concludes his
interpretation:

> You are to be driven from human society,
> and live with the wild animals;
> you will feed on grass like the oxen,
> you will be drenched by the dew of heaven;
> seven times will pass over you
> until you have learnt
> that the Most High rules over the kingship of men,
> and confers it on whom he pleases (Dn 4:22).

Daniel then gives Nebuchadnezzar some advice:

> May it please the king to accept my advice:
> by virtuous actions break with your sins,
> break with your crimes by showing mercy to the poor,
> and so live long and peacefully (Dn 4:24).

We may ascertain from the advice that Daniel gives Nebuchadnezzar that the gloomy fate foretold by the dream can still be avoided by an appropriate change of attitude on the king's part. However, Nebuchadnezzar is too egocentric to give up his Neroposture, and consequently the Self, represented by the Watcher from heaven, now intervenes. This Power is greater than that of the Ego, and the dream declares it will render the Ego helpless and divest the Ego of its arrogance by forcing the king to live like an animal. Put in psychological language, the dream says that the Self has the power to overcome the Ego, and to create, if necessary, disagreeable, even incapacitating symptoms. Nevertheless, the ultimate purpose is not to destroy the Ego but to cure it of its egocentricity, and restore it to a correct relationship with the Self.

In spite of the dream's dramatic warning that he is on the way to a disaster, Nebuchadnezzar persists in his egocentric stance. Twelve months later while strolling on the roof of his palace, Nebuchadnezzar says,

> Great Babylon! Imperial palace! Was it not built by me alone,
> by my own might and power to the glory of my majesty? (Dn
> 4:28).

At this very moment Nebuchadnezzar is struck by the power of God; he is driven from human society, feeds on grass like an ox, lives outdoors in the rain, grows his hair long like an eagle's feathers, and his nails become like the claws of a bird. In short, he goes through a shattering Ego-crisis akin to a psychotic episode in which his once seemingly powerful Ego is rent apart and humbled.

Eventually, however, Nebuchadnezzar's time of punishment comes to an end, and he returns to himself, aware now that whatever power his Ego may have comes from God, who must be acknowledged as its source. With this realization, Nebuchadnezzar is restored to his throne and acquires his former dominion. Now he says:

> Praise and extol and glorify the King of heaven,
> his promises are always faithfully fulfilled,
> his ways are always just,
> and he has power to humble those who walk in pride
> (Dn 4:34).

Let us now turn to some contemporary dream material. The following three dreams came in close succession to a middle-aged businessman. The first one shows the initial posture of the Ego:

> It is during a war and we are under attack. We prepare to defend our position. Now I suddenly find myself outside the defended area among the enemy, but under cover. No one knows I am here but they might find me out. I must change my clothes, especially my trousers, but when I do so they will see the American coins and know who I am. Someone is looking at me.

The opening line of the dream shows that the Ego is intent on defending its position. This is an apt way to picture an egocentric Ego whose defenses are being attacked from within. At first it looks as though the Ego might hold out, but suddenly the apparently strong position which seemed to be capable of being defended is non-existent, and the dreamer finds himself hiding helplessly in the midst of the enemy. We may assume that the Self has won the day, and the egocentricity of the dreamer can no longer hold out against it, so the Ego has been forced to find another way of hanging on to its egocentricity: hiding. The switch may be from a Nero to a Turtle posture. However, this means of defense is not going to work either; the dreamer would like to remain invisible but can't because his American coins and clothing will give him away. To make his attempt to conceal himself even more impossible "someone" is looking at him. This reminds us of the "watcher" who saw all that Nebuchadnezzar was up to. Clearly the Ego can't escape from the all-seeing eye of this mysterious person in the dream who sees him no matter how he tries to conceal himself.

The second dream occurred only a few days later. In this dream the dreamer tries to destroy dangerous snakes, but undergoes a change of attitude. The dream has two parts:

> I am in the woods. There is an encounter with another man. Snakes arrive and the man shoots at them but cannot damage them. I have a .45 and also shoot at the snakes. How beautiful they are! I must bring them back. I must capture or shoot them.
>
> Now I am in the woods again. I see two huge beautiful snakes in the water. One is green and brown, the other is red and black. The sun hits the colors and they are clearly seen. I could not hurt them with my .45.

In the first scene the dreamer and another man are approached by snakes and meet them with a belligerent attitude. The dreamer has a .45 revolver, which symbolizes the extension of his egocentric power, and he is determined to kill the snakes, which he perceives as dangerous. However, neither he nor his companion can hurt the snakes, which appear to be protected by some invisible force. The snakes can be understood as a channel through which the power of the Self is expressed, and it is this power that makes them immune to the threats of the Ego. Meanwhile, the dreamer becomes intrigued by the snakes, and decides that he must kill or capture them so he can have them. So far in the dream the dreamer's posture is clearly egocentric. First he sees the snakes as a threat and is concerned with protecting and defending himself at all costs; then he wants to possess them.

However, in the second scene his attitude toward the snakes changes, and now he likes them so much that he knows he can't hurt them. Whether he can't hurt them with the .45 because he recognizes that the snakes are too powerful, or because he can't bring himself to do it, is not clear. But in any event, there is a recognition on the part of the dreamer that he is neither able nor willing to do away with the snakes as he had originally desired.

As the dreamer's hostile attitude changes the figures in the dream lose their threatening character. At first the Self expressed

itself through the soldiers about to storm the dreamer's defensive
position. Then the Self appeared as the silent person who was
watching the dreamer as he was hiding. Then the Self was seen in
the beautiful snakes, which, though they are initially feared by the
dreamer, are not threatening him, and which eventually bring
about a change in him through their beauty. We could say that
sometimes we are won over by the wrath of God and sometimes
by the love of God.

In the third dream we find out that the dreamer and his
erstwhile adversaries are reconciled:

> Now I am in a cabin in the woods again. The green snake is
> here now but is a woman. I talk with her. The red and black
> snake now arrives and I pick him up. I fear he will be slimy
> but he is not. It felt heavy. Now the snake becomes a man and
> I am comfortable with them.
> Now my hunting license must be revoked for five years.

The Self approaches the Ego again, but this time the approach is peaceful and the Ego meets the Self without fear, and
makes friends. The green snake, transformed into a woman,
engages the dreamer in conversation. The dreamer is not afraid
any longer of the red and black snake but picks him up and
handles him; then that snake also changes and becomes a man. All
of this suggests that the Self is coming closer to the Ego and can
establish a companionate relationship. Notice, however, that the
dreamer must give up his hunting license for five years. That is,
the rapacious Ego-attitude must be sacrificed; that is the price to
be paid for getting along with the snakes.

The next dream we will consider came to a businessman in
late middle-age who had an incurable disease. He dreamed as
follows:

> I see many wildly plunging horses. Then people come to
> attack and kill me. I am trying to pull off my mask and say, "If
> only they could see my face they would know that I am not the
> villain."

The dreamer is under attack; this suggests that the inner
forces are unhappy with the posture the Ego is in. We soon

discover why: the dreamer is wearing a mask. Evidently this man has been going through life with a false front, i.e., he has used his persona for egocentric reasons. Consciously in his waking life this man knows nothing about all this, but in the dream he realizes that he has kept people from seeing his face, and he also knows that he is regarded as a villain. Frantically he tries to pull off his mask so his face can be seen and he will not be looked at in this way. Once again we are forced to ponder Kunkel's thesis that it is the egocentric Ego that is the devil.

The next dream came to a middle-aged woman. What makes this dream especially interesting is that many years earlier this woman lost her small son in a swimming pool accident. She dreams:

> I dreamed that I was bathing a little baby boy. I had to leave him a minute. I came back and he was drowned. I picked him up and massaged his little chest with my palms and as I pushed, water squirted out of his mouth in a pulse-like fashion. When no more water came out I breathed into his mouth and got his lungs going. Then I looked at him, and he was pale but he smiled at me. I gathered him up and cuddled him and walked home with him.

This dream shows the dream-Ego in a positive light. The little boy in the dream who drowned might well have brought out a terrified response in any dreamer but especially in this woman who had actually lost a son this way. But the dreamer does not panic. Panic would have been a reaction from her egocentricity, but in the dream she acts from the Self. The dream is an example of the creative Ego response taking place on the level of a dream. The hard work the dreamer had done on herself since the tragic death of her son has evidently borne fruit.

A similar motif occurs in the following dream that came to a woman who reports that embroidery is something at which she is extremely awkward. She dreams:

> I am in a room with others in something like a factory where we are all sitting at various tables working on cloth. A person could work at straight sewing for a while and then move on to another spot and work on embroidery. It is cream colored

cloth. It seems to be blouses we are making. I move from straight sewing to embroidery work while talking to some of the others . . . and am somewhat surprised at myself that I *do* seem able to do the embroidery.

The dream shows that she has the power, via the Self, to succeed even where she feels inadequate and inferior. Inferiority feelings are an aspect of egocentricity. Where the Ego is connected to the Self we may not be able to do everything, but we no longer feel inferior. The dream points this out to her.

In the previous chapter we mentioned that there were dreams in which the dreamer is accused of something, feels convinced of his innocence, but is nevertheless judged guilty by others in the dream. The following dream that came to a middle-aged man is an example.

I am inside a lumber yard building with a friend of mine and one or two others. We are piling fresh new lumber into my station wagon, selecting what we need. No one else is around. I assume this is okay, for naturally I intend to buy the lumber. I feel perfectly honest about the whole thing, so think nothing of it even when my friend makes a certain remark, which, upon hindsight, I see should have been a warning. At last we are ready to go when the lights suddenly go on. There are a lot of young men here—they run the lumber yard. They act as though they have caught us stealing. Suddenly I realize that my friend must have known it would be bad for us if we were seen loading the lumber without attendants around. I know now what his remark was about and wonder how I could have missed its significance. I realize how bad it looks for us. Naturally these men will not believe my story of my innocence, even though I know my intentions were honest and trusting. Lots of people seem to be there now—lots of them and lots of us. We are lined up so they can take pictures of us. I take out my comb to comb my hair which is unruly. I wonder how this situation will look to others when they realize I have been arrested for stealing.

A motif that is similar to the one in this dream can be found in Franz Kafka's book *The Trial*. In Kafka's story the protagonist is accused of a crime he knows nothing about; he is persuaded of his innocence and is sure he will be vindicated; nevertheless he is ultimately sentenced. Kafka's novel, and dreams such as the above, come from the same archetypal situation: in spite of its assumed innocence the Ego is really guilty as long as it is egocentric.

We are so unaware of our egocentricity that we don't realize we have committed a psychological crime; the crime is our betrayal of the Self, and hence of life's purposes. If there was any doubt in the above dream about the egocentricity of the dreamer it is resolved in the final sentence of the dream where the dreamer's main concern is what others will think about him once they know he has been arrested.

Our final example is a dream that occurred to the same man. It illustrates the two Ego states we can fall into: the narrow, frightened egocentric state, and the extraordinarily vital and expansive Ego state that comes from a contact with the Self. The dream is in two sections:

> *First Section:* I am in a mental hospital and am treated as a patient. I am alone in my room on an upper floor. I will be here for several days. It is night. I read about the other patients, though I don't see them. They are elsewhere in the building. According to my reading, one of them is dangerous. This person is especially a threat in the eyes of the other people. I am afraid.
>
> I go to the head of the stairs and call. A staff doctor and nurse come to see what is wrong with their patient. The atmosphere resembles the atmosphere in the film *One Flew Over the Cuckoo's Nest.* They look at me suspiciously. I answer weakly, "I was just lonely, I guess." I didn't want any trouble from them.
>
> I return to my room. The nurse comes up to see me. She is touched by my plight and acts now in a friendly, motherly way. I decide to learn her name and cultivate the relationship. An ally in this strange and fearful place would be welcome.

The dreamer said about this part of the dream:

> I was frightened, lonely and weak. It was a terrible place to be. I felt helpless in a hostile environment. I planned to

take advantage of the motherly woman and use her to better my situation. The staff people were vague in the dream. They seemed gigantic and frightening to me.

Second Section: The same scenario as the first. I am still a patient, still in a humble role, dressed, as before, in a hospital type of gown. But now I am a totally different person. I am happy, and, curiously enough, am respected. And I am no longer in the building of the first scene but am outside, although I'm supposed to be quite crazy. I sing a song now and dance and clap my hands in a great rhythm. It is as if I *know* something or have seen something, some great important secret or piece of knowledge. It's a breakthrough experience of some kind it seems.

There are several episodes of my singing, dancing, and clapping joyfully—even humorously. In one of these there was a soldier who was ill. Perhaps he was a major. A young doctor and nurse were attending to him, and I was also there in my hospital gown. I am like a person who must be either crazy or a sage. Lo! Our prayers cure the soldier!

In another scene I approach a man with a large dog. The dog rushes at me to charge and attack, but when he gets up to me and sees who I am he stops and is friendly.

In a third scene it appears that I have also become a famous doctor. I am an unknown person who took a certain part in a drama and because of a keen sense of the dramatic have become highly successful. I was able to do so well because of the previous breakthrough experience. I am now half-clown, half-sage.

In the last scene there is a climactic occurrence. A certain man has put a detective on the trail of his wife because he suspects her of infidelity. This man receives messages indicating that his wife had indeed been with another man. I am there too and am somehow implicated in all of this, but am without guilt. I know the woman and see her in a flashback scene. In this flashback scene the woman is in the military. She meets a man who is lonely, and the two of them make love together, in the way a soldier might who is far away on dangerous duty and meets a woman whom he likes and who likes him. The love-making is sort of archetypal. Surely the woman must be forgiven for this one love-making incident. There was something right about it.

The dreamer comments on this section of the dream:

> The feeling in this part of the dream was extremely positive. I
> was incredibly happy and vibrant. The music I made, the
> skipping, singing, dancing, and clapping was vivid in the
> dream almost beyond imagination.

It would be tempting to analyze the rich symbolism of this
dream, but our purpose is to focus on the posture of the Ego. The
first part of the dream shows a timid, fearful, Turtle of an Ego,
imprisoned in its own egocentricity. Such a person is incapable of
courage or love; even when the woman offers a friendly hand he
can only see her offer of friendship as an opportunity to be
exploited for his egocentric purposes. This scene shows graphically how it looks and feels to be egocentric, and the kind of narrow
and frightened existence we then lead.

The second part is the direct opposite. In this part the dreamer is vital, alive, full of joy and humor, and has remarkable
curative powers. But there is no trace of hubris in this part of the
dream; instead the dreamer recognizes and rejoices in a marvelous power that he feels and expresses through his singing and
dancing and rhythm, and he knows this power comes as a gift
from a source beyond himself.

In life we may be in one ego state one day and the other ego
state the next day; we continually move in and out of egocentricity depending on many factors. But many people live their whole
lives in the egocentric condition represented so graphically in the
first part of the last dream; they don't know there is any other way
to feel, and accept the fearful, limited state of their egos as the
norm; as long as their Ego system isn't totally breaking down
society may even pronounce them healthy. But once a person has
entered into the positive Ego state engendered by a surrender of
egocentricity and a relationship to the Self it is never forgotten.
Even though we can't always remain in the positive state, and
frequently lapse back into an egocentric posture, we can always
hope to find again the creative life that we now know is possible
for us.

Index

active imagination: 158
Adler, Alfred: 20, 21, 290
alchemy(ist): 24, 329, 375, 378; philosopher's stone, 374, 375, 376, 378
Alchemy, von Franz: 369fn, 375fn
"Aim and Goal of Jungian Analysis", Stein: 372
Androgyny: 357
anima: 293, 306, 308, 371, 376, 381–383; compensates, 381–383; and egocentric Ego, 381, 383; and persona, 381
animus: 305, 308, 383
Answer to Job, Jung: 358, 362
Aquinas, Thomas: 355
archetype(s) (al): 367, 368
Archetypes of the Collective Unconscious, The, June: 379fn
Aristotle: 355
Augustine, St.: 355, 356

Beatitudes: 340–341
Black Giant(s): 13, 89–93, 97, 117, 122, 124, 128, 196, 208, 215–218, 220–221, 223, 298, 300–302, 309, 321; diagram, 297, 299;
blunder(s): 40, 41, 175–178, 183, 189, 280; psychological, 276
Buddha: 46, 271, 287
Burch, Beatrice: 14

Caesar and Christ, Durant: 381fn
Caligula, Emperor: 381

Center: 23, 29, 50–52, 56–57, 161, 170, 232, 241, 243, 248, 258, 266–268, 278–279, 288, 311–312, 339, 343, 374; creative, 61, 161, 172, 232, 251, 279, 335, 340; Diagram 389–390; real, 53, 57, 61–62, 161–162, 173, 177, 181, 232, 234, 236, 238–243, 249, 252, 257, 260, 265–266, 274, 282, 288–289, 292, 306; as Self, 25, 52, 61, 177, 268, 356; and Shadow, 181, 390; sham, 61
Christ: 13, 23, 52, 240, 271, 278, 280, 335, 352, 357, 377; Child, 334–335; our burdens, 347; false, 183; Gospel of, 346, 357; and redemption, 363; resurrection of, 350; and the Self, 335, 377; temptations, 335–337; within, 23, 335
Christianity: 31, 58, 151, 157, 211, 244–245, 269, 272, 278, 286, 289, 347, 353; and evil, 354, 388; and Jung, 356, 361; and Kunkel, 22, 361; and the Self, 377
Clement of Alexandria: 31
Clinging Vine: 12, 66, 108–111, 115–116, 126, 136, 138, 140, 142–144, 194, 196, 202–204, 213, 215, 218, 321–322, 337, 345–347, 382–383, 385; and Nero, 121, 126, 144; and perso-

404